Eclipse 2 for Java Developers

Eclipse 2 for Java Developers

Berthold Daum

JOHN WILEY & SONS, LTD

Other Wiley Editorial Offices

John Wiley & Sons, Inc., Hoboken, NJ 07030, USA

Jossey-Bass, 989 Market Street, San Francisco, CA 94103-1741, USA

Wiley-VCH Verlag GmbH, Boschstr. 12, D-69469 Weinheim, Germany

John Wiley & Sons Australia Ltd, 33 Park Road, Milton, Queensland 4064, Australia

John Wiley & Sons (Asia) Pte Ltd, 2 Clementi Loop #02-01,
Jin Xing Distripark, Singapore 129809

John Wiley & Sons Canada Ltd, 22 Worcester Road,
Etobicoke, Ontario, Canada M9W 1L1

Wiley also publishes its books in a variety of electronic formats. Some content that appears in print may not be available in electronic books.

Library of Congress Cataloging-in-Publication Data (to follow)

British Library Cataloguing in Publication Data
A catalogue record for this book is available from the British Library
ISBN 0 470 86905 4

Typeset in Helvetica Neue and Times Roman by WordMongers Ltd, Treen, Cornwall TR19 6LG, England
Printed and bound in Great Britain by Biddles Ltd., Guildford and Kings Lynn
This book is printed on acid-free paper responsibly manufactured from sustainable forestry
in which at least two trees are planted for each one used for paper production.

Contents

Introduction

What is Eclipse?

The first version of Eclipse was released in November 2001. Eclipse was announced by IBM as a $40 million donation to the Open Source community. The first reactions to this gift, however, were mixed. While many Java programmers hailed the release of Eclipse enthusiastically (when would one not be enthusiastic about a $40 million present?), Sun Microsystems was initially less than amused. First, there was the name issue, then Sun felt it was being ignored. In fact, Sun Microsystems was not invited to the Eclipse initiative. IBM claimed the contrary: that Sun had belonged to the group of invited companies. This circle is not at all small: the Eclipse consortium has about 150 member companies, and people from Borland Software Corp., Merant International Ltd., Oracle, QNX Software Systems, Rational Software Corp., Red Hat Inc., Suse Inc., TogetherSoft Corp., and of course IBM belong to the board (Microsoft is not a member). The atmosphere between IBM and Sun Microsystems has cooled considerably.

By now, this public relations noise has calmed, and both companies see Eclipse as an important chance to meet the challenge of Microsoft's .NET initiative, and – most important – to get Java back to the desktop.

So, the question is, what is Eclipse? Is it a Java IDE? Is it a new GUI for Java applications? Is it an application platform or framework?

According to www.eclipse.org Eclipse is a platform for "everything and nothing in particular". That we can use Eclipse to develop Java programs (in fact, it is one of the finest Java IDEs), is just a special application of this platform. But its real application domain reaches far beyond Java development. Because of its plug-in architecture, Eclipse is as adaptable as a chameleon and can find a habitat in quite different environments. The Eclipse Java IDE is, in fact, only an eminent example of an Eclipse plug-in. A large number of other plug-ins have been developed for Eclipse already by various companies and developers, or are currently in development (see Appendix A for a small selection of such developments). For example, there is a plug-in for a C++ IDE, while plug-ins for other programming languages such as RPG or COBOL are in preparation. In this book, however, we will concentrate on Java development with Eclipse.

Eclipse is more than a pure development environment. With its SWT and JFace libraries it provides an alternative to Sun's Java libraries, AWT and Swing. SWT and JFace allow creation of Java applications that closely match native applications (i.e. applications written in C or C++) in both 'look and feel' and in responsiveness. In contrast, applications implemented on the basis of Swing often lack responsiveness and sometimes differ – despite the possibility to switch skins – from the 'look and feel' of a native application. Such applications are notoriously hard to sell, as end users expect applications that fulfill the standards of the host platform. SWT and JFace could therefore be a breakthrough for Java applications on the desktop. No wonder therefore that there is a heated debate for and against SWT/JFace in the respective discussion forums (for example `www.javalobby.com`), and that the SWT was voted as the 'most innovative Java component'.

Last but not least, Eclipse provides a large framework for implementing Java applications. Besides the GUI libraries SWT and JFace, we find higher level components such as editors, viewers, resource management, task and problem management, help system, and various assistants and wizards. All these components are used by Eclipse to implement features such as the Java IDE or the workbench, but can also be used for your own applications. The Eclipse license model allows users to embed these components into their own applications, to modify them, and to deploy them as part of their own applications – all without paying a cent in license fees. The complete Eclipse code is available as source code, can be browsed online, and used within own projects.

With Eclipse V3, which is planned for the second quarter of 2004, this concept will be widened further. While Eclipse V2 allows IDE-like applications to be built on the basis of the Eclipse platform, Eclipse V3 will provide a framework for the construction of generic client applications. The desktop battle goes on…

The Eclipse culture

Of course, Eclipse was not just 'invented': it has a history. The author of this book, who has used *Visual Age for Java* for years, can detect many of the Visual Age construction elements within Eclipse. In fact, the same company that stood behind the development of Visual Age is also responsible for the development of Eclipse. This company is OTI (`www.oti.com`). As long ago as 1988, OTI developed a collaborative development environment for Smalltalk called ENVY®, which was later licensed to IBM under the name Visual Age®. What followed was the development of Visual Age for Java, but this was still implemented in Smalltalk. Now, OTI has started the next generation of development tools with Eclipse. Of course, we find many of the design elements of Visual Age in Eclipse. The difference is, however, that Eclipse is implemented in Java and that it features a much more open architecture than Visual Age.

Eclipse was licensed by IBM and than donated to the Open Source community. This was not done without self-interest: Eclipse basically is nothing more than the community edition of IBM's *WebSphere Studio Application Developer* (WSAD). The core platform and the core plug-ins are all the same. The main difference is that Eclipse 2.1 consists of about 70 plug-ins, while WSAD features about 500–700 plug-ins, thus offering greatly extended functionality, such as plug-ins for developing Web and database applications.

About this book

It is practically impossible to write a single book about Eclipse. The sheer complexity of Eclipse would require quite a few books. I have tried to emphasize those topics where Eclipse makes significant contributions to the Java world. In particular, these are the new GUI libraries (SWT and JFace) and the use of Eclipse as a platform and framework for desktop applications. What had to be excluded from this book are WebSphere specific topics such as J2EE and servlet development. Also, after writing several books about Web themes and electronic business, I wanted to take a close look again at desktop programming. Developing desktop applications is currently one of the strong points of Eclipse. For developing Web applications, in contrast, Eclipse still lacks good support for JSP.

This book is not an introduction to Java programming. We assume that readers have a good knowledge of Java and of object-oriented programming concepts. Most of the examples used in this book are not trivial. Two examples come from the multi-media area. Here, readers have the possibility of 'getting their feet wet' with cutting-edge Java technology such as speech processing and MP3 (all in pure Java!). In the third example, we do something useful and implement a spell checker plug-in for Eclipse. I am sick and tired of bad orthography in Java comments!

This book therefore addresses the Java programmer – from the student to the professional – who want to implement their own desktop applications with the help (or on the basis) of Eclipse. We will learn all the techniques that are required to create applications of professional quality.

How this book is organized

The novice to Eclipse is first overwhelmed – even when an experienced Java programmer – by the sheer number of functions. But the functions visible to the user are only the tip of the iceberg. If we start to explore the inner workings of Eclipse, its API, we can get lost easily. Currently the Eclipse download has a size of 62 Mbytes.

Faced with this huge amount of information, this book uses a pragmatic approach. Following the motto that 'perception works from the outside to the inside', we first investigate how Eclipse presents itself to the end user. The benefit is twofold: first, each programmer is an end user of the Eclipse Java IDE; second, the various components of the Eclipse workbench such as editors, views, menus, dialogs, and much more, can also be used in personal applications. Experienced programmers, however, may find an introduction into the Java IDE trivial and superfluous. Nevertheless, it is useful to get well acquainted with the Eclipse user interface, as many of the concepts and details can be later utilized when designing applications.

In *Part 1* of this book we therefore first introduce practical work with Eclipse, in particular with the Java development environment. Eclipse presents itself as a very powerful Java IDE that continues the positive traditions of *Visual Age for Java*, but also introduces new concepts such as code completion for refactoring code, assistants that make intelligent proposals for fixing program errors, and a local history that allows return to previous code versions.

In this part we also discuss the organization of the workbench, the resources of the Eclipse workspace such as projects, folders, and files, how these resources are related to the native file system, and the tools for navigation. We explain what perspectives are and how they can be used effectively. We discuss the Eclipse Java debugger, the integration of JUnit into Eclipse, and give a short introduction about Eclipse's support for working in a team.

When implementing examples, we still restrain ourselves and implement all examples as usual on basis of the AWT and Swing.

However, this will quickly change in *Part 2*. Here, we introduce the secrets of the SWT and JFace libraries. For SWT we discuss event processing, the various GUI elements such as text fields, tables, buttons, trees, etc., the various layout options, graphics operations and how Java2D can coexist with the SWT, and printer output. We also explain the specialities of thread and resource management in context of the SWT.

In case of the JFace library, we present the higher user interface levels such as windows, dialogs, viewers, actions, menus, text processing, wizards, and preferences. As an example we implement an MP3-player completely with SWT and JFace that can be deployed independently of the Eclipse platform. An interesting detail in this example is how the SWT library is used in a multi-threaded application.

In *Part 3* we explain how to develop your own products on the basis of the Eclipse platform: either as a plug-in to Eclipse or as a stand-alone application. Since Eclipse consists more or less only of plug-ins, we first introduce the plug-in architecture of Eclipse. We discuss the requirements for a minimal platform, show how workspace resources are used in Eclipse, and how plug-ins are declared via a manifest. Then we discuss the various components of the Eclipse workbench such as editors, views, actions, dialogs, wizards, preferences, perspectives, and the help system. All these components are available to the application programmer as building blocks, a fact that can speed up application development considerably.

Finally, we show how your own products can be packaged for deployment. Eclipse offers integrated support for all tasks here too: from the creation of a feature, via the definition of an *Update Site*, to the automated installation of updates. As an example we develop a universal and fully functional plug-in for spell checking on Eclipse platforms.

In Appendix A we list some more interesting third-party plug-ins. In Appendix B we discuss the migration to another version of the Eclipse platform. Appendix C contains download addresses for the third-party software and the source code used in the examples.

Acknowledgements

Books are always team work, even if only the author's name appears below the title. This is also the case with this book, and here is the place to acknowledge the contribution of all the other team members.

Special thanks go to the publisher John Wiley & Sons, in particular to Gaynor Redvers-Mutton who acted as the publishing editor. Thanks go also to the publisher of the original German edition, dpunkt verlag, and the responsible editor there, René Schönfeldt. Steve Rickaby of WordMongers did the copy-editing for the English edition, and the cover design was done by Lou Page.

Many important tips that found their way into this book came from the (anonymous) reviewers, but also from developers and employees of OTI who had looked at the first manuscript version. Many thanks! And of course, without the development of Eclipse this book would not have been written, and Eclipse is indeed a tool that I don't want to miss. Thanks again!

Berthold Daum

October 2003

berthold.daum@bdaum.de

Part 1
The Java IDE

In *Part 1* we use Eclipse just like a normal Java IDE. We explain the functionality of the workbench and provide tips for efficient code authoring and how development projects are organized correctly. Then we start with our first example, a program for converting written text into speech. In this example we still use the standard Java GUI-classes of the AWT and Swing libraries: the Eclipse GUI-libraries SWT and JFace are discussed in *Part 2* and *Part 3*. A discussion of the Eclipse debugger and of the Javadoc export function concludes this part.

1 Going places

In this chapter we use the classical `HelloWorld` example to show how to create effectively Java programs under Eclipse. We first discuss the most important workbench preferences, and then introduce various utilities for code creation.

1.1 Installing Eclipse

Installing Eclipse is very easy. In most cases, the only thing to do is to unpack the downloaded ZIP-file onto a disk drive with sufficient free space.

But let's start from the beginning. What do we need to run Eclipse?

Requirements

1. A suitable platform. While Eclipse 1 was limited to Windows and Linux, Eclipse 2.1 runs on a wide variety of platforms: Windows, Linux, Solaris, QNX, AIX, HP-UX and Mac OS X. However, in this book we mostly refer to the Windows platform, and occasionally give hints for the Linux platform.

2. Sufficient disk space. 300 Megabytes should be enough.

3. Sufficient RAM. 256 MB should be fine.

4. Java SDK 1.4. Eclipse also runs under JDK 1.3. However, for our examples, we require JDK 1.4. If this SDK is not installed on your machine, you can download it from `www.javasoft.com` and install it by following the instructions given on this site. The `bin` subdirectory of the SDK should be specified in your `PATH` environment variable so that the Java VM can be called by issuing the command `java` from the command prompt.

5. Eclipse SDK 2.1 for your platform.

6. The Eclipse example files (`eclipse-examples-2.1`) for your platform.

How do you proceed?

Installation
1. Unpack the Eclipse SDK into the target directory. For example, on Windows that could be the root directory `C:\`. In effect, the Eclipse libraries will be contained in directory `C:\eclipse`. Under Linux we could use the `/opt/` directory so that the Eclipse files would be stored under `/opt/eclipse/`.

2. Immediately afterwards we unpack the Eclipse example files into the same root directory. By doing so, the example files are automatically placed into the just-created `eclipse` subdirectory.

3. That's all. Under Windows we can now invoke Eclipse by clicking on the icon with the darkened sun (in the `eclipse` subdirectory). After a short while we should see the screen shown in Figure 1.1.

   Under Linux we would issue the shell command

   ```
   ./eclipse -data /root/workspace
   ```

   under directory `/opt/eclipse/`. By using the option `-data` we make sure that the Eclipse workspace is stored in the users root directory (named `root` here).

   Also under Windows you are recommended to use the `-data` option. By using this option we can keep the workspace directory out of the Eclipse installation directories. This will make the upgrade to later Eclipse versions easier (see also Appendix A). In addition, it becomes easier to back-up the workspace.

   Important: When backing up the Eclipse workspace you should always create complete back-ups – never incremental back-ups. Eclipse treats the archive attribute of files in a somewhat unconventional way, which can lead to a corrupt workspace when restoring a workspace from an incremental back-up. This is a known bug in Eclipse that has not been fixed with the release of Eclipse 2.1.

4. It is a good idea to create a desktop short-cut for Eclipse. Under Windows we simply pull the Eclipse icon onto the desktop by pressing the right mouse button. In the context menu we select *Create Shortcut here*. We can add additional command line options to this short-cut, for example the `-data` option discussed above. To do so, we right click the short-cut and select *Properties* from the context menu.

   To learn which command line options are available for Eclipse we look into the Eclipse help system. In Eclipse we invoke the menu point *Help > Help Contents*. Then we choose *Workbench User Guide*, expand the item *Tasks* and select *Running Eclipse*.

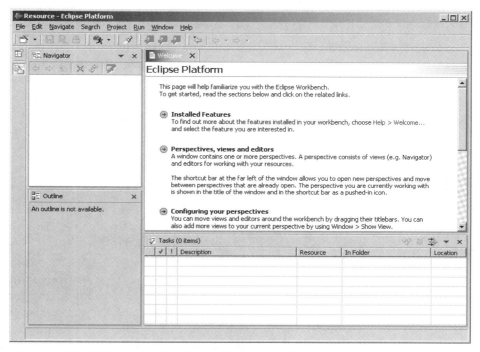

Figure 1.1:   Eclipse after installation: Not a trace of a Java IDE!

Under Linux we can similarly create a desktop shortcut under KDE or Gnome and add the required command line options.

5. One of the most important command line option deals with the selection of the *Java Virtual Machine* (JVM) under which the Eclipse platform is executed. If we don't want to use the standard JVM (the one executed when invoking the java command), we can specify a different JVM by using the command line option -vm.

When the Eclipse loader is invoked it uses a three-stage strategy to determine the JVM under which the platform is executed. If a JVM is explicitly specified with the command line option -vm then this VM is used. Otherwise, the loader will look for a specific JAVA runtime environment (JRE) that was deployed together with the Eclipse platform. Such a JRE must be located in the directory \eclipse\jre\. If such a JRE does not exist (as in our case), then the location of the VM is derived from the PATH environment variable.

By the way, this strategy only affects the JVM under which the platform is executed. Which JVM and which SDK is used for Java development is specified separately in the Eclipse workbench.

6. The command line option -vmargs can be used to specify parameters for the *Java Virtual Machine*. For example:

```
eclipse.exe —vm C:\java13\bin\javaw -vmargs -Xmx256M
```

Here we start Eclipse with a specific JVM and set the JVM heap to 256 Mbytes. With very large projects this can help to prevent instabilities of the workbench.

1.2   The first application: Hello World

Until now we haven't seen much of a Java development environment. Eclipse – which is advertised as a platform for everything and nothing in particular – shows, in fact, nothing in particular when invoked for the first time. We are now going to change this radically.

Perspectives   To see something 'particular' in Eclipse, we first must open an Eclipse perspective. Perspectives consist of a combination of windows and tools that is best suited for particular tasks. Perspectives are contributed to the Eclipse workbench by various Eclipse plug-ins. This is, for example, the case with the user interface of the Java IDE which is nothing more than a big plug-in for the Eclipse workbench. To start developing Java programs, we therefore must first open the Java perspective. To do so, we click the *Open Perspective* symbol, as shown in Figure 1.2.

Figure 1.2:   Use the Open Perspective symbol to open new perspectives.

In the list that appears now we select the item *Java*. Afterwards we should see the screen shown in Figure 1.3.

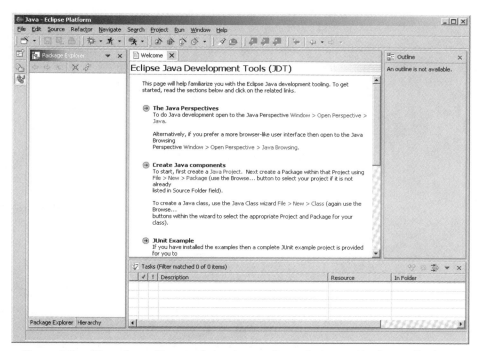

Figure 1.3: The Java Perspective shows the windows (Package Explorer, Hierarchy), menu items and toolbar icons that are typical for Java development. On the left we see a new icon denoting the Java perspective. Above this icon is the icon for the Resource perspective that was active before we opened the Java perspective. We can quickly switch between different perspectives by clicking on these icons.

Projects

Now it's time to say *Hello* to the world and to create our first program. To do so, we first create a new Java project. On the toolbar we click the *Create a Java Project* icon (see Figure 1.4).

Figure 1.4: By clicking on the icons of this group we can create new Java projects, packages, classes, interfaces, and scrapbook pages.

In the following dialog we name the project with HelloWorld. In the *Package Explorer* we now see an entry for the new project.

Create a new class   In the next step we click the *C*-icon on the toolbar (*Create a Java Class*). In the following dialog (Figure 1.5) we make sure that:

- The *Source Folder* is specified as HelloWorld.

- The name of the new class is specified as HelloWorld.

- public is selected as *Modifier.*

- java.lang.Object is specified as *Superclass.*

- The option to *public static void main( )* is checked.

Figure 1.5:   The Create a New Class Wizard is able to generate some class code. The wizard can generate stubs for the inherited methods, especially if a super class and interfaces are specified.

After clicking the *Finish* button the Eclipse workbench looks a bit more like a workbench in use (Figure 1.6).

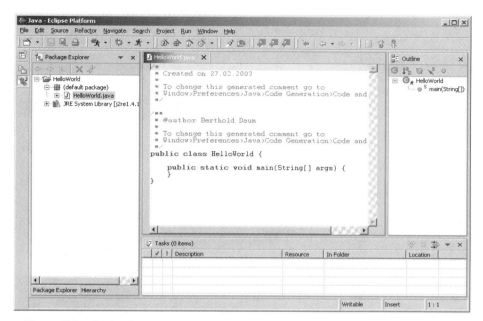

Figure 1.6:   In the Package Explorer we see the content of the new project. This includes the libraries of the Java runtime environment. At any time we can open the classes belonging to these libraries and look at their source code. The center window is occupied by the Java source editor, currently containing the pre-generated code for the HelloWorld class. At the right hand side we can see the Outline window showing the current class with its methods. We can use this window to quickly navigate to any method in the source editor by clicking on the method.

Now we complete the pre-generated code. We change the main() method in the following way:

```
public static void main(String[] args) {
  System.out.println("Hello World");
}
```

By doing this we have finished the programming work for our first project. We save the new class HelloWorld to disk by clicking on the floppy disk icon on the toolbar. (Alternatively, we may use the keyboard shortcut *Ctrl-S.*) This will also compile this class. The program is now ready for execution.

Launch   The *Run* icon is positioned on the right side of the bug icon. Here, we activate the drop down menu by clicking the arrow at the right of the Run icon. From this drop down menu we select *Run as... > Java Application* to start program execution. Now, a new window should open in the area of the *Tasks* window (see Figure 1.7) and should display the text 'Hello World'. Done!

During this first execution, Eclipse creates a new *Run Configuration* named *HelloWorld*. A list of all available Run Configurations is found under the arrow on the right side of the *Run* icon. The Run icon itself is always associated with the Run Configuration that was executed last. To execute our program again, a simple click on the Run icon is therefore sufficient.

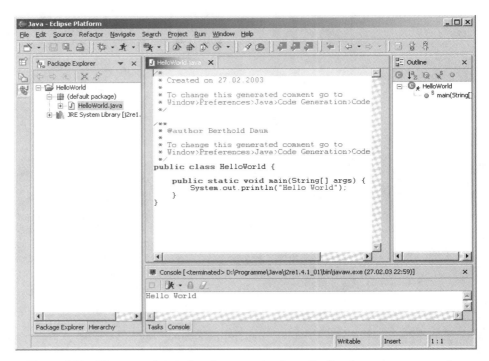

Figure 1.7: The console window is opened automatically when a program writes to System.out or System.err.

1.3 The most important preferences for Java development

Before we continue in our programming efforts, let's first explore our working environment. Under the menu function *Window > Preferences* we get access to all Eclipse preferences (see Figure 1.8).

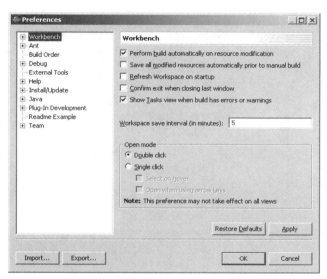

Figure 1.8:   On the left of the Preferences dialog we can select from several preference categories. On the right hand side of the dialog the details of the selected preference category is shown. All settings made here can be stored into an external file by clicking the 'Export...' button, or loaded from an external file by using the 'Import...' button.

At first sight, the sheer mass of preferences shown in this dialog may be overwhelming, as each plug-in may contribute its own set of preference categories to this dialog. In this chapter, we will discuss only those preferences that are most relevant in the context of this book. Readers should take the time to step systematically through all preference categories to get an initial overview. Some of the categories have sub-categories. To expand a category, click on the '+' sign in front of the category name.

Some of the preference settings will only make sense when we discuss the corresponding Eclipse function. In such cases we will postpone the discussion of the preference settings to the discussion of the corresponding workbench function.

1.3.1   Workbench preferences

Keyboard short-cuts   For developers that previously have worked with Emacs, it makes sense to switch the *Key Bindings* in Eclipse so they can continue to use the familiar Emacs shortcuts. To do so, we expand the *Workbench* category and select the sub-category *Key Bindings*. Within the key bindings preference settings we can choose between *Emacs* and *Default*. We can even define own keyboard shortcuts by clicking the button *Customize Key Bindings...*

1.3.2　Installed JREs

We don't always want to create Java applications that require a Java 1.3 or Java 1.4. In some cases we may need to run on Java 1.2 platforms. Within the preferences category *Java*, in sub-category *Installed JREs*, we have the possibility to list all Java Runtime Environments (JRE) that are installed on the host computer (see Figure 1.9).

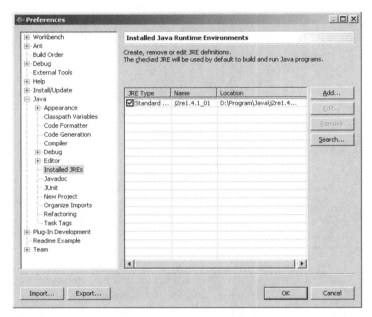

Figure 1.9: In this preference category we declare all the Java Runtime Environments (SDK or JRE) that are installed on the host computer for Eclipse. Among the JREs listed here we checkmark one as the default JRE. This JRE will be assigned to all new Java projects. We will learn later how this can be changed in the project settings and how different JREs can be used in different Launch Configurations.

To add a new JRE, we click the *Add* button (alternatively we may click the *Search* button to scan a whole directory for a JRE or SDK). Then we complete the following dialog (see Figure 1.10).

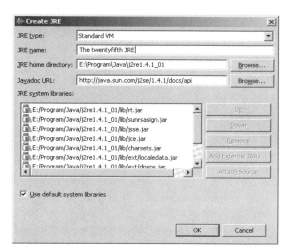

Figure 1.10: A new JRE is added to the Eclipse workbench. We have provided the name and location of the JRE home directory. The location of the corresponding Javadoc is preset by Eclipse and points to the JavaSoft Web site. If the documentation is available locally, this entry should be modified accordingly. For further customization we could uncheck the item 'Use default system libraries'. This would allow us to add further JAR libraries. If any of the JARs does not contain source code we can attach external source code by pressing 'Attach Source...'.

Using V1.1 JREs   If we want to add a version 1.1 JRE (this is necessary when we want to run our application on a Microsoft VM), we must additionally change the *JRE type* to the value *Standard 1.1.x VM*.

Of course is it possible to execute an application on a JVM that is different from the JVM under which the application was developed. For example, if we developed an application under Java SDK 1.1.8 and want to test how the application performs under a version 1.3.1 JVM, we must change the runtime environment before executing the program. We can do this by choosing the appropriate JVM in the Eclipse *Launch Configurator*. The *Launch Configurator* is opened by invoking the menu function *Run > Run...*

For the remainder of this book we use the Java 1.4 SDK.

1.3.3   Compiler preferences

We now take a closer look to the compiler preferences. In the *Preferences* dialog we select the category *Java* and the sub-category *Compiler*. Note that all adjustments made here affect the whole workbench. On a project level (see Section 2.10), however, we have the possibility of overriding the global settings made here under *Preferences*.

Warnings and Errors

On the right hand side of the *Java > Compiler* category we see a tabbed notebook. The page *Problems* shows which compiler events create errors or warnings and which compiler events should be ignored (see Figure 1.11):

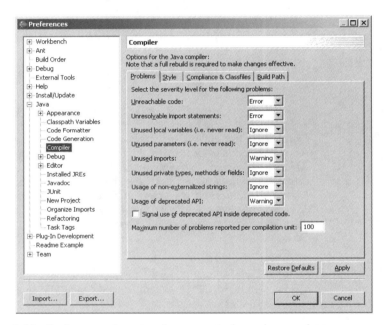

Figure 1.11: Preferences for compiler generated warnings and errors.

Detecting garbage in programs

As we use a lot of third-party code in our examples, we reset the settings for unused imports, unused local variables, and unused parameters to *Ignore*. Otherwise we could face an overwhelming flood of error messages. But if we develop our own applications, it makes sense to set these settings to *Warning*. These settings help us to detect and remove garbage from our code. Just try the following: set *Unused parameters* to *Warning* and press *OK*. The project is re-compiled. At the program line:

```
public static void main(String[] args) {
```

we now see a warning icon, and in the *Tasks* window we see the entry:

```
The argument args is never read
```

Quite right! Within our `HelloWorld` program we did not make use of the parameter that contains the command line arguments.

Classfiles and JDK compliance

The third page of the same preferences category is titled *Compliance & Classfiles*. Here we can specify which symbolic information, such as variable names and line numbers, is to be included in the generated classfiles. This information is required for debugging, and therefore we leave the proposed settings unchanged. However, for a well tested program it may make sense to remove this information from the classfiles: generated files are much smaller without these symbol tables.

On the same page we can determine if the compiler must comply to the Java 1.4 or Java 1.3 syntax. With Java 1.4 one new instruction was added to the language: `assert`. Consequently, the word 'assert' can no longer be used as a field or method name. In addition, `assert` requires support from the JVM. Classes that use this instruction cannot be executed by older JVMs. As we do not plan to use `assert` in our first example program, we leave this setting at the proposed value of Java 1.3.

1.3.4　Formatting code

Formatting code can be very helpful, because it is easier to detect violations of the control structures of a program (such as open `if` or `while` statements) when the program is formatted. In the preference category *Java*, sub-category *Code Formatter* we can configure how the Eclipse code formatter works (see Figure 1.12). The best method is to try some of the settings and to select those that work best for your application. For the examples in this book we have used the default settings.

But how does one apply code formatting? Very simply: just click with the right mouse button on the source code and select *Source > Format* from the context menu. The key shortcut *Ctrl-Shift-F* works even faster. Note that it is also possible to select only a portion of the source code to format just that portion. The only condition is that the selected portion must be a closed syntactical construct, such as an entire class definition, a whole method, or a complete `while` loop.

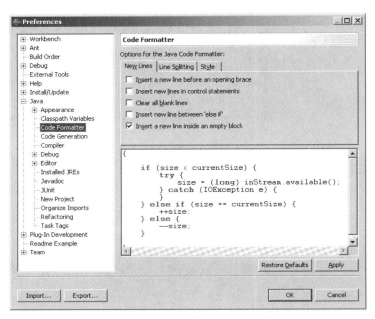

Figure 1.12: Three pages allow us to determine the details of code formatting.

1.3.5   Templates

When we created the new *HelloWorld* class, the following text was generated at the top of the new compilation unit:

```
/*
 * Created on 27.02.2003
 *
 * To change this generated comment go to
 * Window>Preferences>Java>Code Generation>Code and Comments
 */

/**
 * @author Berthold Daum
 *
 * To change this generated comment go to
 * Window>Preferences>Java>Code Generation>Code and Comments
 */
```

The first comment was generated for the new Java file, the second commend was created for the new type (HelloWorld). We now should follow the advice given in these comments and modify the code generation preferences according to our requirements.

We open the preferences category *Java*, sub-category *Code Generation*. There, we bring the page *Code and Comments* to the top (Figure 1.13):

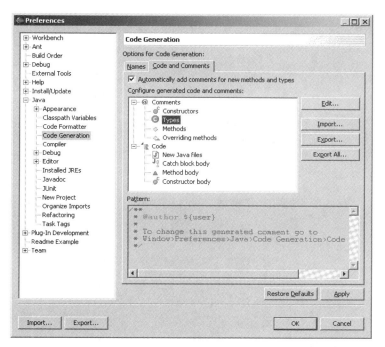

Figure 1.13: The preferences for code generation. For various events, such as the creation of a new type, a new method, or a new constructor, we can specify which code is to be generated.

We select the *Types* entry and press the *Edit* button. In the following dialog (Figure 1.14) we replace the text provided by Eclipse with the string 'created first in project'. Then we press the button *Insert Variable*. From the following list we select the variable named *project_name*. The result should look like that shown in Figure 1.14.

After we have committed these changes new classes and interfaces will be created with a comment containing the user name and the project name.

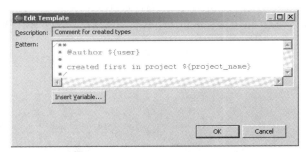

Figure 1.14: Editing a code generation template. All variables are prefixed with the '$' character and are enclosed in curly brackets. Apart from the template pattern, we can in addition supply a description (which will appear in the overview) and a template context (Java or Javadoc).

Afterwards we also change the entry for *New Java File*. The predefined text is here:

```
/*
 * Created on ${date}
 *
 * To change this generated comment go to
 * Window>Preferences>Java>Code Generation>Code and Comments
 */
${package_declaration}

${typecomment}
${type_declaration}
```

The variables used here define the sequence of the different code parts. For example, what happens under *typecomment* was just specified by us in the previous template. Here, we leave everything as is, but delete only the text lines 'To change... Comments'.

1.4   Tasks and Markers

The *Tasks* window is used by Eclipse to notify the user about pending tasks. One task category is problems such as errors or warnings. By clicking on such an entry in the *Tasks* window we can quickly navigate to an erroneous program line.

Other task entries are hints about pending development actions. Some of these hints are created by Eclipse. For example, when we create a new class or a new method, Eclipse creates a hint that the new construct must still be completed. Programmers may create similar task entries at their own discretion.

1.4.1 Problems, problems

In Section 1.3.3 we saw the *Tasks* window in action. The entries in the *Tasks* window correlated to pending problems in the Eclipse workbench. In Figure 1.15 we purposely created a syntax error by inserting a blank into the parameter name `args`. This resulted in three error messages.

Error messages are represented by a white cross in a red circle. In contrast, warnings are represented by a yellow triangle. The third problem type is information tasks, which are represented by a blue 'i' character.

With a double click on the problem entry in the *Tasks* window we can quickly navigate to the problem location. Should the problem be located in a file that currently is not open, the file will be opened in the editor and the editor window is positioned to the error location. Just try it, and click on one of the entries in the *Tasks* window.

Task filter

As the workbench gets more and more busy, the *Tasks* window often overflows with errors, warnings and other tasks. At times it can become difficult to find the *Tasks* window entries that are related to the current project or file, as the *Tasks* window by default shows all problems and other tasks within the whole workspace. Of course, we can suppress some of the warning by setting the compiler options accordingly (see Section 1.3.3). But there is another way: to reduce the information overload: we can make use of the *Task Filter*. We can open the *Task Filter* dialog with a click on the *Filter* button in the toolbar of the *Tasks* window (Figure 1.16).

Here, in the task filter, we may restrict the entries shown in the *Tasks* window to specific types. For example, we may opt to show only Java problems. The entry types shown in this window depend on the installed plug-ins.

In addition, we can restrict the entries by their origin. *On any resource* shows all problems and tasks from the whole workbench. *On any resource in same project* shows only problems and tasks from the current project. An interesting option is also the definition of a *Working Set* – a freely configurable and named set of resources. We select *On any resource in same project* because we only want to see the tasks and problems of the project on which we are currently working.

We also have the option of filtering problems according their severity. To do so, we mark the checkbox *Where problem severity is:* and in addition the checkbox *Error*. By doing so we can suppress all warnings and information entries.

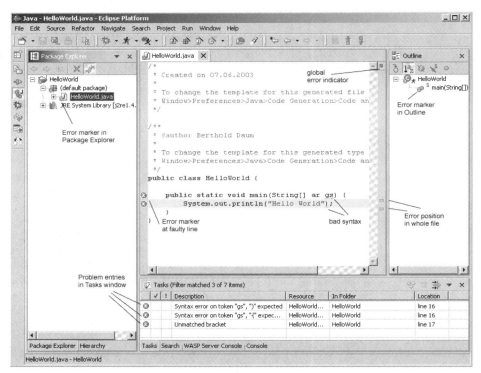

Figure 1.15: After the double click on the problem entries. The faulty expressions are underlined in red. Red error markers on the source editor's left margin mark the faulty lines. The markers on the right margin show the position of the errors relative to the whole file. To scroll to the error position, it is only necessary to pull the scroll bar to the markers. Clicking the markers works just as well.

1.4.2   General tasks

Problem entries generated by the compiler are only a specific type of task entry. In addition, we have the option of creating entries manually. When writing code it often happens that we want to postpone a certain task to a later time. In this case, we can create a task entry that later reminds us of the unfinished work.

Just click with the right mouse button on the left margin of the source editor at the line where you want to create the task marker. Select the *Add Task...* function In the displayed context menu. In the *New Task* dialog, enter a task description. The result could look like Figure 1.17.

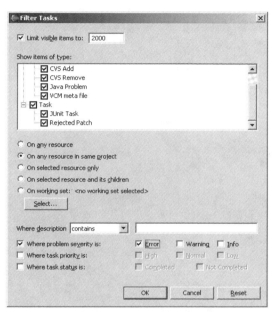

Figure 1.16: The task filter. The setting shown here only allows entries from the current project in the Tasks window. The type of the entry is irrelevant.

A function that was introduced with Eclipse 2.1 is even simpler. Just type a comment starting with the word TODO in a new line. This line will automatically appear in the *Tasks* window as soon as the source code is saved. By the way, in *Preferences > Java > Task Tags* we may define alternative or additional tags such as FIXME, TUNE, etc. Of course, these workbench-wide definitions can be overridden on project level.

1.4.3   Bookmarks

In addition to tasks, Eclipse also has a construct that is quite similar: *Bookmarks*. In the same way that we created a task entry, we can also create a bookmark. Such a bookmark, however, does not appear in the Tasks window, but appears in a separate *Bookmark* window. Since this window is not a standard part of the Java perspective, we first must open it: Select *Window > Show View > Other > Basic > Bookmarks* (see also Section 2.7).

If you like your bookmarks better in a separate list, use this construct. Otherwise, you can achieve the same effect with tasks.

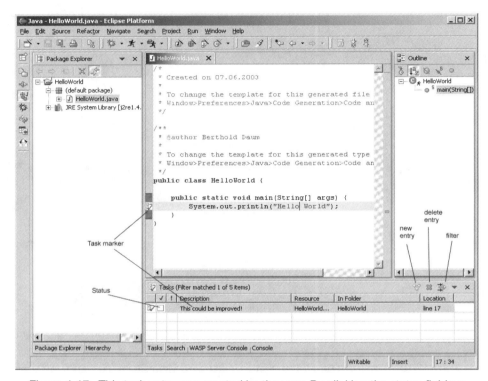

Figure 1.17: This task entry was created by the user. By clicking the status field we can mark the entry as 'completed'. The delete button can be used to select one or several selected tasks. We can create task entries that are not related to specific locations with the new entry button. For example, we could create a task 'Don't forget to buy fresh milk!'

1.5   The Scrapbook

The *Scrapbook* was also inherited by Eclipse from Visual Age. A scrapbook page is nothing other than a small file in which we can try out Java expressions or just jot down a new idea.

We can create a new scrapbook page by clicking the *New Scrapbook Page* button in the Eclipse toolbar, at the right hand side of the *New Java Package* button. In the displayed dialog we specify a name for the new page and – if necessary – the target folder. The result is the creation of a new empty scrapbook page in the target folder. Scrapbook pages have the file extension .jpage.

Experimenting with Java expressions   Now, how do we use a scrapbook page? We simply type in arbitrary Java expressions. If we use external types in these expressions, we either have to qualify the type names fully or add `import` statements. The context function *Set Imports* allows us to add `import` statements for single types or whole packages.

We then select the expressions that we want to execute and call the *Execute* context function with the right mouse button (Figure 1.18).

It is not necessary to save the scrapbook page before executing the selected code. The selected code is compiled by the *Execute* function. In the case of a compilation or execution error, Eclipse inserts the error message either in before or after the selected expression. After reading the error message, we can easily remove it by applying the *Undo* function (*Ctrl-Z*).

Execute is not the only function to run a Java expression. In cases where we want to know the result of an expression, it would be better to use the *Display* function. For example, executing the expression:

```
6*7
```

with the function *Display* returns the result:

```
(int) 42
```

Eclipse inserts this result expression directly after the selected and executed expression. (So we don't forget what the question was…) The easiest method to remove the result expression from the scrapbook page is again the *Undo* function.

A further function for executing selected expressions is *Inspect*. This function shows the result in a separate *Expressions* window (Figure 1.19) that is opened automatically when needed. This function is particularly useful when the result of the executed expression is a complex object. In the *Expressions* window we can open the result object and analyze it in detail.

1.6   Little helpers

Eclipse is equipped with a variety of very useful tools and helpers, which – when used correctly – can save a substantial amount of typing and, in addition, reduce the number of bugs in our programs. In this section we want to introduce most of these little helpers.

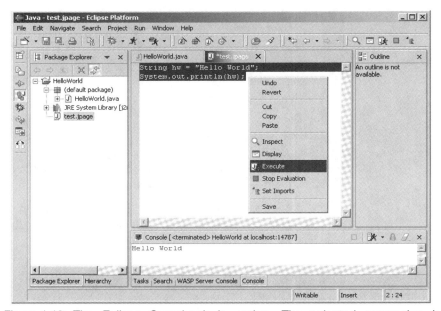

Figure 1.18: The Eclipse Scrapbook in action. The selected expression is executed with the help of the context function Execute. The scrapbook context function appears on the workbench's toolbar at the very right.

1.6.1   System information

Under the menu item *Help > About Eclipse Platform* we find some sections that may be important for our daily work. In particular, the button *Configuration Details* opens a text file that contains all essential information about the current configuration of the Eclipse platform:

- The section *System Properties* contains information about the Java platform under which the Eclipse workbench is executing. In addition, it displays information about the host operating system.

- The section *Features* lists the installed features. A *Feature* usually consists of a set of plug-ins that work together to provide specific functionality. For example, the Java IDE is a feature.

- The section *Plug-in Registry* lists all installed plug-ins separately.

- The section *Update Manager Log* lists information about the tasks performed by the update manager, such as installing new features or checking existing configurations.

Figure 1.19: The Expressions window directly after executing the expression 'new java.util.ArrayList(3);' using the Inspect function.

- The last section, *Error Log*, is important. Here we find a protocol of all error events that occurred during the execution of the Eclipse platform. If we develop own plug-ins this section will prove especially useful. A more comfortable way to view these error messages, however, is the *Error Log* view. We can open this view via *Window > Show View > Other > PDE Runtime > Error Log*. Physically, this error information is stored in file `.metadata/.log` in the workspace directory.

1.6.2 Help and Hover

Help

At this stage we don't want to dig too deep into the Eclipse help system. We need to know that we can invoke Eclipse help via the menu item *Help > Help Contents*. Like many other help systems, Eclipse also uses a client-server solution for its help system. Under the cover, Tomcat works as the help server, and a standard or custom Web browser is used to display the help to the end user.

In a vanilla Eclipse SDK we find the following help chapters:

1. *Workbench User Guide*

2. *Java Development User Guide*

3. *Platform Plug-in Developer Guide*

4. *JDT Plug-in Developer Guide*

5. *PDE Guide*

More chapters can be added by additional plug-ins. In *Part 1* of this book the first two help chapters are the most relevant. During *Part 2* and *Part 3* help Chapters 3 and 5 will also become important.

Since Eclipse 2.0, the Eclipse help function has been equipped with a search function. With the *Search Scope* function we can restrict the search to specific chapters and sections in the help system.

Context sensitive help

In addition to the explicit help function we can call help within Eclipse at any time simply by pressing the *F1* key – provided the currently active plug-in supports this function. After pressing *F1* we get a pop-up window (*Infopop*) where we can select a relevant help topic and jump directly to it within the help pages. In this context the *Show in Table of Contents* button (the second to the left of the printer symbol) is useful: it synchronizes the table of contents with the currently displayed help page. So we can see in which context the current help topic is located.

Hover

You probably know *hover infos* already from other applications: when the mouse hovers over a GUI element, a small pop-up window appears after a short delay that informs you of the purpose and function of the GUI element. Eclipse uses this technique as follows:

- All buttons on the various toolbars are equipped with hover infos.

- For files opened in the editor, you can display the full path information by hovering over the tag of the respective editor page.

- All task and problem markers are equipped with hover infos. You can display the text associated with a particular marker by hovering over the marker, so you don't have to look up the marker in the *Tasks* window.

- Last but not least: hover infos exist for source code as well. Just place the mouse over the type name `String` in our `HelloWorld` example. After a short delay you will see a hover info containing the Javadoc of class `java.lang.String`. Similarly, you display the Javadoc for method `java.io.PrintStream.println` when you hover over the word `println`. Using this technique, you can quickly find out in which class a certain method is defined, instead of browsing up and down the class hierarchies.

  If you press the *Ctrl* key while hovering over source text, your hover info will show the item's source code instead of the Javadoc!

1.6.3   Automatic code completion

The Code Assistant

One of the most powerful utilities for writing code in Eclipse is the *Code Assistant*. Tedious typing and searching in Javadoc or source code can be replaced by just a few keystrokes. Just try the following:

In our `HelloWorld` example open under

```
System.out.println("HelloWorld");
```

enter a new line. In this new line just type three characters:

```
Sys
```

and press *Ctrl-Spacebar*. In the pop-up list that appears, select the class System from the Package java.lang (double click). Now enter a period. A fraction of a second afterwards another pop-up list appears. From this list select the field out of type PrintStream. Once again enter a period and once again you get a pop-up list: select the method println. The cursor is now positioned within the parenthesis for the method parameters. We now complete this method call by entering the string 'Hello Eclipse'. It only remains to type the semicolon at the very end of the expression. The new line should now look like this:

```
System.out.println("Hello Eclipse");
```

I expect you get the idea already: the Code Assistant allows you to enter long class and method names with just a few keystrokes. But what is even more important: it saves you tedious searching and browsing in the documentation. If required, it can automatically insert the necessary import statements as well.

Templates   There is an even quicker method, however. Just try the same again, but now enter only the letters:

```
sy
```

and press *Ctrl-Spacebar*. From the pop-up list, select the entry sysout. (If you continue typing, the pop-up list will get smaller and smaller, as it only displays entries that match the entered string.) If you select the entry sysout with a single click, another pop-up window appears showing a code proposal for the keyword sysout. You can accept this proposal with a double click, while the *Esc* key closes both windows.

The code proposal shown is based on a code template that is associated with the keyword sysout. These templates are defined under *Preferences > Java > Editor > Templates*, where you can also create your own templates. This is done in a similar way to defining entries for code generation (see Section 1.3.5).

It is worth browsing through all these templates, as they can save you substantial typing work. While many templates are named to resemble Java constructs (if, while, catch, etc.), other templates bear the names of design patterns. For example, the template lazy. This template generates the following code:

```
if (name == null) {
  name = new type(arguments);
}
return name;
```

That is a typical pattern for the lazy assignment of a variable. What you have to do with this pattern is just replace the first occurrence of the string 'name' by the name of your own variable, for example with 'myHashMap'. This automatically replaces all occurrences of 'name' with 'myHashMap' throughout the pattern!

In addition to these Java code templates, there are predefined Javadoc templates, too. For example, if you enter the character '@' within a Javadoc comment, a pop-up window appears showing the available Javadoc keywords.

Custom templates   Of course we can define our own templates. In Section 1.3.5 we have already modified the template *typecomment*. Here now is an example for a completely home-grown template. The template generates an `if` instruction that only executes when the `equals()` method in the condition was successful. In addition, we make sure that we don't get a null pointer exception.

Template `equals`:

```
if (${name} != null && ${name}.equals(${cursor})) {
}
```

This template contains the user defined variable `${name}`. When applying this template, this variable will be replaced by a real field name (just as in the `lazy` template). In addition, the template contains the system variable `${cursor}`. This variable marks the position of the cursor. When applying the template, we just replace the first occurrence of 'name' with the real field name. Then we press the *TAB* key to jump to the predefined cursor position. There we can enter the argument for the `equals()` method.

Here are two more templates that occasionally prove useful:

Template `sconst`:

```
public static final String ${name} = "${cursor}";
```

Template `iconst`:

```
public static final int ${name} = ${cursor};
```

Code Assistant   Under *Preferences > Java > Editor > Code Assist* we can make adjustments to influence
preferences   the behavior of the *Code Assistant* (Figure 1.20).

In particular, the option *Automatically add import instead of qualified name* is very useful. When this option is set, we can in most cases avoid adding `import` statements manually – simply by using the *Code Assistant*.

For most of the other options, the default values provided by Eclipse make sense, so we should not need to change these settings. What can be a bit annoying at times is the automatic activation of the *Code Assistant* after entering a period or a '@' character. It could make sense to increase the delay value of this option from 500 msec to 1000 msec.

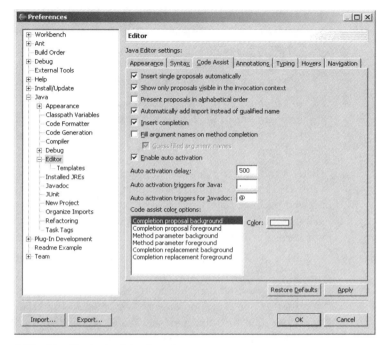

Figure 1.20: The Code Assistant preferences.

Other functions of code completion

Apart from the *Code Assistant*, which appears either automatically after entering an activation character or when pressing *Ctrl-Spacebar*, there are a few more context functions for code completion. Let's take a look at how we can use these functions to create Javadoc comments.

Creating Javadoc In our example program `HelloWorld`, just place the cursor into the main method and invoke the function *Source > Add Javadoc Comment*. This will insert the comment lines

```
/**
 * Method main.
 * @param args
 */
```

in front of the method. The only thing that remains to do is to complete this description.

An even simpler method for creating a Javadoc comment is to open a new line in front of the method and to enter the String `/**` followed by the *Enter* key.

The context submenu *Source* contains more useful functions for code completion:

Importing types
- *Organize Imports*. This function analyzes the whole program and inserts the required `import` statements at the beginning of the program. Should this function discover equally named types from different packages during this task, it will prompt you with a list of those packages. You must then select the required type from this list.

- *Add Import*. This function inserts an `import` statement for the selected type name at the beginning of the program. Similar to the *Organize Imports* function, this function will prompt you for type selection if it discovers equally named types from different packages.

Under *Window > Preferences > Java > Organize Imports* you can specify a threshold value for single type `import` statements. If the program contains more import types from a given package than what was specified under this threshold value, the `import` statements for this package will be combined into a single `import` statement by using wildcards (as in `eclipse.org.*`). The default threshold value is 99.

Overriding methods
- *Override Methods...* This function first shows a selection list for all inherited methods. In this list we can check all methods that we want to override. Afterwards, Eclipse generates method stubs for all these methods. This function is particularly useful if our class implements one or several interfaces. In such a case, we simply invoke this function and check all the methods of the interface (if they are not already checked). Afterwards we simply complete the generated method stubs.

Encapsulating fields
- *Generate Getter and Setter...* This function generates access methods for class fields. For example, if a class contains the field definition

```
private String hi;
```

invoking this function would result in the following generated methods:

```
/**
 * Returns the hi.
 * @return String
 */
public String getHi() {
  return hi;
}
/**
 * Sets the hi.
 * @param hi The hi to set
 */
public void setHi(String hi) {
  this.hi = hi;
}
```

However, this function does not change existing references to the encapsulated field. If you want to change these references, too, are better off using the context function *Refactor > Encapsulate Field...* We will discuss this function in Section 1.8.2.

Creating delegate methods
- *Generate Delegate Methods...* This function can be applied to non-primitive fields and replicates the method of the field's type in the containing type.

Inheriting constructors
- *Add Constructors from Superclass.* This function generates proxies for the inherited constructors. These proxies contain only a super() call. Of course, you can then modify these proxies to override the behavior of the constructor.

i18n
- *Externalize Strings...* This function supports the internationalization of applications. We will discuss this in detail in Section 10.6.1.

- *Generate Delegate Methods...* This function can be applied to all non-primitive fields and replicates the methods of the field's type within the class or interface that contains the selected field.

1.6.4   The Correction Assistant

Even before you compile a program by invoking the *Save* function, the editor tells you how bad a programmer you are. Erroneous expressions are underlined in red – as happened to you in school. (The same metaphor is used by some word processors.) So even before compiling a program, you can notice faulty expressions such as a missing bracket or semicolon, so that you can react accordingly.

QuickFix
Depending on the skills of the programmer, you may also occasionally see a yellow bulb in the left margin of the source editor. This function is called *QuickFix*, and signals that Eclipse has at least one correction proposal for the programmer's mistake. In fact, there are only a few error types where Eclipse loses its wits and is unable to offer a *QuickFix* proposal. To activate the *QuickFix* function, click on the yellow bulb. (The same function can be invoked by pressing *Ctrl-1* when the cursor is above the faulty line.)

Let's try it. Say we purposely make a mistake and write only printl() instead of println(). Immediately we will see a yellow bulb on the left margin (Figure 1.21).

One of the advantages of the *Correction Assistant* is the fast feedback it gives to the program author. The immediate response to a mistake should trigger a learning effect in the programmer, making the same mistake less likely next time.

However, we may also use the *Correction Assistant* to save some typing. For example, when we write some code and refer to a method that has not yet been written, a simple click on the yellow bulb that appears allows us to generate a stub for the missing method instantly.

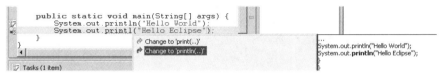

Figure 1.21: The Correction Assistant in action. The erroneous method name 'printl()' is underlined in red. On the left we see the yellow bulb. A click on the bulb brings up a pop-up window with the suggestions 'Change to 'print(..)'' and 'Change to 'println(..)'. The pop-up window on the right shows what the code will look like if we select the second suggestion.

By using the *Correction Assistant* we can therefore adopt a top-down programming style. Instead of thinking ahead and creating every field and method that we might need, we can just start coding the main functionality. Fields and methods encapsulating sub-functions are created by referencing them and then using *QuickFix* to create a declaration for the missing field or a stub for the missing method. Later, we can go and implement the details of this field or method.

You can switch off the *Correction Assistant* completely or in parts under *Preferences > Java > Editor > Problem Indication*.

1.6.5   Convenience functions of the Java editor

Typing aids   Under *Preferences > Java > Editor > Behavior* you can activate or deactivate a variety of typing aids. The Java editor is, for example, able to close open parenthesis or brackets automatically. It can include string literals in quotes automatically and can wrap the text within Javadoc and other comments.

The function *Smart Java string wrapping* is also nice. In our `HelloWorld` example program, just place the cursor between 'Hello' and 'World' and press *Enter*.

The result is the syntactically correct expression:

```
System.out.println("Hello " +
    "World");
```

1.7   Source code navigation

In large projects it is essential to have good navigation tools at hand. Eclipse offers some of them as an editor context function (right mouse click):

- *Open Declaration*. The function opens the definition of the selected type in the editor.

Hyperlinks   Eclipse 2.1 introduced a more convenient route to this function: Just press the *Ctrl* key and move the cursor above the type reference 'String'. This type reference now appears in blue and is underlined – it has become a hyperlink. With a click on it you open the definition of java.lang.String.

- *Open Type Hierarchy.* This function opens a special browser window that will appear in front of the *Package Explorer*. The new window shows the type hierarchy for the selected type. We discuss this browser in detail in Section 2.4.3.

- *Open Super Implementation.* This function opens the super implementation of the selected method, i.e. its implementation in the parent class or the next ancestor class.

- *Show in Package Explorer.* This function synchronizes the *Package Explorer* with the current editor window (see Section 2.4.2).

The arrow buttons in the toolbar of the Eclipse workbench are also useful. These arrow buttons were introduced with Eclipse 2.1 to give the Eclipse workbench a behavior similar to Web browsers. By clicking these buttons we can jump to previously visited code locations (and if necessary back again).

1.8   Refactoring code

Modifications of existing programs usually take a lot of time and may introduce new bugs. Even the simple renaming of a type may affect dozens, hundreds or even thousands of other compilation units. In such cases the computer is superior to the human, and consequently Eclipse offers a rich set of refactoring utilities. The purpose of refactoring is to improve the structure of the code without modifying the behavior of the application. *Refactoring* plays a major role, especially in the context of *Extreme Programming* (XP).

1.8.1   Modifying types

Modifications at the type level (classes and interfaces) are best applied in the *Package Explorer*. The context menu of the *Package Explorer* offers some functions under the subtitle *Refactor* such as *Refactor > Move* and *Refactor > Rename*. In addition is it possible to create a copy of a type by using the context function *Copy*.

Move and rename   • *Moving a compilation unit.* Let us assume that we are happy with the current location of our *HelloWorld* class in the default package of the project. Instead, we would like to create a new package named *HelloPackage* and move the class *HelloWorld* into it.

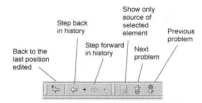

Figure 1.22: We can jump to the most recently edited code location with the 'Goto last edit position' button. Two more buttons allow us to step backwards and forwards in the navigation history of visited code locations. The 'Show source of selected element' button can isolate elements (methods or field definitions) in the editor window.

We create a new package in the usual way (the *Create a Java Package* button). Then we select the compilation unit HelloWorld in the *Package Explorer*. From the context menu we select the function *Refactor > Move...* The following dialog contains another small package explorer. Here, we expand the project HelloWorld by clicking on the '+' character and select the package HelloPackage as the move target. After pressing *OK* the compilation unit HelloWorld is moved into the target package. The source code of HelloWorld now contains the line

```
package HelloPackage;
```

Should other compilation units contain references to the type HelloWorld, these references would be updated accordingly. We can inhibit this by removing the checkmark from *Update references to moved element(s)*.

As a matter of fact, moving a compilation unit can also be achieved by a simple drag-and-drop operation with the mouse. We could have just dragged the compilation HelloWorld from the default package into the package HelloPackage and dropped it there. But in larger projects where packages may have a large distance between them, the context function *Refactor > Move...* usually works better.

• *Moving a type.* Similarly, we may move types (classes and interfaces) within a compilation unit. For example, we can drag the class symbol (the green circle with the 'C') onto another class symbol. The dragged class thus becomes an inner class of the target class. However, in this case the original version of the dragged class remains at its original position, too, so this is a copy function rather than a move.

• *Renaming compilation units and types.* Similarly we can rename compilation units and types by invoking the context function *Refactor > Rename...* (Figure 1.23)

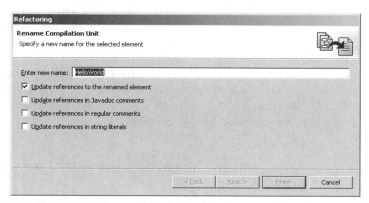

Figure 1.23: Renaming a compilation unit. In addition to updating references in the code, it is also possible to have references in Javadoc comments, normal comments, and string literals updated.

1.8.2 Refactoring code

As well as classes and interfaces, there are many more possibilities for code refactoring. These functions can be invoked from the source editor's context menu, from the context menu of the *Outline* view (see Section 2.5), or from the main menu of the workbench.

Methods

- *Rename*. Nearly everything can be renamed with the function *Refactor > Rename...*: classes and interfaces, methods, fields, parameters, and local variables. References to the renamed elements are updated accordingly. If fields are renamed and if the field has access methods (get...() and set...()), the method names are updated, too.

- *Move*. Static methods (and, with some restrictions, also instance methods) can be moved into other classes with the function *Refactor > Move...* References to these methods are updated accordingly.

- *Pull up*. Non-static methods and fields can be moved into super classes by applying the function *Refactor > Pull up...*

- *Change method signature*. The function *Refactor > Change Method Signature...* allows us to change a method's access modifier, its result type, and the order, names and types of its parameters. References to the method are updated accordingly. When new parameters are introduced into the method, it is necessary to define a default value for each new parameter. This default value is inserted as the value for the new parameter when the corresponding method calls are updated.

- *Extract method*. The function *Refactor > Extract Method...* encapsulates the selected code into a new method definition. Eclipse performs a data flow control analysis for the selected code section. From that it determines the parameters and the result type of the new method. The new method is inserted behind the current method and the selected code is replaced by a corresponding method call. In some cases, however, it is not possible to apply this function, for example if there are multiple result values of the selected code section. In cases where the function cannot be applied, it tells you the reason for the rejection.

Example:

In the following method we select the bold line and apply the *Extract Method* function:

```
public static void main(String[] args) {
  System.out.println("Hello World");
  System.out.println("Hello Eclipse");
}
```

In the following dialog we specify 'helloEclipse' as the name for the new method and receive:

```
public static void main(String[] args) {
  System.out.println("Hello World");
  helloEclipse();
}
public static void helloEclipse() {
  System.out.println("Hello Eclipse");
}
```

Vice versa, we can resolve methods by applying the function *Refactor > Inline...*

Types and classes
- *Extract interface*. With the function *Refactor > Extract Interface...* we can generate a corresponding interface for an existing class. For example, if we select the class name HelloWorld and invoke this function, we are asked for a name for the new interface. If we enter IHelloWorld and press *OK*, a Java interface IHelloWorld is generated and the class definition of HelloWorld is completed with the clause implements IHelloWorld. In addition, Eclipse determines which references to HelloWorld can be replaced with a reference to the interface IHelloWorld. As it happens, the interface generated in this example is empty, as the class HelloWorld contains only static methods.

- *Use Supertype*. After creating the interface IHelloWorld we call the function *Refactor > Use Supertype where possible...* for class HelloWorld. This function offers us a choice between the types IHelloWorld and Object. Both are supertypes of HelloWorld. If we now select IHelloWorld, Eclipse will replace all references to

HelloWorld by references to IHelloWorld, provided that this would not result in compilation errors.

- *Convert nested type to top level.* Inner classes and interfaces can be separated into their own compilation unit (.java file) by applying the method *Refactor > Convert Nested Type to Top Level...* to them. The new compilation unit is equipped with the necessary import statements. In the type definition that previously contained the inner type, a new class field is generated whose type declaration refers to the newly generated top level type. In addition, the constructor of the container type is extended with a new parameter that supplies the new field with an instance of the new top level type.

- *Promote anonymous class to nested class.* We often create anonymous classes that work as event listeners, especially when working with events. Such anonymous classes can be converted easily into named inner classes by applying the function *Refactor > Promote Anonymous to Nested...*

Variables

- *Extract local variable.* The function *Refactor > Extract Local Variable...* replaces the selected expression with the name of a new variable. A suitable variable assignment is inserted before modified expression. For example, in

```
System.out.println("Hello World");
```

we select 'HelloWorld' and apply the function. In the following dialog we specify 'hi' for the variable name. The result is:

```
String hi = "Hello World";
System.out.println(hi);
```

Optionally, all occurrences of 'HelloWorld' are replaced with a reference to the variable hi.

- *Inline local variable.* The function *Refactor > Inline...* works in the opposite way. For example, if we select the variable hi and apply this function, all occurrences of hi are replaced with the value of hi (the string 'Hello World'). Before the replacement is performed, a dialog box shows us the effects of the replacement by comparing the old version with the new version of the compilation unit (see Section 1.10.1).

- *Encapsulate.* The function *Refactor > Self Encapsulate...* allows us to convert a public variable into a private variable. It generates access method for this variable (see also *Generate Getter and Setter...* in Section 1.6.3), and updates all read and write access to this variable accordingly.

Before:

```
public int status;
public void process() {
    switch (status) {
      case 0 :
        System.out.println("Status 0");
        break;
      }
}
```

After:

```
private int status;
public void process() {
  switch (getStatus()) {
    case 0 :
      System.out.println("Status 0");
      break;
    }
}
public void setStatus(int status) {
  this.status = status;
}
public int getStatus() {
  return status;
}
```

- *Convert local variable to field.* The function *Refactor > Convert Local Variable to Field...* can convert a local variable that is defined in a method body into an instance field.

Constants
- *Extract/Inline Constant.* The extract and inline functions that we discussed for variables are also available for constants. For example, let's select the string 'Hello World' and invoke the function *Refactor > Extract Constant...* In the following dialog we assign the name HELLOWORLD to the new constant. Eclipse now inserts the line

```
private static final String HELLOWORLD = "Hello World";
```

and replaces all occurrences of 'Hello World' with HELLOWORLD. Vice versa, the function *Refactor > Inline...* allows us to resolve the names of constants by replacing them with the constant's value.

1.9   Undo and Redo

With *Edit > Undo (Ctrl-Z)* it is possible to revert previous actions. The *Undo* function can be applied over many steps – no limit seems to exist. *Undo* can even undo actions across previous *Save* operations.

With *Edit > Redo* (*Ctrl-Y*) we can once again execute actions that were previously undone by applying the *Undo* function.

Undoing the *Refactor* functions (see Section 1.8) is a special case. The normal *Undo* function can only revert these functions in several steps, and then only partially. To undo a *Refactor* function, it is better to use the special *Undo* (*Ctrl-Shift-Z*) and *Redo* (*Ctrl-Shift-Y*) functions in the *Refactor* submenu.

1.10 Local History

The *Local History* function group belongs to Eclipse's most powerful functionality for maintaining source code. For each compilation unit, Eclipse stores a configurable number of older versions that are updated with each *Save* operation.

The number of stored version can be set in *Preferences > Workbench > Local History*. The default value is 50 versions, with a maximum age of seven days and a maximum file size of 1 Mb. If you use the *Save* key (*Ctrl-S*) as frequently as I do, it is better to increase the maximum number of versions a bit.

The *Local History* functions work for any type of resource, not just for Java source code.

1.10.1 Comparing resources

The context function *Compare > Local History* allows us to compare the current version of a compilation unit with previous versions. First we get a selection list with the previous versions nicely grouped by days. Clicking one of these versions will compare the selected version with the current version.

This function can be invoked from the *Package Explorer* or from the *Resource Navigator*. It can also be called from the editor, where it is applied to the selected element only – for example a method.

1.10.2 Replacing with an older version

The function *Replace > Local History* works very similarly to *Compare > Local History*. The window is additionally equipped with a *Replace* button with which we can replace the current version with the version in the right window. In contrast, this function does not have a *Java Structure Compare* window.

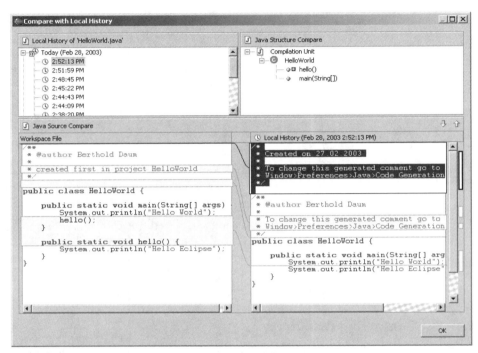

Figure 1.24: Here we have deleted and modified some comments and extracted the 'println()' statement as a separate method. The comparison shows the deleted lines on the right and the inserted lines on the left hand side on a gray background. The right vertical ruler shows all modification to the file: the selected modification has a black border, all other modifications have a gray border. The window at the top right corner (Java Structure Compare) allows the comparison of single methods.

1.10.3   Restore deleted resource

Mistakenly deleting a resource is not a tragedy in Eclipse 2 (it was in Eclipse 1.0). The function *Restore > Local History* shows us a selection list for previously deleted resources that can be restored by simply marking their checkboxes.

2 Organizing your code

In this chapter we first discuss the handling of the different components of the Eclipse workbench: editors, views, and perspectives. Then we look at the basic resource types in Eclipse: projects, folders, and files.

Afterwards we use the new knowledge in a practical example. This time we don't output 'Hello World' on the Java console – but on your computer's sound card! In the context of this example we discuss topics such as the import and export of files and archives, the association of source files with binary files, and how to set the project properties correctly.

2.1 The Workbench

In the *Introduction* we mentioned that the Java IDE is merely one of the many possible plug-ins for the Eclipse workbench (which itself is a plug-in into the Eclipse platform). The Eclipse workbench is completely language-neutral – all functions that are specific to development with Java are packaged in the Java IDE plug-ins.

Let's switch back to the resource perspective for a moment (Figure 2.1). Where we previously saw the *Package Explorer*, we now find the *Resource Navigator*. The Java packages have vanished, and instead we see a structure of nested folders.

Resource perspective

Figure 2.1: The Resource Navigator shows projects, folders, and files. This shows a project in the Navigator that we will develop in Chapter 3.

2.2   Resources

The *Resource Navigator* shows an overview of the set of resources maintained by the Eclipse workbench (the workspace) and supports navigation within this set of resources.

2.2.1   Resource types

The workbench understands three different resource types:

* *Projects.* A project is always the root node of a resource tree. Projects can contain folders and files. Projects cannot be nested.

* *Folders.* A folder can contain files and other (nested) folders.

* *Files.* Files are the leaf nodes in a resource tree, i.e. a file cannot contain other resources.

2.2.2   Where Resources are stored

All resources are stored directly in the file system of the host platform. This is different from Visual Age, where resources were stored in a repository. In contrast, the structure of projects and folders in the Eclipse workspace directly correlates to the directory structure of the host platform. This has advantages in the case of crashes and for back-ups. (In Section 5.1 we will discuss how to connect a repository to Eclipse.)

By default the resources of the Eclipse workbench are stored in the (host) directory `\eclipse\workspace`. Each project is contained in a corresponding sub-directory. For example, the resource `AnimationEvent.java` shown in Figure 2.1 is stored under path `\eclipse\workspace\DukeSpeaks\com\sun\speech\freetts\relp\Animation-Event.java`. Of course is it possible to create a workspace directory in a different location by specifying the command line option `-data` when starting Eclipse:

```
eclipse.exe -data C:\myOldWorkSpace
```

2.2.3   Synchronizing resources

Refresh

For each resource in the workbench Eclipse stores some metadata in the directory `\eclipse\workspace\.metadata`. Sometimes it happens that the state of a resource in `\eclipse\workspace` does not match the state of the corresponding metadata. In particular, this happens when a workspace file is modified outside of Eclipse, for example by modifying that file with an external tool.

This is not a tragedy. All you have to do is select the resource that is out-of-sync and apply the context function *Refresh*. This function can be applied not only to single resources, but also to folders and projects, so that we can easily re-synchronize a whole directory tree.

2.2.4   Navigation

The following context functions in the navigator's context menu are available for navigation:

- *Go into*. This function reduces the current view to the content of the selected project or folder. This function can be particularly useful when your workspace consists of thousands of resources.

- *Go to > Back*. This function returns to the previous view. The function can also be invoked from the navigator's toolbar (arrow to the left).

- *Go to > Forward*. Undoes a previous *Go to > Back* operation. The function can also be invoked from the navigator's toolbar (arrow to the right).

- *Go to > One level up*. Goes into the next higher folder or project. The function can also be invoked from the navigator's toolbar (folder symbol).

- *Open in new Window*. This function works similarly to *Go into*, but opens a new window (with a complete workbench!) in which only the contents of the selected project or folder are shown in the navigator.

The menu of the navigator's toolbar (under the small triangle) offers further functions:

- The *Sort* function allows files to be sorted by name or type.

- The *Filters...* function allows files with specific file name extensions to be excluded from the navigator.

- The function *Select Working Set...* allows you to select a named working set, to restrict the resources shown in the navigator to the resources belonging to the selected working set. This function also allows you to define new working sets.

- The function *Deselect Working Set* removes the working set restrictions from the navigator.

- The function *Edit Active Working Set...* allows you to modify the current working set.

2.3   Associations

In Eclipse the type of a file is usually determined by its file name extension. (It is also possible to assign specific file types to fully qualified file names.) In Figure 2.1 we see text based files such as .java and .html files, but also binary files such as the .class files. The file type (and thus the file name extension) controls what happens when a file is opened.

Open with...

For example, if we click a .java file with the right mouse button, we get a pop-up menu with context functions. When we select the sub-menu *Open with...*, we get another pop-up menu with editors. In the first menu section we see the editor that was used last for this file (in our case that should be the Java source editor). The second section shows all editors that are registered for that file name extension – in our case these are *Text Editor* and *System Editor*. The *Text Editor* is the text editor that is contained in the Eclipse SDK, which can be used for all text based files. The *System Editor* is the editor which is registered under the host platform for that file type. Eclipse is able to start such editors from the workbench: for example, if we open an HTML file, the host platform's Web browser is started.

Defining new associations

Most of the file associations (which editor works with which file type) are determined by the Eclipse plug-ins. However, it is also possible to add or modify such associations manually. To do so, we invoke *Window > Preferences > Workbench > File Associations* (Figure 2.2).

In the upper window we see a list of registered file types. By using the *Add* and *Remove* buttons we can add new file types or delete existing ones. In the lower window the registered editors for the currently selected file name extension are shown. Here, too, we can add new editors or remove existing editors. By using the *Default* button we can declare a specific editor as the default editor for that file type.

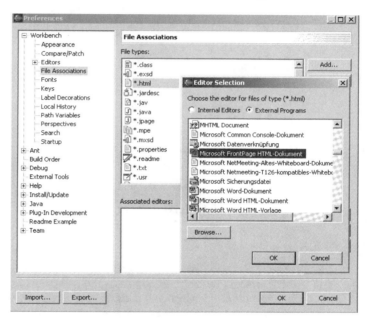

Figure 2.2: Here we define file associations. First we have added the file name pattern '.html', then we associated Microsoft FrontPage with this file type.*

When we press the *Add* button, we first get a list of internal editors, i.e. editors that are implemented as Eclipse plug-ins. If we check the button *External Programs*, we get a list of the applications that are registered in the host operating system for the selected file type. With a double click on such an application, we can select it as a new editor for this file type.

2.4   Packages

Let's switch back to the Java perspective now. The picture we get now is quite different: the *Package Explorer* shows the different projects with their package structure and the compilation units.

2.4.1   Folders and packages

Packages are not real resources but virtual objects. The package structure of a project is derived from the package declaration at the beginning of each Java source file.

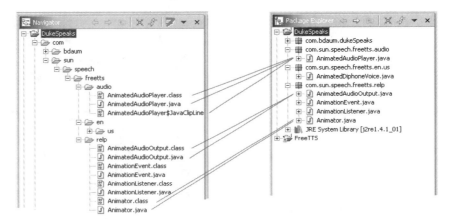

Figure 2.3:   *Each package can be uniquely mapped onto a node in the resource tree. Compilation units, in contrast, can consist of several resources: the source file and one or several binary files. In the case of the class AnimatedAudioPlayer we have two binary files – one for AnimatedAudioPlayer and one for the inner class JavaClipLineListener.*

The Java specification, however, requires that the package structure of a project is isomorphic to the project's directory structure. For example, all resources of the package com.sun.speech.freetts.relp must be stored under the relative path com/sun/speech/ freetts/relp, as shown in Figure 2.3. In Eclipse, the path is always relative to the project's source code root directory. In our case, the relative path com/sun/speech/ freetts/relp is equivalent to the host platform path

        \eclipse\workspace\DukeSpeaks\com\sun\speech\freetts\relp

2.4.2   Navigation

The *Package Explorer* is equipped with similar navigation functions as the *Resource Navigator* (see Section 2.2.4). Here we also have the context functions *Go into* and *Open in new Window*, and in the toolbar we have buttons for the functions *Go to > Back*, *Go to > Forward* and *Go to > One level up*. Under the toolbar's drop-down menu we find the same functions for managing working sets.

The button *Link with Editor* (at the left side of the drop-down menu symbol) is also important. If this button is pushed, the *Package Explorer* is always synchronized with the active editor. When we change between editor pages, the selection in the *Package Explorer* will change correspondingly.

Furthermore, we have the possibility of opening the type hierarchy browser discussed in the next section.

2.4.3   Hierarchy

The type hierarchy shows the super types and subtypes for classes and interface. We can restrict the view to super types or subtypes only, or show the complete hierarchy. By using the *History* function we can quickly change between the different views, or can display previously displayed type hierarchies again (Figure 2.4).

Figure 2.4:   The Type Hierarchy Browser consists of two windows. While the upper window shows the type hierarchy, the lower window displays the fields and methods of the selected type.

In the toolbar of the lower window we can find further functions. The first button affects the upper window. It restricts the view to only those types that implement the field or method selected in the lower window. When we push the second button, the lower window will also show the methods and fields that are inherited by the selected type. The remaining buttons are the same as in the *Outline* view (see the next section).

The *Type Hierarchy Browser* can be useful when we want to analyze existing projects and libraries. When creating a new project we will only need this browser when the project becomes bigger.

2.5   The Outline view

The *Outline* view (Figure 2.5) supports navigation within a source file. In general, the *Outline* view is not restricted to Java sources but supports – depending on the plug-ins installed – other file types as well.

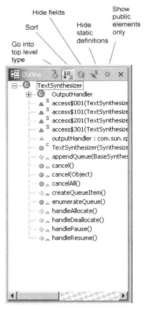

Figure 2.5:   The buttons on the Outline toolbar allow you to restrict the Outline view to specific entry types. Fields and methods can be sorted in alphabetic order by pushing the 'Sort' button (otherwise their order corresponds to their definition sequence in the source file).

For Java programs the *Outline* view displays entries for fields and methods, but also for `import` statements. If inner classes are defined, these classes appear, too, in the outline view: the main type and the inner types form a tree structure.

With a single click on such an entry the source editor is positioned to the corresponding element. Apart from this facility for quick navigation the *Outline* view offers a few more functions. But lets start with the graphical representation of the entries within the *Outline* view.

2.5.1 Representation

The first icon in front of a *Outline* view entry represents the entry type (package, `import` statement, interface, class, method, field) and the visibility (`public`, `protected`, `private`).

Icons

	import statement
	interface
	class
	public method
	protected method
	private method
	default method (without modifier)
	public field
	protected field

▫	private field
△	default field (without modifier)

In addition to this first icon, additional icons can add information about the entry:

C	constructor
S	static element
F	final element
▲	overridden element

Outline preferences The representation of the *Outline* view can be changed under *Window > Preferences > Java > Appearance*:

- *Show method return types*. Displays the result type of methods in the *Outline* view.

- *Show override indicators...* Displays the indicator for methods that override inherited methods.

- *Show member in Package Explorer*. If this option is set, methods and fields are also shown in the *Package Explorer* as child elements of classes and interfaces. Most of the *Outline* View functions are in this case available in the *Package Explorer*, too.

2.5.2   Context functions

The *Outline* view offers a rich variety of context functions. The most important of these functions are available as toolbar buttons, too (see Figure 2.5). Here is an overview of these functions:

- *Open Type Hierarchy*. Shows the type hierarchy for the selected element (see Section 2.4.3). This function can be applied not only to single types, but also to whole packages or projects.

- *Open Supertype Implementation*. This function is only available for elements that override an inherited feature. When applied, the inherited feature is opened in the source editor.

- *Show in Package Explorer.* Synchronizes the *Package Explorer* with the element selected in the *Outline* view.

- *Cut, Copy, Paste, Delete.* The usual copy and delete functions, but applied to the element selected in the *Outline* view.

- *Refactor>...* Various functions for refactoring code (see Section 1.8.2).

- *Source>...* Various functions for automatic source code completion (see Section 1.6.3).

- *References>...* Searches for references to the selected element (see next section).

- *Definitions>...* Searches for definitions of the selected elements (see next section).

- *Read Access>...* Searches for read access to the selected field (see next section).

- *Write Access>...* Searches for write access to the selected field (see next section).

- *Add/Remove Watchpoint.* This function appears only on field entries and belongs to the debugger's tool set (see Chapter 4).

- *Add/Remove Method Breakpoint.* This function appears only on method entries and belongs to the debugger's tool set (see Chapter 4).

- *Compare With>..., Replace With>..., Restore from Local History...* With these functions we can compare the current version of an element with a previous version from the *Local History*, or we can restore a previous version (see Section 1.10).

2.6   Searching

2.6.1   The Search function

The powerful Eclipse *Search* function consists of two components: the *Search* dialog for entering the search criteria (Figure 2.6) and the view containing the search results (Figure 2.7).

Search criteria   If the search function is called from the toolbar of the Eclipse workbench or from the Eclipse main menu, we first get the dialog for entering the search criteria. If we call the function as a context function, this step is omitted, since the search criteria are already defined by the context.

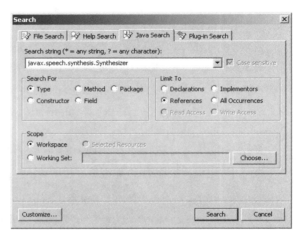

Figure 2.6: The dialog for entering search criteria has several pages (depending on the installed plug-ins). In the above case, the dialog contains a page for searching in generic files, a page for searching within the Eclipse help system, a page for Java specific searching (opened), and a page for searching plug-ins.

In the case of a *Java Search* we can search for the name of a type, of a method, of a package, of a constructor, or of a field. We can qualify this name completely or only partially. In addition, we may restrict the search by constraints. We can just search for declarations, or only for references, or for both. In case of fields we may restrict the search to read or write accesses. The search scope can be limited to the selected resources only or to *Working Sets* (named resource sets).

Besides the *Java Search* the *Search* dialog features additional pages for searching in generic files, for searching in the help system and for searching plug-ins. With the *Customize* button we can hide and show specific search dialog pages.

Search results   The results of a search are always shown in the *Search View*. In the standard Java perspective the Search View is stacked with the *Tasks View*.

By using the up- and down-arrows in the toolbar of the *Search View* we can easily step through all the occurrences of the search item. The corresponding compilation unit is automatically opened in the source editor. The position of the search item is shown on the left margin of the source editor with a yellow arrow.

It is useful to know that the *Search View* keeps track of the search history. Previous search results can be recalled by pressing the *Previous Search Results* button or via the *Search View*s drop-down menu.

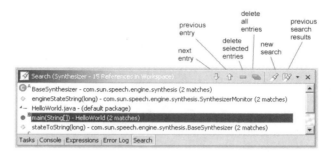

Figure 2.7: The Search View show all compilation units in which the sought item was found. If the sought item occurs several times in the same compilation unit, the number of occurrences is shown in parentheses at the end of the entry. A double click on an entry in the Search View opens the corresponding compilation unit in the source editor.

2.6.2   Find and Replace

Besides the search function discussed above, Eclipse, of course, provides a function for finding and replacing string in text files. With the function *Edit > Find/Replace* we obtain a dialog (see Figure 2.8) where we can enter the search string and additional search options. If we call this function while a string is selected, the selected string will be used as search string.

Figure 2.8: The Find/Replace dialog supports searching for character strings and replacing such strings with others.

When searching, we can search forwards or backwards, and restrict the search to the selected text area. In addition there are further options:

- *Case Sensitive*. If this option is checked, the search is performed in case sensitive mode.

- *Wrap Search*. If this option is checked, searching continues at the beginning of the search area when the end is reached (or at the end of the search area when the beginning is reached, in case of searching backwards). Otherwise, a message prompt is displayed.

- *Whole Word*. If this option is checked, only whole words are searched for.

- *Incremental*. If this option is checked, the search begins immediately when the first character of the search string is entered. When more characters are entered, the search operation is continued as necessary.

Eclipse offers more *Find* functions that correspond to these options, such as: *Edit > Find Next*, *Edit > Find Previous*, and *Edit > Incremental Find*. In addition, this group includes the function *Edit > Go to line...*, which allows us to jump to a line with a specified line number.

2.7   Arranging editors and views

The layout of the different windows in the Eclipse workbench is not fixed and can be configured by the user (with some restrictions). There are essentially three ways in which we can arrange windows within the workbench:

Docked windows
- We can place a window at the left or right of another window, or below or above that window (Figure 2.9). Using this technique, all windows stay visible, however, their size shrinks with each new window. We can dock a window to another window by dragging its title area or tag to the edge of the target window. When the cursor changes to a fat arrow, we drop the window.

Stacked windows
- Another option is to stack several windows in front of each other. By clicking the tag of a window we can bring this window to the top. We can stack a window in front of another window by dragging its title area or tag to the target window. When the cursor changes to a stack symbol, we release it.

FastView
- The *FastView* can minimize a window in the left border of the workbench (under the perspective icons): the window is only represented by an icon. A single click on the icon causes the window to appear, another click and it vanishes again. We can convert a window into a *FastView* by dragging its title area or tag to the left border of the workbench. When the cursor changes to a stack symbol, we release it. This option is only available for windows containing views, not for windows containing

editors. The same is achieved by right clicking a view's title bar and then selecting the context function *Fast View*.

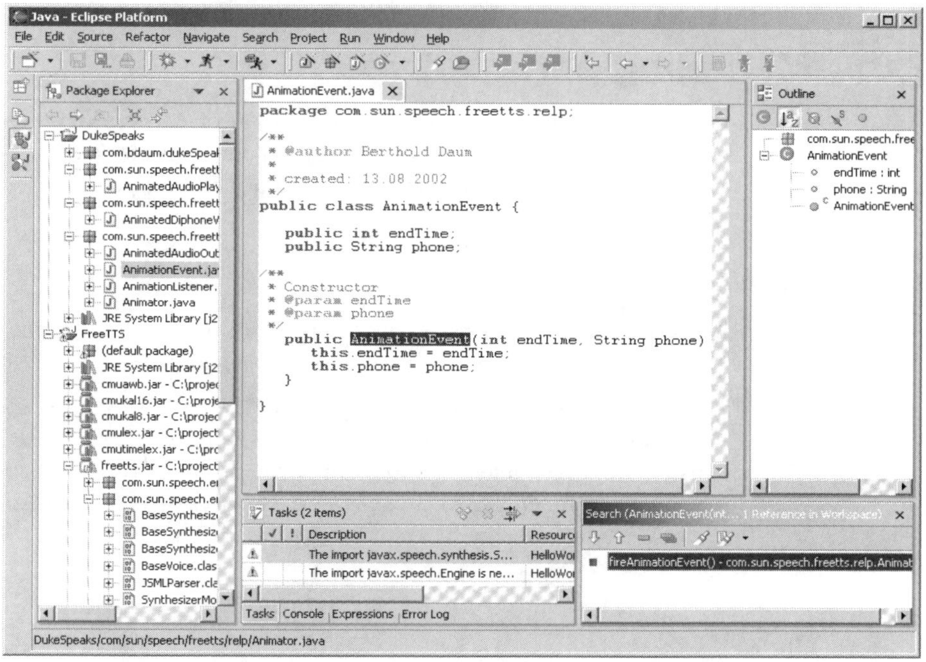

Figure 2.9:   Here we have dragged the Search View to the left edge of the Tasks View so that both views are visible side by side.

Opening and closing windows

Closing a window is trivial: a click on the windows close button in the top right corner or *Ctrl-F4* does the job. But how do we open it again?

- For editor windows this is simple: a double click on the corresponding resource in the *Resource Navigator* or the *Package Explorer* will open the resource under the used editor previously in use.

- For view windows, we use the function *Window > Show View >...* and select the view that we want to open.

By the way, if you want to close all editor windows, just invoke *File > Close All* or press *Ctrl-Shift-F4*.

Maximizing windows

All windows in the workbench can be maximized. A double click on the title area of a view or on the tag of an editor page maximizes the corresponding window, i.e. the window occupies all the space in the workbench window. Another double click restores the previous window layout.

2.8   Managing perspectives

A perspective defines a specific combination of editors, views and menus within the workbench. In this chapter we already encountered the *Resource Perspective* and the *Java Perspective*. In Chapter 4 we will in addition get acquainted with the *Debug Perspective*.

2.8.1   Defining new perspectives

Let's assume that you have now arranged all the windows in the *Java Perspective* to your liking. Is it possible to store these preferences?

You can save this layout with the function *Window > Save Perspective As...* (Figure 2.10). In the name field of this function's dialog you can define a name for the new perspective. If you later want to return to the original Java Perspective, you can do so by invoking the function *Window > Reset Perspective* or by invoking *Window > Close Perspective* followed by *Window > Open Perspective...*

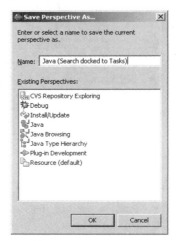

Figure 2.10: The modified workbench configuration shown in Figure 2.9 is stored here as a new perspective under the name Java (Search docked to Tasks).

2.8.2 Configuring perspectives

With the function *Window > Customize Perspective* we can change certain aspects of the current perspective:

- The file types that are available in the submenu *File > New*.

- The perspectives that can be activated from the submenu *Window > Open Perspective*.

- The views that can be opened from the submenu *Window > Show View*.

- The *Action Sets* (buttons and menu functions) that appear in the workbench's toolbar or the main menu (Figure 2.11).

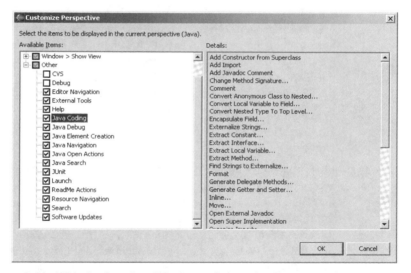

Figure 2.11: With the function 'Window > Customize Perspective' we can remove whole function groups (Action Sets) from a perspective, or add new function groups. The right hand window shows which functions belong to the selected group (here Java Coding).

In addition, under *Window > Preferences > Workbench > Perspectives* we can control how we open a new perspective: either in the current workbench window or in a new workbench window. The latter option, however, only makes sense if you are lucky enough to own a very large screen. On smaller screens you may want to use the Eclipse workbench in its maximum size. In this case the perspective icons on the left border of the workbench window are the perfect way to change perspectives.

Another option allows you to create a new perspective automatically when a new project is created, so that each project has its own perspective. Again, we can open the new perspective in the current workbench window or in a new workbench window.

2.9   Importing files

We now want to start to teach our `HelloWorld` program to talk. Since Version 1.4, Java has contained a speech interface, the *Java Speech API* (JSAPI). A standard implementation of the interface, FreeTTS, is available for free and can be downloaded from the Internet. FreeTTS has its roots in the speech synthesizer *Flite*, but was ported completely to Java. An interesting fact is that FreeTTS is considerable faster than *Flite*. Even in terms of speed, Java seems more and more to outperform C++.

FreeTTS (Version 1.1.1) is found at `//sourceforge.net/projects/freetts`. After downloading the 26 Mbytes (a real flyweight compared to the Eclipse SDK distribution) we unpack the downloaded file into an arbitrary directory. In addition we must also unpack the JSAPI (Java Speech API) because it is distributed under a different license model. To do so, we just need to execute the program `jsapi.exe` in folder `FreeTTS\lib`.

We could now follow the FreeTTS installation guide and make a test run of FreeTTS. However, we don't do that here. Instead, we import the system into the Eclipse workbench.

Importing third party software

First, we create a new project under the name `FreeTTS`. We keep the project selected and invoke the *Import Wizard* with the context function *Import...* In the next dialog we see a list with all sorts of import sources. We select *Filesystem* and press the *Next* button. In the following dialog we press the *Browse* button and navigate to folder...`\FreeTTS\demo\JSAPI\HelloWorld`. This folder now appears in the left window of the dialog. We select it and at the right hand side we see all the files contained in that folder (Figure 2.12). There, we check the file `HelloWorld.java` and press the *Finish* button.

If everything has worked correctly, the imported program `HelloWorld.java` should now be in a default package of project `FreeTTS` (Figure 2.13). But we get a lot of error markers, too!

Figure 2.12: Importing from a file system. The field 'Directory' contains a drop-down list of all import sources used so far. This can save tedious searching for import sources.

This is to be expected – the FreeTTS runtime system is still missing. We have two options:

- We import the JAR files of the FreeTTS runtime system into the workbench. But this would separate us from future version changes. We would need to re-import new versions of these JAR files into the Eclipse workbench.

- We add the JAR files as external files to the *Java Build Path*. This saves us importing these files. An additional advantage is that we don't have to keep two copies of the files. If the original files are replaced by a new version, the changes will automatically affect our project.

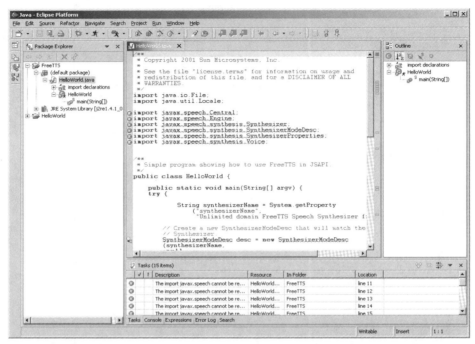

Figure 2.13: After the import. The imported file was compiled immediately, leading to a lot of unresolved references.

2.10 Project properties

The Java build path

In this example we select the second option. To add JAR files to the *Java Build Path* we invoke the function *Project > Properties*. In the selection tree we choose *Java Build Path* and then open the page *Libraries*. Here we see only a single entry: the Java 1.4 runtime system rt.jar.

We press the button *Add External Jars* and navigate to the directory...\FreeTTS\lib. From the JAR files now listed in this dialog (cmuawb.jar,..., JSAPI.jar) we select all files (we may omit demo.jar) and then press the *Open* button. These files are now added to the *Libraries* list (Figure 2.14). Then we press the *OK* button and see what happens. All the error markers have vanished!

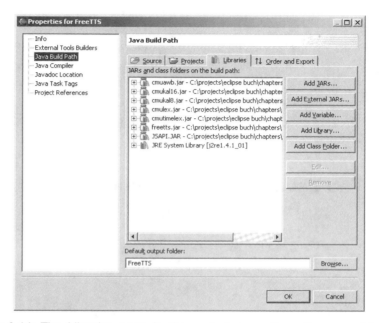

Figure 2.14: The Libraries page in the project properties after we added the FreeTTS JARs.

What is still missing is the source code for the FreeTTS binaries. This code is contained in the FreeTTS distribution in archive src.zip. We must only associate this file with the corresponding packages of the FreeTTS project. Here's how it's done.

In the *Package Explorer* select freetts.jar and invoke the context function *Properties*. In the dialog that appears, select *Java Source Attachment* for the package properties. Then press the button *External File* and navigate to file src.zip. And that's all. If we now open a file from freetts.jar the corresponding source code will appear in the source editor. Of course, this code cannot be edited, only viewed. (We have to repeat this process for the other external JAR files as well.)

Now we should be able to do a test run. Like our very first HelloWorld program, we execute the new HelloWorld program with the same function *Run > Run as > Java Application*.

However, instead of the expected speech output, we only get the following text on the Java console:

Speech properties
```
Can't find synthesizer.
Make sure that there is a "speech.properties" file at either of these
locations:
```

```
user.home : H:\Dokumente und Einstellungen\Berthold Daum
java.home/lib: C:\j2sdk1.4.1\jre\lib
```

Right. Something like this was mentioned in the FreeTTS installation guide. We copy the file speech.properties from FreeTTS into one of the directories mentioned in the error message and execute our program again. We hear:

Hello, World!

Provided of course, that your computer is equipped with a sound card and the speakers are connected...

2.11 The Java Browsing Perspective

The *Java Browsing Perspective* delivers a slightly different view of the structure of a Java project, and is reminiscent of Visual Age. We can install this perspective with a click on the button *Open a Perspective* (see Section 1.2). From the list we then select *Java Browsing*.

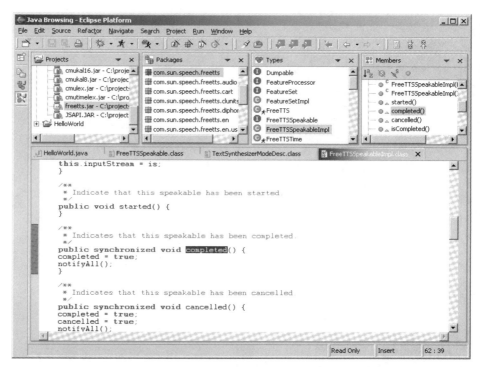

Figure 2.15: The Java Browsing Perspective provides four windows at the top where we can select projects, packages, types and methods or fields in a hierarchical manner. Since we can easily switch between this perspective and the normal Java Perspective, the Java Browsing Perspective is a good way to avoid losing the overview of a project.

3 Project 1 – Duke speaks

In this chapter we are going to implement our first major example project. We learn how to base a new project on an existing project and how to modify and enhance features of the base project. During this task we will use many of the comfortable features of the Eclipse Java IDE.

Our example application is based on the FreeTTS speech synthesizer that we have already introduced in Chapter 2. There we implemented the project FreeTTS with a speaking `HelloWorld` program, which communicated with the synthesizer via the JSAPI interface.

In this chapter we develop a Swing GUI for FreeTTS. This GUI includes an animated face that moves its lips synchronously with the speech output.

Of course, there is also a speech synthesizer manufactured by IBM (*ViaVoice*) that even comes as an Eclipse plug-in. The *Voice Toolkit for WebSphere Studio* runs under Eclipse, too, and cooperates with the *WebSphere Voice Server SDK*. For our purposes, however, FreeTTS is better suited, since it is an Open Source product and supports all platforms supported by Eclipse.

3.1 Setting up the project

To achieve good lip synchronization, it is necessary to have event notification for single phonemes. The JSAPI, however, only supports event notification at word level, and this event notification is currently not supported by the FreeTTS JSAPI implementation. The only choice we have is not to use the JSAPI, but to drive FreeTTS via its native API. In addition, we have to create events for each single phoneme. This requires that we modify the FreeTTS runtime system.

Despite these modifications, we can still use the external FreeTTS JARs as a basis. Where necessary we can subclass the FreeTTS classes to apply our modification. These new classes are stored in packages that bear the same name as the parent class, but are stored in our new project DukeSpeaks.

Let's first create the new Java project DukeSpeaks in the usual way. Again, we modify the *Java Build Path*. This time, however, we do not add external JARs, but open the page *Projects* and checkmark the project FreeTTS. This makes the resources of the project FreeTTS available to the project DukeSpeaks as well. This applies, too, to the external JARs that we added to project FreeTTS. However, these JARs must be marked for export in the project FreeTTS. This is currently not the case.

So we must once again edit the *Java Build Path* of the project FreeTTS. To do so, we select the project in the *Package Explorer*, perform a right click and select the context function *Properties*. In the following dialog we select the category *Java Build Path*. Then we open the page *Order and Export*. There we checkmark all FreeTTS JARs and thus make them available to all projects that build on project FreeTTS.

Working set

To avoid the example files from Chapter 1 littering the *Package Explorer* we create a new working set. To do so, we click the drop-down button (arrow downwards) on the toolbar of the *Package Explorer* and select the function *Select Working Set*. In the dialog that now appears, we press the button *New...* In the following dialog we select *Java* as the working set type and press the *Next* button. Finally, we enter *dukeSpeaks* as the name and checkmark the projects FreeTTS and DukeSpeaks. From now on the *Package Explorer* only displays these two projects. By invoking the function *Deselect Working Set* we can restore the original state.

3.2   A short excursion into speech synthesis

Before we start extending the FreeTTS system, we should get acquainted with the basics of speech synthesis and with the architecture of the FreeTTS system.

Speech synthesis works in several steps:

1. A *Tokenizer* breaks the text into syntactical units (tokens). In general, these are words and numbers including the punctuation.

2. Some tokens such as numbers are converted into words.

3. A *Phraser* analyses the word list and organizes it into phrases (sentences and para-sentences). Phrasing establishes the basis for the later decoration of the speech output with pauses and melody.

4. A *Segmenter* analyses the words and – with the help of a lexicon – assigns a syllable structure to each word.

5. The *Pause Generator* inserts a pause in front of each phrase.

6. The *Intonator* analyses the syllables and assigns an emphasis and a pitch to each syllable.

7. In a further step and depending on the voice used, some phonemes are replaced by others.

8. For each phoneme the duration is determined.

9. The *Contour Generator* assigns an envelope curve to each syllable.

10. In a further step, adjoining phonemes are combined to pairs (*diphones*). This allows a better resolution of the text into speech.

11. The *PitchMark Generator* analyses the results of the contour generator and generates parameters for the later sound synthesis.

12. The results of the *PitchMark Generator* and the list of diphones are now used to select and concatenate the corresponding speech samples.

13. Finally, the concatenated samples are replayed with the help of a suitable *Audio Player*.

Utterances   FreeTTS is designed as a modular system. Each of the steps listed above is processed by a specialized *Utterance Processor*. An `Utterance` is the basic data structure in FreeTTS. It may contain the complete text that is to be spoken, but may later be broken into individual phrases, which again are represented as `Utterance` instances.

Each utterance consists of a set of lists (in FreeTTS these are called 'relations'). This lists include the list of syllables, of words, of segments (result of the *Segmenter*), etc. The various utterance processors perform read and write accesses to these lists.

Detailed information about the architecture of FreeTTS is found in the FreeTTS *Programmer's Guide* (contained in the FreeTTS documentation).

3.3   Extending the FreeTTS system

We can derive the information needed for lip synchronization from the durations computed in step 8 where the duration of each single segment (phoneme) was determined. The best point for invoking the lip synchronization, however, is between steps 12 and 13, as close as possible to audio output.

We generate the events for lip synchronization by implementing our own utterance processor, called `Animator`. This processor derives events (`AnimationEvent`) from the end times stored in each segment and sends this event to an `AnimationListener` at the right time. We control this with our own timer.

3.3.1   Animation events

First we implement the class `AnimationEvent` and the interface `AnimationListener`. Both are stored in package `com.sun.speech.freetts.relp`.

The AnimationEvent.java class

```
package com.sun.speech.freetts.relp;

public class AnimationEvent {

  public int endTime;
  public String phone;

  /**
   * Constructor
   * @param endTime - the end time of the phoneme in msec
   * @param phone - the phoneme string
   */
  public AnimationEvent(int endTime, String phone) {
    this.endTime = endTime;
    this.phone = phone;
  }
}
```

Creating a new class

To create this class, we first create the package `com.sun.speech.freetts.relp` in project DukeSpeaks by pressing the button *Create a Java Package* on the workbench's toolbar. After entering the package name and pressing *Finish* we can now create the new class. To do so, we use the button *Create a Java Class* on the workbench's toolbar. We enter the name of the class (`AnimationEvent`), press the *Finish* button, and start entering code. We don't have to enter much: we only need to create the two fields `endTime` and `phone`, and we must modify the constructor as shown above.

When creating comments we make use of the context function *Source > Add JavaDoc Comment*: if we apply this function on the constructor, Eclipse will create a Javadoc comment in front of the constructor. (The same function can be invoked by entering the string `/**` in a new line in front of the constructor followed by the *Enter* key.) We only have to complete the text strings after '`@param endTime`' and after '`@param phone`'.

However, before creating the class we complete the code generation template for constructors by adding the headline '`Constructor`'. This is done under *Window > Preferences > Java > Code Generation > Code and Comments > Comments > Constructors.*

Then we create the Interface `AnimationListener` in the same package. This one is also quite simple.

The interface AnimationListener.java:

```
package com.sun.speech.freetts.relp;

public interface AnimationListener {

  /**
   * Method processAnimationEvent.
   * @param e AnimationEvent object
   */
  public void processAnimationEvent(AnimationEvent e);
}
```

Creating a new interface

The interface is created by pressing the button *Create a Java Interface* on the workbench's toolbar. Here, too, we use the context function *Source > Add JavaDoc Comment* when entering comments: If we apply this function on method `processAnimationEvent`, we only have to complete the text string after '@param e'.

However, before creating the interface, we complete the method code generation template by adding the headline 'Method ${enclosing_method}.' This is done under *Window > Preferences > Java> Code Generation > Code* and *Comments > Comments > Methods*.

3.3.2 The Animator

Now we can create class `Animator` – also in package `com.sun.speech.freetts.relp`. This class implements the interface `com.sun.speech.freetts.UtteranceProcessor` with the method `processUtterance()`. The Animator receives the `Utterance` instance it has to process via this method. However, we cannot use this method to start animation, because the start-up time needed by FreeTTS and the Java audio system would cause the animation to run ahead of the speech output. To keep the animation fully synchronous, we have to catch the START event of the audio system. For this purpose we additionally implement the interface `javax.sound.sampled.LineListener` with the method `update()`. After receiving the START event we use our own timer to generate animation events. To react to the events of this timer, we implement the additional interface `java.awt.event.ActionListener` with the method `actionPerformed()`. After we have generated the animation events we pass them to all `AnimationListener` objects that had registered via the `addAnimationListener()` method.

Creating a class with interfaces

We create this class, too, with a click on the *Create a Java Class* button, but this time we not only enter the name of the new class into the dialog, but also press the *Add* button to enter the names of the interfaces that this class is going to implement. Usually, it is sufficient to enter just a few characters to qualify the interface. We add the following interfaces: `UtteranceProcessor`, `LineListener`, and `ActionListener`. Then we press the *Finish* button. Eclipse will now generate a class skeleton that includes all the methods declared in the specified interfaces: `processUtterance()`, `update()`, and `actionPerformed()`. However, this is only done if the checkbox *Inherited abstract methods* was marked. If we did not do this, we can easily fix the problem after the creation of the new class by applying the context function *Source > Override/Implement Methods*.

Actually, it didn't matter that we did not have access to the source code of interface `LineListener`. Eclipse is able to retrieve the required information from the binary object.

All generated method stubs are decorated by Eclipse with a `TODO` comment. This comments will show up in the *Tasks* windows as entries and will thus remind us to complete the implementation of these methods.

Using the Code Assistant

When entering the code, we opt not to enter import statements and Javadoc comments at this time. Most of the `import` statements are automatically inserted by subsequently using the code assistant (*Ctrl-Spacebar*) anyway. After we have entered all the code, we can easily add missing import statements by invoking the context function *Source > Organize Imports*. The Javadoc comments are created with the context function *Source > Add JavaDoc Comment* or by entering the string /**. We only have to complete this comments as required.

When entering method code we can use existing code templates: 'pri' followed by *Ctrl-Spacebar* generates a stub for a private method, 'pub' followed by *Ctrl-Spacebar* generates a stub for a public method.

In addition, we don't have to spell out the names of types, methods, and fields. In most cases it is sufficient to type only a few letters, then call the *Code Assistant* by pressing *Ctrl-Spacebar*.

The Animator.java class

```
package com.sun.speech.freetts.relp;

import java.awt.event.ActionEvent;
import java.awt.event.ActionListener;
import java.util.ArrayList;
import java.util.Iterator;
import java.util.List;

import javax.sound.sampled.LineEvent;
import javax.sound.sampled.LineListener;
import javax.swing.Timer;
```

```
import com.sun.speech.freetts.*;

public class Animator
  implements UtteranceProcessor, ActionListener, LineListener {

    // List of AnimationListener instances
    List listeners = new ArrayList(3);
    // Swing Timer object
    Timer timer;
    // Current segment in the segment list
    Item segment;
    // Start time of current segment
    int currentTime = 0;
```

addAnimation
Listener()

```
    /**
     * Method addAnimationListener.
     * @param l AnimationListener object
     */
    public void addAnimationListener(AnimationListener l) {
      listeners.add(l);
    }
    /**
     * Method removeAnimationListener.
     * @param l AnimationListener object
     */
    public void removeAnimationListener(AnimationListener l) {
      listeners.remove(l);
    }
```

processUtterance()

```
    /**
     * @see com.sun.speech.freetts.UtteranceProcessor#
     * processUtterance(Utterance)
     */
    public void processUtterance(Utterance utterance)
      throws ProcessException {
        // Reset current time
        currentTime = 0;
        // Stop time if it is still running (previous utterance)
        if (timer != null && timer.isRunning())
          timer.stop();
        // Fetch first segment of utterance
        segment = utterance.getRelation(Relation.SEGMENT).getHead();
    }
```

actionPerformed()

```
    /**
     * @see
     * java.awt.event.ActionListener#actionPerformed(ActionEvent)
     */
    // Is executed when the timer expires

    public void actionPerformed(ActionEvent e) {
```

```
    // Fire event
    fireAnimationEvent();
}

/**
 * Method fireAnimationEvent.
 */
private void fireAnimationEvent() {
  // If segment == null we have reached the end of the list
  if (segment != null) {
    // Fetch end time from segment and convert to msec
    int end =
      (int) (1000 * segment.getFeatures().getFloat("end"));
    // Get phoneme from segment
    String phone = segment.getFeatures().getString("name");
    // Advance in segment list
    segment = segment.getNext();
    // Create new AnimationEvent object
    AnimationEvent e = new AnimationEvent(end, phone);
    // Send it to all AnimationListener objects
    Iterator iter = listeners.iterator();
    while (iter.hasNext()) {
      AnimationListener listener =
        (AnimationListener) iter.next();
      listener.processAnimationEvent(e);
    }
    // Create new timer that expires at the end time
    // of the current phoneme.
    timer = new Timer(end - currentTime, this);
    timer.setRepeats(false);
    timer.setCoalesce(false);
    timer.start();
    // Update current time
    currentTime = end;
  }
}
```

update()

```
/**
 * @see javax.sound.sampled.LineListener#update(LineEvent)
 */
public void update(LineEvent event) {
  if (event.getType().equals(LineEvent.Type.START)) {
    // Audio output has started — start animation, too.
    // Fire first event
    fireAnimationEvent();
  }
}

/**
 * @see java.lang.Object#toString()
 */
```

```
                public String toString() {
                  return "Animator";
                }
        }
```

3.3.3   Embedding into FreeTTS

Because we want to position the animator as close as possible to the audio output, we will call it from the utterance processor AudioOutput. Of course, we don't want to modify the existing class AudioOutput. Therefore, we create a subclass of this class and override the method processUtterance().

The AnimatedAudioOutput.java class

```java
package com.sun.speech.freetts.relp;

import com.sun.speech.freetts.ProcessException;
import com.sun.speech.freetts.Utterance;
import com.sun.speech.freetts.UtteranceProcessor;

public class AnimatedAudioOutput extends AudioOutput {

  UtteranceProcessor animator;

  /**
   * Method AnimatedAudioOutput.
   * @param animator Animator object for generating animation events
   */
  public AnimatedAudioOutput(UtteranceProcessor animator) {
    // Initialize animator field
    this.animator = animator;
  }

  /**
   * @see com.sun.speech.freetts.UtteranceProcessor#
   * processUtterance(Utterance)
   */
  public void processUtterance(Utterance u) throws ProcessException {
    // In case we got an Animator we invoke its
    // processUtterance method.
    if (animator != null)
      animator.processUtterance(u);
    // Then proceed as usual
    super.processUtterance(u);
  }
}
```

Creating a subclass   Again, we create this class with the *Create a Java Class* button. This time we not only enter the name of the new class, but also press the *Browse* button at the right hand side of the *Superclass* field. There we select the field AudioOutput from the list. After pressing *Finish*, we can start to enter code. In the case of import statements and Javadoc comments we proceed as discussed above.

When entering the method processUtterance() the context function *Source > OverrideMethods...* will save us some work. In this function's dialog box we mark the method processUtterance() below the class AudioOutput. Afterwards we only need to add the lines for calling the processUtterance() method from the Animator instance.

Alternatively, we can make use of the *Code Assistant* to create specific method stubs. For example, to create a stub for the method processUtterance() we need only type the letters 'pro' and press *Ctrl-Spacebar*. Then we select processUtterance from the list.

After we have completed this class we must tell FreeTTS to use AnimatedAudioOutput instead of AudioOutput. Which utterance processor is used for audio output is determined in the subclasses of class com.sun.speech.freetts.Voice in method getAudioOutput(). Since we plan to use the voice

    com.sun.speech.freetts.en.us.CMUDiphoneVoice

for our application, we will extend this class.

For this purpose we create a new package com.sun.speech.freetts.en.us in the project DukeSpeaks. In this package we create a new class named AnimatedDiphoneVoice. When creating this new class, we specify CMUDiphoneVoice as super class. We override the method getAudioOutput() and introduce a new method setAnimator().

The AnimatedDiphoneVoice.java class

```
package com.sun.speech.freetts.en.us;

import java.io.IOException;

import com.sun.speech.freetts.UtteranceProcessor;
import com.sun.speech.freetts.relp.AnimatedAudioOutput;

public class AnimatedDiphoneVoice extends CMUDiphoneVoice {

  UtteranceProcessor animator;

  /**
   * @see com.sun.speech.freetts.Voice#getAudioOutput()
   */
  protected UtteranceProcessor getAudioOutput() throws IOException {
    return new AnimatedAudioOutput(animator);
  }
```

```
/**
 * Sets the animator.
 * @param animator The animator to set
 */
public void setAnimator(UtteranceProcessor animator) {
  this.animator = animator;
}
}
```

Here, too, we make use of the context function *Source > Override Methods...* In the following dialog we mark the method getAudioOutput() below class CMUVoice. Afterwards, we just complete the method as shown above.

Now, we only have to create the field animator. After we have created this field we select it and invoke the context function *Source > Generate Getter and Setter...* to generate the method setAnimator(). Since we are only interested in the set-method we remove the checkmark from getAnimator.

3.3.4 Connection with the Java audio system

What is still missing is the program logic for starting the animator. Here, we must first register the Animator as LineListener with a javax.sound.sampled.Line object. Such an object is created by the player com.sun.speech.freetts.audio.JavaClipAudio-Player in method end() in the disguise of a javax.sound.sampled.Clip object.

Structural imitation The correct way to extend JavaClipAudioPlayer would be to subclass it. But unfortunately JavaClipAudioPlayer proves to be a stubborn beast. Too many private fields prevent us from applying the required extensions. Therefore, we choose a different path: We simply create a copy[1] of JavaClipAudioPlayer, which we than can modify easily.

Theoretically, we could use the *Copy* function of the *Package Explorer*, but unfortunately this function cannot be applied to the contents of external JARs (why?). Therefore, we first create the new package com.sun.speech.freetts.audio in project DukeSpeaks and create in this package the new class AnimatedAudioPlayer. Then we open the class JavaClipAudioPlayer in package FreeTTS, select the whole text with *Ctrl-A* and copy it with *Ctrl-C* to the clipboard. Then we select in the new class AnimatedAudioPlayer with *Ctrl-A* the whole text and replace it with *Ctrl-V* with the contents of the clipboard. Now, we can start modifying this class for our requirements. (Modifications are printed in bold type.)

First, we create a new private field:

private LineListener externalLineListener;

---

1. Eclipse programmers, however, don't use this naughty word. The official speak for copying modules is according to Erich Gamma: "to imitate a module structurally".

In the constructor we insert an equally named parameter and initialize the field `exter-nalLineListener` with the parameter value:

```
/**
 * Constructs a default AnimatedAudioPlayer
 */
public AnimatedAudioPlayer(LineListener externalLineListener) {
  this.externalLineListener = externalLineListener;
  debug = Boolean.getBoolean
    ("com.sun.speech.freetts.audio.AudioPlayer.debug");
  closeDelay = Long.getLong
    ("com.sun.speech.freetts.audio.AudioPlayer.closeDelay",
      150L).longValue();
  setPaused(false);
}
```

Then we register `externalLineListener` in method `end()` with the `Clip` object:

```
...
DataLine.Info info = new DataLine.Info(Clip.class, currentFormat);
Clip clip = (Clip) AudioSystem.getLine(info);
clip.addLineListener(lineListener);
clip.addLineListener(externalLineListener);
clip.open(currentFormat, outputData, 0, outputData.length);
setVolume(clip, volume);
...
```

Finally, we apply the function *Source > Organize Imports* to remove all unnecessary `import` statements.

3.4   The user interface

We implement the user interface with Swing. Since we don't use any Eclipse components at all, we can easily execute this application outside of Eclipse.

A second reason for using Swing is that we want to use anti-aliasing for drawing operations. Face and lips of our animation would look too rough-edged without this smoothening technique. Anti-aliasing, however, is only available under Java2D.

As this is all standard Java programming, there is not much to learn about Eclipse in this section. Therefore, we don't show the full source code but provide only a short overview over the structure of the user interface. The complete source code can be downloaded from the author's Web site at www.bdaum.de.

3.4.1   The animated face

The face with the lip synchronization is implement as a sub-class of the Swing class `JPanel`. We give this class the name `Face` and create it in package com.bdaum.duke-

Speaks. The class implements the interface `AnimationListener` which we had created in section 3.3.1. This allows us to register the face as `AnimationListener` with an `Animator` instance. It will receive `AnimationEvents` from the Animator and can then react accordingly to these events.

The class `Face` works as follows:

- The method `processAnimationEvent()` receives animation events (`AnimationEvent`). From the transmitted phoneme it computes size and shape of the mouth and the position of the eye pupils. The mouth is always drawn as an ellipsoid but with varying positions and diameters. After these values are computed the method `repaint()` is called. This enforces the re-drawing of the component `Face`.

- The method `paintComponent()` is called when the component `Face` is redrawn. The graphical context is passed as a parameter. Via a type cast (`Graphics2D`) we convert it into a Java2D context. Then we enable anti-aliasing and employ the usual graphical methods such as `fillOval()`, `drawOval()`, or `drawPolyline()` to draw the face. The size and position of the mouth and the eye pupils depend on the values previously computed from the transmitted phonemes.

3.4.2   The control panel

Now we can begin to construct the control panel. This unit must contain the animated face in its center, below the face a field for text entry, at the left and right of the face sliders for adjusting volume, speed, pitch, and variation.

Two new classes and one interface are needed to implement this control unit:

- The interface `PlayerModel` specifies the interface of the control panels domain model.

- This interface is implemented by the class `PlayerModelImpl`.

- The class `PlayerPanel` implements the presentation of the data and the various control instruments with the help of Swing.

So, we use a typical MVC design pattern (Model-View-Controller). `PlayerPanel` acts as both a viewer and a controller.

3.4.3   The model

When implementing the domain model we have the choice to write the implementation class first, or to start with the definition of the interface. In fact, we could omit the interface altogether but a separate interface adds some flexibility.

- When we opt to create the interface `PlayerModel` first, we can later, when we create the class `PlayerModelImpl` specify the interface during class creation. Eclipse will then generate all the method stubs for us. This method is in particular interesting if we already have a clear idea of the domain models API.

- Otherwise, when we opt to create the implementation `PlayerModelImpl` first, we can later easily generate the interface `PlayerModel` from the implementation with the help of the context function *Refactor > Extract Interface...* This technique is recommended when the API of the model is shaped during the implementation. Actually, in the beginning we can work without an interface altogether. We simply use the methods of the implementation. Later, when our domain model has matured and is stable, we derive the interface with the mentioned context function. This function will also replace all implementation methods references with references to interface methods, provided this does not lead to compilation problems.

The main task of a `PlayerModel` instance is to encapsulate a FreeTTS-Voice and to provide access methods to control volume, speed, pitch and variation. In addition, there is a method `play()` which runs the `speak()` method of the `Voice` instance in a separate thread. For this task we use a `SwingWorker` instance, so that the speech process does not lock up the GUI.

3.4.4   The presentation

After defining the domain model we can implement the visible part of the user interface. This is done in class `PlayerPanel`, which is implemented as a sub-class of the Swing class `JPanel` in package `com.bdaum.dukeSpeaks`.

Implementing the presentation part is just grinding Swing programming. We have to place the face (an instance of Face) on the `JPanel`, and also the sliders for volume, speed, pitch and variation. In addition, we need a text input field for the text to be spoken, a few buttons and, of course, the necessary event processing for all these control elements.

When creating this class, we can save substantial typing work by consequently using the *Code Assistant*. Again, we generate the `import` statements and the Javadoc comments with the help of the context functions *Source > Organize Imports* and *Source > Add JavaDoc Comments* after we have done all other coding.

3.4.5   The complete application

Finally, we need a root class `Player` for the whole application. This class contains the `main()` method. Within this method we create a new Player instance. This causes the `Players` constructor to create a `Face` and a `Voice` instance and to connect both with the help of the Animator class. Furthermore, a PlayerModel instance and a PlayerPanel instance are created and wired together.

The class Player is implemented as an extension of the Swing class JFrame. When we create this class we therefore specify JFrame as super class. In addition, we checkmark the option *public static void main(...)*. This will generate us a stub for the main() method.

The Player.java class

```java
package com.bdaum.dukeSpeaks;

import java.awt.BorderLayout;
import java.awt.Dimension;
import java.awt.event.WindowAdapter;
import java.awt.event.WindowEvent;

import javax.swing.*;

import com.sun.speech.freetts.audio.AnimatedAudioPlayer;
import com.sun.speech.freetts.en.us.AnimatedDiphoneVoice;
import com.sun.speech.freetts.en.us.CMULexicon;
import com.sun.speech.freetts.relp.Animator;

public class Player extends JFrame {

  private PlayerPanel playerPanel;

  /**
   * @see java.awt.Frame#Frame(String)
   */
  public Player(String title) {
    super(title);
    // Set Look&Feel for Swing
    setDefaultLookAndFeelDecorated(true);
    // WindowListener for close button event handling
    addWindowListener(new WindowAdapter() {
      public void windowClosing(WindowEvent e) {
        System.exit(0);
      }
    });

    // Create new Animator object
    Animator a = new Animator();
    // Create Voice object
    AnimatedDiphoneVoice voice = new AnimatedDiphoneVoice();
    // Use CMULexicon
    voice.setLexicon(new CMULexicon());
    // Use AnimatedAudioPlayer as audio player
    // for this voice
```

Constructor

```
                    // Register Animator object as LineListener
                    voice.setAudioPlayer(new AnimatedAudioPlayer(a));
                    // Create Face object
                    Face face = new Face();
                    // Set face border area
                    face.setBorder(BorderFactory.createEmptyBorder(30, 30, 10, 30));
                    // Set face size
                    face.setPreferredSize(new Dimension(400, 300));
                    // Register Face object as
                    // AnimationListener with Animator object
                    a.addAnimationListener(face);
                    // Pass Animator object to voice
                    voice.setAnimator(a);
                    // Load the voice (mainly the lexicon)
                    voice.load();
                    // Create a PlayerModel instance with the new voice
                    PlayerModelImpl impl = new PlayerModelImpl(voice);
                    // Create a PlayerPanel instance and pass the PlayerModel object
                    // and the Face-Objekt to it.
                    playerPanel = new PlayerPanel(impl,face);
                    // Use the size of the PlayerPanel for the whole Player
                    setSize(playerPanel.getSize());
                    // Insert the PlayerPanel into the Player
                    getContentPane().add(playerPanel, BorderLayout.CENTER);
                  }
```

main()

```
                  /**
                   * Method main.
                   * The main() method of the Player.
                   *
                   * @param args (not used)
                   * @throws Exception
                   */
                  public static void main(String[] args) throws Exception {
                    // Set Metal Look&Feel for Swing
                    try {
                      UIManager.setLookAndFeel(
                        "javax.swing.plaf.metal.MetalLookAndFeel");
                    } catch(Exception e) {
                      System.err.println("Error setting look&feel: " + e);
                    }
                    // Create new Player instance
                    Player player = new Player("Animated FreeTTS Player");
                    // and display it
                    player.show();
                  }
                }
```

Program launch   Now we have completed our application. In the *Package Explorer* we select the class
                    Player in the project DukeSpeaks and then call the function *Run > Run as... > Java*

Application. If everything was done correctly, we should now see the window shown in Figure 3.1.

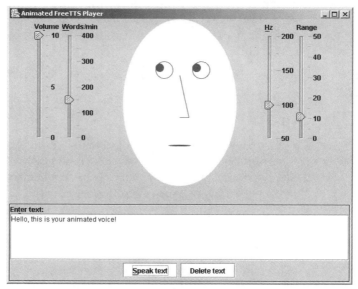

Figure 3.1: *"Hello, this is your animated voice!"*

Now you can play around a bit with the speaking face. Change the speed, the pitch, or the variation. Copy other texts into the text input field (using *Ctrl-V*). Note that the lexicon is based on US English. If you copy foreign language texts into the input field, expect Duke to speak these languages with a fat US accent...

3.5 Exporting the application

Deploy

To be able to run our application outside Eclipse we export it as a JAR file. To do so, we select the project DukeSpeaks and call the context function *Export...* In the dialog that appears, we select the category *JAR File.*

In the next dialog we checkmark the field *Export generated class files and resources* and remove the checkmark from the field *Export java source files and resources.* In addition, we expand the project node DukeSpeaks and checkmark all packages.

Finally, we specify a target location under *JAR file.* We use dukeSpeaks.jar as the file name.

All binary objects of our project DukeSpeaks are now combined in a single JAR file. To run the player successfully outside Eclipse we obviously also need the FreeTTS JARs that we previously added as external JARs to the project's *Java Build Path* in the *Classpath* of the JVM. So the Classpath must contain the JARs: dukeSpeaks.jar, cmuawb.jar, cmukal16.jar, cmukal8.jar, cmulex.jar, cmutimelex.jar and freetts.jar.

A JRE of Version 1.4.0 or higher is required to run this program successfully.

3.6   Bibliography

The main purpose of this chapter has been to get acquainted with practical work in the Eclipse workbench. We have shown how third party projects can be imported into the Eclipse workspace, how they can be navigated and modified. We also have shown how the various assistants are used to create code efficiently.

In the course of this example we could only scratch the surface of the technologies used. Therefore we want to give some pointers where to get more information about these technologies:

- There are several excellent Swing tutorials. In particular, we want to mention the chapter 'User Interfaces that Swing' in the official Java tutorial from JavaSoft (www.javasoft.com). A remarkable book about Swing has been written by Matthew Robinson and Pavel Vorobiev [Robinson2000].

- The FreeTTS documentation contains valuable information about speech synthesis in general and FreeTTS speech synthesis in particular. You will also find some links to related articles there.

- The application implemented here only shows lip synchronization of the simplest kind. Also the rendering of the face is rather minimalist. The current state of the art are 3-D animations in which each facial muscle can be moved separately. Depending on the text content it is even possible to express emotions. Searching the Web for 'lip synchronization' will result in some interesting links. The *DECFace* project is particularly interesting: details can be found at crl.research.compaq.com/projects/facial/facial.html.

3.7 What did we learn?

With this project we have now had our first experiences with Eclipse. Based on these experiences we can derive some 'best practices' for the creation of applications with Eclipse:

Best practices
- If the API of a module is well understood, we should create an interface before we create the implementation. This allows us to use the interface when generating the method stubs in the implementing class. At the same time these method stubs are automatically equipped with Javadoc comments that use the Javadoc keyword @see to refer back to the method description in the interface.

  If the API is not well understood or subject to change, we should create the implementation first. Later we can derive the interface from the implementation (Section 1.8.2).

- If it later becomes necessary to extend the interface definition, we pull down these extensions into the implementation with the context function *Source > Override Methods...* or by using the *Content Assistant*.

- Javadoc comments should be always created with the context function *Source > Add JavaDoc Comment* or by entering /**. This helps to achieve a consistent and complete API documentation.

- Completing the *Create a new Java Class* dialog carefully is well worth the effort. By specifying super classes and interfaces and by marking the various options we can save considerable typing work, because method and constructor stubs will be generated by Eclipse.

- After larger changes in a compilation unit we should call the context function *Source > Organize Imports*. This function adds missing import statements and removes unused ones.

- Using the *Code Assistant (Ctrl-Spacebar)* for program constructs, type and field-names saves us a lot of typing, a lot of searching in the documentation, and can possibly protect us from RSI (repetitive strain injury). At the same time, the *Code Assistant* can generate the necessary import statements (if this option was set in the preferences). *Ctrl-Spacebar* should become the typical gesture of an Eclipse programmer.

4 Project development

In the first part of this chapter we discuss the *Eclipse Java Debugger* in detail. We show how the debugger can be configured, introduce the *Debug Perspective*, and explain how to create and manage breakpoints and watchpoints. In the second part we introduce the test tool *JUnit*, part of the Eclipse SDK distribution. Finally, in the third part we show how we can export *Javadoc* documentation.

4.1 Debugging

Searching for bugs in a complex application is always a time consuming task. A powerful debugger can be of great help here. Fortunately, the Eclipse Java IDE is equipped with a full-featured debugger that leaves hardly anything to be desired.

This debugger has two operation modes: *local* and *remote*. We will first restrict ourselves to the discussion of local debugging. In Section 4.1.6 we then show how the debugger is used in its remote operation mode.

4.1.1 The debug configuration

Like many other parts of the Eclipse workbench the Debugger can be configured by the user in various ways. For example, under *Window > Preferences > Java > Debug > Appearance* we can specify how the values of primitive Java data types (byte, short, char, int, long) are to be displayed, and if final values or static variables should be displayed.

Under *Window > Preferences > Java > Debug > Step Filtering* we can specify which classes should be skipped when stepping though a program. These settings are used during the *Step with Filters* operation (see below).

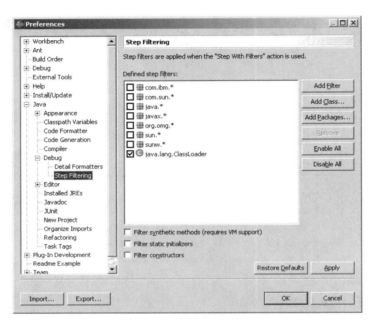

Figure 4.1: Some step filters are already predefined, so that we can activate them with a simple checkmark (by default only the Java class loader is skipped). We can also add other classes, packages, or generic filter expressions to the list, however.

4.1.2   The Debug Perspective

Debugging is started with a click on the bug symbol in the workbench's toolbar. This function is very similar to the *Run* function (see Section 1.2), with the difference that the function opens the *Debug Perspective* and that execution is interrupted at break points. The *Debug Perspective* contains the same windows as the *Java Perspective* plus two more.

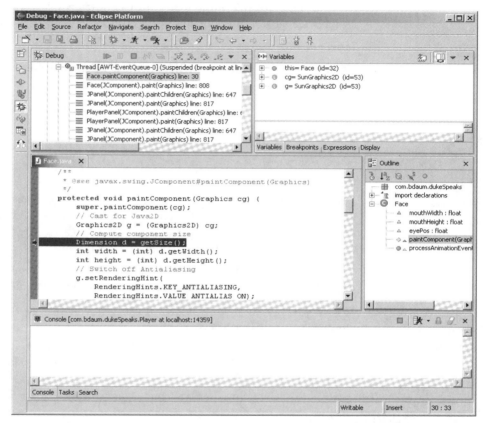

Figure 4.2: The Debug Perspective: in the top left corner we see the Debug window listing the active threads. Under the thread '[AWT-Event-Queue-0]' the execution stack with the method call hierarchy is displayed. In the top right corner the variables of the current execution context are shown. Behind this view are three more stacked views: Breakpoints, Expressions, and Display.

4.1.3 Controlling program execution

The toolbar of the *Debug* window is equipped with all the buttons needed to control the execution of the current program. Most of these functions, however, can be called via function keys, which is much faster. From left to right we see:

• *Resume* (*F8*). Continues the execution of an interrupted thread.

- *Suspend*. Interrupts the execution of a running thread. This function is especially useful when the thread is looping.

- *Terminate*. The execution of a running or interrupted program is terminated.

- *Disconnect*. This function is required to finish debugging a remote program (remote debugging).

- *Remove All Terminated Launches*. This function removes 'garbage' from the Debug window.

- *Step with Filters (Shift-F5)*. When using this function the step operation is influenced by the step filters defined in the preferences (see Section 4.1.1). All other functions ignore the step filters.

- *Step Into (F5)*. Used on a method call this function will step into the invoked method. In program lines containing multiple method calls, however, this function steps through all of them. In such cases it is better to select the method call in question and use the context function *Step into selection*.

- *Step Over (F6)*. Used on a method call this function will step over the invoked method (provided the method does not contain active breakpoints).

- *Step Return (F7)*. The current method is executed in normal mode. When the method returns, step mode is activated again.

Setting breakpoints How do we start a debug session? We would usually set a breakpoint at an interesting location in our program. This is easily done with a double click on the left margin of the Java source editor. It doesn't matter if we do this in the *Java Perspective* or in the *Debug Perspective*. We can remove the breakpoint again with another double click to the same position.

Now, let's set a breakpoint onto the instruction `Dimension d = getSize()` in method `paintComponent()` in class `Player`, as shown in Figure 4.2. When we start the debug process with a click on the *Debug* button the program will stop at this instruction. In the window at the right hand side the variable values of the current object show up.

Testing interactively We have now the following possibilities:

- We can continue the execution of the program with *F8*. The program will only be interrupted when it passes this breakpoint again.

- We can stop execution with a click on the *Terminate* button.

- We can execute the method `getSize()` step by step by pressing the *F5* key.

- We can step over method `getSize()` by pressing the *F6* key.

- We can set further breakpoints, or we can remove breakpoints.

Variables

- We can view the content of variables by hovering with the cursor over a variable name in the source editor.

- In the *Variables* view we can take a closer look at the variables of the current execution environment. Complex objects can be expanded with a click on the '+' character (or with a double click on the variable name) so that we can view their details.

- In the execution stack in the *Debug* window we can select a different execution environment. For example, we may select:

  `Player(java.awt.Container).paint(java.awt.Graphics)` line 1123.

  The source editor automatically shows the corresponding source code, and the *Variables* view shows the variables of this execution environment.

- We can modify variables. With a double click on a variable in the *Variables* view we can open an editor for the variable's value and modify the value.

- By applying the context function *Watch* to individual variables we can add those variables to the *Expressions* window. As we step through the program, the variables in the *Expressions* window will be updated when their value changes. So this offers a way to monitor specific variables during program execution.

HotSwap

- During a debug session we may apply changes to the program code and save (and compile) the changed code. In many cases – provided we run under JDK 1.4 – the debug session need not to be restarted, but can continue with the modified module in place (*HotSwap*). In some cases however – for example, when the signature of a public method was changed – HotSwap is impossible, and program execution is aborted with an error message.

Testing expressions

- In the *Display* view (and also in the *Details* area of the *Expression* view) we can enter expressions that can be executed within the current execution context (see also our discussion of the *ScrapBook* in Section 1.5). To do so, we select the entered expression and invoke the context function *Inspect* or *Display*. For example, if we execute the expression `getBackground()` while in the execution context of `Player.paint()` (see above), the function *Display* will deliver us the background color of `player`.

4.1.4   Managing breakpoints

The *Breakpoints* view shows an overview over all defined breakpoints. Here, we can delete breakpoints that we don't need anymore, or position the source editor to a breakpoint position by double clicking it.

With the context function *Disable* we can disable a breakpoint temporarily. With *Enable* we can activate it again. The context function *Properties* allows further customization of breakpoints (see Figure 4.3).

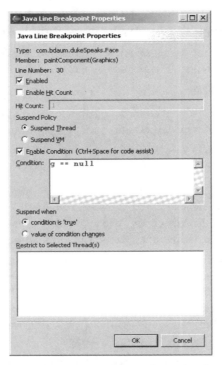

Figure 4.3: The breakpoint properties dialog allows for detailed instrumentation of a breakpoint. By setting a hit count, the breakpoint is activated only after several passes through it. We can also specify an additional condition under which the breakpoint should become active. The breakpoint is activated either when the Boolean value of the condition is 'true' or when the value of the condition changes, depending on the option chosen.

Exception breakpoints

Another useful function of the *Breakpoints* view is the function *Add Java Exception Breakpoint* (the button with the exclamation mark). When invoking this function we can select an exception type from a list.

Usually, Eclipse aborts program execution when an uncaught exception occurs and shows us the stack trace. But with this function, we can interrupt directly at the point where the exception occurs and look into variables, etc. Better still, we can even optionally trap exceptions that are caught in a try/catch block. It is a good idea to set *Java*

Exception Breakpoints for common uncaught exception types such as NullPointerEx-
ception, ClassCastException and IndexOutOfBoundsException.

If we have trapped an exception with such a breakpoint, program execution is interrupted when the exception occurs. In the *Debug* window we now have the possibility of
selecting a method within the stack trace shown under the current thread. The *Variables*
view shows us the variables of the method's execution environment, so that in most
cases we easily can determine the reason for the exception.

4.1.5   The Java console

Although the debugger equips us with a rich arsenal of tools to find bugs in programs,
we should not ignore the Java console. To find a problem, it is sometimes simpler to
program a test output into a method or constructor instead of spending ages stepping
through program code. Such outputs are accomplished with System.out.println() or
System.err.println(). By using the *Code Assistant* (see Section 1.6.3), entering
sysout or syserr is sufficient to create such an instruction.

In the case of a program crash the console is a valuable source of information, too, since
it displays the execution stack. Eclipse here offers additional help: a double click on a
stack entry opens the corresponding compilation unit and positions the editor window to
the specified line!

4.1.6   Remote debugging

Remote debugging is used for applications that run on a remote JVM, especially for
application which run outside of the Eclipse platform. Typical targets for remote debugging are servlets which have neither a GUI nor a console.

To make a Java application accessible to an external debugger we must specify additional command line parameters when starting the application's JVM. In the following
example – assuming that this application has already been installed outside Eclipse – we
show how DukeSpeaks can be made accessible to a remote debugger:

```
java.exe -Xdebug -Xnoagent -Djava.compiler=NONE
   -Xrunjdwp:transport=dt_socket,server=y,suspend=y, address=8787
   -classpath %LOCALCLASSPATH%
   com.bdaum.dukeSpeaks.Player
```

First we switch into debug mode. The sun.tools.debug agent is switched off, as well as
the JIT and HotSpot compilers. With –Xrunjdwp we load the reference implementation
of the *Java Debug Wire Protocols* (JDWP). As transport mode we select a socket
connection. The parameter server=y specifies that the application acts as a debug server,
and the parameter suspend=y specifies that the application must not start autonomously,
but must wait on a connection with the debug client. Finally, the parameter

address=8787 specifies the debug port number that can be selected from the host computer's free ports.

Now, let's start the application and execute the command. Nothing happens. The application waits on the debug client. We are now going to create a remote debug configuration in Eclipse. To do so, we invoke the function *Run > Debug...* In the selection list at the left hand side of the dialog we select *Remote Java Application* and press the *New* button.

Then we enter a name for the new configuration (for example '*DukeSpeaksRemote*') and select the project (*DukeSpeaks*). This specification is actually not used to tell the Eclipse debugger the location of the binary files, but to inform it about the location of the source files.

The field *Connection Type* remains unchanged: *Standard (Socket Attach)*. Since our remote application runs on the same host computer we enter the value *localhost* under *Host*. For *Port* we specify exactly the same value we had used above in the java command. So we enter *8787*. Finally we mark the checkbox *Allow termination of remote VM*. This allows us to terminate the application via remote control from the Eclipse debugger.

Now the configuration is properly set up. We can start the debugging process with a click on the *Debug* button. From now on everything works just as with local debugging. We can set breakpoints, look at variables, and even modify the values of variables. The only thing that does not work with remote debugging is, of course, *HotSwapping*.

4.2   JUnit

JUnit is an Open Source tool that allows us to create and execute test suites quickly and systematically. The people behind JUnit are Kent Beck and Erich Gamma. Since Erich Gamma is also significantly involved in the development of Eclipse, it is no surprise that JUnit is contained in the Eclipse SDK distribution. Detailed information is available at www.junit.org or in [Hightower2001].

Test tools such as JUnit are used to test program modules repeatedly, especially after changes have been applied to a module. Using such automated test tools allows testing frequently and after each small incremental development step, following the XP motto: *Code a little, test a little*.

Of course, the quality of the test results stands or falls with the quality of the test suite. A good test suite should cover the whole functional range of a program module. This is, however, easier said than done!

4.2.1   Setting up JUnit

To be able to work with JUnit we must first make the JUnit-JAR file available to the project that we want to test. To do so, we add junit.jar as external JAR file to project DukeSpeaks, as described in Section 2.10.

junit.jar is found under \eclipse\plugins\org.junit_3.8.1.

TestCase wizard   In our project DukeSpeaks we can now create a test case class (a subclass of the JUnit class TestCase), which we call PlayerTest. We can create such a class manually, or we can use the *JUnit Wizard*. This wizard is invoked via the function *New > Other > Java > JUnit > Test Case*. In the first page of the wizard we press the *Browse* button at field *Test class* and select the class that we want to test (Player). The name PlayerTest in the field *Test case* is generated automatically but may be changed if required. In the field *Package* we can select a target package (within our project) for the new TestCase class. Additional options allow us to generate a main() method, a setUp() method, and a tearDown() method.

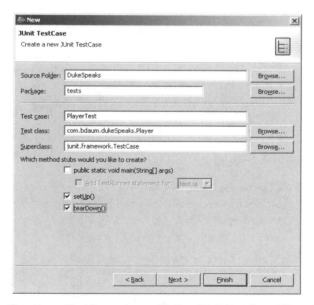

Figure 4.4:   Creating a TestCase class with the JUnit TestCase Wizard.

On the next page we can select for which methods of the test class test methods are to be generated.

Figure 4.5: Selecting methods for testing. Here we have selected only two methods. Normally we would first select all methods, then explicitly de-select all the methods that we don't want to test. Optionally, we can decorate all generated methods with the modifier 'final'. TODO comments can be generated into the method stubs.

4.2.2   Creating a test suite

All generated test methods start with the string 'test'. JUnit recognizes such method names and executes them when running a test. Since the wizard has already generated the method stubs, we only need to add the code inside the method body. If we need to initialize variables or other resources, we do this in method setUp().

Implementing
TestCase

```
import junit.framework.TestCase;
import com.bdaum.dukeSpeaks.Player;

public class PlayerTest extends TestCase {
  Player player;

  /**
   * Constructor for TestCase1.
   * @param arg0
   */
  public PlayerTest(String arg0) {
    super(arg0);
```

```
        }
        /**
         * Initialize the player
         */
        protected void setUp() throws Exception {
          super.setUp();
          player = new Player("Animated FreeTTS Player");
        }

        final public void testGetWidth() {
          assertTrue("width != 600: "+player.getWidth(),
            player.getWidth() == 600);
        }
        final public void testGetHeight() {
          assertTrue("height != 500: "+player.getHeight(),
            player.getHeight() == 500);
        }

        /**
         * Dispose of everything
         */
        protected void tearDown() throws Exception {
          super.tearDown();
          player = null;
        }
      }
```

Here, we have implemented two tests (testWidth() and testHeight()). In these tests we use the JUnit method assertTrue() to test a condition and throw an exception if the condition is not met. Both methods use the variable player that was initialized in method setUp(). This method is called by JUnit before executing the run() method. Similarly, the method tearDown() is called after all tests were executed. This method may be used to dispose of resources.

Creating a test suite   When we have created several TestCase classes it makes sense to combine these classes in a test suite. The *JUnit Wizard* will help us with this task, too. We only have to invoke the function *New > Other > Java > JUnit > Test Suite*. In the wizard's selection list we checkmark all TestCase classes that we want to add to the test suite (in our example this is only class PlayerTest). At this point it is even possible to add other test suites to the new test suite, i.e. we may nest test suites. In the field *TestSuite* we can change the proposed name *AllTests* according to our requirements.

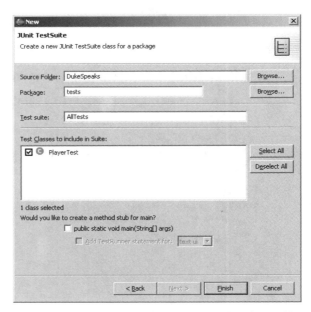

Figure 4.6:   Creating a TestSuite class with the JUnit TestSuite Wizard.

After pressing the *Finish* button the wizard will generate the resulting `TestSuite` class:

```
import junit.framework.Test;
import junit.framework.TestSuite;

public class AllTests {

  public static Test suite() {
    TestSuite suite = new TestSuite("Test for tests");
    //$JUnit-BEGIN$
    suite.addTest(new TestSuite(PlayerTest.class));
    //$JUnit-END$
    return suite;
  }
}
```

Here, we have created a test suite solely for demonstration purposes. If we want to run a single `TestCase` class only, the creation of a test suite is not really required.

4.2.3   Running a test suite

Now, we execute all tests. We invoke the function *Run > Run as > JUnit Test*. Eclipse opens the JUnit view (in front of the *Package Explorer*) and runs the test suite.

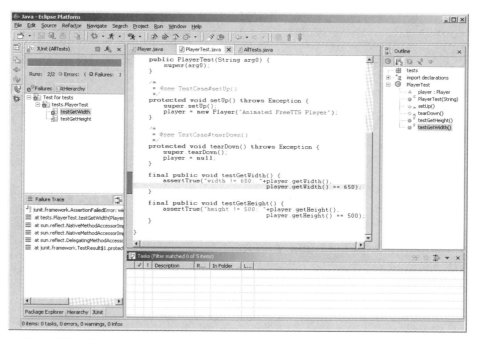

Figure 4.7: In the upper part of the JUnit view all errors are collected (to a maximum of one error per single test case). The other stacked window in the upper area shows the hierarchy of test suites and single test cases. In the lower part of the view JUnit shows the execution stack for the currently selected error. Here, to enforce an error, we specified a panel width (650) in the test case that was different from the panel width we specified in the application.

4.3   Documentation

In Section 1.6.3 we discussed how Javadoc comments can be conveniently added to source code. In this section we will discuss how these comments can be exported as an HTML Javadoc documentation.

4.3.1   Configuring Javadoc

First we must tell Eclipse where the Javadoc generator is located. This is done in the Eclipse preferences under *Window > Preferences > >Java > Javadoc* (see Figure 4.8).

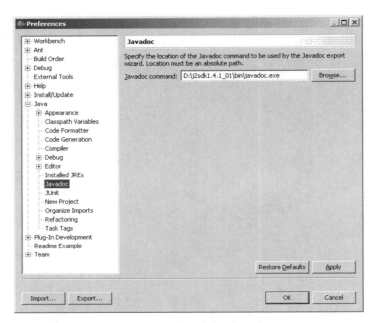

Figure 4.8:   Here we specify the location of the Javadoc generator.

Then we must specify a target location for the generated Javadoc pages. To do so, we select project DukeSpeaks and apply the context function *Properties > Javadoc Location* (see Figure 4.9).

4.3.2   Generating Javadoc documentation

To generate the Javadoc documentation for our completed project DukeSpeaks we select the project and invoke the context function *Export*. On the first page of the *Export* wizard we select *Javadoc* from the list and press the *Next* button. On the following page we can specify in detail what should be exported to Javadoc.

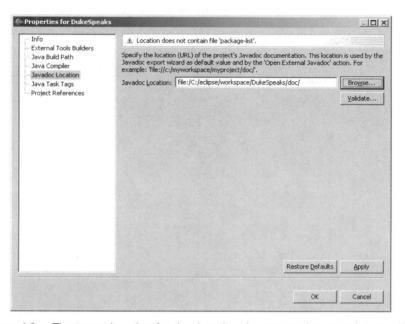

Figure 4.9:   The target location for the Javadoc documentation must be specified as a URL. This allows us to specify locations within and outside the Eclipse workspace.

Javadoc options   In the following step we determine the content and the layout of the single Javadoc pages. The following options exist:

- *Generate use page.* This option allows us to generate a cross reference for each class and each package.

- *Generate hierarchy tree.* When checking this option, a page is generated displaying the hierarchy of packages, classes and interfaces.

- *Generate navigator bar.* This option generates a navigation bar at the top and at the bottom of each page.

- *Generate index.* This option generates one or several index pages.

- *Generate index per letter.* We check this option to generate a separate index page for each letter in the alphabet.

- *@author, @version, @deprecated.* When these options are set, the corresponding key words in the Javadoc comments are evaluated and their information is included in the generated pages.

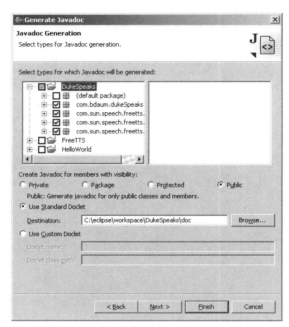

Figure 4.10: On this page we specify for which packages and for which methods Javadoc is to be generated. In addition, we have the option of using a custom doclet instead of Sun Microsystem's reference implementation.

- *Deprecated list.* This option allows a separate page to be generated listing all elements marked as 'deprecated'.

In addition, we can create links to other Javadoc documentations.

Command line options

On the next wizard page we can specify additional command line options for javadoc.exe, if necessary. In addition we may specify a file containing additional text for the Javadoc *Overview* page.

The option *JRE 1.4 source compatibility* must be checked if our source code contains the Java keyword assert. Without this option set, Java 1.4 programs that contain this instruction would cause errors during the Javadoc generation. Checking this option is equivalent to the specification of command line option -source 1.4.

We can also optionally create an Ant script for Javadoc generation. We will discuss Ant in more detail in Chapter 11.

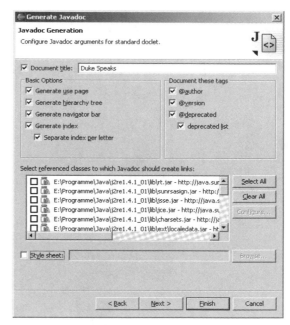

Figure 4.11: On this page we can configure the contents and layout of individual Javadoc pages. Here we have specified a title line. We can mark the listed JARs in the table to create links to their documentation. Finally we have the option of using a custom CSS style sheet instead of the standard style sheet.

After we press *Finish*, the Javadoc generation is started as a batch job. The output of the batch job appears on the Eclipse Java console.

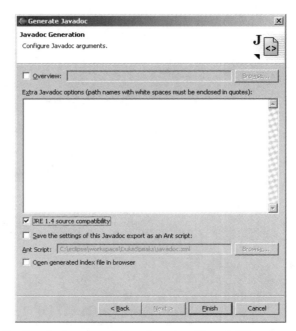

Figure 4.12: On the last page of the Javadoc Export Wizards we can specify additional command line options.

5 Advanced topics of project development

In this chapter we will briefly discuss how development teams can organize their work by using a CVS repository with Eclipse. We also show how external tools can be embedded into Eclipse.

5.1 Developing in a team

In this book, we only want to take a short excursion into Eclipse's support for development teams. Detailed information can be found in the Eclipse help pages under *Workbench User Guide > Tasks > Working in the team environment.*

Different concepts exist for working collaboratively on the same project. These concepts range from sequential or semi-sequential workflow oriented techniques to completely synchronous techniques such as Microsoft's NetMeeting. Eclipse uses the CVS concept (*Concurrent Versions System*) by default. CVS is an Open Source project that has practically become the de-facto standard for the collaborative development of software projects. The CVS is based on a central repository. However, the individual members of the development team work on their own local copies of the repository content. In fact, they are only able to work on these local copies. For resolving clashes, the CVS uses an optimistic concept: it assumes that the same software artifact is only rarely modified simultaneously by multiple team members. Therefore, the software artifacts – even if they are currently worked on – are not locked against the access of other team members. All team members continue to have access to the central repository, may own a local copy of any artifact in the central repository, and may modify this local copy without restrictions.

From time to time the local copies are synchronized with the copies in the central repository. Usually, only the central repository is updated with the newest versions. Some care should be taken when doing so: since software artifacts are usually highly dependent from each other, the global repository should only be updated when the local resources are in a consistent state, for example when the project's test suite was executed without errors.

However, such an optimistic concept allows conflicts. Such conflicts must be resolved. For example, if the local copy of a resource and its original version in the central repository have *both* been modified since the last synchronization, a simple replacement of the central copy with the local copy would cause loss of information. In such a case, the CVS offers several strategies for resolving such a conflict. For example, it is possible to *merge* both copies either manually or automatically.

Another option is to open a new development *branch*. The initial code base of the project forms the *trunk* or *HEAD* of a development tree with many possible branches. Later, these different branches can be brought together with the help of the mentioned conflict solution strategies (see Section 5.1.4).

In addition, the CVS allows software artifacts to be given version numbers. Eclipse builds on this facility. The version management known from Visual Age is only supported by Eclipse if Eclipse collaborates with a CVS. In addition to explicit version numbers, the CVS uses internal revision numbers to identify each change in the central repository uniquely. The CVS stores the complete history of a software artifact. This allows the comparison of a given software artifact with previous versions and revisions at any time, or its replacement with a previous version or revision. This feature can be very helpful, especially for maintenance and debugging.

Detailed information about the CVS can be found in [Fogel2003] and [Vesperman2003], and on the CVS Web site under www.cvshome.org.

5.1.1   Setting up a repository

It is a prerequisite for working in a team under Eclipse that the team members' Eclipse workbenches all have access to the central repository. Since Eclipse by default supports the CVS access protocol, direct access is possible to the following systems:

* *Concurrent Versions System* (CVS) for Linux/Unix. This CVS server is freeware and can be downloaded from www.cvshome.org.

* Also *CVS for Windows* is freeware and can be downloaded from www.cvsnt.org. However, *cvsnt* is not officially supported by Eclipse, since it does not have the same maturity and robustness as the CVS for Linux or Unix.

In addition to these popular CVS there are some commercial systems, too, that support central code management:

- *Microsoft Visual Source Safe.* A special plug-in connects Eclipse with the VSS client module. This module organizes the access to the central VSS server (see Appendix A).

- *Rational ClearCase.* Here also a special plug-in is required to access the source files in the ClearCase repository (see Appendix A).

Now, how do we connect Eclipse with a repository? Let's assume that we have already installed a CVS. Under C:\cvs\eclipse we have created and initialized the root directory of the repository. We further assume that we access the repository via the pserver protocol.

Eclipse offers its own perspective for managing connected repositories (yes, we may connect more than one repository). The *CVS Repository Perspective* is opened with *Window > Open Perspective > Other > CVS Repository Perspective.* In the *CVS Repositories* view we invoke the context function *New > Repository Location...* In the following dialog we specify the domain name of the host computer, the access protocol, the absolute path of the repository's root directory, and, if necessary, a user name and a password. After we press *Finish* the new repository appears in the *CVS Repositories* view.

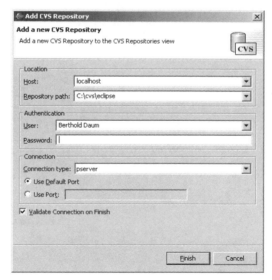

Figure 5.1:   The wizard for setting up a new repository. In our case the repository is located on the same host computer (localhost) as Eclipse.

In addition to these external repositories, Eclipse comes with a simple default repository based on the file system of the host platform. However, this default repository does not support version management.

5.1.2   Projects in the repository

If we want to share a project with a team, we apply the context function *Team > Share Project...* to the project. In the dialog that follows we select a repository from the list. After pressing the *Finish* button, Eclipse should now create a corresponding directory within the repository. However, depending on the system used, it may be necessary to create such a directory beforehand by executing an appropriate command in the host operating system. For example, if we want to create a directory for project DukeSpeaks in cvsnt, we would use cvs import DukeSpeaks bdaum start.

Details about this command line syntax are found in the manuals of the respective repository systems.

Now, we can add source files to the repository. We select all Java files in project Duke-Speaks. We apply the context function *Team > Commit...* to this selection. Then we switch back to the *CVS Repository Perspective* to view the result (Figure 5.2).

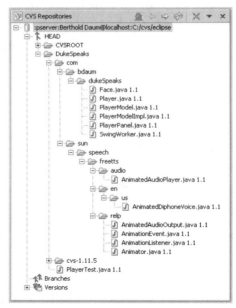

Figure 5.2:   The CVS Repositories view after we have committed all source files from DukeSpeaks to the repository.

5.1.3 Version management

Now, we can mark our current project state as Version 1. It is this function which makes a CVS interesting even for a sole developer. Without a CVS, Eclipse cannot manage project versions.

We select all Java files from the project DukeSpeaks. We apply the context function *Team > Tag as Version...* to this selection. Then we enter the version number. We should apply this function only to files that we have previously synchronized with *Team > Commit...*

In principle, working on a repository based project is not different from working on a private project. All modifications are applied to the local resources without accessing the repository. The local resources are only synchronized with the resources in the repository when we apply the context function *Team > Commit...* to selected resources.

5.1.4 Working in a team

When several developers work on the same project, not only may the local version be newer than the central version: the reverse situation is also possible if resources were changed and committed by other team members. We should always first import the changes made by other team members into our local project before committing our changes to the repository. This import is done with the function *Team > Update*.

Conflicts

In cases where several team members work simultaneously with the same resource, it may happen that the resource gets changed by more than one team member. Here, we differentiate between three conflict types:

1. *No conflict.* Either the local or the central copy of the file was changed, but not both.

2. *A conflict that can be resolved by automatic merging.* This only works if the same lines of code have not been modified in both the local and the central version.

3. *A conflict that can only be resolved manually.* Here the resource contains lines that were modified both in the local and the central version.

The various functions for synchronization of resources react differently under these different conflict cases. The *Update* function, for example, replaces the local copy in any case with the central copy. However, in cases 2 and 3 the previous local version is saved under a modified name as a backup. In case 3, the function adds comments into the file to make the conflicts visible.

Figure 5.3: The Synchronize view shows the difference between the local workspace and the central repository. Here we have applied a change to the file 'PlayerTest.java'. The 'Synchronize...' function embellishes this file with an arrow to the right, indicating an outgoing change.

The *Synchronize...* function, in contrast, opens the *Synchronize* view (see Figure 5.3). For each resource the type of conflict is shown. We may then apply an appropriate context function to a selected resource. With *Override and Update* we can resolve conflict cases of type 1 and 2. Type 3 cases, however, need manual treatment. For this purpose we invoke the function *Show Content Comparison*, which will show us the differences between the copies. We can now include the changes in our local copy by using cut and paste. Finally, we invoke the function *Mark as Merged* to release the local file for a later *Commit* command.

Generally, we have the following possibilities for resolving a conflict:

- We discard our own modifications and copy the new central version into the workbench. *Our own code is lost!*

- We enforce our own version on the repository (but we should ask team members for permission). *Other people's code is lost!*

- We manually merge the local version with the repository version.

- We merge the local version with the repository version using the automated merge.

- We open a new development branch (*Team > Create Branch...*). The local version becomes the root of a new branch. Later we may merge this branch with the trunk.

- Finally, we have the option to extract the local changes as a *patch* and send it to another team member. This team member may apply the patch and include it into the central version. Eclipse provides the necessary functions to extract patches (*Team > Create Patch...*) and to apply patches to resources (*Team > Apply Patch...*). If you don't want to fall out with other team members, you should only use this option (delegating work to others) if you do not have the necessary access rights to apply the changes yourself.

5.1.5 Other functions

Besides the context functions of the *Team* group there are some more context functions that refer to repositories. For example the comparison functions *Compare with > Latest from...*, *Compare with > Another Branch or Version*, *Replace with > Latest from...*, or *Replace with > Another Branch or Version*. In addition, there is a *Team* group in the preferences (*Window > Preferences > Team*). Here we can set several options for the CVS. For example, we can set the content type (ASCII or binary) for different file types, and we may exclude specific file types from the repository.

5.2 External tools and file associations

Eclipse allows us to embed external tools (i.e. tools that were not developed as plug-ins for Eclipse). All we have to do is to create a configuration for the external tool. To do so, we invoke the menu function *Run > External Tools > External Tools...* In the following dialog (see Figure 5.4) we find two configuration types: *ANT-Build* and *Program*. (We discuss Ant in more detail in Section 11.1.) We select type *Program* and press the *New* button. Now we can enter the parameters of the new configuration, such as the name of the configuration, the location of the external tool, the working directory, and possible command line options (*Argume*nts).

Refresh   On the page *Refresh* we can specify whether, and which, workspace resources should be refreshed after the tool has executed. This is necessary if the tool modifies the Eclipse workspace, i.e. if it inserts, modifies, or deletes resources. We can specify in which scope the resources should be refreshed: the selected resource only, all resources in the current folder or project, etc.

Associations   Another method for embedding external programs is to define file associations. This is done with function *Window > Preferences > Workbench > File Associations*.

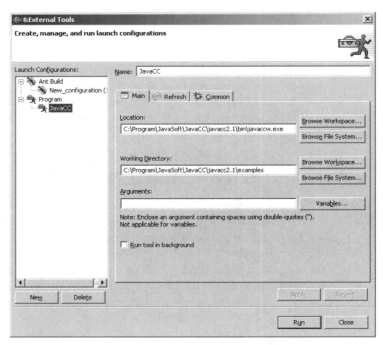

Figure 5.4:   Here we have declared JavaCC as an external tool. In addition, on the Common page we have marked the option 'Display in favorites menu'. This allows us to call this tool conveniently with the function Run > External Tools > Java CC in the following calls to JavaCC.

In this dialog (see Figure 5.5) we select a field type or enter a new file type. In the second step we specify the editor for this file type. We have the option of using either an existing editor registered with the Eclipse workbench or an external editor. In the second case a selection list shows all applications registered with the host operating system. It is possible to select more than one editor for a given file type. By pressing the button *Default...* we may declare an editor as the default editor. If we later want to open a file of this type with another editor, we must use the context function *Open with...*

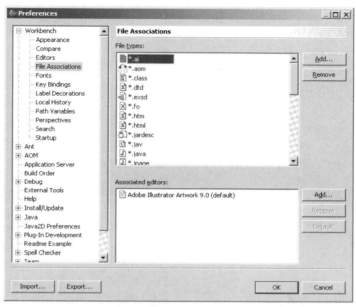

Figure 5.5: Here we have declared Adobe® Illustrator® as the editor for files of type '.ai'. It is also possible to qualify filenames fully. For example, the file type 'plugin.xml' is opened with a different editor than the file type 'build.xml'.

Part 2

Replacing Swing

Eclipse not only has an excellent Java IDE, but with SWT and the JFace it also provides libraries that can serve as a replacement for the Java AWT and Swing. The Java AWT implements its own GUI elements and graphics operations in Java and C. Swing builds on this basis with a pure Java implementation of more advanced GUI elements. In contrast, the SWT is not much more than a platform independent interface to the host windowing system (see Figure 6.0). In most cases, the SWT classes simply delegate the various method calls to the functions of this native windowing system. To do so, SWT uses the *Java Native Interface* (JNI), which allows C-programs to be invoked from Java. Using this technology, it was possible to implement most of the SWT in Java: only a small native library is required.

The advantage of this concept is that, because of the close integration with the host operating system, the 'look and feel' and the responsiveness of SWT-implemented applications is no different than native applications. For Java this could mean a breakthrough on the desktop. Although the performance of Swing has improved with Java 1.4, Java applications that rely on Swing are still unable to match native applications in presentation quality and responsiveness.

In contrast to SWT, JFace does not talk directly to the native windowing system. JFace is completely written in Java and uses the classes and methods of SWT to implement complex GUI elements. Because of this, JFace components also exhibit the native 'look and feel', despite the fact that JFace GUI-elements do not have native siblings.

For our book, however, SWT-based applications are a problem. Because of their closeness to the host windowing system, the SWT examples in this book appear in the 'look and feel' of the author's operating system, Windows 2000. When you run these examples on a different operating system, they will match the appearance of that operating system.

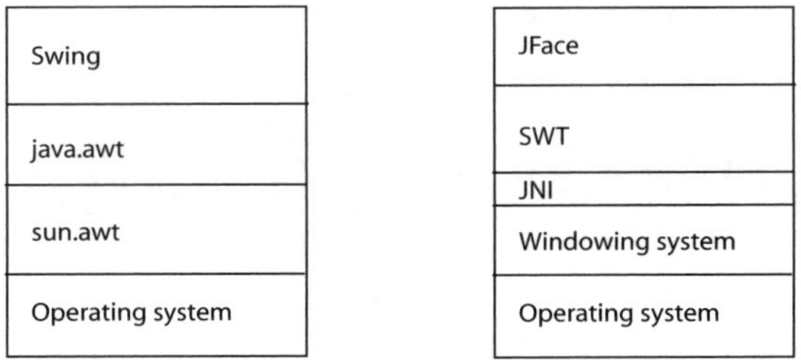

Swing
java.awt
sun.awt
Operating system

JFace
SWT
JNI
Windowing system
Operating system

Figure 6.0:   Unlike AWT, where GUI elements are implemented in the C library sun.awt and only access low-level graphics functions of the host operating system, SWT uses the higher levels of the host windowing system.

6 The SWT library

The *Standard Widget Toolkit* provides a set of basic GUI classes. In this chapter we first present an overview of the SWT's function groups and discuss the pros and cons of SWT compared to Java AWT. Then we explore the various function groups in detail.

During this exploration, however, we will refrain from presenting a full API specification. Instead, we concentrate on the significant features of the individual function groups and how they interact. The API description for the various SWT packages is in the Eclipse help system under *Platform-Plugin Developer Guide > Reference > API Reference > Workbench*.

6.1 SWT function group overview

The SWT classes are organized in the following packages:

`org.eclipse.swt`	This package contains all SWT specific constants and exceptions.
`org.eclipse.swt.accessibi lity`	This package contains all classes for the implementation of GUI support for disabled people.
`org.eclipse.swt.custom`	This package contains widgets for the Eclipse platform that do not have an equivalent in the native windowing system. These widgets are implemented in Java.
`org.eclipse.swt.dnd`	This package supports functions for data transfer, such as 'drag and drop' or operations using the clipboard.
`org.eclipse.swt.events`	This package contains all SWT-specific event classes and listener interfaces.

`org.eclipse.swt.graphics`	This package contains classes for graphics operations.
`org.eclipse.swt.layout`	This package contains various layout classes for automatic positioning of GUI elements.
`org.eclipse.swt.ole.win32`	This package supports OLE (Object Linking and Embedding) for 32-bit Windows operating systems.
`org.eclipse.swt.printing`	This package implements printer support.
`org.eclipse.swt.program`	This package contains only the class `program`. Instances of this class represent file associations and support starting external programs (see Section 5.2).
`org.eclipse.swt.widgets`	This package contains all widget classes of the SWT API. This is the package that implements the main functionality of the SWT.

6.2   SWT – pros and cons

6.2.1   Advantages of SWT

The main advantage of SWT is the seamless integration of an SWT-based application into the host environment. Since SWT-based widgets don't emulate the native user interface, as Swing does, but act only as an adapter to the native widgets, SWT-based user interfaces are indistinguishable from user interfaces of native applications to normal end users. Under Windows 2000 an SWT-button looks exactly like a Windows 2000 button, under Windows XP exactly like a Windows XP button, and on a Mac exactly like a Mac button. Under Swing this is not always the case. Of course, Swing comes with some skins that mimic native user interfaces, but the right skin is not always available.

Better interaction   In the case of responsiveness, Eclipse also has an advantage. In this aspect SWT does not show different behavior compared to native applications, since it uses native event processing. Swing, in contrast, is a bit slower, and this can be annoying to the end user at times. In addition, SWT is less resource-hungry than Swing.

Since the Eclipse platform is completely implemented on basis of SWT, SWT should be the first choice when implementing Eclipse plug-ins and when using GUI components of the Eclipse workbench in plug-ins.

More robust   Last but not least, since most SWT based widgets are only adapters to the native widgets of the host windowing system, we can expect that SWT is more robust and tolerant in regards to heterogeneous hardware and the various accelerator settings of the graphics subsystem. In fact, under Windows I find that SWT based applications run without problems, while AWT- and Swing-based applications have occasionally brought my machine to a full halt because of DirectX incompatibilities.

6.2.2   Disadvantages of SWT

However, there are also a few 'lemons' an SWT programmer has to deal with:

- SWT-based application only run on platforms for which SWT is implemented. These are presently the various Windows platforms, Linux with the GTK or Motif, various Unix derivatives (Solaris, QNX, AIX, and HP-UX), and Mac OS X.

- In general, the various implementations of SWT are functionally equivalent. But as you probably know, the devil is in the detail. For some functions, the behavior of GUI elements can differ from platform to platform. If you plan to deploy a software product on multiple platforms, it is essential to test the product thoroughly on each platform.

- Higher software layers based on AWT cannot by default be used under SWT. These are APIs such as *Java 2D*, *Java 3D*, *Java Advanced Imaging*, *Apache Batik*, etc. In Section 6.7 we will discuss how this problem can be solved.

- In contrast to AWT, SWT requires explicit resource management. SWT uses resources of the host windowing system for images, colors, and fonts. These resources must be released with `dispose()` when they are no longer needed. We will discuss this in detail in Section 6.9.

6.3   The package SWT

Package `org.eclipse.swt` contains only three classes: `SWT`, `SWTException` and `SWTError`. While the last two classes support error handling (recoverable and non-recoverable errors), the class SWT defines all SWT-specific constants such as constants for key identifications, predefined colors, layout variations for widgets, text styles, cursor variations, mouse actions, predefined buttons, and more.

For example, the constant `SWT.LINE_DASHDOT` represents, as the name indicates, a dash-dotted line style, or `SWT.MouseDoubleClick` represents a mouse double click event. We will meet some of these constants in the following examples.

6.4   Events

The package org.eclipse.swt.events contains three different groups: Listener interfaces, Event classes and Adapter classes. In case of events we differentiate between two categories: typed events such as ControlEvent or MouseEvent, and untyped events (Event). Similarly, the Listener interfaces are divided into typed and untyped ones.

6.4.1   Listeners

For each different event type there is also a different Listener class. For example, we can add to a button (Button) a SelectionListener instance with method addSelectionListener(). The method widgetSelected() of this instance is invoked when the button is selected (clicked). The SelectionListener instance is passed to the method as a parameter.

Example:

```
public void createButton(Composite parent) {
  Button myButton = new Button(parent, SWT.PUSH);
  myButton.addSelectionListener(new SelectionListener() {
    public void widgetSelected(SelectionEvent e) {
      System.out.println("Button pressed!");
    }
    public void widgetDefaultSelected(SelectionEvent e) {
    }
  });
}
```

Here, we have added an instance of the inner anonymous SelectionListener class to the new button as a listener.

As a matter of fact, there is a method remove...Listener() for each method add...Listener(). In complex systems in particular, we should deregister (remove) listening components that are currently not active to avoid overhead. Later, when the component becomes active again, we can add it again as a listener with add...Listener().

It is precisely for this reason that we should not make assumptions about the order in which registered listeners are called. While it is true that the list of listeners is processed sequentially when an event is fired, the sequence within this list is practically unpredictable, as components can register and deregister at their own discretion.

6.4.2   Adapters

An adapter is a standard implementation of a given interface that does nothing. They contain empty methods for each method defined in the interface.

The only purpose of an adapter is convenience for the programmer. Instead of having to implement all the methods of an interface, the programmer has only to declare a subclass of the corresponding adapter and to override the methods of interest.

In the example from the previous section we can replace `SelectionListener` by a `SelectionAdapter` to avoid the definition of the empty `widgetDefaultSelected()` method:

```
public void createButton(Composite parent) {
  Button myButton = new Button(parent, SWT.PUSH);
  myButton.addSelectionListener(new SelectionAdapter() {
    public void widgetSelected(SelectionEvent e) {
      System.out.println("Button pressed!");
    }
  });
}
```

6.4.3 Events

All SWT event classes, with the exception of class `Event`, are subclasses of class `TypedEvent`, which in turn is a subclass of class `java.util.EventObject`.

> **Note**: `TypedEvent` is not a subclass of `Event`!

Each event type has a number of public fields that contain specific data about the event represented by the event object. For example, the type `MouseEvent` contains the integer fields `x`, `y`, `stateMask`, and `button`. All those fields must be accessed directly (without a `get...()` method). In addition, each `TypedEvent` class contains the method `getSource()`. Not surprisingly, this method is used to retrieve the source of the event.

In contrast, the generic event class `Event` contains a field `type`, from which we may retrieve the type of event. The source of the event is contained in the field `widget`.

6.4.4   Overview of Listeners, Adapters, and Events

Typed events

Listener	Event	Adapter
ArmListener	ArmEvent This event happens when a widget such as a menu is prepared (armed) for selection. In particular, this is the case when the mouse is moved over the widget.	–
ControlListener	ControlEvent This event happens when a GUI-element is moved or modified in size.	ControlAdapter
DisposeListener	DisposeEvent This event happens when a widget is disposed.	–
FocusListener	FocusEvent This event happens when a GUI-element gains or looses focus.	FocusAdapter
HelpListener	HelpEvent This event happens when help for a GUI-element is requested (*F1* key).	–
KeyListener	KeyEvent This event happens when a key is pressed or released.	KeyAdapter
MenuListener	MenuEvent This event happens when a menu is shown or hidden.	MenuAdapter

Listener	Event	Adapter
ModifyListener	ModifyEvent This event happens after text is modified.	—
MouseListener This listener is notified when a mouse button is pressed or released.	MouseEvent Generic mouse event.	MouseAdapter
MouseMoveListener This listener is notified when the mouse is moved.	MouseEvent Generic mouse event.	—
MouseTrackListener This listener is notified when the mouse is moved over a GUI element or hovers over a GUI element.	MouseEvent Generic mouse event.	MouseTrackAdapter
PaintListener	PaintEvent This event happens when a GUI element must be redrawn.	—
SelectionListener	SelectionEvent This event happens when a GUI element is selected.	SelectionAdapter
ShellListener	ShellEvent This event happens when the state of a shell instance changes (default, minimized, maximized).	ShellAdapter

Listener	Event	Adapter
TraverseListener	TraverseEvent This event happens when the user transfers the focus to another GUI element by pressing TAB, or when the traverse() method was called.	–
TreeListener	TreeEvent This event happens when a tree node expands or collapses.	TreeAdapter
VerifyListener	VerifyEvent This event happens before text is modified. By assigning the value 'false' to the doit field of the event objects, the modification can be vetoed.	–

Generic events

Listener	Event	–
Listener	Event Untyped event used internally within the SWT. This event type is only generated by non-widget objects.	–

6.5   Widgets

In this section we discuss the various GUI elements and their position in the inheritance tree (see Figure 6.1). At the top is the class Widget. The inheritance tree includes of course the obvious control elements such as buttons (Button), text fields (Text), or sliders (Slider). Elements that are used to organize other elements into groups are also included, such as the classes Group or Composite.

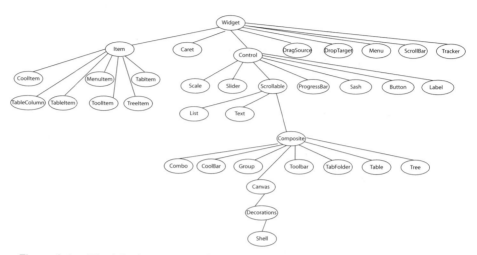

Figure 6.1:   The inheritance tree of the most significant Widget classes

The Widget class

All GUI elements are derived from the abstract class Widget. This class implements some of the common methods for GUI elements such as dispose() or addDisposeListener(). On execution of dispose(), a DisposeEvent object is send to all registered DisposeListener instances.

The Control class

The class Control is an immediate derivative of class Widget. Instances of this class represent window related GUI elements and correspond directly with GUI elements of the host windowing or operating system.

The class Control may send event objects of the following types to registered listeners: ControlEvent, FocusEvent, HelpEvent, KeyEvent, MouseEvent, MouseTrackEvent, MouseMoveEvent, PaintEvent. For this purpose Control provides the necessary add...Listener()- and remove...Listener() methods for the corresponding listeners.

In addition, Control provides a rich set of methods that allowing the various properties of the specific GUI elements to be set and retrieved. In particular, the methods setVisible() and setEnabled() allow a GUI element to be shown or hidden, enabled or disabled.

Size and position   The size of a Control instance is set initially to a default value. In many cases this is the minimum size (0x0), allowing the GUI element to remain invisible. The method setBounds() allows the size of a GUI element to be set, and also its position relative to the containing Composite (see Section 6.5.5). Alternatively, the containing Composite can be equipped with a layout (see Section 6.6) that organizes the sizing and positioning for all Control instances contained in the Composite. The method pack() is used to re-compute the size of a GUI element from the preferred size setting or from the layout.

6.5.1 Visual overview

The best overview of the various widgets in SWT is obtained with the help of one of the example applications for Eclipse. In Section 1.1 we installed the Eclipse example applications, so now we only need to start the required application. To do this we invoke the function *Window > Show View > Other...* In the dialog we select *SWT Examples > SWT Controls*. This view then appears in the window at the bottom right corner. Because we need all the space we can get with this application, we double click the view's title bar to maximize it.

Since this application is perfectly suited to visualize widgets in varying configurations, we will in most cases refrain from depicting widgets on the following pages.

6.5.2 Displays and Shells

The classes Display and Shell form the basis for the construction of a user interface. The class Display represents the GUI process (thread); the class Shell represents windows.

Display

The class Display connects the Java application with the operating system. Each application with an SWT-based GUI creates at least one instance of this class. Or, to be more precise: as long as only one GUI thread is needed, only one Display instance is needed. Should we want to execute GUI operations in multiple threads, we would then need one Display instance for each thread. With the help of the static method Display.getCurrent() we can retrieve the active Display instance for the current thread.

SWT thread

Unlike the AWT and Swing, the SWT enforces an SWT object to only be used from the thread in which is was created. To allow for multi-threaded applications, the class Display provides two methods that allow the execution of arbitrary code in the context of the SWT thread. A Runnable object can be passed as a parameter to the methods syncExec() and asyncExec(), which in turn execute the run() method of the Runnable. In the following chapters we will make use of this technique frequently.

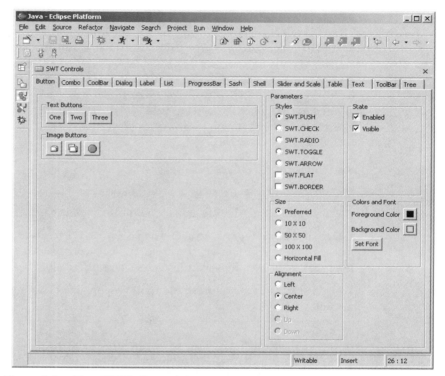

Figure 6.2: The 'SWT Controls' example application organizes the different widget types in different pages. On the right we can configure the selected widget type by specifying parameters. The names of the buttons reflect the names of the corresponding SWT constants (see Section 6.3). The configured widgets are shown on the left.

In addition to these services the Display class provides methods that allow us to retrieve GUI properties of the host windowing system, such as getSystemFont() and getDoubleClickTime(). Display also manages the resources of the host windowing system.

Finally, the class Display provides methods for general management of widgets such as getActiveShell() and getFocusControl().

A Display instance generates events of class Event (see Section 6.4.3) and of type SWT.Open or SWT.Close respectively.

Shell

The class Shell represents a window on the desktop of the host windowing system. A Shell instance can be in one of three different operation modes: *maximized*, *default* and *minimized*. When the operation mode changes, the Shell generates an event of type ShellEvent.

> **Warning**: You must not subclass Shell. (An exception is thrown at runtime in such a case.) To implement your own window types, it is better to subclass the JFace class Window (see Section 7.2).

Shell types

SWT supports two different shell types:

- Top level shells are used to implement the main window of an application.

- Dialog shells are shells that are subordinate to other shells.

Which of the two types is created when a new Shell instance is created depends from the constructor's parameter: If a Display instance is passed to the constructor, a top level shell is created; if a Shell instance is passed, a dialog shell is created.

When a shell is created we can optionally supply one or several style parameters from the following list:

SWT.NONE	Default window. Layout depends on host system.
SWT.BORDER	Bordered window (depends on host platform).
SWT.CLOSE	Window has a title bar with a *Close* button.
SWT.MIN	Window has a title bar with a *Minimize* button.
SWT.MAX	Window has a title bar with a *Maximize* button.
SWT.NO_TRIM	Window has neither a title bar nor a border.
SWT.RESIZE	Window can be resized by using a mouse action.
SWT.TITLE	Window has a title bar.
SWT.SHELL_TRIM	Combination of styles suitable for a top level window: (SWT.CLOSE | SWT.TITLE | SWT.MIN | SWT.MAX | SWT.RESIZE).
SWT.DIALOG_TRIM	Combination of styles suitable for a dialog window: (SWT.CLOSE | SWT.TITLE | SWT.BORDER).

There are further constants that control the modal behavior of the window: SWT.APPLICATION_MODAL, SWT.MODELESS, SWT.PRIMARY_MODAL, and SWT.SYSTEM_MODAL.

A modal window in the foreground does not allow other windows (of the same application or even of the whole system) to come to the foreground. Such a window should be instrumented with a *Close* button, so that the end user may close the window.

If no style parameter was specified, the default style depends on the host system and on the shell type. For example, for Windows CE the default style is SWT.NONE. For other Windows versions, however, the default style is SHELL_TRIM for top level shells and DIALOG_TRIM for dialog shells.

Figure 6.3: A shell with two buttons. The shell was created with the options SWT.BORDER, SWT.TITLE, SWT.CLOSE, SWT.MIN and SWT.MAX, so it is equipped with a 3D-border, a title bar, a close button, a minimize button, and a maximize button.

Setting up the workbench

To write a first example program for a shell, we first need to prepare the workbench. We create a new project called widgets. In this project we create a new class called widget-Test. The SWT library is not yet known to this project. We must therefore add it as an external JAR file to the *Java Build Path*. How to do this was described in Section 2.10.

When running under Windows we find the SWT library under

    \eclipse\plugins\org.eclipse.swt.win32_2.1.0\ws\win32\swt.jar[1]

Under Linux we need two JAR files:

    /opt/eclipse/plugins/org.eclipse.swt.gtk_2.1.0/ws/gtk/swt.jar
    /opt/eclipse/plugins/org.eclipse.swt.gtk_2.1.0/ws/gtk/swt-pi.jar

Under other operating systems you will find the SWT libraries in similar places.

The first SWT program

We can now write a first SWT-based program. First we create a new Display instance, then a new top level shell. This is done by passing the Display instance to the Shell constructor. (For a dialog shell we would instead pass another Shell instance.)

```
import org.eclipse.swt.widgets.Display;
import org.eclipse.swt.widgets.Shell;

public class widgetTest {

  public static void main(String[] args) {
    // Create Display instance
```

---

1. Under later Eclipse versions such as 2.1.1 you need to modify these paths accordingly!

```
final Display display = new Display();
// Create top level Shell (pass display as parent)
final Shell toplevelShell = new Shell(display);
// Set title line
toplevelShell.setText("TopLevel.Titelzeile");
// Display shell
toplevelShell.open();
// Create a dialog shell (pass toplevelShell as parent)
final Shell dialogShell = new Shell(toplevelShell);
// Set title line
dialogShell.setText("Dialog.Titelzeile");
// Display shell
dialogShell.open();
// Wait until top level shell is closed
while (!toplevelShell.isDisposed()) {
  // Check for waiting events
  if (!display.readAndDispatch()) display.sleep();
}
  }
}
```

The while loop at the end of this program is very important. Under SWT the programmer is responsible for the event loop! Without this loop, the user interface would lock up while this program is running. This problem is solved in the while loop with the method readAndDispatch(), which reads events waiting at the Display instance and passes them to the listening GUI-element. If no more events are waiting, we invoke the method sleep(), which waits until a new event occurs.

SWT run configuration

Now we can execute this little program. For this purpose we must create a new *Run* configuration of type *Java Application*. To do so, invoke the function *Run > Run...* and press the *New* button. Specify widgetTest as name for the new configuration, and the same under *Main Class*. Under *Project* specify widgets.

However, these specifications are not sufficient to run this program successfully. The SWT requires native modules, and these modules must be made known to the *Java Virtual Machine*. The path of the module library is specified in the *Run* configuration on the page *Arguments* under *VM Arguments*. In the case of a Windows host system, we have to specify the following parameters[1]:

```
-Djava.library.path=
    C:\eclipse\plugins\org.eclipse.swt.win32_2.1.0\os\win32\x86
```

Under Linux/GTK we specify:

```
-Djava.library.path=
    /opt/eclipse/plugins/org.eclipse.swt.gtk_2.1.0/os/linux/x86
```

---

1. Under later Eclipse versions such as 2.1.1 you need to modify these paths accordingly!

Under other host systems you will find this module library in a similar place.

Afterwards this we can press the *Run* button, and be rewarded with a new window on our desktop.

6.5.3 Dialogs

The class `Dialog` is an abstract class from which we may derive concrete native dialogs. The necessary code would look like this:

```
public class MyDialog extends Dialog {
  Object result;
  // Constructor with style parameter
  public MyDialog (Shell parent, int style) {
    super (parent, style);
  }
  // Constructor without style parameter
  public MyDialog (Shell parent) {
    this (parent, 0);
    // The 0 can be replaced by own default style parameters.
  }
  public Object open () {
    // Get containing shell (as set in the constructor)
    final Shell parent = getParent();
    // Create new dialog shell
    final Shell shell = new Shell(parent, SWT.DIALOG_TRIM |
      SWT.APPLICATION_MODAL);
    // Transfer dialog title to shell title
    shell.setText(getText());
    // TODO Create all widgets here
    // Usually the result variable is set in the
    // event processing of the widgets
    shell.open();
    // Wait until dialog shell is closed
    final Display display = parent.getDisplay();
    while (!shell.isDisposed()) {
      if (!display.readAndDispatch())
        display.sleep();
    }
    return result;
  }
}
```

Predefined dialogs Some concrete subclasses of `Dialog` are already contained in the SWT, such as:

`ColorDialog`	Dialog for selecting a color.
`DirectoryDialog`	Dialog for selecting a directory in the host file system.

FileDialog	Dialog for selecting a file in the host file system. The style parameters `SWT.OPEN` and `SWT.SAVE` are used to determine the purpose for which the file is selected.
FontDialog	Dialog for selecting a text font.
MessageBox	Dialog for displaying a message. With various style parameters we can determine which buttons are used to instrument the dialog. The following combinations are possible: `SWT.OK` `SWT.OK	SWT.CANCEL)` `SWT.YES	SWT.NO)` `SWT.YES	SWT.NO	SWT.CANCEL)` `SWT.RETRY	SWT.CANCEL)` `SWT.ABORT	SWT.RETRY	SWT.IGNORE)`  In addition, we can determine which icon is displayed with the message:  `SWT.ICON_ERROR` `SWT.ICON_INFORMATION` `SWT.ICON_QUESTION` `SWT.ICON_WARNING` `SWT.ICON_WORKING`

The 'look and feel' of these dialogs depend, of course, on the host system. To get an idea of what these dialogs look like on your platform, take a look on the Eclipse example application *SWT Controls*.

MessageBox   In the following code we show how we can create and use a MessageBox dialog in an example program or our own (see Figure 6.4):

```
import org.eclipse.swt.SWT;
import org.eclipse.swt.widgets.Display;
import org.eclipse.swt.widgets.MessageBox;
import org.eclipse.swt.widgets.Shell;

public class widgetTest {

  public widgetTest() {
    super();
  }

  public static void main(String[] args) {
    // Create Display instance
    final Display display = new Display();
    // Create top level shell (pass display as parent)
    final Shell toplevelShell = new Shell(display);
    // Set title line
```

```
        toplevelShell.setText("TopLevel.titleLine");
        // Show shell
        toplevelShell.open();
        while (true) {
          // Create message box
          MessageBox box =
            new MessageBox(
            toplevelShell,
            SWT.RETRY
            | SWT.CANCEL
            | SWT.APPLICATION_MODAL
            | SWT.ICON_QUESTION);
          // Set title
          box.setText("Test");
          // Set message
          box.setMessage("Do you want to try again?");
          // Open message box
          if (box.open() == SWT.CANCEL)
          break;
        }
      }
    }
```

Figure 6.4: The message box created by our example. You can tell from the picture that this dialog is native, indeed. I run a German language version of Windows 2000. The 'Retry' button (Wiederholen) and the 'Cancel' button (Abbrechen) are generated by Windows.

However, for our own complex dialogs we will probably not use the SWT class Dialog, but rather the similarly named JFace class (see Chapter 7), because the JFace version is much more convenient to use. Most of the Eclipse workbench dialogs, for example, build upon the JFace Dialog class and not on SWT dialogs.

6.5.4 Composites, Groups and Canvas

Usually we will not mount widgets directly into a shell, but will rather put one or several hierarchies of Composite instances in between. Composites are used to organize widgets into groups. For example, the buttons of a dialog can be combined into one group with the help of a Composite. This is important for radio buttons, where pressing one button releases all other buttons in the same group. Another possibility is organizing several input fields and labels into a group to improve the layout or the navigation.

Constructing composites

If we want to add widgets to a `Composite`, we will search in vain for an appropriate `add()` method. Instead, we construct a GUI in a completely different way. Each time we create a new widget, the containing `Composite` is passed as a parameter to the constructor. The widgets in the `Composite` are ordered in the sequence of their creation.

Since `Composites` are widgets, too, we must specify a containing `Composite` instance when we create a new `Composite` (shells are also `Composites`). We will usually transfer the background and foreground color and the type font from the containing composite. Also, we may specify the position and the dimensions of the new `Composite` in relation to the containing `Composite`.

```
// Create new Composite instance
final Composite composite = new Composite(parent,0);
// Get properties from the containing composite
composite.setBackground(parent.getBackground());
composite.setForeground(parent.getForeground());
composite.setFont(parent.getFont());
// Set position and size
composite.setBounds(X,Y,WIDTH,HEIGHT);
```

We can optionally specify the constant `SWT.NO_RADIO_GROUP` as a second parameter in the constructor if we don't want the composite to interfere with the release mechanism of radio buttons.

The class `Group` is a subclass of class `Composite`. This class in addition is equipped with a border line that clearly demarcates the group area. The style of this line can be influenced with the constants `SWT.SHADOW_ETCHED_IN`, `SWT.SHADOW_ETCHED_OUT`, `SWT.SHADOW_IN`, `SWT.SHADOW_OUT`, and `SWT.SHADOW_NONE`, provided that the host windowing system supports this. The method `setText()` can be used to place a title into this border line. In many cases `Groups` are a better choice than `Composites`. When dialogs become complex, groups allow a better navigation with the keyboard, and thus are more user friendly for disabled people (see Section 6.11).

For `Composite` and `Group` instances that contain other widgets we usually will set a layout. We will discuss this in more detail in Section 6.6.

Canvas

The class `Canvas` is a subclass of `Composite`. Its purpose is not to contain other GUI-elements (although this is possible) but to serve as a canvas for drawing operations. In particular, if we want to invent our own GUI elements, we can draw them on a `Canvas` instance.

In addition, the `Canvas` class supports a caret (`setCaret()` and `getCaret()`).

6.5.5   Buttons

Buttons come in many flavors. The button type created by the `Button()` constructor depends on the style constant passed to this constructor:

SWT.ARROW		Button with a small arrow. Normally used for drop-down menus and the like.
SWT.CHECK		Checkbox that can be marked. The button text is printed beside the checkbox.
SWT.PUSH		Pushbutton with the button text on the button face.
SWT.RADIO		Radio button. Radio buttons within the same group release each other when pressed.
SWT.TOGGLE		A toggle button is similar to a pushbutton. The difference is that the button remains pushed after the first click. The second click will release it again.

In addition, we have the option of controlling the look and the alignment of a button:

SWT.FLAT	The button is not drawn in 3D-fashion but in a "flat" fashion.
SWT.BORDER	The button is enclosed by a frame.

However, not all platforms support these attributes.

Text and image buttons

Using the methods `setText()` and `setImage()` we can assign text or an image to a button. For push-buttons and toggle buttons the text or the image appears on the button face. For checkboxes and radio buttons text or image are shown beside the button. Buttons of type ARROW show neither text nor image.

Both methods are mutually exclusive. Either:

```
final Button button = new Button(composite,SWT.PUSH);
button.setText("Press me!");
// React to click events
button.addSelectionListener(new SelectionAdapter() {
  public void widgetSelected(SelectionEvent e) {
    System.out.println("Key was pressed");
  }
});
```

or:

```
final Button button = new Button(composite,SWT.PUSH);
Display display = composite.getDisplay();
final Image image = new Image(display, "images/button1.gif");
button.setImage(image);
// React to click events
button.addSelectionListener(new SelectionAdapter() {
  public void widgetSelected(SelectionEvent e) {
    System.out.println("Key was pressed");
  }
});
// Dispose image when button is disposed
button.addDisposeListener(new DisposeListener() {
  public void widgetDisposed(DisposeEvent e) {
    image.dispose();
  }
});
```

In the second case we needed additional logic to dispose of the Image resource when it was no longer needed. This is necessary as images allocate resources in the host operating system.

> **Tip**: A good source for images for buttons, tool bars and other purposes are the icons directories in the various Eclipse plug-ins, for example \eclipse\plugins\org.eclipse.pde.ui_2.1.0\icons\full\obj16.

6.5.6   Sliders, Scales and Progress Bars

Sliders and Scales

Both classes Slider and Scale support entry of a numeric value via a sliding control. Usually the class Slider is used for the positioning of window contents (*scroll bar*) while Scale is used for adjusting numeric parameters such as volume, brightness, contrast, etc.

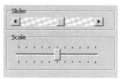

Figure 6.5: Slider and Scale, both enclosed by a group.

The following style constants influence the presentation of these widgets:

SWT.HORIZONTAL	Horizontal or vertical orientation
SWT.VERTICAL	
SWT.BORDER	Scales are surrounded with a frame. This option has no effect for class Slider.

The following example creates a simple slider:

```
final Slider slider = new Slider(composite,SWT.HORIZONTAL);
// Set minimum value
slider.setMinimum(0);
// Set maximum value
slider.setMaximum(1000);
// Set increment value for arrow buttons
slider.setIncrement(50);
// Set increment value for clicks on the slider face
slider.setPageIncrement(200);
// Set current position
slider.setSelection(500);
// Set size of handle
slider.setThumb(200);
// React to slider events
slider.addSelectionListener(new SelectionAdapter() {
  public void widgetSelected(SelectionEvent e) {
    System.out.println("Slider was moved to: "
      +slider.getSelection());
    }
});
```

With the corresponding get...() methods we can retrieve these values, too. Scale provides the same methods, except the setThumb() and getThumb() methods.

ProgressBar

The class ProgressBar supports the presentation of a progress indicator. The API is very similar to that of class Slider, except that ProgressBar does not generate events.

There are also two more style constants:

- `SWT.SMOOTH` enforces a continuous progress indicator. Otherwise, the progress indicator is broken into segments.

- `SWT.INDETERMINATE` is used to create a constantly moving progress indicator. When the progress indicator reaches maximum size it starts again with minimum size. With this option set we don't use `setSelection()` for indicating progress.

Using this class is not as easy as it seems, as the progress indicator is only updated when the event loop is not locked.

Scrollable and ScrollBar

Some widgets are already equipped with scroll bars. All these widgets are subclasses of `Scrollable`. Which sliders are active for a `Scrollable` instance can be controlled with the style constants `SWT.H_SCROLL` and `SWT.V_SCROLL`. The class `Scrollable`, by the way, does not use `Slider` instances to implement the scroll bars, but instead uses instances of class `ScrollBar`. In contrast to `Slider` and `Scale`, `ScrollBar` is not a subclass of `Control`, i.e. it is not a native widget.

6.5.7   Text fields and Labels

Instances of class `Text` are used to display, enter or modify text. The following style constants can be used to configure `Text` instances:

`SWT.MULTI` `SWT.SINGLE`	Determines if the text field has multiple or only a single line.
`SWT.READ_ONLY`	When this option is set, the end user cannot modify the text in the text field.
`SWT.WRAP`	When the option is set, automatic word wrapping is supported.

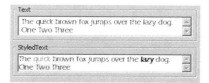

Figure 6.6: The upper field is a Text instance, the lower field is a StyledText instance (see also Section 6.5.13). For both fields we set the font Eras Book, and for the lower field we applied additional formatting. In addition, for each field we specified a vertical scroll bar with SWT.VERTICAL.

Instances of class Text create the following event types:

SelectionEvent	When the *Enter* key is pressed, the method widgetDefaultSelected() is called for all registered SelectionListeners.
ModifyEvent	This event is fired after text is modified.
VerifyEvent	This event is fired before the widget's text content is modified. By assigning the value false to the event objects doit field we can veto the modification of the text.

The following example creates a text field with a VerifyListener to reject invalid modifications:

```
final Text text = new Text(composite,SWT.SINGLE);
text.setText("Input text");
text.addSelectionListener(new SelectionAdapter() {
  public void widgetDefaultSelected(SelectionEvent e) {
    System.out.println("Enter was pressed: "+text.getSelection());
  }
});
text.addModifyListener(new ModifyListener() {
  public void modifyText(ModifyEvent e) {
    System.out.println("Text after modification: "+text.getText());
  }
});
text.addVerifyListener(new VerifyListener() {
  public void verifyText(VerifyEvent e) {
    String s = text.getText();
    System.out.println("Text before modification: "+s);
    // Veto: Text longer than 10 characters is prohibited
    if (s.length() >= 10) e.doit = false;
  }
});
```

The class Text has a rich variety of methods for processing text input. In particular, it has methods for exchanging text content with the host systems clipboard (cut(), copy(), paste()).

Labels   Not surprisingly, instances of class Label are used to label other widgets. In addition, we may use labels to display an image or a horizontal or vertical line. Label presentation and purpose can be controlled with the following style constants:

SWT.SEPARATOR	The label is displayed as a horizontal or vertical line.
SWT.HORIZONTAL SWT.VERTICAL	Determines the orientation of the label.
SWT.SHADOW_IN SWT.SHADOW_OUT SWT.SHADOW_NONE	Determines the shadowing effects of the label.
SWT.CENTER SWT.LEFT SWT.RIGHT	Determines the alignment of text or image labels.
SWT.WRAP	When the option is set, automatic word wrapping is supported for text labels.

The following code can be used to create a text label:

```
final Label label = new Label(composite, SWT.NULL);
label.setText("Enter");
```

For image labels, the image is set with the method setImage(). Just as with Buttons (Section 6.5.5), Image instances should be released when they are no longer needed.

6.5.8   Tables, Lists and Combos

Tables and lists are used to present contents in columns. Both widget types support the selection of single or multiple elements. Combos are a space saving variant for selecting items from a list.

Tables

The class `Table` is responsible for the presentation of tables. In addition to the `Composite` style constants, `Table` provides the following additional style constants:

SWT.SINGLE SWT.MULTI	The end user may select only single or multiple table rows respectively.
SWT.FULL_SELECTION	The whole table row is selectable. (Normally, only the first element of a row can be selected.)
SWT.CHECK	Each table row is equipped with a checkbox placed in front of the row. The state of the checkbox can be accessed with the methods setChecked() and getChecked().

`Table` instances generate `SelectionEvent` objects when a table element is selected. The `SelectionListener` method `widgetDefaultSelected()` is called when *Enter* is pressed for a table element or when a table element is double clicked.

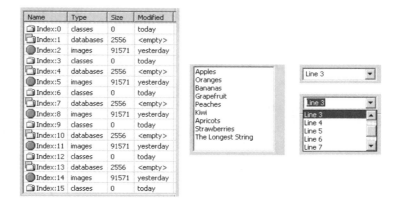

Figure 6.7: From left to right: Table, List and Combo. At the right, the top widget shows the combo in its normal state, the bottom widget shows the same combo in expanded state after a click on the arrow button. For the table we made the grid lines and the column headers visible.

Table columns

To configure individual table columns we can assign `TableColumn` to a `Table` instance. This is done in the same way as widgets are added to a `Composite` – the `Table` instance is passed to the `TableColumn()` constructor as a parameter. In addition, we may specify a column header and a width (in pixels) for each table column, using the methods setText() and setWidth().

The end user is still able to modify the width of table columns. In addition, the column headers act as buttons. In consequence, TableColumn instances can create a variety of events. A ControlEvent is fired when a table column is moved or modified in size. A SelectionEvent is fired when a column header is clicked.

The alignment of table columns can be specified with the help of the style constants SWT.LEFT, SWT.CENTER, and SWT.RIGHT.

Table rows   In a similar way we can create table rows as TableItem objects. The method setText() is used to set the content of a table row. The content is passed to this method as a string or, in the case of multi-column tables, as an array of strings.

The Table methods setHeaderVisible() and setLinesVisible() are used to show or hide the column headers and grid lines.

The following code creates a table with three columns and two lines:

```
final Table table = new Table(composite,
  SWT.SINGLE | SWT.H_SCROLL |
  SWT.V_SCROLL | SWT.BORDER |
  SWT.FULL_SELECTION );
// Create three table columns
final TableColumn col1 = new TableColumn(table,SWT.LEFT);
col1.setText("Column 1");
col1.setWidth(80);
final TableColumn col2 = new TableColumn(table,SWT.LEFT);
col2.setText("Column 2");
col2.setWidth(80);
final TableColumn col3 = new TableColumn(table,SWT.LEFT);
col3.setText("Column 3");
col3.setWidth(80);
// Make column headers and grid lines visible
table.setHeaderVisible(true);
table.setLinesVisible(true);
// Create table rows
final TableItem item1 = new TableItem(table,0);
item1.setText(new String[] {"a","b","c"});
final TableItem item2 = new TableItem(table,0);
item2.setText(new String[] {"d","c","e"});
// Add selection listeners
table.addSelectionListener(new SelectionAdapter() {
  public void widgetDefaultSelected(SelectionEvent e) {
    processSelection("Enter was pressed: ");
  }
  public void widgetSelected(SelectionEvent e) {
    processSelection("Table element was selected: ");
  }
```

```
private void processSelection(String message) {
  // Get selected table row
  TableItem[] selection = table.getSelection();
  // Because of SWT.SINGLE only one row was selected
  TableItem selectedRow = selection[0];
  // Format the table elements for output
  String s = selectedRow.getText(0)+", "+
    selectedRow.getText(1)+", "+selectedRow.getText(2);
  System.out.println(message + s);
}
});
```

Lists

If we only want to offer a single-column list of string elements for selection, using the class List is much simpler than creating a table. List instances generate the same event types as Table instances, but the method widgetDefaultSelected() is only called in the case of a double click on a list element. The style constants SWT.SINGLE and SWT.MULTI can be used to specify whether the end user may select only a single or multiple list entries.

In the following code we construct a list with three entries. We allow, and process, the selection of multiple entries:

```
final List list = new List(composite,SWT.MULTI);
list.add("Element1");
list.add("Element2");
list.add("Element3");
list.addSelectionListener(new SelectionAdapter() {
  public void widgetDefaultSelected(SelectionEvent e) {
    processSelection("Enter was pressed: ");
  }
  public void widgetSelected(SelectionEvent e) {
    processSelection("List entry was selected: ");
  }
  private void processSelection(String message) {
    // Get selected entries
    String[] selection = list.getSelection();
    // Format entries for output
    StringBuffer sb = new StringBuffer();
    for (int i = 0; i < selection.length; i++) {
      sb.append(selection[i]+" ");
    }
    System.out.println(message + sb);
  }
});
```

Combos

Finally, we have the class `Combo`, which combines selection from a list and text input.

Instances of class `Combo` generate the following event types:

SelectionEvent	If the *Enter* key is pressed on a list entry the `SelectionListener` method `widgetDefaultSelected()` is invoked.
	If a list entry is selected, the method `widgetSelected()` is called instead.
ModifyEvent	This event is fired when the text is changed via keyboard or via list selection.

The following style constants influence the presentation and the function of `Combo` instances:

SWT.DROP_DOWN	The selection list is only shown after a click on the arrow button.
SWT.READ_ONLY	When this option is specified, values may only selected from the list, but not entered by keyboard.
SWT.SIMPLE	The selection list is always visible if this option was specified.

The following code creates a Combo instance:

```
final Combo combo = new Combo(composite,SWT.DROP_DOWN);
// Create three list elements
combo.add("Element1");
combo.add("Element2");
combo.add("Element3");
// Supply default value for text field
combo.setText("Select");
// Add selection listener
combo.addSelectionListener(new SelectionAdapter() {
  public void widgetDefaultSelected(SelectionEvent e) {
    System.out.println("Enter was pressed: " + combo.getText());
    }
    public void widgetSelected(SelectionEvent e) {
      System.out.println("List entry was selected: " +
        combo.getText());
      }
  });
  // Add ModifyListener
  combo.addModifyListener(new ModifyListener() {
  public void modifyText(ModifyEvent e) {
  System.out.println("Text was modified: "+combo.getText());
  }
});
```

6.5.9   Trees

The class Tree is responsible for the presentation of trees. The presentation and functionality of the tree can be influenced by the following style constants:

SWT.SINGLE SWT.MULTI	The end user may select only single or multiple tree nodes respectively.
SWT.CHECK	Each tree node is equipped with a checkbox in front of the node. The state of the check box can be accessed via the methods setChecked() and getChecked().

Figure 6.8:   Two trees. The tree on the left only has text nodes, while the tree on the right has images assigned to the tree nodes.

Tree instances generate the following event types:

SelectionEvent	In case of a double click or when the *Enter* key is pressed on a tree node, the SelectionListener method widgetDefaultSelected() is called. The method widgetSelected() is invoked when a tree node is selected.
TreeEvent	The TreeListener method treeExpanded() is called when a tree node is expanded. The method treeCollapsed() is called when a tree node is collapsed. The node in question is passed in field item in the TreeEvent object.

The individual tree nodes are implemented as TreeItem instances. When such an instance is created, we pass either the Tree object or another TreeItem instance as parent node via the constructor. The text content of a TreeItem instance is set via method setText(). In addition, we may assign an image to each tree node using the method setImage(). As already discussed with Buttons (see Section 6.5.5), Image instances should be disposed of when they are no longer needed.

The following code creates a simple tree with three node. The first node has two child nodes:

```
final Tree tree = new Tree(composite,SWT.SINGLE);
// Create first node level
final TreeItem node1 = new TreeItem(tree,SWT.NULL);
node1.setText("Node 1");
final TreeItem node2 = new TreeItem(tree,SWT.NULL);
node2.setText("Node 2");
final TreeItem node3 = new TreeItem(tree,SWT.NULL);
node3.setText("Node 3");
// Create second node level
final TreeItem node11 = new TreeItem(node1,SWT.NULL);
node11.setText("Node 1.1");
final TreeItem node12 = new TreeItem(node1,SWT.NULL);
node12.setText("Node 1.2");
// Add selection listener
tree.addSelectionListener(new SelectionAdapter() {
  public void widgetDefaultSelected(SelectionEvent e) {
    System.out.println("Enter was pressed: " +
      tree.getSelection()[0].getText());
  }
  public void widgetSelected(SelectionEvent e) {
    System.out.println("Tree node was selected: " +
      tree.getSelection()[0].getText());
  }
});
// Add TreeListener
tree.addTreeListener(new TreeAdapter() {
  public void treeCollapsed(TreeEvent e) {
    System.out.println("Tree node was collapsed: " +
      ((TreeItem) e.item).getText());
  }
  public void treeExpanded(TreeEvent e) {
    System.out.println("ree node was expanded: " +
      ((TreeItem) e.item).getText());
  }
});
```

For larger trees we will usually refrain from constructing the tree completely before displaying it. A better way is to construct a tree lazily, meaning to create nodes when they become visible, i.e. when their parent nodes are expanded.

6.5.10 Sashes

The class Sash is responsible for representing sashes. Sashes can be used to segment a *Composite* into separate areas. The end user is able to reposition the sashes so that the size of the areas may change. As the sashes don't control the size of the adjoining areas themselves, the programmer is responsible for reacting to events from Sash instances and adjusting the size and position of these areas accordingly. Sash instances create events of type SelectEvent. The orientation of a sash can be controlled via the style constants SWT.HORIZONTAL and SWT.VERTICAL.

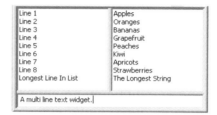

Figure 6.9:   A vertical and a horizontal Sash separating three text fields from each other. Both Sashes can be moved with the mouse.

In the following example we first create a group. On this group we position a Combo instance, a sash, and a tree:

```
// Create group
final Group group = new Group(composite, SWT.NULL);
group.setText("Group");
// Create layout (see section 6.6)
group.setLayout(new RowLayout());

// Create combo
final Combo combo = new Combo(group, SWT.DROP_DOWN );
...

// Create sash
final Sash sash = new Sash(group, SWT.VERTICAL | SWT.BORDER);

// Create tree
final Tree tree = new Tree(group, SWT.SINGLE);
...
// Event processing for sash
sash.addSelectionListener(new SelectionAdapter() {
  public void widgetSelected(SelectionEvent e) {
    if (e.detail != SWT.DRAG) {
      moveSash(group, combo, sash, tree,
        e.x, e.y, e.width, e.height);
    }
  }
});
// Event processing for group Group
group.addControlListener(new ControlAdapter() {
  // React to size changes
  public void controlResized(ControlEvent e) {
    Rectangle groupClientBounds = group.getClientArea();
```

```
        moveSash(group, combo, sash, tree,
        groupClientBounds.x + groupClientBounds.width / 2,
        groupClientBounds.y, 8, groupClientBounds.height);
      }
  });
  ...
  private void moveSash(final Composite parent, final Control c1,
    final Sash sash, final Control c2,
      int x, int y, int width, int height) {
    // Reposition sash
    sash.setBounds(x, y, width, height);
    // retrieve the client area of the group
    Rectangle r = parent.getClientArea();
    // adapt the left widget in size
    c1.setBounds(r.x, r.y, x - r.x, r.height);
    // adapt the right widget in size and position
    c2.setBounds(x + width, r.y, r.width - (x + width), r.height);
  }
```

The positioning of the sash and the other GUI elements is done in method moveSash(). This method is called from the event processing of the sash. In addition, it must also be called for each size change of the group widget.

6.5.11 Tabbed folders

The class TabFolder implements a tabbed folder, a multi-page unit in which a page can be brought to the front by clicking on the page's tab. Each TabFolder instance is a Composite which may contain one or several TabItem instances. Each TabItem object relates to a tab, and the tab's text can be set with the method setText(). With the method setControl() we can assign a Control instance (such as a Composite) to each TabItem object. The Control instance is made visible when the corresponding TabItem object is selected. The Control instance must be created as a part of the TabFolder (i.e. by specifying the TabFolder instance in the constructor when the Control is created).

TabFolder only supports the style constant SWT.BORDER.

TabFolder instances generate SelectionEvents on selection of a TabItem.

The following code creates a tabbed folder with two tabs:

```
import org.eclipse.swt.SWT;
import org.eclipse.swt.events.SelectionAdapter;
import org.eclipse.swt.events.SelectionEvent;
import org.eclipse.swt.layout.FillLayout;
import org.eclipse.swt.widgets.*;

public class widgetTest {

  public static void main(String[] args) {
```

```java
        // Create display instance
        final Display display = new Display();
        // Create top level shell (pass display as parent)
        final Shell toplevelShell = new Shell(display);
        // Set title
        toplevelShell.setText("TopLevel.Titelzeile");
        // Fill the shell completely with content
        toplevelShell.setLayout(new FillLayout());
        // Create tabbed folder
        TabFolder folder = new TabFolder(toplevelShell, SWT.NONE);
        // Protocol selection event
        folder.addSelectionListener(new SelectionAdapter() {
          public void widgetSelected(SelectionEvent e) {
            System.out.println(
              "Tab selected: " + ((TabItem) (e.item)).getText());
          }
        });
        // Fill tabbed folder completely with content
        folder.setLayout(new FillLayout());
        Composite page1 = createTabPage(folder, "tab1");
        // We can now place more GUI elements onto page1
        //...
        Composite page2 = createTabPage(folder, "tab2");
        // We can now place more GUI elements onto page2
        //...
        // Display shell
        toplevelShell.open();
        // Event loop
        while (!toplevelShell.isDisposed()) {
          if (!display.readAndDispatch())
          display.sleep();
        }
      }

    private static Composite createTabPage(TabFolder folder,
      String label) {
      // Create and label a new tab
      TabItem tab = new TabItem(folder, SWT.NONE);
      tab.setText(label);
      // Create a new page as a Composite instance
      Composite page = new Composite(folder, SWT.NONE);
      //... and assign to tab
      tab.setControl(page);
      return page;
    }
  }
```

6.5.12   Tool bars and Menus

Tool bars

The class `ToolBar` implements tool bars. Each `ToolBar` instance is a `Composite` that contains one or several `ToolItem` instances.

We can control the presentation of tool bars with the following style constants:

`SWT.FLAT`	Use a two-dimensional representation instead of three-dimensional presentation, provided this is supported by the host platform.
`SWT.WRAP`	Use automatic word wrapping.
`SWT.RIGHT`	Align right.
`SWT.HORIZONTAL` `SWT.VERTICAL`	Horizontal or vertical orientation respectively.

`ToolItem` instances represent the buttons on the tool bar. The button type can be controlled via the following style constants:

`SWT.PUSH`	Normal button that releases immediately.
`SWT.CHECK`	Locking button (similar to toggle buttons).
`SWT.RADIO`	Radio button that releases other radio buttons in the same tool bar when pressed.
`SWT.SEPARATOR`	Passive element to separate button groups.
`SWT.DROP_DOWN`	Normal button with an associated arrow button.

Tool items are labeled with the method `setText()`. Image buttons can be created with the method `setImage()`. With the method `setHotImage()` we can set an additional image that appears when the mouse hovers over the button. With the method `setDisabledImage()` we can set an image that is shown when the tool item is disabled. So we can visualize the different operation modes of a tool item. As we already have discussed for `Buttons` (see Section 6.5.5), `Image` instances must be disposed of when they are no longer needed. With `setToolTipText()` we can add an additional text to the tool item that is shown when the mouse is moved over the tool item.

When activated, `ToolItem` instances generate `SelectionEvent` objects. In the case of `DROP_DOWN` tool items we have to find whether the main button or the arrow button was pressed. This can be done by checking the condition (`event.detail == SWT.ARROW`).

The event listener can then create a menu list for the drop-down menu, allowing the selection of a function.

Moveable tool groups (CoolBar)

The CoolBar class can be used to combine several ToolBar instances into so-called CoolItems, i.e. tool groups that can be repositioned by the end-user. Each single Toolbar instance is embedded into a CoolItem instance. These CoolItem instances are placed onto a CoolBar and can be moved within the area of the CoolBar. The association between CoolItem and ToolBar is achieved with the CoolItem method setControl(). Initially we must assign a minimum size for each CoolItem instance. We show how this is done in the second example below.

If we assign the style constant SWT.DROP_DOWN for a CoolItem instance, an arrow symbol appears when all tools within the tool group cannot be displayed. We need to implement the necessary event processing in such a case: we must construct a drop-down menu, as we had to do for drop-down tool items (see above).

Menus

The class Menu is used to implement menus. The following style constants influence the presentation of a Menu instance:

SWT.BAR	The instance represents a menu bar.
SWT.DROP_DOWN	The instance represents a drop-down menu.
SWT.POP_UP	The instance represents a pop-up menu.

Menu instances generate events of type HelpEvent and MenuEvent. When a menu appears on the screen, the MenuListener method menuShown() is invoked. When the menu disappears, the method menuHidden() is called.

MenuItem

Menu items are implemented by MenuItem instances. The type of item is controlled via a style constant:

SWT.CHECK	The menu item is equipped with a check symbol. This symbol is toggled with each click on the menu entry.
SWT.CASCADE	The menu item implements a cascading menu.
SWT.PUSH	Normal menu item.

| SWT.RADIO | Menu item with a check symbol. When this symbol is set, other radio menu items in the same menu are reset. |
| SWT.SEPARATOR | Passive item implementing a separator line. |

Menu items are labeled with the help of method setText().

MenuItem instances create events of the types SelectionEvent, ArmEvent, and HelpEvent. ArmEvents are fired when the menu item is armed, i.e. when the mouse cursor is moved over the item.

If we want to create the typical menu bar, we first must create a Menu instance of type SWT.BAR. When doing so, we must specify the Shell for which the menu is created as parent Composite. The creation of the menu bar is not enough, however. We must also activate the menu bar for the parent shell. This is done in the Shell instance by calling the method setMenuBar().

The individual menu titles are then created as cascading MenuItem instances. The submenus belonging to these instances are created as independent SWT.DROP_DOWN menus under the Shell instance. Then we use the MenuItem method setMenu() to assign the submenus to the cascading menu items.

The following example shows the construction of a simple menu with a single menu title:

```
// Create menu bar
Menu menuBar = new Menu(toplevelShell, SWT.BAR);
toplevelShell.setMenuBar(menuBar);
// Create menu title
MenuItem fileTitle = new MenuItem(menuBar, SWT.CASCADE);
fileTitle.setText("File");
// Create submenu for this menu title
Menu fileMenu = new Menu(toplevelShell, SWT.DROP_DOWN);
fileTitle.setMenu(fileMenu);
// Create menu item
MenuItem item = new MenuItem(fileMenu, SWT.NULL);
item.setText("Exit");
// Event processing for menu item
item.addSelectionListener(new SelectionAdapter() {
  public void widgetSelected(SelectionEvent e) {
    toplevelShell.close();
  }
});
```

In the next example we create a CoolBar consisting of two moveable groups with five different buttons. We also have a drop-down button that expands a menu with two menu items when pressed.

```
// Create CoolBar
final CoolBar coolbar = new CoolBar(composite, SWT.NULL);
// Create ToolBar as a component of CoolBar
final ToolBar toolbar1 = new ToolBar(coolbar, SWT.NULL);
// Create pushbutton
final ToolItem toolitem1 = new ToolItem(toolbar1, SWT.PUSH);
toolitem1.setText("Push");
toolitem1.setToolTipText("Push button");
// Create event processing for pushbutton
toolitem1.addSelectionListener(new SelectionAdapter() {
  public void widgetSelected(SelectionEvent e) {
    System.out.println(
      "Tool button was pressed: " + toolitem1.getText());
  }
});
// Create check button
final ToolItem toolitem2 = new ToolItem(toolbar1, SWT.CHECK);
toolitem2.setText("Check");
toolitem2.setToolTipText("Check button");
// Create CoolItem instance
final CoolItem coolitem1 = new CoolItem(coolbar, SWT.NULL);
// Assign this tool bar to the CoolItem instance
coolitem1.setControl(toolbar1);
// Compute size of tool bar
Point size = toolbar1.computeSize(SWT.DEFAULT, SWT.DEFAULT);
// Compute required size of CoolItems instance
size = coolitem1.computeSize(size.x, size.y);
// Set size for this CoolItem instance
coolitem1.setSize(size);
// The minimum size of the CoolItem is the width of the first button
coolitem1.setMinimumSize(toolitem1.getWidth(), size.y);

// Create second ToolBar instance
final ToolBar toolbar2 = new ToolBar(coolbar, SWT.NULL);
// Create two radio buttons
final ToolItem toolitem3a = new ToolItem(toolbar2, SWT.RADIO);
toolitem3a.setText("Radio");
toolitem3a.setToolTipText("Radio button a");
final ToolItem toolitem3b = new ToolItem(toolbar2, SWT.RADIO);
toolitem3b.setText("Radio");
toolitem3b.setToolTipText("Radio button b");
// Create separator
new ToolItem(toolbar2, SWT.SEPARATOR);
// Create drop-down menu button
final ToolItem toolitem5 = new ToolItem(toolbar2, SWT.DROP_DOWN);
toolitem5.setText("Drop-down-Menu");
// Add event processing to drop-down menu button
toolitem5.addSelectionListener(
  // In class DropDownSelectionListener we construct the menu
  new DropDownSelectionListener(composite.getShell()));
```

```
// Create second CoolItem, assing Toolbar to it and set size
final CoolItem coolitem2 = new CoolItem(coolbar, SWT.NULL);
coolitem2.setControl(toolbar2);
size = toolbar2.computeSize(SWT.DEFAULT, SWT.DEFAULT);
size = coolitem2.computeSize(size.x, size.y);
coolitem2.setSize(size);
coolitem2.setMinimumSize(toolitem3a.getWidth(), size.y);
```

The class DropDownSelectionListener is responsible for menu construction, and is defined as follows:

```
class DropDownSelectionListener extends SelectionAdapter {
  private Menu menu;
  private Composite parent;

  public DropDownSelectionListener(Composite parent) {
    this.parent = parent;
  }

  public void widgetSelected(final SelectionEvent e) {
    // Create menu lazily
    if (menu == null) {
      menu = new Menu(parent);
      final MenuItem menuItem1 = new MenuItem(menu, SWT.NULL);
      menuItem1.setText("Item1");
      // Set SelectionListener for menuItem1
      menuItem1.addSelectionListener(new SelectionAdapter() {
        public void widgetSelected(SelectionEvent m) {
          processMenuEvent(e, menuItem1);
        }
      });
      menuItem1.addArmListener(new ArmListener() {
        public void widgetArmed(ArmEvent m) {
          System.out.println("Mouse is over menu item 1");
        }
      });

      final MenuItem menuItem2 = new MenuItem(menu, SWT.NULL);
      menuItem2.setText("Item2");
      // Set SelectionListener foür menuItem1
      menuItem2.addSelectionListener(new SelectionAdapter() {
        public void widgetSelected(SelectionEvent m) {
          processMenuEvent(e, menuItem2);
        }
      });
      menuItem2.addArmListener(new ArmListener() {
        public void widgetArmed(ArmEvent m) {
          System.out.println("Mouse is over menu item 2");
        }
      });
    }
```

```
                    // Check, if it was the arrow button that was pressed
                    if (e.detail == SWT.ARROW) {
                      if (menu.isVisible()) {
                        // Set visible menu invisible
                        menu.setVisible(false);
                      } else {
                        // Retrieve ToolItem and ToolBar from the event object
                        final ToolItem toolItem = (ToolItem) e.widget;
                        final ToolBar toolBar = toolItem.getParent();
                        // Get position and size of the ToolItem
                        Rectangle toolItemBounds = toolItem.getBounds();
                        // Convert relative position to absolute position
                        Point point =
                        toolBar.toDisplay(
                          new Point(toolItemBounds.x, toolItemBounds.y));
                        // Set menu position
                        menu.setLocation(point.x, point.y + toolItemBounds.height);
                        // Make menu visible
                        menu.setVisible(true);
                      }
                    } else {
                      final ToolItem toolItem = (ToolItem) e.widget;
                      System.out.println(
                      "Tool button was pressed: " + toolItem.getText());
                      }
                  }
                  private void processMenuEvent(
                    final SelectionEvent e,
                  final MenuItem item) {
                    // Get text of menu item
                    final String s = item.getText();
                    // Get ToolItem
                    final ToolItem toolItem = (ToolItem) e.widget;
                    // Replace ToolItem label with text of the menu item
                    toolItem.setText(s);
                    // Hide menu
                    menu.setVisible(false);
                  }
                }
```

6.5.13 Custom widgets

The package org.eclipse.swt.custom contains further widgets that are not mapped to native widgets of the host platform, but are pure Java implementations.

The following table lists the most important ones of these widget classes:

BusyIndicator	This class is used to replace the mouse pointer with a busy symbol (hourglass, etc.). To do this, we call the method showWhile(display, runnable). The second parameter must be of type java.lang.Runnable. The run() method of this Runnable contains the processing logic to be executed while the busy symbol is shown.
ControlEditor	This class is used to attach a Composite to another GUI element. When the Composite is moved or modified in size, the position of the attached element is also changed. Normally, we use ControlEditor to attach an editor to a non-editable Composite. The Eclipse API reference documentation contains an example in which a button is attached to a Canvas instance (see Section 6.7). When the button is pressed, the background color of the canvas changes. When the canvas is moved, the button is moved with the canvas.
PopupList	This class works similarly to the List class (see Section 6.5.8). However, the list appears in its own shell in front of the Shell instance that is specified in the PopupList() constructor. Normally, this class is used to select values from a list within a table element.
StyledText	This class implements a single- or multi-line text input field, similar to the class Text. In addition, some text attributes are supported: background and foreground color, text font, bold and normal text style. This functionality is sufficient for programming program editors, but insufficient for implementing word processors.
	The text can be formatted with the help of the methods getStyleRangeAtOffset(), getStyleRanges(), setStyleRange(), and setStyleRanges() that allow StyleRange instances to be retrieved and set. In addition, the methods getLineBackground() and setLineBackground() allow us to retrieve and set the background color of a text line.
	As an alternative to these methods, we may implement our own text style processing as LineStyleListener and LineBackgroundListener instances.

TableTree	This class has similar functionality as the class Tree (see Section 6.5.9). However, the graphical representation is different: The tree structure appears as a series of hierarchically indented tables; lines representing the tree branches are not shown. The individual tree nodes are implemented by TableTreeItem instances.
TableEditor TreeEditor TableTreeEditor	These classes are similar to the class ControlEditor but are specialized for the target classes Table, Tree, and TableTree. The Eclipse API reference documentation contains examples that show how to attach text fields to TableItem, TreeItem, and TableTreeItem instances.

6.6   Layouts

After this *tour de force* through the land of widgets, we now have a look at layouts. Layouts are used to position GUI elements on a Composite in an automated way. The layout computes the size and position of each GUI element that belongs to a Composite. Should the size of the Composite change – either under program control or by user inter-action – the layout of the GUI elements is recomputed automatically.

By default, all GUI elements within the Composite are treated as equal by the layout. However, it is possible to influence the layout process for each GUI element individually by assigning specific layout data to GUI elements. This is done with the Control method setLayoutData().

Eclipse provides five predefined layout classes. In addition, it offers the possibility of creating our own layout classes. The names of the predefined layout classes all follow the pattern '*Layout'. The names of the corresponding classes for the individual layout data follow the pattern '*Data'. With the exception of the class StackLayout, which is part of the package org.eclipse.swt.custom, all predefined layout classes are contained in package org.eclipse.swt.layout.

An excellent article about layouts is *Understanding Layouts in SWT* by Carolyn MacLeod and Shantha Ramachandran [MacLeod2002].

6.6.1   Visual overview

The best way to gain an overview of the different layouts and their options is to activate one of the Eclipse example application under *Window > Show View > Other...* In the displayed dialog, select the application *SWT Examples > SWT Layouts*, which then shows up in the bottom right corner of the workbench window (Figure 6.10). Because we need all the space we can get, we maximize this application window by double clicking its title bar.

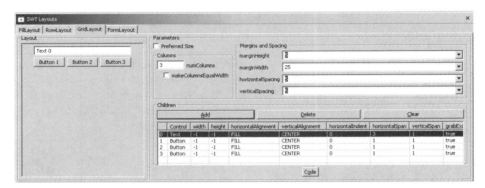

Figure 6.10: The 'SWT Layouts' example application can be used to try the various options for FillLayout, RowLayout, GridLayout, and FormLayout. We can generate the corresponding source code with the Code button, so this example application can be used as a (very) minimal GUI designer.

Since this application is perfectly suited for visualizing the various layouts and their options, we will refrain from showing the corresponding screen shots.

6.6.2   The FillLayout class

FillLayout is the simplest of the predefined layouts. The effect of a FillLayout is that the GUI elements completely fill the containing Composite. There are neither spaces nor margins between the GUI elements. Also, automatic wrapping in the event of insufficient space is not possible. All GUI elements are sized to the same size. The height is determined by the GUI element with the largest preferred height, and the width is determined by the GUI element with the largest preferred width. FillLayouts are typically used for tool bars where the individual buttons are not separated by spaces. They are also used in cases where a single GUI element completely fills a Composite.

By default, all GUI elements are concatenated in the horizontal direction. However, we can enforce a vertical orientation by specifying the style constant SWT.VERTICAL to the layout's type field:

```
FillLayout fillLayout = new FillLayout();
fillLayout.type = SWT.VERTICAL;
composite.setLayout(fillLayout);
new Button(composite, SWT.RADIO).setText("One");
new Button(composite, SWT.RADIO).setText("Two");
new Button(composite, SWT.RADIO).setText("Three");
```

In the case of FillLayouts we have no option to set the size of the contained GUI elements individually.

6.6.3   The RowLayout class

Similar to FillLayout, the RowLayout positions the contained GUI elements in a row. However, RowLayout provides the following fields for additional options:

type	As in FillLayout.
wrap	If this option is set to true (the default), GUI elements that do not fit into a line are wrapped onto the next line.
pack	If this option is set to true (the default), GUI elements are displayed in their preferred size and at the left-most position. Otherwise, the GUI elements fill all the available space, similar to FillLayout.
justify	If this option is set to true, GUI elements are distributed evenly over the available space. The default is false.
marginLeft marginTop marginRight marginBottom	These fields control the size of the margins in pixels.
spacing	This field controls the minimum space between the GUI elements in pixels.

The following example shows how to set the various options of a RowLayout instance:

```
RowLayout rowLayout = new RowLayout();
rowLayout.wrap = false;
rowLayout.pack = false;
rowLayout.justify = true;
rowLayout.type = SWT.VERTICAL;
rowLayout.marginLeft = 10;
rowLayout.marginTop = 5;
rowLayout.marginRight = 10;
rowLayout.marginBottom = 8;
rowLayout.spacing = 5;
composite.setLayout(rowLayout);
```

RowData For GUI elements within a `RowLayout` instance we can set the size of each GUI element individually by assigning a `RowData` instance to it. In the following example we create two buttons and assign height and width to both of them:

```
Button button1 = new Button(composite, SWT.PUSH);
button1.setText("70x20");
button1.setLayoutData(new RowData(70, 20));
Button button2 = new Button(composite, SWT.PUSH);
button2.setText("50x35");
button2.setLayoutData(new RowData(50, 35));
```

6.6.4 The GridLayout class

The class `GridLayout` is the most useful and powerful of the predefined layout classes. However, it is not trivial to manage, because of its many parameters and their interactions. If you have experience of the layout of HTML pages using tables you will know what I mean.

`GridLayout` has, indeed, some similarity to HTML tables. Here, we also have rows and columns, and it is possible to fuse adjoining table elements horizontally or vertically.

The following options are available for `GridLayout`s:

numColumns	The number of columns. The number of rows is determined automatically from the number of GUI elements and the number of columns.
makeColumnsEqualWidth	If this field is set to `true`, all columns are laid out with the same width. The default is `false`.
marginHeight	This field controls the height of the upper and lower margins in pixels.
marginWidth	This field controls the width of the left and right margins in pixels.
horizontalSpacing	This field controls the minimal distance between columns in pixels.
verticalSpacing	This field controls the minimal distance between rows in pixels.

The following example shows how to set the various options of a `GridLayout` instance:

```
GridLayout gridLayout = new GridLayout();
gridLayout.numColumns = 3;
gridLayout.marginWidth = 10;
gridLayout.makeColumnsEqualWidth = true;
```

```
gridLayout.marginHeight = 5;
gridLayout.horizontalSpacing = 6;
gridLayout.verticalSpacing = 4;
gridLayout.makeColumnsEqualWidth = true;
composite.setLayout(gridLayout);
```

GridData The layout options that we may set for individual GUI elements with the help of Grid-Data instances are quite rich. GridData objects have the following public fields:

grabExcessHorizontalSpace	If this field is set to true, the GUI element fills all the remaining horizontal space. The default is false.
grabExcessVerticalSpace	If this field is set to true, the GUI element fills all the remaining vertical space. The default is false.
heightHint	This field specifies a minimum height in pixels. If a value is specified, the vertical scroll function of a corresponding scrollable GUI-element is disabled.
horizontalAlignment	This field specifies how the GUI element is aligned horizontally in its table cell. The following constants can be specified: GridData.BEGINNING (default) GridData.CENTER GridData.END GridData.FILL
horizontalIndent	This field specifies how many pixels a GUI element is indented from the left.
horizontalSpan	This field specifies how many table cells the GUI element consumes in the horizontal direction (the cells are fused).
verticalAlignment	This field specifies how the GUI element is aligned vertically in its table cell. The following constants can be specified: GridData.BEGINNING GridData.CENTER (default) GridData.END GridData.FILL

verticalSpan	This field specifies how many table cells the GUI element consumes in vertical direction (the cells are fused).
widthHint	This field specifies a minimum width in pixels. If a value is specified, the horizontal scroll function of a corresponding scrollable GUI-element is disabled.

Some of this options may already be specified in the GridData() constructor. For this purpose, the following style constants are available:

Constant	Equivalent
GridData.GRAB_HORIZONTAL	grabExcessHorizontalSpace = true
GridData.GRAB_VERTICAL	grabExcessVerticalSpace = true
GridData.HORIZONTAL_ALIGN_BEGINNING	horizontalAlignment = GridData.BEGINNING
GridData.HORIZONTAL_ALIGN_CENTER	horizontalAlignment = GridData.CENTER
GridData.HORIZONTAL_ALIGN_END	horizontalAlignment = GridData.END
GridData.HORIZONTAL_ALIGN_FILL	horizontalAlignment = GridData.FILL
GridData.VERTICAL_ALIGN_BEGINNING	verticalAlignment = GridData.BEGINNING
GridData.VERTICAL_ALIGN_CENTER	verticalAlignment = GridData.CENTER
GridData.VERTICAL_ALIGN_END	verticalAlignment = GridData.END
GridData.VERTICAL_ALIGN_FILL	verticalAlignment = GridData.FILL
GridData.FILL_HORIZONTAL	HORIZONTAL_ALIGN_FILL | GRAB_HORIZONTAL

GridData.FILL_VERTICAL	VERTICAL_ALIGN_FILL | GRAB_VERTICAL
GridData.FILL_BOTH	FILL_VERTICAL | FILL_HORIZONTAL

We do not give a code example here, but refer to Section 8.3 that shows the use of the GridLayout class in a real application.

Should all these layout options be not sufficient, we still have the possibility of nesting GridLayouts by nesting Composites. This technique should be well known to all those who have laid out HTML pages with the help of nested tables.

The FormLayout class

FormLayout was introduced with Eclipse 2.0. It allows us to position GUI elements on a two-dimensional surface in relation to another GUI element or in relation to the borders of the Composite. This is done by using FormAttachment instances.

For FormLayouts we have the following options:

marginHeight	This field controls the height of the upper and lower margins in pixels.
marginWidth	This field controls the width of the left and right margins in pixels.

FormData

Most of the layout options of form layouts are contained in the classes FormData and FormAttachment. FormData provides the following options that are applied to individual GUI-elements:

height	The preferred height of the GUI element in pixels.
width	The preferred width of the GUI element in pixels.
top bottom left right	These fields accept a FormAttachment instance that specifies to which item the upper/lower/left/right edge of the GUI-element relates.

FormAttachment

For FormAttachment instances we have two variants:

- Specification of a relative position with the Composite
- Specification relative to another GUI-Element

Composite position   For the first variant there are two constructors:

```
FormAttachment fa = new FormAttachment(percent,offset);
```

and

```
FormAttachment fa = new FormAttachment(numerator, denominator,
    offset);
```

The position p is computed from the width and height of the Composites respectively, as follows:

```
p = d*numerator/denominator+offset
```

If a percent value was specified, the following formula is used:

```
p = d*percent/100+offset
```

Let's assume that our Composite is 400 pixels wide and 300 pixels high. When we create a FormAttachment instance with a constructor FormAttachment(30,10) and assign it to the top field of a FormData instance, we get:

```
p = 30/100*300+5 = 95
```

The upper edge of our GUI element will therefore be positioned 95 pixels below the upper border of the Composite's client area. If we were to assign the same FormAttachment instance to the bottom field of the FormData instance, the lower edge of our GUI element would be 95 pixels above the lower border of the Composite's client area.

If we assign the same FormAttachment instance to the left field of the FormData instance, we would get a distance of:

```
p = 30/100*400+5 = 125
```

The left edge of our GUI element will therefore be 125 pixels to the right from the left border of the Composite's client area. So what happens when we assign the FormAttachment instance to the right field? By now, you should be able to find the answer yourself.

Reference GUI element   For the second variant (positioning relative to another GUI element) we have three constructors:

```
FormAttachment (control, offset, alignment)
FormAttachment (control, offset)
FormAttachment (control)
```

The parameter control accepts a Control instance (the GUI element to which we relate).

The parameter offset specifies the distance to the reference element. If this parameter is omitted, the distance is 0.

The parameter `alignment` specifies to which edge of the reference element we relate. When we assign this `FormAttachment` instance to a `top` or `bottom` field, we can use the style constants `SWT.TOP`, `SWT.BOTTOM`, and `SWT.CENTER`. If we assign it to a `left` or `right` field, we can use the constants `SWT.LEFT`, `SWT.RIGHT`, and `SWT.CENTER`. If the `alignment` parameter is omitted, we will relate to the closest edge of the reference element.

6.6.5 The StackLayout class

Unlike the previous classes, this class is not contained in `org.eclipse.swt.layout`, but in `org.eclipse.swt.custom`. In contrast to the other layout classes, this layout can only show a single GUI element at a time within a `Composite`. The reason is that all GUI elements contained in the `Composite` are made equal in size and are positioned at the same spot on top of each other, so only the front-most element is visible. The class `StackLayout` is useful when we want to switch between GUI elements. We only need to move the `Control` instance to be shown to the front-most position.

The class `StackLayout` has the following public fields:

`marginHeight`	This field controls the height of the upper and lower margins.
`marginWidth`	This field controls the width of the left and right margins.
`topControl`	This fields accepts the top (visible) `Control` instance.

In the following example we position two `Button` instances on top of each other. When a button is pressed, the other button becomes visible:

```
// Create new composite
final Composite stackComposite = new Composite(composite,SWT.NULL);
final StackLayout stackLayout = new StackLayout();
// Create text buttons
final Button buttonA = new Button(stackComposite, SWT.PUSH);
buttonA.setText("Button A");
final Button buttonB = new Button(stackComposite, SWT.PUSH);
buttonB.setText("Button B");
// React to clicks
buttonA.addSelectionListener(new SelectionAdapter() {
  public void widgetSelected(SelectionEvent e) {
    stackLayout.topControl = buttonB;
    // Enforce new layout
    stackComposite.layout();
    // Set focus to visible button
    buttonB.setFocus();
  }
});
buttonB.addSelectionListener(new SelectionAdapter() {
  public void widgetSelected(SelectionEvent e) {
```

```
        stackLayout.topControl = buttonA;
        // Enforce new layout
        stackComposite.layout();
        // Set focus to visible button
        buttonA.setFocus();
    }
});
// Initialize layout
stackLayout.topControl = buttonA;
stackLayout.marginWidth = 10;
stackLayout.marginHeight = 5;
// Set layout
stackComposite.setLayout(stackLayout);
```

6.7   Graphics

The interfaces and classes for graphical operations are contained in the package org.eclipse.swt.graphics. The functionality of this package is based on the graphical functionality of the supported platforms. While the functionality of the package exceeds those of the basic classes of the Java AWT, it does not match the functionality of the Java2D API. We discuss how this functionality can be extended in Section 6.7.5.

6.7.1   The Graphics Context

The class GC contains all the methods needed for drawing, such as drawLine(), drawOval(), drawPolygon(), setFont(), getFontMetrics(), and much more.

We can draw onto instances of all those classes that implement the Drawable interface. This is in particular the case for the classes Image, Control, and its subclasses such as Canvas and Display. Usually we will draw on an Image when implementing *double buffering* (for a description of this technique, see Section 6.7.4). We will draw on a Canvas when we want to display a drawing to the user. We draw on a Display when we don't want to draw inside a window, but all over the screen instead. We select the medium for drawing operation by passing the Drawable to the constructor GC().

When we create a graphics context with the help of a GC() constructor, we must dispose of the GC instance when it is no longer needed, as GC instances allocate resources in the host system. However, more often than not we will not need to create a graphics context ourselves, but will instead use a context given to us by a PaintEvent.

The golden rule for graphics processing is:

All graphical operations must be executed within the paintControl() method of a PaintListener object, i.e. within the PaintEvent processing of a Control instance.

In the following example we show how we can decorate a `Composite` with a green key line:

```
composite.addPaintListener(new PaintListener () {
  public void paintControl(PaintEvent event){
    // Get Display intsance from event object
    Display display = event.display;
    // Get a green system color object – we don't
    // need to dispose that
    Color green = display.getSystemColor(SWT.COLOR_DARK_GREEN);
    // Get the graphics context from the event object
    GC gc = event.gc;
    // Set line color
    gc.setForeground(green);
    // Get size of the Composite's client area
    Rectangle rect = ((Composite) event.widget).getClientArea();
    // Now draw an rectangle
    gc.drawRectangle(rect.x + 2, rect.y + 2,
      rect.width - 4, rect.height - 4);
  }
});
```

6.7.2 Colors

Within a graphics context we can set line and text colors – as shown above – with the help of the method `setForeground()`. Fill colors are set with `setBackground()`.

To set colors, we first have to supply ourselves with color objects. There are two ways to obtain colors:

- We can fetch a system color from a `Device` instance. Since `Display` is a subclass of `Device`, we can fetch a system color from the widget's `Display` instance with the help of the method `getSystemColor()`. The necessary `COLOR_...` constants for the color names are defined in the class `SWT`.

  Color objects that are obtained in this or another way from other instances must not be released with `dispose()`, as they may still be in use elsewhere!

- We can create our own color objects:

  ```
  Color red = new Color(device, 255,0,0)
  ```

  or

  ```
  Color blue = new Color(device, new RGB(0,255,0));
  ```

  The parameter `device` accepts objects of type `Device`. `RGB` is a simple utility class for representing RGB color tuples.

The representation of colors is exact on all devices with a color depth of 24 bits. On devices with a lower color depth, Eclipse will approximate the color as well as possible [Moody2001].

If we create colors in this way, we *must* release them with dispose() when they are no longer needed.

6.7.3   Fonts

Fonts work similarly to colors. The current font of a graphics context is set with the method setFont().

- We can obtain the current system font from a Device instance with the help of the method getSystemFont(). Such a font instance must not be disposed of with the method dispose().

- New Font instances can be created with one of the following constructors:

  ```
  Font font = new Font(device,"Arial",12,SWT.ITALIC)
  ```

  or

  ```
  Font font = new Font(device,new FontData("Arial",12,SWT.ITALIC))
  ```

  If we create fonts in this way, we *must* release them with dispose() when they are no longer needed.

In the following example we fetch the current system font, create an italic variant, configure the graphics context with this new font and draw the word 'Hello':

```
// Get Display instance
Display display = composite.getDisplay();
// Fetch system font
Font systemFont = display.getSystemFont();
// FontData objects contain the font properties.
// With some operating systems a font may possess multiple
// FontData instances. We only use the first one.
FontData[] data = systemFont.getFontData();
FontData data0 = data[0];
// Set the font style to italic
data0.setStyle(SWT.ITALIC);
// Create a new font
Font italicFont = new Font(display, data0);
// Set the new font in the graphics context
gc.setFont(italicFont);
// TODO: call italicFont.dispose() in the DisposeListener
// of composite
// Draw text at position (4,4) with a transparent background (true).
gc.drawText("Hello",4,4,true);
```

In the class GC there are a few more text methods for text processing. For example, the method getFontMetrics() delivers a FontMetrics object that contains the characteristic measurements of the current font. The methods stringExtent() and textExtent() allows us to compute the pixel dimensions of a string if it were drawn with the currently active font. Unlike textExtent(), the method stringExtent() ignores TAB and CR characters when computing the text extent.

6.7.4 Images

The class Image is responsible for the device dependent representation of images. Image instances can be created in many ways: by specifying a java.io.Stream object, by specifying a file name (absolute or relative to the current project), or by specifying an ImageData object.

In contrast to Image, the class ImageData is responsible for the device independent representation of images. Instances of this class can be created by specifying a java.io.Stream object or by specifying a file name. Alternatively, an ImageData instance can be obtained from an Image object via the method getImageData().

Both Image and ImageData support images in RGB format as well as in indexed format. Transparency is possible (alpha channel for RGB images, transparent color for indexed images). The following file formats are supported when reading an image from file: .bmp, .gif, .jpg, .png, and .ico. In Section 6.5.6 we have already shown how an image is read from a file.

In the following example we use an Image instance to implement double buffering. This technique is frequently used to avoid screen flicker when drawing images. First, we create an Image instance large enough to contain the drawing. Then we create a GC instance for the Image instance and perform all drawing operations within this graphics context. Finally, we draw the complete Image instance onto the target Drawable.

```java
// Create canvas
final Canvas canvas = new Canvas(composite,SWT.BORDER);
// Get white system color
Color white = canvas.getDisplay().getSystemColor(SWT.COLOR_WHITE);
// Set canvas background to white
canvas.setBackground(white);
// Add paint listener
canvas.addPaintListener(new PaintListener() {
  public void paintControl(PaintEvent e) {
    // Get Display instance from the event object
    Display display = e.display;
    // Get black and red system color - don't dispose these
    Color black = display.getSystemColor(SWT.COLOR_BLACK);
    Color red = display.getSystemColor(SWT.COLOR_RED);
    // Get the graphics context from event object
```

```
GC gc = e.gc;
// Get the widget that caused the event
Composite source = (Composite) e.widget;
// Get the size of this widgets client area
Rectangle rect = source.getClientArea();
// Create buffer for double buffering
Image buffer = new Image(display,rect.width,rect.height);
// Create graphics context for this buffer
GC bufferGC = new GC(buffer);
// perform drawing operations
bufferGC.setBackground(red);
bufferGC.fillRectangle(5,5,rect.width-10,rect.height-10);
bufferGC.setForeground(black);
bufferGC.drawRectangle(5,5,rect.width-10,rect.height-10);
bufferGC.setBackground(source.getBackground());
bufferGC.fillRectangle(10,10,rect.width-20,rect.height-20);
// Now draw the buffered image to the target drawable
gc.drawImage(buffer,0,0);
// Dispose of the buffer's graphics context
bufferGC.dispose();
// Dispose of the buffer
buffer.dispose();
    }
});
```

6.7.5   Higher graphics layers

Because of its closeness to the host windowing system, the SWT represents a new, fresh approach to the implementation of the lower layers of a graphical user interface. However, the question is – what about the higher layers?

As far as windows, dialogs, and menus are concerned, the answer is simple. Functionality as provided by Swing is provided by the JFace library in Eclipse.

The answer becomes more difficult when we are interested in higher level graphical operations, such a those provided by the *Java2D* and the *Java3D* API, by Apache's *Batik* SVG implementation (www.apache.org), or by the bitmap manipulation operations defined in the *Java Advanced Imaging* API (JAI). None of these APIs are compatible with SWT. Advanced functions such as anti-aliasing, transparent vector graphics, or text rotation cannot be easily implemented on top of SWT.

However, it is possible to embed this functionality into SWT using a free Java2D plug-in that can be downloaded from www.holongate.org. The same Web site also offers plug-ins for embedding *Java Advanced Imaging* and *Batik*. The trick used here is to perform all advanced graphical operations on a internal bitmap first, then to draw this bitmap (as an Image instance) onto an SWT Canvas, in the same way as we have shown in the double buffering example in the previous section.

To use this plug-in, we need to download the *Core plug-in* and its documentation from the Web site. For Windows and Linux/Gtk platforms there are also optional native code plug-in fragments that act as accelerators. We just unpack the ZIP archives into directory `\eclipse\plugins`.

Java2D example   In the following code we demonstrate how we can apply Java2D and SWT drawing operations onto the same `Canvas`. For Java2D we have enabled anti-aliasing. Unlike SWT, where drawing operations are performed within the `PaintEvent` event processing, the drawing happens here within an `IPaintable` object which is passed to the `J2DCanvas()` constructor.

```java
import java.awt.Color;
import java.awt.Font;
import java.awt.Graphics2D;
import java.awt.RenderingHints;
import org.eclipse.swt.SWT;
import org.eclipse.swt.graphics.GC;
import org.eclipse.swt.layout.FillLayout;
import org.eclipse.swt.layout.GridLayout;
import org.eclipse.swt.widgets.Composite;
import org.eclipse.swt.widgets.Control;
import org.eclipse.swt.widgets.Display;
import org.eclipse.swt.widgets.Shell;
import org.holongate.eclipse.j2d.IPaintable;
import org.holongate.eclipse.j2d.J2DCanvas;

public class TestJava2D {

  class CombinedPaintable implements IPaintable {
    /**
     * responsible for all Java2D operations
     * @see org.holongate.eclipse.j2d.IPaintable
     * #paint(org.eclipse.swt.widgets.Control, java.awt.Graphics2D)
     */
    public void paint(Control control, Graphics2D g2d) {
      // Switch anti-aliasing on
      g2d.setRenderingHint(
      RenderingHints.KEY_ANTIALIASING,
      RenderingHints.VALUE_ANTIALIAS_ON);
      // Set graphics context color to red
      g2d.setColor(Color.RED);
      // Draw ellipsoid
      g2d.fillOval(10, 10, 35, 25);
      // Set color to white
      g2d.setColor(Color.WHITE);
      // Create new Font
      // Note: We need not to dispose of Java2D resources
      Font arialBold12 = new Font("Arial", Font.BOLD, 12);
      // Activate font
```

```java
        g2d.setFont(arialBold12);
        // Write white text into red ellipsoid
        g2d.drawChars("J2D".toCharArray(), 0, 3, 17, 27);
    }

    /**
     * Responsible for all SWT drawing operations
     * @see org.holongate.eclipse.j2d.IPaintable#redraw(
     * org.eclipse.swt.widgets.Control, org.eclipse.swt.graphics.GC)
     */
    public void redraw(Control control, GC gc) {
        // Get current Display instance
        Display display = control.getDisplay();
        // Get blue system color
        org.eclipse.swt.graphics.Color blue =
        display.getSystemColor(SWT.COLOR_BLUE);
        // Set text color
        gc.setForeground(blue);
        // Draw blue text
        gc.drawText("SWT", 30, 30, true);
    }
}

public static void main(String[] args) {
    TestJava2D test = new TestJava2D();
    test.run();
}
public TestJava2D() {
    super();
}
public void run() {
    // Create new Display instance
    final Display display = new Display();
    // Create top level shell (pass display as parent)
    final Shell toplevelShell = new Shell(display);
    // Set title
    toplevelShell.setText("J2D/SWT-Test");
    // Create shell layout
    toplevelShell.setLayout(new FillLayout());
    // Create J2DCanvas instance
    // An IPaintable object must be passed as third parameter
    J2DCanvas canvas =
        new J2DCanvas(toplevelShell, SWT.BORDER,
            new CombinedPaintable());
    // Adapt shell size to content
    toplevelShell.pack();
    // Display shell
    toplevelShell.open();
    // Wait until top level shell is closed
    while (!toplevelShell.isDisposed()) {
```

```
            // Prüfen ob Ereignisse warten
            if (!display.readAndDispatch())
            display.sleep();
        }
    }
}
```

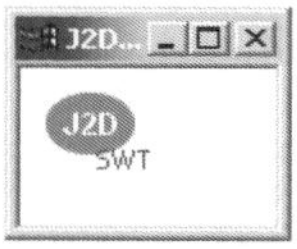

Figure 6.11: Yes, it is possible: Java2D and SWT drawing operation on the same Canvas.

Despite the accelerators for Windows and Linux/GtK, we should use this plug-in only for fairly small drawings. Since the plug-in copies the Java2D drawable pixel by pixel to an SWT drawable, large drawings would cause a high CPU load, reducing the speed and responsiveness of the user interface.

6.8 Output to printer

Output to a printer is performed with the help of the classes `PrintDialog`, `Printer-Data`, and `Printer`. `PrintDialog` is a subclass of the abstract class `Dialog` and represents the printer selection dialog of the host operating system. As a result `Print-Dialog` either delivers a `PrinterData` instance or null. The `PrinterData` instance contains all the specifications made in the printer selection dialog, such as number of copies, printing scope, etc. By accessing the corresponding fields (`copyCount`, `scope`, etc.) we can use these specifications for the resulting output process.

For the actual printing process, we create an instance of the `Printer` class, which is a `Device` subclass. This is then used to create a new graphics context (`GC`). We perform all output operations necessary of filling the printed pages with content on this graphics context.

First, we call the `Printer` method `startJob()` to create a new print task. Then we call the method `startPage()` for each page. Afterwards we apply all drawing operations on the printer's graphics context. When each page is filled we call the method `endPage()`. When all pages are printed, we close the printing task by calling the method `endJob()`. Finally, we must dispose of the graphics context and the `Printer` object by calling their `dispose()` methods. The following code shows how it's done:

```
// Create button for starting printing process
final Button printButton = new Button(composite, SWT.PUSH);
printButton.setText("Print");
```

```java
// React to clicks
printButton.addSelectionListener(new SelectionAdapter() {
  public void widgetSelected(SelectionEvent e) {
    // Get Shell instance
    Shell shell = composite.getShell();
    // Create printer selection dialog
    PrintDialog printDialog = new PrintDialog(shell);
    // and open it
    PrinterData printerData = printDialog.open();
    // Check if OK was pressed
    if (printerData != null) {
      // Create new Printer instance
      Printer printer = new Printer(printerData);
      // Create graphics context for this printer
      GC gc = new GC(printer);
      // Open printing task
      if (!printer.startJob("Hello"))
        System.out.println("Starting printer task failed");
      else {
        // Print first page
        if (!printer.startPage())
          System.out.println("Printing of page 1 failed");
        else {
          // Get green system color from printer
          // and set it as text color
          Color green =
            printer.getSystemColor(SWT.COLOR_DARK_GREEN);
          gc.setForeground(green);
          // Draw text
          gc.drawText("Hello World", 4, 4, true);
          // Close page
          printer.endPage();
        }
        // Print second page
        if (!printer.startPage())
          System.out.println("Printing of page 2 failed");
        else {
          // Get blue system color from printer
          // and set it as text color
          Color blue = printer.getSystemColor(SWT.COLOR_BLUE);
          gc.setForeground(blue);
          // Draw text
          gc.drawText("Hello Eclipse", 4, 4, true);
          // Close page
          printer.endPage();
        }
        // Close printing task
        printer.endJob();
      }
      // Release operating system resources
```

```
            gc.dispose();
            printer.dispose();
        }
    }
});
```

In fact this code shows only the simplest case. Processing becomes more complicated if we have to consider `PrinterData` specifications such as the number of copies, collating options, or printing scope. In addition, it makes sense to fetch the printer's resolution from the `Printer` instance via the method `getDPI()` and to scale the graphical operations accordingly.

6.9 Resource management

In the course of this chapter we have met several resource types that need to be disposed of when no longer needed. In particular, they are instances of the classes `Color`, `Font`, `Image`, `GC`, `Printer`, `Display`, and `Shell`.

For all of these resources the golden rule is:

> If you created something you must also dispose of it, but if you got a resource from somewhere else (e.g. with `getSystemColor()`), you must *not* dispose of it.

However, you don't need to dispose of resources at the end of a program – the host operating system will do this for you. So the above rule applies only to resource that are used temporarily within an application.

This sounds quite simple, but can become complicated in larger applications. In many cases we want to use the same color, font, or image in several places in an application. Who is responsible for disposing of the resource in such a case? And is it really necessary to dispose a resource if it can be reused later somewhere else?

In such cases we can make use of a 'store' concept. We implement a *Resource Store* that manages the lifecycle of our resources. The managed resources are disposed of by the *Resource Store* when the *Resource Store* is itself disposed of. This allows us to reuse resources. This is useful in particular with `Image` instances, as images can be very memory hungry.

In the following example we show a simple *Resource Stores* for color resources. When we ask the class `ColorStore` for a `Color` object, it will return us an existing `Color` object if it is already in the store, otherwise a new `Color` object is created. When the `ColorStore` is disposed of by calling its `dispose()` method, all `Color` objects in the store are disposed of, too.

```java
import java.util.HashMap;
import java.util.Iterator;
import java.util.Map;
import org.eclipse.swt.graphics.Color;
import org.eclipse.swt.graphics.Device;

public class ColorStore {

  private static Map store = new HashMap();

  /**
   * Method getColor.
   * @param name some Color name
   * @param device Device instance
   * @param r red-value
   * @param g green-value
   * @param b blue-value
   * @return Color requested color
   */
  public static Color getColor(String name,Device device,
    int r, int g, int b) {
    Object obj = store.get(name);
    if (obj == null) {
      Color newColor = new Color(device,r,g,b);
      store.put(name,newColor);
      return newColor;
    }
    return (Color) obj;
  }

  /**
   * Method dispose.
   */
  public static void dispose() {
    Iterator iter = store.values().iterator();
    while (iter.hasNext()) {
      Color color = (Color) iter.next();
      color.dispose();
    }
  }
}
```

Here is how we obtain a Color object from the store:

```java
Color green = ColorStore.getColor("green",display,0,255,0);
```

Since all methods in the class ColorStore are static, ColorStore can manage all the colors of an application. Only when we need no more colors do we dispose of the whole store with:

```java
ColorStore.dispose();
```

In Section 7.1 we will discuss some predefined registries for fonts and images.

6.10 Windows32 Support (OLE)

SWT provides a special library to support the OLE mechanism of Microsoft's Windows operating systems. The *Microsoft Win32 Object Linking and Embedding* (OLE) mechanism is supported by the classes in the package `org.eclipse.swt.ole.win32`. OLE allows OLE documents and other *ActiveX* control elements to be embedded in other (*Container*) applications. This allows us, for example, to use *Microsoft Internet Explorer* as an SWT GUI element, or to embed a *Microsoft Office* document into an SWT user interface. Using these classes requires sufficient knowledge of the OLE API. A small example plug-in is found in the Eclipse example collection under `org.eclipse.swt.examples.ole.win32_2.1.0`.

6.11 Accessibility

Finally, we discuss how SWT supports the creation of user interfaces that are suitable for disabled people. Accessibility is an important topic in the context of commercial application development. Many public institutions are only allowed to purchase software that conforms to certain standards regarding its usability by disabled people.

The Eclipse documentation contains a special chapter about this topic in the *Platform Plug-in Developer Guide* under *Reference > Other Reference Information > Tips For Making User Interfaces Accessible*.

Many operating system support special hardware devices designed for disabled people and provide an API for these devices. Eclipse supports the *Microsoft Active Accessibility (MSAA) API*. This support is provided by the classes defined in package `org.eclipse.swt.accessibility`. All SWT `Control` instances can provide an instance of class `Accessible` via the method `getAccessible()`. This instance serves as a link to the *Accessibility API*.

7 JFace

The JFace API is based on the SWT API and provides the programmer with higher level GUI components such as viewers, actions, dialogs, wizards, and much more. In the following sections we discuss the most important function groups.

Some of the JFace components are specific to the Eclipse workbench, and are packaged in the archive workbench.jar as an integral part of the Eclipse workbench plug-in. Most of the components of JFace, however, can be used independently from the Eclipse workbench and are therefore packaged in the archive jface.jar and are deployed in a separate JFace plug-in.

7.1 Resource management

We begin this chapter with the topic with which we ended the previous chapter: resource management. JFace provides some classes that support the management of resources such as fonts, colors, and images. The classes of this group are contained in the package org.eclipse.jface.resource.

7.1.1 The FontRegistry class

The FontRegistry class is able to manage all the fonts used within an application. A FontRegistry instance is always created for a concrete Display instance. If no Display instance is passed to the FontRegistry() constructor, the current Display instance will be used.

We don't need to specify a Display instance when adding a font to the FontRegistry with the help of the put() method, because the FontRegistry can supply the Display instance by itself if it needs to create a new font instance. It is sufficient to specify the symbolic font name and a FontData instance (see Section 6.7.3). We can retrieve a font from the FontRegistry with get() by specifying a symbolic name.

What is convenient with a `FontRegistry` is that we don't have to care at all about the disposal of font resources. When a `FontRegistry` is created it links itself into the `DisposeEvent()` processing of its `Display` instance. When this `Display` instance is disposed of, the `FontRegistry` and all fonts contained in the registry are disposed of as well. It is important that we *must not* explicitly dispose of a font contained in the `FontRegistry` by calling its `dispose()` methods.

7.1.2   The ImageRegistry class

The `ImageRegistry` class works quite similarly to `FontRegistry`, but is responsible for the management of images. `ImageRegistry` instances are also associated with a concrete `Display` instance. Images are added to the registry with the `put()` method and are addressed with a symbolic name. They can be retrieved again with `get()`. In Section 7.2.1 we show a code example of how to use the `ImageRegistry`. As with `FontRegistry`, the disposal of the `ImageRegistry` instance and of the contained images is linked to the `DisposeEvent()` processing of the corresponding `Display` instance.

In lieu of an `Image` instance, we can add an `ImageDescriptor` instance to the registry using `put()`. `ImageDescriptor` instances act as proxies for images: they contain only the image metadata, and know where and how to fetch the corresponding image. The image is only loaded when it is really needed – in the case of the `ImageRegistry`, this is when it is retrieved with `get()`.

7.1.3   The JFaceColors class

This class organizes consistent color management for all GUI components of JFace. Various static methods allow the retrieval of specific colors, such as the color of error messages, of hyperlinks, or of other GUI elements.

7.1.4   The JFaceResources class

This class organizes consistent font and registry management for all JFace GUI components. Various static methods allow the retrieval of specific fonts, such as fonts for dialogs, texts, banners, etc. We can also retrieve the current `FontRegistry` and `ImageRegistry` instances.

7.2   Dialogs and windows

The package `org.eclipse.jface.dialogs` provides some classes implementing standard dialogs. All these classes are subclasses of the abstract JFace class `Dialog`, which is itself a subclass of the abstract class `Window`.

Window

The class Window can be used to implement our own windows. The typical life cycle of a window is:

```
new
create()
open()
close()
```

create() can be omitted: the open() method will then automatically execute the create() method. Among other things, create() creates the window's Shell instance. Consequently, retrieving the shell via method getShell() only makes sense after create() has been executed. The shell is disposed of automatically when close() is executed. In addition, create() invokes the methods createContents() and initializeBounds(), which may be overridden or extended by subclasses. For example, one would override createContents() to construct the window content.

With the help of the getReturnCode() method we can retrieve the current state of an opened window. We obtain the value Window.OK for a window with an opened shell, and the value Window.CANCEL when the window's shell is closed.

Dialog

As the class Dialog is a subclass of Window, its life cycle is similar. But unlike Window, we would not override the createContents() method to add content to a Dialog instance. Instead, we override one or several of the methods createDialogArea(), createButtonBar() and createButtonsForButtonBar(). By default, the latter method creates an *OK* button and a *Cancel* button.

To create additional buttons, the class provides the createButton() method. This also creates the necessary event processing for each button. When a button is pressed, the buttonPressed() method is called. For the *OK* button and the *Cancel* button, this method in turn invokes the methods okPressed() and cancelPressed(). Both of these methods close the dialog with close(). All of these methods may be overridden or extended using subclasses.

We can get the code of that button with which the dialog was closed with the getReturnCode() method or as the result of the open() method: this will be Window.OK for the *OK* button and Window.CANCEL for the *Cancel* button.

7.2.1 Some Dialog subclasses

The InputDialog class

This class creates a simple dialog with a text field (see Figure 7.1), an *OK* button and a *Cancel* button. Creating such a dialog requires only a few instructions:

```
InputDialog inputDialog = new InputDialog(shell,
  "Input","Please enter text","text",null);
```

```
if (inputDialog.open() == Dialog.OK) {
  String result = inputDialog.getValue();
  System.out.println(result);
}
```

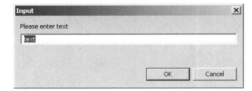

Figure 7.1:   InputDialog is the simplest of the predefined JFace dialogs.

The MessageDialog class

This class generates a simple dialog for displaying messages. The number of buttons and their labeling can be configured. In addition, an icon may be shown in the title bar of the dialog window. Usually, we would use a GIF image of size 16x16 pixels.

```
// Create image registry
ImageRegistry imageRegistry = new ImageRegistry();
// Load icon for title line
final Image image = new Image(shell.getDisplay(),
  "images/envelop.gif");
// Register image
imageRegistry.put("envelope",image);
// Create message dialog
MessageDialog messageDialog = new MessageDialog(shell,
  "Message", imageRegistry.get("envelope"),
  "You have mail!", MessageDialog.INFORMATION,
  new String[] {"View", "Dispose", "Abort"}, 0);
// Open dialog and retrieve the index of the button pressed
int buttonPressed = messageDialog.open();
System.out.println("Button pressed: "+buttonPressed);
```

In the third parameter we pass an image for the title line. (We retrieve this image from the image registry.) If we don't want to use an image, we just specify null. In the fifth parameter we specify a style constant declaring the type of dialog and the icon shown in front of the message:

MessageDialog.NONE	No specification, no icon shown
MessageDialog.ERROR	Error message
MessageDialog.INFORMATION	Info message

MessageDialog.QUESTION	Question
MessageDialog.WARNING	Warning

In the sixth parameter we specify a `String[]` array containing all the button labels. The seventh parameter specifies the index of the default button.

Figure 7.2:   The MessageDialog from the code example shown above

The class `MessageDialog`, in addition, provides some static methods implementing simple standard dialogs such as `openConfirm()`, `openError()`, `openInformation()`, `openQuestion()`, and `openWarning()`. Here is an example with the `openConfirm()` method:

```
if (MessageDialog.openConfirm(shell,
    "General question", "System crash!\nPlease acknowledge!")) {
    System.out.println("OK was pressed");
}
```

The TitleAreaDialog class

This class defines a basic pattern for more complex dialogs. We will usually not instantiate this class directly, but will rather define own subclasses (see Section 7.2.2). The class `TitleAreaDialog` provides the following features:

- Title line.

- Message area. A text with usually one or two lines. This area also displays an error message when present. Optionally, we may specify an own image for this area with `setTitleImage()`. Figure 7.3 shows the Eclipse default image for the `TitleAreaDialog` on the right hand side of the message area. This image has a size of 72x72 pixels. Since this image controls the height of the message area, we can make room for additional message lines by specifying a taller image.

- An *OK* button and a *Cancel* button.

The following code shows how a `TitleAreaDialog` instance is created and initialized. Before we can set features such as title, message, or image, we must invoke the `create()` method:

```
TitleAreaDialog titleAreaDialog = new TitleAreaDialog(shell);
titleAreaDialog.create();
titleAreaDialog.setTitle("Important message");
titleAreaDialog.setMessage(
  "You have mail!\nIt could be vital for your career…");
if (titleAreaDialog.open() == Dialog.OK) {
  System.out.println("OK was pressed");
}
```

Figure 7.3:   The TitleAreaDialog allows for the display of longer messages within its message area.

7.2.2   Implementing our own dialog classes

We can derive own subclasses from the dialog classes discussed above (and of course also from the mother of all JFace dialogs, the class `Dialog`). This makes sense, in particular, for the class `TitleAreaDialog`. This dialog still has a big empty space in the center that needs to be filled.

The various areas in such a dialog are all created using different methods. By overriding one or several of those methods, we can change the configuration of the dialog considerably. For example, by overriding the method `createButtonsForButtonBar()` we may add further buttons to the *OK* button and the *Cancel* button, or even replace those buttons.

The following code implements the `MailDialog` class, which is based on the `TitleArea-Dialog` class. The center area contains a List widget that displays mail messages that have arrived. The *OK* button and the *Cancel* button are replaced with the buttons *Open*, *Delete*, and *Abort*. The *Delete* button does not close the dialog, but simply removes an item from the list. When no items are selected, the *Open* button and the *Delete* button are disabled, and an error message is shown in place of the normal message.

```java
import org.eclipse.jface.dialogs.TitleAreaDialog;
import org.eclipse.swt.SWT;
import org.eclipse.swt.events.SelectionAdapter;
import org.eclipse.swt.events.SelectionEvent;
import org.eclipse.swt.layout.GridData;
import org.eclipse.swt.layout.GridLayout;
import org.eclipse.swt.widgets.Button;
import org.eclipse.swt.widgets.Composite;
import org.eclipse.swt.widgets.Control;
import org.eclipse.swt.widgets.List;
import org.eclipse.swt.widgets.Shell;

public class MailDialog extends TitleAreaDialog {
  // IDs for MailDialog buttons
  // We use large integers because we don't want
  // to conflict with system constants
  public static final int OPEN = 9999;
  public static final int DELETE = 9998;
  // List widget
  List list;
  // Initial content of the list
  String[] items;
  // Selected items
  String[] itemsToOpen;
  /**
   * Constructor for MailDialog.
   * @param shell - Containing shell
   * @param items - Mail messages passed to the dialog
   */
  public MailDialog(Shell shell, String[] items) {
    super(shell);
    this.items = items;
  }
  /**
   * @see org.eclipse.jface.window.Window#create()
   * We complete the dialog with a title and a message
   */
  public void create() {
    super.create();
    setTitle("Mail");
    setMessage(
      "You have mail!\n It could be vital for this evening…");
  }
  /**
   * @see org.eclipse.jface.dialogs.Dialog#
   * createDialogArea(org.eclipse.swt.widgets.Composite)
   * Here we fill the center area of the dialog
   */
  protected Control createDialogArea(Composite parent) {
    // Create new composite as container
```

```
        final Composite area = new Composite(parent, SWT.NULL);
        // We use a grid layout and set the size of the margins
        final GridLayout gridLayout = new GridLayout();
        gridLayout.marginWidth = 15;
        gridLayout.marginHeight = 10;
        area.setLayout(gridLayout);
        // Now we create the list widget
        list = new List(area, SWT.BORDER | SWT.MULTI);
        // We define a minimum width for the list
        final GridData gridData = new GridData();
        gridData.widthHint = 200;
        list.setLayoutData(gridData);
        // We add a SelectionListener
        list.addSelectionListener(new SelectionAdapter() {
            public void widgetSelected(SelectionEvent e) {
                // When the selection changes, we re-validate the list
                validate();
            }
        });
        // We add the initial mail messages to the list
        for (int i = 0; i < items.length; i++) {
            list.add(items[i]);
        }
        return area;
    }
    private void validate() {
        // We select the number of selected list entries
        boolean selected = (list.getSelectionCount() > 0);
        // We enable/disable the Open and Delete buttons
        getButton(OPEN).setEnabled(selected);
        getButton(DELETE).setEnabled(selected);
        if (!selected)
            // If nothing was selected, we set an error message
            setErrorMessage("Select at least one entry!");
        else
            // Otherwise we set the error message to null
            // to show the intial content of the message area
            setErrorMessage(null);
    }
    /**
     * @see org.eclipse.jface.dialogs.Dialog#
     * createButtonsForButtonBar(org.eclipse.swt.widgets.Composite)
     * We replace the OK and Cancel buttons by our own creations
     * We use the method createButton() (from Dialog),
     * to create the new buttons
     */
    protected void createButtonsForButtonBar(Composite parent) {
        // Create Open button
        Button openButton = createButton(parent, OPEN,
            "Open", true);
```

```
                      // Initially deactivate it
                      openButton.setEnabled(false);
                      // Add a SelectionListener
                      openButton.addSelectionListener(new SelectionAdapter() {
                        public void widgetSelected(SelectionEvent e) {
                          // Retrieve selected entries from list
                          itemsToOpen = list.getSelection();
                          // Set return code
                          setReturnCode(OPEN);
                          // Close dialog
                          close();
                        }
                      });
                      // Create Delete button
                      Button deleteButton =
                        createButton(parent, DELETE, "Delete", false);
                      deleteButton.setEnabled(false);
                      // Add a SelectionListener
                      deleteButton.addSelectionListener(new SelectionAdapter() {
                      public void widgetSelected(SelectionEvent e) {
                        // Get the indices of the selected entries
                        int selectedItems[] = list.getSelectionIndices();
                        // Remove all these entries
                        list.remove(selectedItems);
                        // Now re-validate the list because it has changed
                        validate();
                      }
                    });
                    // Create Cancel button
                    Button cancelButton =
                      createButton(parent, CANCEL, "Cancel", false);
                    // Add a SelectionListener
                    cancelButton.addSelectionListener(new SelectionAdapter() {
                      public void widgetSelected(SelectionEvent e) {
                        setReturnCode(CANCEL);
                        close();
                      }
                    });
                  }
                  /**
                   * Method getItemsToOpen.
                   * @return String[] - the selected items
                   */
                  public String[] getItemsToOpen() {
                    return itemsToOpen;
                  }
              }
```

We then can use the `MailDialog` class as follows:

```
MailDialog mailDialog = new MailDialog(shell,
new String[] {"Carol", "Eve", "Claudia", "Alice" });
if (mailDialog.open() == MailDialog.OPEN) {
  String[] itemsToOpen = mailDialog.getItemsToOpen();
  for (int i = 0; i < itemsToOpen.length; i++) {
    System.out.println(itemsToOpen[i]);
  }
}
```

7.2.3   Making dialogs persistent

The interface `IDialogSettings` is used to save and restore the state of `Dialog` instances across sessions, such as the state of checkboxes, entries in text fields, etc.

For this purpose `IDialogSettings` defines methods that allow us to set and retrieve name/value pairs. With `get()` and `getArray()` we can read scalar string values or string arrays respectively, and with `put()` we can write both scalars and arrays. There is also a variety of data type specific `get…()` methods, such as `getInt()`, `getLong()`, `getFloat()`, `getDouble()`, and `getBoolean()`.

In addition, we have the option to store and retrieve whole subsections of dialog settings with the `addSection()`, `addNewSection()`, and `getSection()` methods. Each subsection is represented by another `IDialogSettings` instance. Consequently, subsections may be nested. We can thus construct a deeply nested tree.

With the `load()` method we can read an `IDialogSettings` instance from a file or from an input stream, and with `save()` we can write an `IDialogSettings` instance to a file or to an input stream.

The class `DialogSettings` is the standard implementation for the interface `IDialogSettings`. It uses XML as the file format for persistent storage of the settings.

In the following example we create a `DialogSettings` instance with two subsections:

```
IDialogSettings settings = new DialogSettings("dialog");
IDialogSettings section1 = new DialogSettings("dialogPage1");
settings.addSection(section1);
section1.put("volume",4.5);
section1.put("pitch",300);
IDialogSettings section2 = new DialogSettings("dialogPage2");
settings.addSection(section2);
  section2.put("Languages", new String[]{"english",
    "german","french"});
settings.save("settings/test/dialog.xml");
```

7.3 Viewers

Despite the name *Viewer*, the classes in the package org.eclipse.jface.viewers do not only support viewing contents. All ...Viewer classes also support the modification of contents. In fact, some of the editors in the Eclipse workbench are constructed with the help of these viewer classes. The name *Viewer* is derived from the *Model-Viewer-Controller* (MVC) design pattern. This pattern defines a cooperation between three component types: the *Model* component manages the domain data, the *Viewer* component is responsible for the representation of the data on the screen, and the *Controller* component handles user interaction. Besides a clear separation of concerns, this design pattern has the advantage that it allows several *Viewer* instances for a single *Model* instance. This allows us to display the same data in different ways simultaneously.

7.3.1 The Viewer event model

In the context of the MVC design pattern, JFace establishes its own event model. It features those events that are sent from the *Viewer* component to the *Controller*. The following event types are available:

Event	Listener	Description
CheckStateChangedEvent	ICheckStateListener	This event is generated when the state of a checkbox within the viewer changes.
DoubleClickEvent	IDoubleClickListener	This event is generated when a data element representation in the viewer is double clicked.
OpenEvent	IOpenListener	This event is generated when a data element shown in the viewer is opened with a double click or by pressing the *Enter* key.

Event	Listener	Description
SelectionChangedEvent	ISelectionChangedListener	This event is generated when the selection in the viewer changes.
TreeExpansionEvent	ITreeViewerListener	This event is generated when a tree node expands or collapses.

All these event types are subclasses of class java.util.EventObject.

7.3.2   The Viewer hierarchy

The abstract class Viewer is the mother of all viewer classes in JFace. Most notably, each Viewer instance wraps an SWT widget that is responsible for the representation of data, such as widgets of type Table, Tree, TableTree, etc. The class Viewer provides the basis for the concrete viewer implementation but also provides some methods of general interest, such as functions supporting the help system.

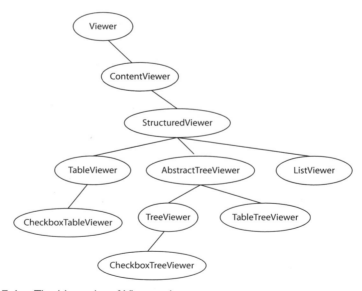

Figure 7.4:   The hierarchy of Viewer classes.

ContentViewer   The class ContentViewer is an immediate subclass of class Viewer and implements the MVC design pattern. ContentViewer retrieves the domain data from an IContentProvider instance that has been registered with the ContentViewer via the setContentProvider() method. The IContentProvider instance may deliver the data in its raw format: the later transformation of the single data elements into their representational format is done via an IBaseLabelProvider instance that has been registered with the ContentViewer via the setLabelProvider() method. For example, if we want to display a table containing the various file attributes for a set of files, the IContent-Provider would just deliver the File instances. The IBaseLabelProvider would retrieve for each table column the corresponding attributes from a single File instance and would deliver the representation of the attribute. IBaseLabelProviders may deliver both text and image representations.

Both IContentProvider and IBaseLabelProvider are 'abstract' interfaces, i.e. they don't declare methods to retrieve or transform contents. They only declare general methods such as dispose() or inputChanged().

ILabelProvider   The definition of the actual methods for data transformation are left to 'concrete' interfaces such as ILabelProvider, with the methods getImage() and getText(), ITableLabelProvider with the methods getColumnImage() and getColumnText(), and IStructuredContentProvider with the methods getChildren(), hasChildren() and getParent().

StructuredViewer   The class ContentViewer is the direct parent class for the (still) abstract class StructuredViewer. This class is the basis for most of the concrete viewer implementations in JFace. It provides a wealth of additional methods – in particular, methods that allow to sort and filter the dataset displayed in the viewer. The abstract classes ViewerSorter and ViewerFilter act as a basis for implementations of custom sorters and filters. In section 8.6 we will see a TableViewer as a concrete example of the StructuredViewer in full action.

TreeViewer   The abstract class AbstractTreeViewer provides the basis for all concrete tree-oriented viewer implementation such as TreeViewer (and its derivative CheckboxTreeViewer) and TableTreeViewer. In particular, this class provides methods for the management of trees, such as methods for expanding and collapsing tree nodes.

7.3.3   Cell editors

All table-oriented viewers such as TableViewer and TableTreeViewer can be equipped with cell editors. It becomes possible then not only to view table contents, but also to edit them. Eclipse provides a variety of predefined cell editors:

CheckboxCellEditor	This editor allows the modification of a Boolean value.
ColorCellEditor	This editor supports the selection of a color.

ComboBoxCellEditor	This editor allows the selection of a value from a list, but also the free input of an arbitrary value.
DialogCellEditor	This editor allows the invocation of arbitrary dialogs. The result value of the dialog is then assigned to the cell.
TextCellEditor	This editor allows unrestricted input into the cell.

All these editors are derivatives of the abstract class CellEditor. To make table and table-trees editable, several components must cooperate:

- We need a suitable viewer (TableViewer or TableTreeViewer).

- We need a suitable cell editor (see above). The editor is registered with the viewer via the method setCellEditors(). We may register an individual editor for each column.

- With each editor we can register an ICellEditorValidator instance via the setValidator() method. These instances are responsible for validating the editor input.

- We must register an ICellModifier instance with the viewer via method setCellModifier(). This instance is responsible for the data flow between the viewer and the editor. Each ICellModifier instance must implement the following three methods:

  - getValue() retrieves from the domain data the value that will appear in the editor.

  - canModify() checks whether a given value can be modified.

  - modify() gets the result data from the editor and modifies the domain data accordingly.

- *Column Properties* identify each column uniquely. The CellModifier can recognize the column it works on with the help of these column properties. We can assign a column property to each viewer column via the method setColumnProperties().

In Section 8.6 we will see cell editors in action.

7.4   Text processing

The text processing functional group is another main functional area of JFace. In particular, the different editors of the Eclipse workbench are based on JFace's text processing. However, it is possible to use JFace text processing isolated from the Eclipse workbench.

The text processing functionality is deployed in the archives `jfacetext.jar` and `text.jar` and consists of the packages:

```
org.eclipse.jface.text
org.eclipse.jface.text.*
```

7.4.1 Text processing base classes

The text processing function group is separated into a data domain layer and a presentation layer. The representation is done by the `TextViewer` class, while the data model is described by the interface `IDocument`. For the interface `IDocument`, Eclipse provides the standard implementation `AbstractDocument` and `Document`.

The document model

Classes that implement the `IDocument` must provide the following services:

- *Text manipulation.* Modifying the text content of a document is done with the help of the `replace()` method. This method can replace a specified text area with another string. Such operations generate `DocumentEvents` that inform registered `Listeners` and `IPositionUpdaters` (see below) about the text modification.

- *Positioning.* `Position` instances represent a position or an area within a document. We may add any number of `Position` instances to an `IDocument` instance and may assign each `Position` instance to a category. For the Java editor, for example, we have breakpoints, problem markers, and other position categories. Remembering a document position in a `Position` instance, however, raises a problem. When the document changes, the real position may change, too. It is therefore necessary to update all `Position` instances in the case of document modification. This is done with the help of `IPositionUpdate` instances. (The `DefaultPositionUpdater` class is the standard implementation of this interface). We can add any number of these instances to a document. When a document is modified, all registered `IPositionUpdate` instances are invoked in their registration order via their `update()` method, and a `DocumentEvent` instance is passed to this method.

- *Partitioning.* Partitions are non-overlapping sections within a document. For example, a source code document could be segmented into partitions of the types *comment*, *declaration*, and *instruction*. Each partition is characterized by its position, its length, and its type. A document is segmented into separate partitions with the help of an associated `IDocumentPartitioner` instance. If a document does not have such an `IDocumentPartitioner`, it consists of only a single partition – the entire document. When a partition is changed, the method `documentPartitioningChanged()` is called for a registered `IDocumentPartitioningListener` instance.

- *Searching.* The method search() supports searching for a character string. It can search forwards and backwards, allows case sensitive or case insensitive searching, and can search for words or generic character strings.

- *Line tracking.* The line tracking functions are only found in the standard implementations AbstractDocument and Document, but don't belong to the IDocument interface. With an ILineTracker instance (standard implementations are Abstract-LineTracker, DefaultLineTracker, and ConfigurableLineTracker) we can create a relationship between document position and line number. Initially, the whole text is parsed for line separation characters. Later modifications are made known to the ILineTracker instance, so that this instance may update its internal line number associations. It is not the client's responsibility to register an ILineTracker instance with a document. Instead an ILineTracker is associated with an IDocument instance by implementation, i.e. when a subclass of AbstractDocument is implemented. For example, the class Document uses the standard implementation DefaultLineTracker.

IDocument implementations throw a BadLocationException or a BadPositionCategoryException when we try to access beyond the document bounds, or when we use an unknown position category.

The TextViewer

The class TextViewer implements the presentation layer of the text processing function group. It uses the SWT class StyledText (see Section 6.5.13) for displaying and editing text. Writing a bare-bone text editor with the help of this class is almost trivial. For example:

```
Document doc = new Document("Some text");
TextViewer textViewer = new TextViewer(composite,SWT.MULTI
  | SWT.H_SCROLL | SWT.V_SCROLL);
textViewer.setDocument(doc);
```

Despite this minimalist example, the class TextViewer provides such rich functionality that it would require a complete book to cover the topic. Here, we only want to list the most important functions.

The event processing for class `TextViewer` is handled by four `Listener` interfaces:

Listener	Event	Description
ITextInputListener	–	The `inputDocumentAboutToBeChanged()` method is called before the current document is replaced by a new document. After the replacement the method `inputDocumentChanged()` is invoked.
ITextListener	TextEvent	The `textChanged()`method is invoked when text is changed. The `TextEvent` describes the replaced text and the replacement.
IViewportListener	–	The `viewportChanged()` method is invoked when text is changed within the visible window of the viewer.
VerifyKeyListener	VerifyEvent	The `VerifyEvent` of the `StyledText` widget.

Selection
The methods `getSelectedRange()`, `setSelectedRange()`, `getSelection()`, and `setSelection()` allow clients to retrieve and set text selections. These methods use `TextSelection` instances for parameters and results. With `setTextColor()` or `changeTextPresentation()` we can assign a different color to a selected text area. In addition, we can set and retrieve text markers with `setMark()` and `getMark()`.

Viewport
The viewport describes the editor's visible window onto the text. This viewport can be managed with the `getTopIndex()`, `setTopIndex()`, `getBottomIndex()`, `getTopIndexStartOffset()`, and `getBottomIndexEndOffset()` methods. We can therefore get and set the line number of the top line in the viewport, the line number of the bottom line in the viewport, the text position of the top left viewport corner, and the text position of the bottom right corner of the viewport. With `revealRange()` we can position the editor window to the specified area.

Visible text region
The visible text region consists of all text lines that can be displayed in the editor window. Apart from these lines, a document may contain lines that always remain invisible. The following methods can be used to manage the visible region:

```
getVisibleRegion()
setVisibleRegion()
resetVisibleRegion()
overlapsWithVisibleRegion()
```

Hover

We can set or retrieve an `ITextHover` instance for each text partition with the methods `setHover()` and `getHover()`. These instances organize the display of explanation texts that are displayed when the mouse hovers over a text area. They implement the method `getHoverInfo()`, which computes the explanation text from the text area, and the method `getHoverRegion()`, which computes the text area for which the explanation is provided from a text position.

Apart from these basic functions, the `TextViewer` establishes a framework for implementing a complete text editor. This includes support for operations and support for installing plug-ins.

Operations

Instances of type `ITextOperationTarget` represent operations typically performed by the user. This interface is implemented by the `TextViewer` with the methods `canDoOperation()` and `doOperation()`. The latter method must only be invoked if `canDoOperation()` is successful. In addition, the `TextViewer` implements the method `enableOperation()` from the interface `ITextOperationTargetExtension`.

Operations can be identified with the following predefined constants (defined in interface `ITextOperationTarget`): `COPY`, `CUT`, `DELETE`, `PASTE`, `PREFIX`, `PRINT`, `REDO`, `SELECT_ALL`, `SHIFT_LEFT`, `SHIFT_RIGHT`, `STRIP_PREFIX`, and `UNDO`. For example, the following code deletes all text:

```
textViewer.doOperation(ITextOperationTarget.SELECT_ALL);
if (textViewer.canDoOperation(ITextOperationTarget.DELETE))
    textViewer.doOperation(ITextOperationTarget.DELETE);
```

Configuring the TextViewer

Some of these operations are only available if we have previously created an appropriate manager for the `TextViewer`. In particular, this is the case for `UNDO` and `REDO` operations. Before we can perform these operations, we first must add an `IUndoManager` instance to the `TextViewer` via the `setUndoManager()` method. In the following code we install the `IUndoManager` standard implementation, the class `DefaultUndoManager`:

```
// maximum 99 Undos
IUndoManager undoManager = new DefaultUndoManager(99);
undoManager.connect(textViewer);
textViewer.setUndoManager(undoManager);
```

The operations `PREFIX` and `STRIP_PREFIX` can be configured by setting a default prefix with the `setDefaultPrefixes()` method. This allows us to set a different default prefix for each text category. Similarly, we can use the method `setIndentPrefix()` to specify category specific prefixes for text indentation used by the operations `SHIFT_LEFT` and `SHIFT_RIGHT`.

The indentation of text can, in addition, be automated by specifying an `IAutoIndent-Strategy` instance. For each text modification the `customizeDocumentCommand()` of this instance is called. A `DocumentCommand` is passed as a parameter to this method and informs us how the text was changed. The IAutoIndentStrategy instance may then decide how to indent the text. The IAutoIndentStrategy standard implementation, for example, always indents a line by left aligning it with the previous line. The following code shows how this strategy is installed:

```
try {
  textViewer.setAutoIndentStrategy(new DefaultAutoIndentStrategy(),
    doc.getContentType(0));
} catch (BadLocationException e) {}
```

7.4.2   The SourceViewer class

The SourceViewer class is a subclass of TextViewer. In addition to the TextViewer, it offers a vertical ruler on which we can place annotations and mark text areas. There are some new operations, too:

CONTENTASSIST_PROPOSALS

CONTENTASSIST_CONTEXT_INFORMATION

FORMAT

INFORMATION

The SourceViewer is, in particular, suited to implement source code editors. An example for the application of the SourceViewer is given in Chapter 8.

Configuration

The SourceViewer combines most of its configuration settings and managers in a separate configuration object, which is an instance of the SourceViewerConfiguration class. Here we can specify all kind of settings such as prefixes, UndoManager, hover behavior, or content assistant in complete isolation from the SourceViewer. Later we can assign the configuration object to a SourceViewer instance via the configure() method. Usually we would want to create subclasses of SourceViewerConfiguration to create editors of different behavior. Instead of subclassing the class SourceViewer, we subclass SourceViewerConfiguration and use the instances of these subclasses to configure the SourceViewer.

Annotations

Annotation for a document are managed outside the IDocument instance. The package org.eclipse.jface.text.source provides the interface IAnnotationModel for this purpose with the standard implementation AnnotationModel. With the connect() method we can connect this model with the document instance. The SourceViewer is told about the annotation model as an additional parameter in the setDocument() method (together with the IDocument instance).

The `IAnnotationModel` interface provides a number of methods to add `Annotation` instances to the model, or to remove or retrieve annotations. When doing so, the position of the annotation is specified with a `Position` instance (see Section 7.4.1). This guarantees that the annotation remains in the right position, even when the document content is changed.

In addition, we have the option of adding an `IAnnotationModelListener` instance to the model. The `modelChanged()` method of this instance is invoked when the model changes.

The abstract class `Annotation` defines some methods for the graphical representation of annotations. We have the option of specifying a *layer* for each `Annotation` instance, so we can position annotations on top of each other.

The interface `IAnnotationHover` also belongs to the annotation mechanism. Instances of type `IAnnotationHover` can be registered with the `SourceViewer` via the method `setAnnotationHover()`. Implementations of `IAnnotationHover` must implement the method `getHoverInfo()`. This method generates a text that is displayed when the mouse hovers over the annotation for each given line number.

Text formatters

Text formatters modify the content of a document. They insert characters or remove characters to mold the text into a given format. An example for a text formatter is the *Java Formatter* introduced in Section 1.3.4.

Text formatters are passed from a `SourceViewerConfiguration` to a `SourceViewer` instance via method `getContentFormatter()`. All these formatters must implement the interface `IContentFormatter`. The standard implementation `ContentFormatter` can work in two operation modes: being aware of text categories or insensitive to text categories. For each text category, we can specify a special formatting strategy via the method `setFormattingStrategy()`. The formatting strategies must implement the interface `IFormattingStrategy`. The actual formatting is done in the `format()` method. The methods `formatterStarts()` and `formatterStops()` inform the `IFormattingStrategy` instance about the start and the end of the formatting process.

Content assistants

Content Assistants (or *Code Assistants*) suggest content completion proposals to the end user. After selection of a proposal and commitment by the end user, the document is modified by the content assistant.

Content assistants are passed from a `SourceViewerConfiguration` to a `SourceViewer` instance via the method `getContentAssistant()`. All these assistants must implement the interface `IContentAssistant`. The standard implementation of this interface is the class `ContentAssistant`. Usually, instances of this class are configured appropriately before they are used. This can be done with the `enableAutoActivation()` and `setAutoActivationDelay()` methods. With these methods we can specify that the content assistant automatically appears on the screen after a specified time, even when no activation key (such as *Ctrl-Spacebar*) is pressed. When we want to activate the content assistant via a key press we must explicitly call the `SourceViewer` method `doOperation(SourceViewer.CONTENTASSIST_PROPOSALS)`.

The proposals of the content assistant are compiled with the help of `IContentAssistProcessor` instances. Such instances can be registered for each text category separately with the `ContentAssistant` via the method `setContentAssistProcessor()`. These processors implement the method `computeCompletionProposals()`, which computes appropriate proposals based on the current position in the document. The method returns an array of `CompletionProposal` instances. Each of these proposals contains the string to be inserted into the document, the position at which to insert the string, the length of text to be replaced, and the new position of the cursor relative to the inserted string.

A simple example for a content assistant is given in Section 8.7.

Text presentation

The classes in the package `org.eclipse.jface.text.presentation` are responsible for presenting the text content on the screen. These operations do not modify the document. The interface `IPresentationReconciler` covers the presentation process when text parts are modified. Instances of this interface are passed from a `SourceViewerConfiguration` to a `SourceViewer` instance via the `getPresentationReconciler()` method. The standard implementation of this interface is the class `PresentationReconciler`. This class uses two cooperating processors: an instance of `IPresentationDamager` and an instance of `IPresentationRepairer`. The `IPresentationDamager` computes the document area for which the current representation has become invalid because the document was changed. The `IPresentationRepairer` decorates this text area with new text attributes. The standard implementation `DefaultDamagerRepairer` implements both interfaces.

When creating a `DefaultDamagerRepairer` instance, an `ITokenScanner` instance is passed in the constructor. Usually, a subclass of `RuleBasedScanner` is used here. (`RuleBasedScanner` implements `ITokenScanner`). And so we come to the package `org.eclipse.jface.text.rules`.

Since `RuleBasedScanners` can be programmed by supplying an ordered list of rules, they are quite flexible. They analyze the specified text area with the help of these rules and deliver a series of tokens, which can then be interpreted by the client (in this case the `DefaultDamagerRepairer`). In our case, these tokens contain only `TextAttribute` instances that specify color and style attributes for the corresponding text sections.

All rules must implement the `IPredicateRule` interface. They search in the specified text area for a given pattern. Such a pattern can be specified by supplying a string with which the pattern begins and a string with which it ends. When a rule finds a pattern in the text, it will return the specified token. If not, the `RuleBasedScanner` will continue the process with the next rule.

The various concrete rule types, such as `SingleLineRule`, `WordRule`, `MultiLineRule`, etc., differ in how they treat space characters and line separation characters. For example, the `SingleLineRule` does not search for patterns across line breaks, and the `WordRule` does not search across word breaks, etc. In addition, there are special rules such as the `NumberRule`, which recognize numeric values.

A simple example for the rule based text presentation is given in Section 8.7.

7.5   Actions and menus

7.5.1   The IAction interface

The `IAction` interface is contained in the package `org.eclipse.jface.action`. `IAction` instances represent abstract user actions such as 'Save to file', 'Search', or 'Go to marker'. Actions can be represented on the user interface in many ways, for example as a menu item, or as toolbar button, or as both.

The `IAction` interface defines a set of methods with which the properties of an action may be set or retrieved. For example. we may assign a unique identification (string) to an action via the method `setId()`. With the method `setText()` we can define a display text that is shown when the action is represented as a menu text or a toolbar button. This text can contain a display text for a keyboard shortcut, separated by an '@' or '\t' character. If the keyboard shortcut consists of several keys we must concatenate the key names using the '+' character. With the method `setToolTipText()` we can specify a text that appears on the screen when the mouse hovers over the action representation. In addition, we can use the method `setDescription()` to specify a longer descriptive text. This text is shown in a status line when the action is selected.

With the `setImageDescriptor()` method we can set an icon that represents the action on a tool bar. With `setDisabledImageDescriptor()` we can specify a special variant of that icon that is shown when the action is disabled. With `setHoverImageDescriptor()` we can specify an icon variant that is shown when the mouse hovers over the action. We can disable or enable an action by invoking `setEnabled()`. With `setChecked()` we can set an action to 'checked' or reset the action again. How the 'checked' state is represented on the user interface depends on the representation of the action itself: in menus a checkmark is displayed; in tool bars the button remains pushed.

With the setAccelerator() method we can specify a keyboard shortcut for the action. If this shortcut consists of several keys we must combine the key codes using the "|" operator for binary OR. To specify alphanumeric keys we just specify the character. Codes for other keys are defined in the class SWT. For example, we can specify SWT.CTRL | 'Z' for the keyboard shortcut *Ctrl-Z*.

With the method setHelpListener() we can register the action's HelpListener. This listener will receive an appropriate event object when the *F1* key is pressed for the selected action.

Finally, each IAction instance must implement the run() method. This action is called when the end user activates the action.

7.5.2   The Managers

We discussed menus and toolbars in Section 6.5.12. The question here is how to organize the cooperation between menus, toolbars, status lines and actions. All this cooperation is handled by IContributionManager instances that come in various derived types such as IMenuManager, IToolBarManager, and IStatusLineManager and their standard implementations MenuManager, ToolBarManager, and StatusLineManager.

MenuManager   We will now briefly discuss the MenuManager (the ToolBarManager works quite similarly) and finally the StatusLineManager.

We can create a new menu manager with the constructor MenuManager(). Optionally we may pass a text and an identification with this constructor. Then we tell the menu manager to create a menu. With the method createContextMenu() we can create a context menu, and with createMenuBar() we can create a menu bar.

The addMenuListener() method allows us to register an IMenuListener instance with the menu manager. The menuAboutToShow() method of this instance is called before the menu is displayed. We will usually construct the menu each time from scratch when this method is invoked, and especially when the menu content depends on the context. This is not difficult: we just add IAction instances (and possibly also Separator instances) to the menu manager using the add() method. One thing still remains to be done: We must tell the menu manager to remove all entries after the menu has been shown. This is achieved with the method setRemoveAllWhenShown(). Otherwise, we would create double entries next time the method menuAboutToShow() is invoked.

In Section 11.6.1 we show how to construct a context menu with the help of a menu manager as a practical example.

StatusLineManager   The StatusLineManager creates a StatusLine object when the method createCon-
trol() is called. The StatusLineManager provides several methods for the output of
information messages and error messages into this status line, such as setMessage() and
setErrorMessage(). With the method getProgrMonitor() we can access the
progress monitor built into the status line. For this progress monitor we can allow
cancellation of an operation by the end user by calling the setCancelEnabled() method.
We can determine if the end user has cancelled an operation with isCancelEnabled().

7.6   Wizards

Wizards consist of a series of dialogs that guide the user through several steps of a task.
The user can step forwards and backwards within the task. Typical examples for such
wizards are the *New File* wizard, the *Import* wizard, or the *Export* wizard.

The package org.eclipse.jface.wizard provides four classes with which we may
implement such wizards:

- The abstract class Wizard forms the basis on which all wizards are implemented.
  This class is the standard implementation of the interface IWizard.

- The class WizardDialog implements the dialog that presents the wizard to the end
  user. This dialog may have several pages.

- The abstract class WizardPage forms the basis on which all wizard pages may be
  implemented.

- Finally, we have the class WizardSelectionPage. This class allows the end user to
  select a specific wizard from a list of possible wizards.

7.6.1   The Wizard class

The implementation of a new wizard begins by extending the class Wizard. This class
offers various wizards that we can use to configure the concrete wizard subclass. This
configuration is usually done in the method addPages() that is called when the wizard is
initialized.

addPage()	This method can be used to add new pages of type WizardPage to the wizard.
setHelpAvailable()	This method can be invoked to indicate that help is available for the wizard.
setDefaultPageImageDescriptor()	This method is called to decorate the default page with an image (ImageDescriptor).

setDialogSettings() getDialogSettings()	These methods allow us to set and retrieve instance of type IDialogSettings (see Section 7.2.3) to make wizard properties persistent.
setNeedsProgressMonitor()	This method is called to equip the wizard with a ProgressMonitor.
setTitleBarColor()	We can use this method to set the title bar color.
setWindowTitle()	We can use this method to set a title.

Concrete subclasses of Wizard will, in addition, override some wizard methods to implement application logic. In particular, we may want to override the methods performCancel() and performFinish(), possibly also the methods createPageControls(), addPages(), and dispose(). In the method performFinish() we will start all operations that need to be performed after the *Finish* button has been pressed. The method performCancel() is called when the *Cancel* button was pressed. In this method we may want to undo operations that have been performed on the single wizard pages. In method createPageControl() the wizard content is constructed. The construction of the single pages is done in the individual WizardPage instances, but the corresponding method calls IDialogPage.createControl() are invoked from the createPageControls() method.

7.6.2 The WizardPage class

To implement a concrete wizard we will construct wizard pages by subclassing the abstract class WizardPage. When a page instance is created, we pass a unique identification with the constructor, and optionally a page title and a title image (ImageDescriptor).

This class, too, offers various methods that support the configuration of the wizard page:

setDescription()	This method can be used to supply a longer explanatory text that is shown below the page title.
setErrorMessage()	With this method we can set an error message. This error message replaces an information message previously set with setMessage(). To reset the error message, supply null as a parameter.

`setImageDescriptor()`	With this message we can set an image (`ImageDescriptor`) to be displayed on the page. Here we will not use small 16x16 icons, but rather images of size 48x48 pixels or larger.
`setMessage()`	With this message we can display an information message to the end user. Typically we would use it to ask the end user to do something.
`setPageComplete()`	This method can be used to set an internal indicator when the page is completed by the end user. This indicator can be retrieved via the method `isPageComplete()`.
`setPreviousPage()`	This method sets the page to be shown when the end user presses the *Back* button.
`setTitle()`	This method can be used to set the page title.

Here, too, the concrete subclasses may override several methods of class `WizardPage` to implement specific implementation logic. In particular, we may want to override the methods:

`performHelp()`	This method shows the help information for the wizard page.
`canFlipToNextPage()`	This method enables the *Next* button.
`isPageComplete()`	This method finds out if the page was completed by the end user. The standard implementation just returns the value set by the method `setPageComplete()`.
`setDescription()`	See above.
`setTitle()`	See above.
`dispose()`	This method can be extended if we need to release page specific resources.

7.6.3   The WizardSelectionPage class

The `WizardSelectionPage` class is an abstract subclass of class `WizardPage`. It is used as a basis for wizard pages that allow the selection of nested wizards. This allows us to concatenate wizards with each other. The class `WizardSelectionPage` only introduces two new methods: using `setSelectedNode()` and `getSelectedNode()` we can set or retrieve the selection on the page.

7.6.4   The WizardDialog class

Instances of type WizardDialog act as GUI containers for a wizard and support the end user in stepping through the wizard's pages. To execute a wizard, we first create a new instance of this wizard. Then we create a new instance of the class WizardDialog and pass the Wizard instance in the constructor as a parameter. Then we can open the WizardDialog instance via method open():

```
IWizard wizard = new FancyWizard();
WizardDialog dialog = new WizardDialog(shell, wizard);
dialog.open();
```

We would usually use the class WizardDialog in its original form. However, in special cases it may be necessary to create subclasses and to override individual methods. In particular, it can become necessary to override the methods backPressed() and next-Pressed() if we need to perform special processing during a page change.

7.7   Preferences

To manage application specific preferences, several components need to cooperate. The package org.eclipse.jface.preference provides these components. First, there is the class PreferenceStore, which can store preferences in the form of name/value pairs. Next, there is class PreferenceConverter that can convert popular object types into string values. The user interface can be constructed with the help of the classes Preference-Page, PreferenceDialog, PreferenceManager, and PreferenceNode. Using FieldEditors in PreferencePages can save some hard coding.

7.7.1   The PreferenceStore and PreferenceConverter classes

To be precise, PreferenceStore doesn't store preferences as name/value pairs, but as triples, which consist of an identifier, a value and a default value. The identification must be unique within the context of a PreferenceStore instance. When we read a preference from the store, we will get the previously set value (usually, a value that has been set by the end user). If such a value does not exist, the default value defined by the application is returned.

The interface IPreferenceStore defines various data type specific access methods for values and default values. The methods getDefaultxxx() return the default value, and the getxxx() methods return the previously set value, or the default value if no value has been set. With setDefaultxxx() we can set the default value, and with setxxx() we can set the current value. All these methods have variants for the following data types: boolean, int, long, float, double, and String.

For example:

```
store.setDefaultBoolean("use_animation",true);
```

or

```
double speed = store.getDouble("animation_speed");
```

Of course, these data types are not sufficient by themselves. The class PreferenceConverter therefore provides a set of conversion methods, with which we can convert popular object types into string values and vice versa. In particular, the types RGB (colors), FontData (fonts), Point (coordinates), and Rectangle (areas) are supported.

Events

Since the modification of preference values can influence the behavior and the appearance of an application, we must have a means to react to changes of preference values. It is therefore possible to register an IPropertyChangeListener instance with the PreferenceStore via the method addPropertyChangeListener(). This instance is notified immediately when a preference value within the PreferenceStore is changed: it receives an event object of type PropertyChangeEvent via the method propertyChanged(). This object passes information about the identification of the modified preference value, both the new value and the old value. We can thus react to such a modification and may adapt the applications appearance accordingly.

We can specify a file name when we create a new PreferenceStore instance. Using the methods load() and save() we can load the preference store content from the specified file or save its content to the file. Only the actual values are written to file, not the default values: the default values of the preference store must always be set by the application. This is best done during the initialization of the application so that the PreferenceStore is always correctly configured.

7.7.2   The PreferencePage class

The abstract PreferencePage is the base class for implementing our own preference pages. By default this class is equipped with four buttons. The end user may commit the entered values with the *OK* button. The *Cancel* button is used to abort the modification of preference values. The *Apply* button allows the user to modify the values in the PreferenceStore without closing the preference dialog. The *Default* button can be pressed to reset all values to the default value.

The last two buttons can be suppressed by calling the method noDefaultAndApplyButton(). This method must be called before the method createControl() is invoked; it is a good idea to call it in the constructor.

Each concrete subclass of PreferencePage must implement the method createControl(). Here we will set up all the input fields for the preference values, usually with the help of field editors (see Section 7.7.3).

In addition, we should extend or override the method `doComputeSize()`. This method computes the size of the area constructed in the `createControl()` method.

7.7.3 Field editors

We could construct a `PreferencePage` 'manually' with the help of SWT widgets and set the PreferenceStore values using the `setxxx()` methods. But it is far simpler to construct a preference page based on the abstract class `FieldEditorPreferencePage` and to use field editors.

To do this, we just define our own preference page as a subclass of `FieldEditorPreferencePage` and override the methods `createFieldEditors()`. Within this method we add field editors, one for each preference value, to the page by using `addField()`.

All field editors are based on the abstract class `FieldEditor`. When creating a new field editor, we pass as parameters in the constructor the identification of the preference value (see Section 7.7.1), a display text, and the containing `Composite`. We must fetch this `Composite` with the method `getParent()` from the preference page for each field editor, as the `FieldEditorPreferencePage` may create a new `Composite` each time a new field editor is added.

JFace provides the following concrete subclasses of `FieldEditor`:

`BooleanFieldEditor`	A field editor for a Boolean value. This field editor is represented as a checkbox.
`ColorFieldEditor`	A field editor for entering a color value. By pressing a button, the end user may select the color from a host system specific color selection dialog.
`DirectoryFieldEditor`	A field editor for selecting a directory. This field editor is a subclass of the `StringButtonFieldEditor`.
`FileFieldEditor`	A field editor for selecting a file. This field editor is a subclass of the `StringButtonFieldEditor`.
`FontFieldEditor`	A field editor for entering a type font. By pressing a button, the end user may select the font from a host system specific font selection dialog.
`ListEditor`	An abstract field editor for entering multiple values that are organized as a list. Concrete subclasses must implement the methods `parseString()`, `createList()`, and `createNewInputObject()`.

PathEditor	This field editor is a subclass of `ListEditor`. With the help of this editor the end user can compile a list of file and directory paths from the host operating system. Besides a *New* and a *Remove* button, this editor features *Up* and *Down* buttons with which the order in the path list may be changed. An additional title line for the pop-up path selection dialog must be specified in the constructor of this class.
IntegerFieldEditor	A field editor for entering an integer value. This field editor is a subclass of `StringFieldEditor`.
RadioGroupFieldEditor	A field editor that presents an enumeration of radio buttons for selection. This class requires some additional parameters in the constructor: the number of columns, and a two-dimensional array containing all the number/value pairs available for selection. We may optionally specify an additional parameter that places the specified radio buttons into a `Group` widget (see Section 6.5.5).
StringButtonFieldEditor	An abstract field editor that displays a *Change* button next to the input field. Pressing this button will lead to a pop-up dialog in which the new value may be entered.
StringFieldEditor	A field editor for entering a string value.

An example of the use of field editors in connection with the `FieldEditorPreference-Page` is shown in Section 11.9.1.

7.7.4   Preference page trees

The classes `PreferenceNode`, `PreferenceManager` and `PreferenceDialog` can be used to organize multiple `PreferencePages` into a preference page tree. In a larger application (and, in particular, on an open platform such as Eclipse) it is neither possible nor desirable to place all preferences into a single page. It is better to distribute the preferences across multiple pages and to order these pages according to topics. A tree structure is best suited to support the organization of preference pages.

The PreferenceNode class

The class `PreferenceNode` with the corresponding interface `IPreferenceNode` is used to implement such a tree structure. Each node within a preference page tree is implemented by an instance of this class. The class features all the usual methods to construct and manage trees such as add(), remove(), getSubNodes(), and findSubNode().

Each PreferenceNode has a unique identification that is specified in the constructor when an instance is created. In addition, we can specify a PreferencePage instance that belongs to this node in the constructor. Later we can retrieve this page via the method getPage(), and we can modify the page via method setPage().

A further variant of the constructor allows us to create PreferencePage instances lazily, i.e. at the time they are first displayed. This can be achieved by specifying the class name of the concrete PreferencePage in lieu of the PreferencePage instance. Using the *Java Reflection* function, the PreferenceNode will create the PreferencePage instance when it is actually needed. This makes sense for applications with many preference pages, the Eclipse workbench being one of them.

In addition to the PreferencePages the PreferenceNode instances also take care of the display information needed for the presentation of the preference page tree. This information consists of a label and an icon (ImageDescriptor). These objects can also be specified in the constructor.

The PreferenceManager class

This class provides methods allowing us to navigate within preference page trees by just specifying a path. Each path consists of a series of PreferenceNode identifications that are separated with a separator character. This character can be specified in the constructor of the PreferenceManager.

Other methods allow the modification of preference page trees: in particular, the methods addTo(), remove(), and find() use path expressions. We may add child nodes to a node specified by a path with addTo(). Similarly, remove() removes the child node addressed by the specified path from its parent node. The method find() returns the node at the specified path. There are further utility methods such as removeAll() or addToRoot(). All these PreferenceManager methods allow us to completely construct and manage a preference page tree.

The PreferenceDialog class

The class PreferenceDialog is an extension of the class Dialog (see Section 7.2). In addition to the Dialog methods, it features the methods setPreferenceStore() and getPreferenceStore() to set and retrieve a PreferenceStore instance. We must also specify a PreferenceManager instance as an additional parameter in the PreferenceDialog() constructor. This instance is used by the PreferenceDialog to organize the user interaction. The PreferenceDialog displays the tree managed by PreferenceManager on the left hand side of the dialog. When the user clicks on a tree node, the attached PreferencePage is opened on the right hand side of the dialog.

8 Project 2 – Jukebox

In this chapter we use a longer example to demonstrate the various techniques employed in the use of SWT and JFace. The example is a Java version of a 'jukebox', a device that can play sound files or lists of sound files, known as 'playlists'. We plan to implement the player's user interface using SWT and JFace. However, we don't want to implement the player as an Eclipse plug-in, but as a stand-alone application.

To make our jukebox a bit more interesting, we allow the association of a background image and a descriptive text with each entry in the playlist. By doing this we achieve nearly the same multimedia experience as with an old vinyl album collection, but without the crackles and hisses.

8.1 Design goals and how to achieve them

Before we begin the implementation, we should first perform a short requirements analysis:

- Our jukebox should be able to play diverse sound file formats, including MP3.

- We should be able to associate a title, a background image and a descriptive text with each sound file.

- We should be able to mark-up descriptive texts in some way. End users should get some assistance when editing descriptions, for example when inserting keywords into the text.

- We should be able to define individual playlists, to store the playlists, and to navigate within the playlists.

Constraints   During the implementation of these design goals we must take into consideration some technological constraints:

- For replaying sound files we need external modules. For this project we select the *JavaZoom* sound modules (www.javazoom.net). These modules support many sound formats, including MP3, and are completely written in Java. The modules are freely available and come with source code. They also include a nice player skin. However, the player GUI is different than what we want to implement.

- For the storage of playlists we have different options. For example, we could store the different playlist entries in a relational database and could query this database via SQL. Another possibility is to store a whole playlist in a single XML document. Access to the playlist entries can be organized via a DOM API (Eclipse already contains the Xerces DOM). We select the latter option for our implementation. Because of space limitations we only present the interface for the playlist's data model here and skip the discussion of its implementation. The complete source code is available from this book's Web site at www.bdaum.de.

What we want to learn

Apart from implementing a jukebox and listening to music, we also want to do some real work – that is, apply the topics discussed in previous chapters to a real world example. In particular, we discuss the following issues:

- Creation of GUI elements, layouts, and of SWT event processing. This applies in particular when implementing the main window of the jukebox.

- The application of a TableViewer for the presentation of playlists. This includes the implementation of custom cell editors for modifying playlists.

- Syntax highlighting in an editor based on a SourceViewer. In this editor we also demonstrate the implementation of a *Content Assistant*. We also equip the viewer with an *Undo* and *Redo* function.

- Communication between the SWT thread and other threads within the player.

8.2   Installing the project

First, we need the module for replaying sound files. We download the module *jlGui 2.1.1* from www.javazoom.net/jlgui/sources.html. The ZIP file found there is completely adequate for our purposes: the installer module is not required. After downloading the file we unzip it into an empty directory.

Now, we can create a new Eclipse Java project called Jukebox. You should already know how to do this. After entering the name on the first page of the *New Java Project wizard*, just click *Next*. On the second page we need to complete the *Java Build Path*.

First, we need some Eclipse JARs. Obviously, we need the JARs for SWT and for JFace, but we also need the JARs for text processing, and finally the Apache JARs for Xerces.

These are:

swt.jar   jface.jar   jfacetext.jar
(plus swt-pi.jar under Linux)

text.jar   xercesImpl.jar   XMLParserAPIs.jar

In addition, we need the JARs boot.jar and runtime.jar. Both belong to the Eclipse platform and are needed because JFace relies on them. This dependency should be dropped with Eclipse 3.0.

All these JARs are located in subfolders of the directory \eclipse\plugins. Because the names of these subfolders differ depending on the Eclipse version and on the platform, we only specify the above short names here. Your best option is to search these JARs with the search function of your operating system.

We also need all the JARs from the lib directory of the unpacked *jlGui* ZIP-file. These are:

j1020.jar   jogg-0.0.5.jar   jorbis-0.0.12.jar

mp3sp.1.4.jar   vorbissp0.6.jar.

Figure 8.1: The Java Build Path for the Jukebox project, here shown under Windows 2000.

After we have created this project, we import (see Section 2.9) three more files from the src directory of the unpacked *jlGui* archive:

`javazoom/jlGui/BasicPlayer.java`

`javazoom/jlGui/BasicPlayerListener.java`

`javazoom/Util/Debug.java`

By now, our project should have two Java packages: `javazoom.jlGui` and `javazoom.Util`.

Images   Finally we need a folder for images. Directly under the project we create a new folder named `icons`. In this folder we place a little warning icon that we "borrow" from Eclipse. We import the image named `alert_obj.gif` from the directory `\eclipse\plugins\org.eclipse.pde.ui_2.1.0\icons\full\obj16` into the newly created folder.

Actually, we do not necessarily have to invoke the import wizard to perform this task. Depending on the host operating system, we can just drag and drop the object that we want to import from the native directory into the target folder of the Eclipse navigator.

8.3   The player module

To get an idea of what the player should look like, we first make a sketch of its layout (see Figure 8.2). The windows for the descriptive text of the current tune and the window for the playlist should only be shown on demand. So, we allow for some buttons for opening and closing these windows.

Layout   In the main window we install a `Canvas` object that covers the full window. We will use this canvas to display the background image. On top of the `Canvas` object we mount the player's instrumentation and the status display. The instrumentation includes the usual player buttons *Start*, *Stop*, *Pause*, *Forward*, *Backward*, and the buttons for opening and closing the additional windows. We combine all the buttons in a toolbar.

In addition, we install a `Scale` instance. This scale should always display the current position in the playing tune. In addition, it should allow the user to freely navigate (scroll) in the tune. However, the *jlGui* engine supports this functionality only for WAV files. In case of other sound file formats, therefore, we lock the scale against modifications by the user.

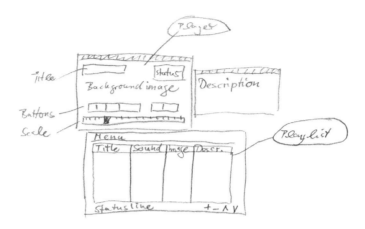

Figure 8.2: We design the layout of the jukebox using a sketch. This shows the main window, the windows for the playlist and the current tune's descriptive text.

The status display includes the status panel in the upper right corner and the title display in the upper left corner. The status panel shows the total length of the current tune and the current operational state. Both status display and tool bar are only shown as long as the mouse hovers over the canvas. When the mouse is gone, the background image is shown in its full beauty.

Threads　All these GUI elements must be updated during the operation of the player. For example, the operational state changes when the current tune is finished. The scale's handle must move during the player's operation from left to right, and the push buttons for the additional windows must be released when these windows are closed.

During the operation of the player two threads are active:

- The main() thread in which our player operates. This thread acts, too, as the SWT thread in which all SWT operations are performed.

- The thread of the *jlGui* engine. This must be a separate thread, otherwise our jukebox would be locked against user interaction as long as a tune plays.

Of course, this set-up causes some complications. The *jlGui* engine produces events that must be reflected in the user interface, so the SWT thread must react to those events. Unfortunately, SWT only accepts method calls from its own thread: method calls from other threads are rejected by throwing an exception.

We solve this problem by first storing the events from the *jlGui* engine in a field of the Player instance. Then we call the method updateGUI(). This method creates a new Runnable instance by calling the method display.asyncExec(). Within the run() method of this Runnable we update the GUI elements and – if necessary – start a new replay process. This is possible because this run() method is executed in the SWT thread (see also Section 6.5.3).

In the following sections we walk step by step through our player's source code. Of course, each compilation unit starts with the necessary package and import declarations. Then follows the class declaration and the declarations of all instance variables. Here we also define the fields holding the various GUI elements such as buttons, scale and windows. In addition, there are a few fields for storing the current state of the player.

The Player.java class

```
package com.bdaum.jukebox;

import java.io.File;
import java.io.IOException;

import javax.sound.sampled.LineUnavailableException;
import javax.sound.sampled.UnsupportedAudioFileException;

import javazoom.jlGui.BasicPlayer;
import javazoom.jlGui.BasicPlayerListener;

import org.eclipse.swt.SWT;
import org.eclipse.swt.events.*;
import org.eclipse.swt.graphics.GC;
import org.eclipse.swt.graphics.Image;
import org.eclipse.swt.graphics.Rectangle;
import org.eclipse.swt.layout.GridData;
import org.eclipse.swt.layout.GridLayout;
import org.eclipse.swt.layout.RowLayout;
import org.eclipse.swt.widgets.*;

/**
 * Player module. This module demonstrates the various techniques
 * of the SWT, in particular the coordination between SWT thread
 * and other threads.
 */
public class Player implements BasicPlayerListener {

    // Operation states
    private static final int PLAY = 1;
    private static final int PAUSE = 2;
    private static final int STOP = 3;
    private static final int EOM = 4;
```

```
                    // Text representation of operation state
                    private static final String PLAYING = "Playing";
                    private static final String PAUSED = "Paused";
                    private static final String IDLE = "Idle";

                    // Features in the playlist data model
                    public final static String TITLE = "title";
                    public final static String SOUNDFILE = "soundfile";
                    public final static String IMAGEFILE = "image";
                    public final static String DESCRIPTION = "description";

                    /* Data model of the player model */

                    // Current operation state
                    private int state = STOP;
                    // The player engine
                    private BasicPlayer soundPlayer;
                    // The playlist's data model
                    private IPlaylist playlistModel;
                    // Duration of current tune
                    private double lengthInSec = 0;
                    // Current position
                    private int currentPosition = 0;
                    // Maximum position
                    private int maxPosition = 0;
                    // Text representation of current operation state
                    private String mediaState = "Stopped";
                    // Current background image
                    private String currentImage;
                    // Title of current tune
                    private String currentTitle = "";
```

GUI elements

```
                    /*** GUI elements ***/
                    /* Widgets of player windows */

                    // Player shell
                    private Shell toplevelShell;
                    // Current Display instance
                    private Display display;
                    // Canvas for background image
                    private Canvas canvas;
                    // Status Panel
                    private Composite statusPanel;
                    private Label statusLabel, lengthLabel;
                    // Toolbar with buttons
                    private ToolBar toolbar;
                    private ToolItem backButton, playButton, pauseButton,
                      stopButton, forwardButton, playlistButton,
                        descriptionButton;
```

```
// Scale
private Scale scale;

// Additional windows
private DescriptionWindow descriptionWindow;
private PlaylistWindow playlistWindow;
```

main()

```
/**
 * Method main.
 * @param args - unused
 */
public static void main(String args[]) {
  Player player = new Player();
  player.run();
}
```

The method run() is similar to the SWT programs shown in Chapter 6. We create a Shell instance and construct the content of this shell in the constructPlayer()method. After opening the shell, we stay in the event loop, ensuring that the GUI is supplied with all occurring events.

In addition, we initially create the domain model of the playlist (see Section 8.4). Before the shell is opened, we create an instance of the *jlGui* engine by calling new Basic-Player(). When doing so, our player instance registers as a BasicPlayerListener with the engine.

```
/**
 * Method run. Initialize Player
 */
private void run() {
  // Create Playlist domain model
  playlistModel = new PlaylistModel();
  // Create Display instance
  display = new Display();
  // Create top level shell with the usual controls
  toplevelShell = new Shell(display, SWT.SHELL_TRIM);
  // Set title
  toplevelShell.setText("Jukebox");
  // Create rest of Player GUI
  constructPlayer(toplevelShell);
  // Adapt shell size to content
  toplevelShell.pack();
  // Create the jlGui-engine
  soundPlayer = new BasicPlayer(this);
  // Display shell
  toplevelShell.open();
  // Event loop
   while (!toplevelShell.isDisposed()) {
     // Check for waiting events
     if (!display.readAndDispatch())
```

```
            display.sleep();
        }
        // If necessary stop playing
        stop();
        // Force session exit -
        // otherwise the Java audio system would remain active
        System.exit(0);
    }

    /**
     * Method getPlaylist.
     * @return IPlaylist - the Playlist model
     */
    public IPlaylist getPlaylist() {
        return playlistModel;
    }
```

Create GUI We instrument the surface of the player in the method `constructPlayer()`. As we want to use the whole area as a canvas for the background images, we first add a `Canvas` instance to which we later can apply graphical operations. On this `Canvas` instance we place the controls (with the help of the methods `createToolbar()` and `createScale()`) and the status panel (`createStatusPanel()`). We register a `PaintListener` with the `Canvas` instance, because the correct method to draw something onto a `Canvas` is to do this in the `paintCanvas()` method of a `PaintListener`.

In addition, we register a `MouseTrackListener` with the `Canvas`. The listener allows us to hide the control elements when the mouse leaves the canvas area. When we move the mouse back to the canvas, the control elements appear again. The additional tests in the method `mouseExit()` are required to check that the mouse has really left the canvas area, as this method is called, too, when the mouse is moved over controls that hide the canvas area.

```
    /**
     * Method constructPlayer. Construction of the Player-GUI.
     * @param parent - containing Composite
     */
    private void constructPlayer(Composite parent) {
        // We use a GridLayout for the containing Composite
        parent.setLayout(new GridLayout());
        // Create Canvas
        canvas = new Canvas(parent, SWT.NONE);
        // Set preferred canvas size
        GridData data = new GridData();
        data.widthHint = 320;
        data.heightHint = 240;
        canvas.setLayoutData(data);
        // The Canvas instance acts as a Composite, too.
        // So we apply a GridLayout to it, too.
        GridLayout gridLayout = new GridLayout();
```

```
          gridLayout.marginHeight = 10;
          canvas.setLayout(gridLayout);
          // Construct status panel
          createStatusPanel();
          // Construct Toolbar
          createToolbar();
          // Construct scale
          createScale();
          // Add PaintListener to Canvas to support drawing
          canvas.addPaintListener(new PaintListener() {
            public void paintControl(PaintEvent e) {
              paintCanvas(e.gc);
            }
          });
          // Add MouseTrackListener to Canvas
          canvas.addMouseTrackListener(new MouseTrackAdapter() {
            public void mouseEnter(MouseEvent e) {
              setCanvasControlsVisible(true);
            }
            public void mouseExit(MouseEvent e) {
              Rectangle rect = canvas.getClientArea();
              // Check if mouse has really left the canvas area
              if (!rect.contains(e.x, e.y))
                setCanvasControlsVisible(false);
            }
          });
          setCanvasControlsVisible(false);
        }

        /**
         * Method setCanvasControlsVisible.
         * Shows or hides the control elements on top of the canvas.
         * @param v - true for showing, false for hiding
         */
        private void setCanvasControlsVisible(boolean v) {
          toolbar.setVisible(v);
          scale.setVisible(v);
        statusPanel.setVisible(v);
        }
```

Graphics operations   Here now is paintCanvas(), which is always invoked when the canvas needs to be redrawn. If we have an image file, we create from this image file a new Image instance. Then we draw this image onto the graphics context (GC) of the Canvas instance. Immediately afterwards we dispose of the Image instance (see also Section 6.7.1. and Section 6.7.4).

We then draw the title line over this background. For the background color and the text color we use system colors, so we don't need to dispose these colors.

```
/**
 * Method paintCanvas. Draw all graphical elements on the canvas
 * @param gc. The graphics context
 */
private void paintCanvas(GC gc) {
  // Check if we have an image file
  if (doesFileExist(currentImage)) {
    // Draw image
    Image image = new Image(display, currentImage);
    gc.drawImage(image, 0, 0);
    // Dispose image
    image.dispose();
  } else {
    // Otherwise fill background with gray color
    gc.setBackground(display.getSystemColor(SWT.COLOR_GRAY));
    gc.fillRectangle(canvas.getClientArea());
  }
  // Draw title of current sound file
  if (currentTitle != null && currentTitle.length() > 0) {
    gc.setBackground(display.getSystemColor(SWT.COLOR_DARK_GRAY));
    gc.setForeground(display.getSystemColor(SWT.COLOR_WHITE));
    gc.drawText(" " + currentTitle + " ", 5, 12, false);
  }
}

/**
 * Method doesFileExist.
 * Checks if a file with the specified name exists.
 * @param filename — File name
 * @return boolean - true, if the file exists
 */
private static boolean doesFileExist(String filename) {
  return (
    filename != null
    && filename.length() > 0
    && openFile(filename).exists());
}

/**
 * Method openFile.
 * Get the File instance for the specified file name
 * @param file — File name
 * @return File — File instance
 */
private static File openFile(String file) {
  return new File(file);
}
```

Instrumentation   Now, we place the control element onto the Canvas instance. The scale is used to display the current position in the sound file. In case of WAV files, it is possible to scroll within the sound file by moving the scale's handle. For this purpose we add a SelectionList-ener to the Scale instance. We perform the positioning within a tune in the widgetSelected() method of this listener by invoking the seek() method.

```
/**
 * Method createScale.
 * Creates a scale that shows the current position
 * in the sound file.
 */
private void createScale() {
  scale = new Scale(canvas, SWT.NONE);
  // Set preferred size of scale
  GridData data = new GridData();
  data.horizontalAlignment = GridData.CENTER;
  data.widthHint = 300;
  data.heightHint = 20;
  scale.setLayoutData(data);
  // Add event processing
  scale.addSelectionListener(new SelectionAdapter() {
    public void widgetSelected(SelectionEvent e) {
      seek();
    }
  });
}
```

The toolbar contains the usual buttons for operating a player. In addition, we implement two more buttons to allow us opening and closing the playlist and description windows. These buttons are created with the style constant SWT.CHECK to achieve a toggling behavior. We separate these two buttons from the rest of the buttons with another button that has the style constant SWT.SEPARATOR.

The event processing for all buttons is done in the method processButton(). Depending on the button – and in case of the last two buttons, also depending on the state of the button – this method calls the appropriate methods for controlling the player and opening and closing windows respectively.

By specifying a GridData instance appropriately we position the toolbar at the lower border of the player area.

```
/**
 * Method createToolbar.
 * Create toolbar with all buttons
 */
private void createToolbar() {
  // Create toolbar
  toolbar = new ToolBar(canvas, SWT.NONE);
  // Create all buttons
  backButton = makeToolItem(toolbar, SWT.PUSH, "<<", "Previous");
  playButton = makeToolItem(toolbar, SWT.PUSH, ">", "Play");
```

```
      pauseButton = makeToolItem(toolbar, SWT.PUSH, "||", "Pause");
      stopButton = makeToolItem(toolbar, SWT.PUSH, "[]", "Stop");
      forwardButton = makeToolItem(toolbar, SWT.PUSH, ">>",
        "Next");
      makeToolItem(toolbar, SWT.SEPARATOR, null, null);
      playlistButton =
        makeToolItem(toolbar, SWT.CHECK, "Playlist", "Show Playlist");
      descriptionButton = makeToolItem(toolbar, SWT.CHECK, "ShowText",
        "Show Description");
      // Create layout data for toolbar
      GridData data = new GridData();
      data.horizontalAlignment = GridData.CENTER;
      data.verticalAlignment = GridData.END;
      data.grabExcessHorizontalSpace = true;
      data.grabExcessVerticalSpace = true;
      toolbar.setLayoutData(data);
    }

    /**
     * Method makeToolItem.
     * Convenience method for creating a toolbar button
     * @param bar - the toolBar
     * @param style — the button type
     * @param text — text for the button face
     * @param tip — tool tip
     * @return ToolItem — the created toolbar button
     */
    private ToolItem makeToolItem(
      ToolBar bar,
      int style,
      String text,
      String tip) {
        ToolItem item = new ToolItem(bar, style);
        if (style != SWT.SEPARATOR) {
          item.setText(text);
          item.setToolTipText(tip);
          // Add event processing for button clicks
          item.addSelectionListener(new SelectionAdapter() {
            public void widgetSelected(final SelectionEvent e) {
              processButton(e);
            }
          });
        }
        return item;
      }
```

```
/**
 * Method processButton.
 * This method processes all ToolItem events.
 * @param e - the event object
 */
private void processButton(SelectionEvent e) {
  Widget widget = e.widget;
  if (widget == playButton) {
    play();
  } else if (widget == stopButton) {
    stop();
  } else if (widget == pauseButton) {
    pause();
  } else if (widget == forwardButton) {
    forward();
  } else if (widget == backButton) {
    back();
    // The following buttons are of type CHECK.
    // We must retrieve their state to react correctly.
  } else if (widget == descriptionButton) {
    if (descriptionButton.getSelection())
    showDescription();
    else
    hideDescription();
  } else if (widget == playlistButton) {
    if (playlistButton.getSelection())
    showPlaylist();
    else
    hidePlaylist();
  }
}
```

Finally, we create a small status panel that displays the current operation mode of the player and the total length of the current sound file. With the help of an appropriate GridData instance we position the panel to the top right corner.

```
/**
 * Method createStatusPanel.
 * Create status panel with total duration and operating mode.
 */
private void createStatusPanel() {
  // Create panel as a new Composite
  statusPanel = new Composite(canvas, SWT.NONE);
  // Create layout data for the panel
  GridData data = new GridData();
  data.horizontalAlignment = GridData.END;
  data.verticalAlignment = GridData.BEGINNING;
  data.grabExcessHorizontalSpace = true;
  statusPanel.setLayoutData(data);
  // We use a vertical RowLayout for the status panel
```

```
                    RowLayout rowLayout = new RowLayout();
                    rowLayout.type = SWT.VERTICAL;
                    rowLayout.wrap = false;
                    rowLayout.pack = false;
                    statusPanel.setLayout(rowLayout);
                    // Now we create the widgets of the status panel
                    lengthLabel = new Label(statusPanel, SWT.RIGHT);
                    lengthLabel.setText(timeFormat(0));
                    statusLabel = new Label(statusPanel, SWT.RIGHT);
                    statusLabel.setText(IDLE);
                }

                /**
                 * Method timeFormat.
                 * Convert the duration into an appropriate display format
                 * @param sec - Seconds
                 * @return String mm:ss.s
                 */
                private static String timeFormat(double sec) {
                    int sec10 = (int) (sec * 10);
                    return twoDigitFormat(sec10 / 600)
                        + ":"
                        + twoDigitFormat((sec10 / 10) % 60)
                        + "."
                        + (sec10 % 10);
                }

                /**
                 * Method twoDigitFormat.
                 * Format an integer into a two-digit string with leading zeros.
                 * @param n — the integer value
                 * @return String — the result string
                 */
                private static String twoDigitFormat(int n) {
                    if (n < 10)
                    return "0" + n;
                    return String.valueOf(n);
                }
```

Updating the SWT thread

The following method updateGUI() is intended to make state changes in the *jlGui* engine visible on the player's GUI. Since the engine runs in a different thread and this method is invoked from the thread, we cannot directly access the GUI elements, because they run in the SWT thread. We therefore encapsulate all these accesses into a Runnable which we pass to the Display instance via the asyncExec() method. For each event we update the status panel (see above). When the engine reaches the end of a sound file, we start playing the next sound file in the playlist.

```
/**
 * Method updateGUI.
 * Updates SWT-Widgets, caused by events from other threads, are
 * executed via this method. By performing the updates under the
 * SWT-thread (display.asyncExec()) we avoid an SWT thread error.
 */
private void updateGUI() {
  display.asyncExec(new Runnable() {
    public void run() {
      if (!toplevelShell.isDisposed()) {
        // Update scale
        scale.setMaximum(maxPosition);
        scale.setSelection(currentPosition);
        // Update operation mode
        updateText(statusLabel, mediaState);
        // Update total length
      updateText(lengthLabel, timeFormat(lengthInSec));
        // Check if we have to start the next sound file
        if (state == EOM) {
          state = STOP;
          forward();
        }
      }
    }
  });
}

/**
 * Method updateText.
 * @param c - the Label instance
 * @param s - the new text
 */
private void updateText(Label c, String s) {
  // test against current content to avoid screen flicker
  if (!c.getText().equals(s))
  c.setText(s);
}
```

Button functions   Now we implement some player functions that are invoked by a button press. All we
have to do in such a case is to update the player mode, update the status panel via the
method updateGUI(), and pass the invoked function to the *jlGui* engine.

Only the play() method is more elaborate. Here we fetch the data from the playlist
model (title, image, name of the sound file, and description). The Canvas instance is
updated with a new background image, and the window with the descriptive text is
updated. Then we initialize the *jlGui* engine and – depending on the file type of the
sound file – disable or enable the scale.

```java
/**
 * Method seek.
 * Positions in the sound file when the scale is modified
 * by the end user (only for .WAV files).
 */
private void seek() {
  try {
    double position =
    ((double) scale.getSelection()) /
    ((double) scale.getMaximum());
    soundPlayer.setSeek(position);
    updateGUI();
  } catch (IOException e) {
    System.out.println(e.toString());
  }
}

/**
 * Method stop. Stops playing.
 */
private void stop() {
  if (state != STOP) {
    soundPlayer.stopPlayback();
    state = STOP;
    mediaState = IDLE;
    lengthInSec = 0;
  }
  updateGUI();
}

/**
 * Method pause. Pauses the playing process.
 */
private void pause() {
  switch (state) {
    case PLAY :
      soundPlayer.pausePlayback();
      state = PAUSE;
      mediaState = PAUSED;
      break;
    case PAUSE :
      soundPlayer.resumePlayback();
      state = PLAY;
      mediaState = PLAYING;
  }
  updateGUI();
}
```

```
/**
 * Method play.
 * Starts playing.
 */
private void play() {
  if (state == PLAY)
  // Stop a current play process.
  stop();
  try {
    switch (state) {
      case PAUSE :
        // If the playing process was paused, we resume it.
        soundPlayer.resumePlayback();
        break;
      case STOP :
        // Otherwise we start all over again.
        // Fetch name of background image and title
        currentImage = playlistModel.getFeature(IMAGEFILE);
        currentTitle = playlistModel.getFeature(TITLE);
        // Update description window
        updateDescription();
        // Fetch name of sound file
        String filename =
          playlistModel.getFeature(SOUNDFILE);
        // We enforce a redraw of the canvas
        canvas.redraw();
        // Do nothing if the sound file does not
        // exist any more.
        if (!doesFileExist(filename))
          return;
        // Otherwise configure the engine
        soundPlayer.setDataSource(openFile(filename));
        soundPlayer.startPlayback();
        soundPlayer.setGain(0.5f);
        soundPlayer.setPan(0.5f);
        // We fetch the total duration of the sound file
        lengthInSec = soundPlayer.getTotalLengthInSeconds();
        maxPosition = (int) lengthInSec;
        // If the sound format is not WAV we deactivate
        // we disable the scale (no scrolling possible).
        boolean canSeek =
          ((soundPlayer.getAudioFileFormat() != null)
          && (soundPlayer.getAudioFileFormat().getType()
          .toString().startsWith("WAV")));
        scale.setEnabled(canSeek);
    }
    // Now we set the operation modus and update the GUI.
    state = PLAY;
    mediaState = PLAYING;
    updateGUI();
```

```
      } catch (UnsupportedAudioFileException e) {
        System.out.println(e.toString());
      } catch (LineUnavailableException e) {
        System.out.println(e.toString());
      } catch (IOException e) {
        System.out.println(e.toString());
      }
    }

    /**
     * Method forward.
     * If the playlist has a next element, we stop playing
     * the current sound file and start again with the next.
     */
    private void forward() {
      if (playlistModel.next()) {
        stop();
        play();
      }
    }

    /**
     * Method back.
     * If the playlist has a previous element, we stop playing
     * the current sound file and start again with the previous.
     */
    private void back() {
      if (playlistModel.previous()) {
        stop();
        play();
      }
    }
```

Managing windows The following three methods are used to open a window for the descriptive text, to update this text, and to close the window. The description window is implemented as the class DescriptionWindow, a subclass of Window. We create and initialize an instance of the class, get its Shell instance, position the window to an appropriate location, and instrument the Shell instance with a ShellListener that informs us when the window is closed. When the window is closed, we also reset the corresponding button on the toolbar.

```
    /**
     * Method showDescription.
     * Creates a new DescriptionViewer if it not yet exists.
     * Supplies the DescriptionViewer with new text content.
     */
    private void showDescription() {
      if (descriptionWindow == null) {
        // Create window
        descriptionWindow = new DescriptionWindow(
```

```
            toplevelShell, playlistModel);
          // Initialize window
          descriptionWindow.create();
          // Fetch Shell instance
          Shell shell = descriptionWindow.getShell();
          Rectangle bounds = toplevelShell.getBounds();
          // Position at the right hand side of the main window
          shell.setBounds(
            bounds.x + bounds.width - 5,
            bounds.y + 10,
            320, 240);
          // React to shell's close button
          shell.addShellListener(new ShellAdapter() {
            public void shellClosed(ShellEvent e) {
              // Update toolbar button
              hideDescription();
            }
          });
          // Open the window
          descriptionWindow.open();
      }
  }

  /**
   * Method hideDescription.
   * Closes the description window
   */
  private void hideDescription() {
    // Reset the description toolbar button
    descriptionButton.setSelection(false);
    // Close window
    if (descriptionWindow != null) {
      descriptionWindow.close();
      descriptionWindow = null;
    }
  }

  /**
   * Method updateDescriptionWindow.
   * Updates the window with new text
   */
  private void updateDescription() {
    if (descriptionWindow != null)
    descriptionWindow.update();
  }
```

Managing the playlist window is very similar:

```
/**
 * Method showPlaylist.
 * Creates a new playlist window
 */
private void showPlaylist() {
  if (playlistWindow == null) {
    // Create new PlaylistWindow instance
    playlistWindow = new PlaylistWindow(toplevelShell,
      playlistModel);
    // Initialize the window to allow us to retrieve
    // the shell instance
    playlistWindow.create();
    Shell shell = playlistWindow.getShell();
    // React to the shell's close button
    shell.addShellListener(new ShellAdapter() {
      public void shellClosed(ShellEvent e) {
        hidePlaylist();
      }
    });
    // Position the shell below the main window
    Rectangle bounds = toplevelShell.getBounds();
    shell.setBounds(
      bounds.x + bounds.width / 8,
      bounds.y + bounds.height - 5,
      400, 240);
    // Open the window
    playlistWindow.open();
  }
}

/**
 * Method hidePlaylist.
 * Closes playlist window
 */
private void hidePlaylist() {
  // Reset playlist toolbar button
  playlistButton.setSelection(false);
  // Close window
  if (playlistWindow != null) {
    playlistWindow.close();
    playlistWindow = null;
  }
}
```

BasicPlayerListener   At last in this section, we show the methods that implement the interface BasicPlayer-
Listener. These methods accept the events from the *jlGui* engine. We use the
updateGUI() method (see above) to update the user interface accordingly.

```
/**
 * @see javazoom.jlGui.BasicPlayerListener#updateMediaData(byte)
 */
public void updateMediaData(byte[] data) {
}

/**
 * @see javazoom.jlGui.BasicPlayerListener#
 * updateMediaState(java.lang.String)
 */
public void updateMediaState(String newState) {
    // At file end set operation mode to IDLE
    if (newState.equals("EOM") && state != STOP) {
        this.state = EOM;
        mediaState = IDLE;
        // Update GUI
        updateGUI();
    }
}

/**
 * @see javazoom.jlGui.BasicPlayerListener#updateCursor(int, int)
 */
public void updateCursor(int cursor, int total) {
    // Save maximum position and current position; update GUI
    maxPosition = total;
    currentPosition = cursor;
    updateGUI();
}
}
```

8.4   The playlist domain model

The domain model of the playlist does not offer much possibility to apply what we have learned in the previous chapters – it has nothing at all to do with user interfaces. Instead, the responsibility of this model is to manage the playlist data. We therefore only represent the API of the model, and refrain from including the implementation in this book. The complete code is available at www.bdaum.de.

The concept of the playlist domain model is quite generic. Entries within the playlist may be decorated with any kind of features that can be configured through the API. In class Playlist (Section 8.3) we saw that the playlist model is configured with the feature identifications TITLE, SOUNDFILE, IMAGEFILE, and DESCRIPTON. The functions of the playlist domain model include setting and retrieving the values of these features, the positioning within the playlist, and adding or removing playlist entries.

In addition to these basic functions, the playlist model also includes the methods of the ISelectionProvider interface. These methods allow adding and removing Selection-Listener instances in the playlist model. The model can inform these listeners when its content or state changes. The methods of the IStructuredContentProvider interface such as getElements(), inputChanged(), and dispose() are also included. The getElements() method is used by the PlaylistViewer to fetch the playlist entries to be displayed. The PlaylistViewer signals to the model that a new playlist was opened via the method inputChanged(). Finally, dispose() is called when the PlaylistViewer is disposed of. Here the model implementation could, for example, close open files.

The IPlaylist.java interface

```
package com.bdaum.jukebox;

import org.eclipse.jface.viewers.ISelectionProvider;
import org.eclipse.jface.viewers.IStructuredContentProvider;

public interface IPlaylist
   extends IStructuredContentProvider, ISelectionProvider {

  /**
   * Method getPlaylistName.
   * Returns the name of the current playlist
   * or null if no playlist active
   * @return String — Name of current playlist
   */
  public String getPlaylistName();
  /**
   * Method getFeature.
   * Returns the specified feature of the current playlist entry.
   * @param feature — Feature identification
   * @return String — Feature value
   */
  public String getFeature(String feature);
  /**
   * Method getFeature.
   * Returns the specified feature of the specified playlist element.
   * @param record - Playlist element
   * @param feature - Feature identification
   * @return String — Feature value
   */
  public String getFeature(Object record, String feature);
  /**
   * Method setFeature.
   * Sets the specified feature of the specified playlist element
   * to the specified value.
   * @param record - Playlist element
   * @param feature - Feature identification
```

```
 * @param value – new Feature value
 */
public void setFeature(Object record, String feature,
  String value);
/**
 * Method next.
 * Positions to the next playlist entry.
 * @return boolean - true if successfull
 */
public boolean next();
/**
 * Method hasNext.
 * Tests if we have a next entry in the playlist
 * @return boolean - true if successfull
 */
public boolean hasNext();
/**
 * Method previous.
 * Positions to the previous playlist entry.
 * @return boolean - true if successfull
 */
public boolean previous();
/**
 * Method hasPrevious.
 * Tests if we have a previous entry in the playlist
 * @return boolean - true if successfull
 */
public boolean hasPrevious();
/**
 * Method setCurrent.
 * Sets the current position of the playlist onto
 * the specified playlist element.
 * @param current – The new current playlist entry
 */
public void setCurrent(Object current);

/**
 * Method deleteCurrent.
 * Deletes the current playlist entry.
 * The next playlist entry becomes the current entry.
 * If none exists, the previous playlist entry becomes the
 * current entry. If this does not exist, too, the
 * current playlist entry is undefined (null).
 */
public void deleteCurrent();
```

```
/**
 * Method insert.
 * Creates a new playlist entry in front of the current playlist
 * entry. The new playlist entry becomes the current
 * playlist entry.
 * @return Object — The new playlist element
 */
public Object insert();

/**
 * Method moveUpwards.
 * Moves the current playlist entry one position
 * towards the beginning
 * of the playlist.
 * @return boolean - true if successfull
 */
public boolean moveUpwards();

/**
 * Method moveDownwards.
 * Moves the current playlist entry one position towards the end
 * of the playlist.
 * @return boolean - true if successfull
 */
public boolean moveDownwards();
}
```

8.5   The description window

The description window is based on the JFace class Window (see Section 7.2). It shows the descriptive text of the current playlist entry as long as the entry is being played. The window is positioned at the right hand side of the player window and is updated with each new playlist entry replayed.

This window gives us the opportunity to show StyledText in action (see Section 6.5.13). Text is displayed multi-colored: specific keywords within the text are shown in a different color and bold text style.

We do this with the help of class KeywordLineStylers, which we create as a subclass of LineStyleListener. The method lineGetStyle() from this class is called by the StyledText widget for each displayed text line. In this method call the whole text of a line and the position of the line in the complete text is passed to KeywordLineStylers. We then search for all words starting with '$' (our keywords) and create a StyleRange instance for each of these words. In this instance we set the text color and the text style differently than the rest of the text, and specify the absolute position of the word and its length.

The DescriptionWindow class

```
package com.bdaum.jukebox;

import java.util.ArrayList;
import java.util.List;

import org.eclipse.jface.window.Window;
import org.eclipse.swt.SWT;
import org.eclipse.swt.custom.LineStyleEvent;
import org.eclipse.swt.custom.LineStyleListener;
import org.eclipse.swt.custom.StyleRange;
import org.eclipse.swt.custom.StyledText;
import org.eclipse.swt.graphics.Color;
import org.eclipse.swt.layout.FillLayout;
import org.eclipse.swt.widgets.Composite;
import org.eclipse.swt.widgets.Control;
import org.eclipse.swt.widgets.Display;
import org.eclipse.swt.widgets.Shell;

public class DescriptionWindow extends Window {

  /**
   * This LineStyleListener a StyleRange instance
   * for each keyword in a text line in order
   * to display that keyword in a different color and
   * bold text style
   */
  class KeywordLineStyler implements LineStyleListener {

    /*
     * Is called by the StyledText widget for formatting a text line
     */
    public void lineGetStyle(LineStyleEvent event) {
      List styles = new ArrayList();
      String lineText = event.lineText;
      // Get system color. We must not dispose this color
      // as it was not created by us.
      Color color = display.getSystemColor(SWT.COLOR_DARK_CYAN);
      int e = 0;
      while (e < lineText.length()) {
        // Find start of keyword
        int dollar = lineText.indexOf('$', e);
        if (dollar < 0)
          break;
        // Find end of keyword
        e = lineText.indexOf(' ', dollar);
        if (e < 0)
          e = lineText.length();
```

```
            // Create StyleRange instance for keyword
            // We specify a text color and a text style
            // but no background color (null)
            StyleRange style =
              new StyleRange(event.lineOffset + dollar,
              e - dollar, color, null);
            style.fontStyle = SWT.BOLD;
            styles.add(style);
          }
          // Return an array of StyleRange instances
          event.styles = new StyleRange[styles.size()];
          styles.toArray(event.styles);
      }
    }
```

When instantiating the `DescriptionWindow` instance, the playlist domain model is passed to this instance. It is used when the window is opened or updated: the text is retrieved from the `DESCRIPTION` feature of the current playlist entry and replaces the content of the `StyledText` widget.

This widget was created in the method `createContents()`, which is called by the parent class `Window` when `create()` is executed. In addition, the `StyledText` widget is configured, it is locked against user interaction and the `KeywordLineStyler` shown above is registered via the method `addLineStyleListener()`.

```
    // The text area
    private StyledText textArea;
    // The playlist model
    private IPlaylist model;
    // The current Display instance
    private Display display;
    // The LineStyleListener instance for text formatting
    private KeywordLineStyler lineStyler = new KeywordLineStyler();

    /**
     * Constructor.
     * @param parent – The containing shell
     * @param model – The playlist model
     */

    public DescriptionWindow(Shell parent, IPlaylist model) {
        super(parent);
        display = parent.getDisplay();
        this.model = model;
    }
```

```
/**
 * This method is called from parent class Window.
 * Here, we construct the window content.
 */
protected Control createContents(Composite parent) {
  parent.setLayout(new FillLayout());
  Composite composite = new Composite(parent, SWT.NONE);
  composite.setLayout(new FillLayout());
  // Create text field
  textArea = new StyledText(composite,
    SWT.BORDER | SWT.MULTI | SWT.V_SCROLL | SWT.H_SCROLL);
  textArea.setEditable(false);
  textArea.addLineStyleListener(lineStyler);
  Color bg = parent.getDisplay().getSystemColor(SWT.COLOR_WHITE);
  textArea.setBackground(bg);
  return composite;
}

/**
 * Method update.
 * Set content of text area
 */
public void update() {
  String description = model.getFeature(Player.DESCRIPTION);
  textArea.setText((description == null) ? "" : description);
}
/**
 * Overriden open() method from class Window.
 * We want to update the text field when the window is opened.
 */
public int open() {
  update();
  return super.open();
}
}
```

8.6   The Playlist viewer

The playlist viewer runs in its own window (PlaylistWindow) and allows opening, creating, and modifying a playlist. The viewer is equipped with specialized cell editors for the individual playlist entries. The playlist domain model serves as a *Content Provider* for the playlist viewer.

To visualize the cooperation between player, playlist viewer, playlist window, and playlist domain model, we show the event processing for the playlist as an interaction diagram (Figure 8.3).

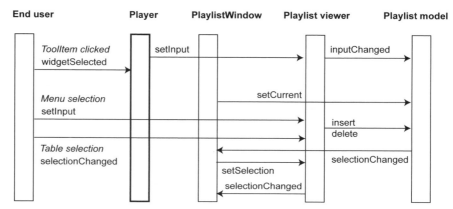

Figure 8.3: The interaction between the different playlist components. In principle there is a possibility of event loops. However, we can avoid these loops by passing events only when an event means a real change (for example in the playlist model).

An interesting problem occurred when performing the insert() operation. This method causes a change of selection. Consequently, the model sends a selectionChanged event to the playlist window, which passes it on to the viewer via method setSelection(). The viewer performs this selection. However, at this time, the new element has not yet been inserted into the Table widget. Consequently, setting the selection for this element results in a null selection. This, again, is send as an selectionChanged to the playlist viewer. The viewer then also sets the selection in the model to null by calling method setCurrent()! This is certainly not our intention. We solve this problem by invoking the viewer's refresh() method from the selectionChanged() method before calling setSelection(). By doing this we enforce an update of the Table instance according to the content of the playlist model.

The PlaylistWindow class

```
package com.bdaum.jukebox;

import org.eclipse.jface.viewers.ISelectionChangedListener;
import org.eclipse.jface.viewers.IStructuredSelection;
import org.eclipse.jface.viewers.SelectionChangedEvent;
import org.eclipse.jface.window.Window;
import org.eclipse.swt.SWT;
import org.eclipse.swt.layout.FillLayout;
import org.eclipse.swt.widgets.Composite;
import org.eclipse.swt.widgets.Control;
import org.eclipse.swt.widgets.Shell;
```

```
public class PlaylistWindow extends Window
   implements ISelectionChangedListener {

  PlaylistViewer viewer;
  Player player;
  IPlaylist model;

  /**
   * Constructor.
   * @param parent — The containing shell
   * @param player - The player
   */
  public PlaylistWindow(Shell parent, IPlaylist model) {
    super(parent);
    this.model = model;
  }
```

In the createContents() method that is called from the parent class Window (see Section 7.2), PlaylistWindow constructs the window content. In particular, an instance of the class PlaylistViewer (a subclass of TableViewer) is created. This viewer is configured with the help of style constants: we allow horizontal and vertical scrolling, only single table rows may be selected, and the whole table row appears selected.

Then the viewer is equipped with event processing. When a row is selected, the selectionChanged() method is invoked. This method retrieves the selection object from the event object. The selected table entry is the first element in the selection object. This table entry is passed, via the method setCurrent(), to the playlist model to update the selection there.

Finally, we initialize the viewer by fetching the file name of the current playlist from the playlist model and passing this name to the viewer via the setInput() method.

```
protected Control createContents(Composite parent) {
  parent.setLayout(new FillLayout());
  Composite composite = new Composite(parent, SWT.NONE);
  composite.setLayout(new FillLayout());
  viewer = new PlaylistViewer(composite,
  SWT.SINGLE | SWT.VERTICAL | SWT.H_SCROLL
    | SWT.V_SCROLL | SWT.BORDER | SWT.FULL_SELECTION, model);
  // Add event processing for selection events
  viewer.addSelectionChangedListener(new
    ISelectionChangedListener() {
    public void selectionChanged(SelectionChangedEvent e) {
      IStructuredSelection selection =
        (IStructuredSelection) e.getSelection();
      // Get selected table entry
      Object selected = selection.getFirstElement();
      // and pass to playlist model
```

```
            model.setCurrent(selected);
        }
    });
    // Get current playlist
    String playlistFile = model.getPlaylistName();
    // and set as input data
    viewer.setInput(playlistFile);
    return composite;
}
```

In the following code we have overridden the two Window methods open() and close().
In the open() method we update the selection of the viewer and register as a Selection-
Listener with the playlist model. Changes in the playlist model are consequently
passed to the method selectionChanged(). In this method we update the viewer's Table
widget by calling refresh(). Then we update the selection of the viewer. Finally, in
method close() we deregister as a SelectionListener from the playlist model.

```
/*
 * Open window and register with the model
 */
public int open() {
    // Update the viewers selection
    viewer.setSelection(model.getSelection());
    // Register as a SelectionChangedListener
    model.addSelectionChangedListener(this);
    // Open window
    return super.open();
}

/*
 * Close window and deregister from the model
 */
public boolean close() {
    // deregister as a SelectionChangedListener
    model.removeSelectionChangedListener(this);
    // Close window
    return super.close();
}

/*
 * Model has changed — we have to update the viewer
 */
public void selectionChanged(SelectionChangedEvent event) {
    // Force table update
    viewer.refresh();
    // Update selection
    viewer.setSelection(model.getSelection());
}
}
```

The PlaylistViewer class

The playlist viewer is defined as a subclass of the JFace class TableViewer. First, we instrument the PlaylistViewer instance with a ContentProvider, a LabelProvider, cell editors, modifiers and column identifications. For a cell editor, we use the standard TextCellEditor, but with the following exceptions: we edit file names with our own FileCellEditor (see below), and for descriptions we use the DescriptionCellEditor discussed in Section 8.7.

Then we modify the layout and the presentation of the table somewhat, and we add a menu, a status line and a toolbar. For the layout we use a nested GridLayout. First, we place the status line and the toolbar into a two-column GridLayout (which results in one row). Then we place the Composite together with the Table instance into a one-column GridLayout.

The menu is added directly to the shell of the playlist window. The menu functions bring up file selection dialogs for opening existing playlists and for creating new playlists.

The toolbar contains functions for creating, deleting and moving playlist elements. The ToolItem events directly result in the invocation of the corresponding operations in the playlist model. Such operations may, of course, change the current element in the playlist model. The model therefore creates an appropriate SelectionChangedEvent, which is received by the playlist window. The window instance then uses the method setSelection() to update the selection in the PlaylistViewer.

```
package com.bdaum.jukebox;

import java.io.File;
import org.eclipse.jface.dialogs.MessageDialog;
import org.eclipse.jface.viewers.*;
import org.eclipse.swt.SWT;
import org.eclipse.swt.events.SelectionAdapter;
import org.eclipse.swt.events.SelectionEvent;
import org.eclipse.swt.layout.GridData;
import org.eclipse.swt.layout.GridLayout;
import org.eclipse.swt.widgets.*;

/**
 * This class implements a viewer for playlists
 */
public class PlaylistViewer extends TableViewer {

  // File extension for for playlists
  public final static String PLS = ".jpl";
  // Filter for the selection of playlist files
  public final static String[] PLAYLISTEXTENSIONS =
    new String[] { "*" + PLS };
```

```
// Filter for the selection of sound files
public final static String[] SOUNDEXTENSIONS = new String[] {
"*.m3u;*.wsz;*.mpg;*.snd;*.aifc;*.aif;*.wav;*.au;*.mp1;" +
"*.mp2;*.mp3;*.ogg", "*.*" };
// Filter for the selection of image files
public final static String[] IMAGEEXTENSIONS =
new String[] { "*.gif; *.jpg; *.jpeg; *.png; *.bmp", "*.*" };

// the playlist model instance
private IPlaylist playlistModel;
// the label provider for the table
private ITableLabelProvider labelProvider;

// Widgets
private MenuItem newPlaylistItem;
private MenuItem openPlaylistItem;
private Label statusLine;
private ToolItem insertButton;
private ToolItem deleteButton;
private ToolItem upButton;
private ToolItem downButton;
```

CellModifier

Here we define an instance of type ICellModifier as a singleton. This instance organizes the data transfer between the model and the table cells. To set the value of a table cell, the method getValue() is called. The parameter property contains the feature identification that corresponds to the respective column of the table cell. We use this identification to fetch the cell value from the playlist model.

Vice versa, when a cell value is modified by the end user, we also must set it in the model. Here again we receive the feature identification in the parameter property. The feature value is passed in the value parameter. However, the use of this method is not consistent in regards to the element parameter. In some cases, the data element of the table row as passed in this parameter, in other cases, the TableItem instance of the table row is passed instead. We therefore check the type of the parameter value and act accordingly. In addition, we validate all entered values: empty titles and empty sound file names are not allowed.

```
private ICellModifier cellModifier = new ICellModifier() {
  // Get value from model
  public Object getValue(Object element, String property) {
    return playlistModel.getFeature(element, property);
  }
  // All elements may be modified by the end user
  public boolean canModify(Object element, String property) {
    return true;
  }
  // Set value in the model
  public void modify(Object element, String property,
    Object value) {
```

```
        // ATTENTION: A TableItem instance may be passed as element
        // In this case we retrieve the playlist entry from
        // the TableItem
        if (element instanceof Item)
          element = ((Item) element).getData();
        // To be safe we validate the new value
        if (validateFeature(property, (String) value) == null) {
          // OK, we set the new value in the model
          playlistModel.setFeature(element, property,
            (String) value);
          // Refresh the viewer so that the new value is
          // shown in the table
          PlaylistViewer.this.refresh();
        }
      }
    };

    /**
     * Method validateFeature.
     * Validates a feature
     * @param tag – Feature name
     * @param value - Value
     * @return String – Error message or null
     */
    public String validateFeature(String tag, String value) {
      if (tag == Player.TITLE) {
        // Empty titles are not valid
        if (value == null || value.length() == 0)
          return "Must specify a title";
      } else if (tag == Player.SOUNDFILE) {
        // Empty sound file names are not valid
        if (value == null || value.length() == 0)
          return "Must specify a sound file";
      }
      return null;
    }
```

In the constructor of the PlaylistViewer we configure the viewer instance. As a ContentProvider (the instance that provides the table entries) we register the playlist model. As a LabelProvider (the instance that is responsible for formatting the table elements) we create a new PlaylistLabelProvider instance (see below).

Then we fetch the viewer's table object. We attach a special cell editor and a validator to each column of the table. The individual columns are identified by the feature identifications. For the column containing the song titles we create a TextCellEditor, for the columns with the sound files and the image files we create FileCellEditors, and for the column containing the descriptions we create a DescriptionCellEditor. While the TextCellEditor already belongs to the JFace functionality, the other two editors must be implemented by us. The validators are created as anonymous inner classes of type ICellEditorValidator with the help of the setCellValidator() method.

Finally, we register the CellModifier created above, create column headers, make column headers and grid lines visible, and add the menu and the status line to the viewer.

```
/**
 * Constructor for PlaylistViewer.
 * @param parent - containing Composite
 * @param style — Style constants
 * @param model — Playlist domain model
 */
public PlaylistViewer(Composite parent, int style,
    IPlaylist model) {
    // Viewer erzeugen (TableViewer)
    super(parent, style);
    playlistModel = model;
```

Content- and LabelProvider

```
    // Create LabelProvider
    labelProvider = new PlaylistLabelProvider(playlistModel);
    // Set Content- and LabelProvider
    setContentProvider(playlistModel);
    setLabelProvider(labelProvider);
```

Cell editors

```
    // Create cell editors and validators
    // First the editor for song titles
    Table table = getTable();
    TextCellEditor titleEditor = new TextCellEditor(table);
    setCellValidator(titleEditor, Player.TITLE);
    // Then the editor for the sound file
    FileCellEditor soundFileEditor = new FileCellEditor(table,
        "Select sound file", SOUNDEXTENSIONS);
    setCellValidator(soundFileEditor, Player.SOUNDFILE);
    // Then the editor for the image file
    FileCellEditor imageFileEditor = new FileCellEditor(table,
        "Select image file", IMAGEEXTENSIONS);
    setCellValidator(imageFileEditor, Player.IMAGEFILE);
    // Then the editor for the description
    DescriptionCellEditor descriptionEditor =
        new DescriptionCellEditor(table, playlistModel);
    setCellValidator(descriptionEditor, Player.DESCRIPTION);
    // Now we pass all editors to the viewer
    // The sequence corresponds with the column sequence
    setCellEditors(new CellEditor[] {titleEditor, soundFileEditor,
        imageFileEditor,descriptionEditor });
    // Set cell modifier
    setCellModifier(cellModifier);
    // Set column identifiers
    setColumnProperties(new String[] {Player.TITLE,
        Player.SOUNDFILE, Player.IMAGEFILE, Player.DESCRIPTION });
```

Presentation

```
// Create column headers
createColumn(table, "Title", 80);
createColumn(table, "Sound file", 120);
createColumn(table, "Image file", 100);
createColumn(table, "Description", 240);
// Make column headers and grid lines visible
table.setHeaderVisible(true);
table.setLinesVisible(true);
// We still need a menu, a toolbar, and a status line
```

Additional widgets

```
constructMenu(parent.getShell());
// Add status line
addStatusLineAndButtons(table);
}
```

Validator for cell editors

```
/**
 * Method setCellValidator.
 * Set validators for cell editors
 * @param editor – The cell editor
 * @param feature – The feature identification
 */
public void setCellValidator(CellEditor editor,
  final String feature) {
  editor.setValidator(new ICellEditorValidator() {
    // isValid is called by the cell editor when the
    // cell content was modified
    public String isValid(Object value) {
      // We validate the cell content
      String errorMessage =
        validateFeature(feature, (String) value);
      // and show the error message in the status line
      setErrorMessage(errorMessage);
      // The cell editor wants the error message
      // What it does with it is unknown
      return errorMessage;
    }
  });
}

/**
 * Method createColumn.
 * Create column header
 * @param table - Table
 * @param header - Label
 * @param width – Column width
 */
private void createColumn(Table table, String header, int width) {
  TableColumn col = new TableColumn(table, SWT.LEFT);
  col.setText(header);
```

```
        col.setWidth(width);
    }
```

Nested grid layout   Since the inherited TableViewer only contains a table, we need to 'improve' it a bit. In addition to the table, we add the status line and the toolbar. To do so, we fetch the parent Composite of the table. On this Composite we apply a one-column GridLayout via the setLayout() method (see Section 6.6.4). Then we add a new Composite (statusGroup) to this Composite. This new Composite will appear below the table. Now we apply a two-column GridLayout to statusGroup. Then we add a new Label to statusGroup, which will appear at the left hand side. This new label acts as a status line. Finally, we add a ToolBar to statusGroup. This toolbar will appear at the right hand side of status-Group. By using different GridData instances, we make the table as big as possible, we give statusGroup and the status line the maximum width, and we align the toolbar to the right. Finally, we set the text color of the status line to red.

```
/*
 * Method addStatusLineAndButtons.
 * Adds a status line and a toolbar
 * @param table - the viewers Table instance
 */
private void addStatusLineAndButtons(Table table) {
    // fetch parent Composite
    Composite parent = table.getParent();
    // we use a one-column GridLayout for this Composite.
    GridLayout gridLayout = new GridLayout();
    gridLayout.marginHeight = 0;
    gridLayout.marginWidth = 2;
    gridLayout.verticalSpacing = 3;
    parent.setLayout(gridLayout);
    // Create Composite for statusline and toolbar
    Composite statusGroup = new Composite(parent, SWT.NONE);
    // For this Composite we use a two-column GridLayout
    gridLayout = new GridLayout();
    gridLayout.numColumns = 2;
    gridLayout.marginHeight = 0;
    gridLayout.marginWidth = 0;
    statusGroup.setLayout(gridLayout);
    // Create status line
    statusLine = new Label(statusGroup, SWT.BORDER);
    // Create toolbar
    ToolBar toolbar = createToolbar(statusGroup);
    // Set table to maximum size
    GridData data = new GridData();
    data.horizontalAlignment = GridData.FILL;
    data.verticalAlignment = GridData.FILL;
    data.grabExcessHorizontalSpace = true;
    data.grabExcessVerticalSpace = true;
    table.setLayoutData(data);
    // Set statusGroup to maximum width
```

```
                  data = new GridData();
                  data.horizontalAlignment = GridData.FILL;
                  data.grabExcessHorizontalSpace = true;
                  statusGroup.setLayoutData(data);
                  // Set status line to maximum width
                  data = new GridData();
                  data.horizontalAlignment = GridData.FILL;
                  data.grabExcessHorizontalSpace = true;
                  statusLine.setLayoutData(data);
                  data = new GridData();
                  // Align the toolbar to the right
                  data.horizontalAlignment = GridData.END;
                  toolbar.setLayoutData(data);
                  // Set status line text color to red
                  statusLine.setForeground(
                    parent.getDisplay().getSystemColor(SWT.COLOR_RED));
              }

              /**
               * Method setErrorMessage.
               * @param errorMessage — error message or null
               */
              public void setErrorMessage(String errorMessage) {
                statusLine.setText((errorMessage == null) ? "" : errorMessage);
              }
```

Toolbar   The toolbar (see Section 6.5.13) is equipped with four buttons for adding new songs to
                 the playlist, deleting songs, and moving entries upwards or downwards. The event
                 processing for these buttons is done in the processToolEvent() method. Depending on
                 the button pressed, the appropriate operation is performed.

```
              /**
               * Method createToolbar.
               * Creates toolbar with all buttons
               * @param parent - containing Composite
               * @return ToolBar - created ToolBar instance
               */
              private ToolBar createToolbar(Composite parent) {
                ToolBar toolbar = new ToolBar(parent, SWT.VERTICAL | SWT.FLAT);
                // Create buttons
                insertButton = makeToolItem(toolbar, "+", "Insert new entries");
                deleteButton = makeToolItem(toolbar, "-",
                  "Delete selected entry");
                upButton = makeToolItem(toolbar, "^",
                  "Move selected entry one step up");
                downButton = makeToolItem(toolbar, "v",
                  "Move selected entry one step down");
                return toolbar;
              }
```

```
/*
 * Method makeToolItem.
 * Create button.
 * @param parent — The toolbar
 * @param text - Label
 * @param toolTipText — The hover text
 * @return ToolItem — the created ToolItem instance
 */
private ToolItem makeToolItem(ToolBar parent, String text,
  String toolTipText) {
  ToolItem button = new ToolItem(parent, SWT.PUSH);
  button.setText(text);
  button.setToolTipText(toolTipText);
  // Add event processing
  button.addSelectionListener(new SelectionAdapter() {
    public void widgetSelected(SelectionEvent e) {
      processToolEvent(e);
    }
  });
  return button;
}

/*
 * Method processToolEvent.
 * @param e — The event object
 */
private void processToolEvent(SelectionEvent e) {
  // Get ToolItem instance form event object
  ToolItem item = (ToolItem) e.widget;
  if (item == insertButton) {
    // Create new playlist entries
    getSoundFiles(item.getParent().getShell());
  } else if (item == deleteButton) {
    // Delete playlist entry
    playlistModel.deleteCurrent();
  } else if (item == upButton) {
    // Move playlist entry upwards
    playlistModel.moveUpwards();
  } else if (item == downButton) {
    // Move playlist entry downwards
    playlistModel.moveDownwards();
  }
  refresh();
}
```

File selection dialogs

A FileDialog (see Section 6.5.4) is used to add new sound files to a playlist. It allows the selection of one or several sound files from the file system. We explicitly enable the option to select more than one file in one step. We restrict the selection list to the sound file types declared in constant SOUNDEXTENSIONS with the method setFilterExtensions(). Finally we create a new entry in the playlist model for each selected file. The required song title is initially derived from the file name.

```
/**
 * Method getSoundFiles.
 * @param shell – Parent shell of dialog
 */
private void getSoundFiles(Shell shell) {
  // Create file selection dialog
  FileDialog dialog =
    new FileDialog(shell,SWT.OPEN | SWT.MULTI);
  dialog.setFilterExtensions(SOUNDEXTENSIONS);
  dialog.setText("Select sound files");
  String title = "New playlist entry";
  if (dialog.open() != null) {
    String root = dialog.getFilterPath() + File.separatorChar;
    String[] filenames = dialog.getFileNames();
    for (int i = filenames.length - 1; i >= 0; i--) {
      // Compute the absolute file name
      String filename = root + filenames[i];
      // Derive the initial song title from the file name
      File file = new File(filename);
      title = file.getName();
      int p = title.lastIndexOf('.');
      if (p > 0)
        title = title.substring(0, p);
      // Insert new playlist entry into model
      Object record = playlistModel.insert();
      playlistModel.setFeature(record, Player.TITLE, title);
      playlistModel.setFeature(record, Player.SOUNDFILE,
        filename);
    }
  }
}
```

Menu

Finally, we create a menu for the playlist viewer (see Section 6.5.13). The menu functions enable us to create new playlists or to open existing playlists. The menu instance is added directly to the shell. The single *File* menu title is created as a MenuItem instance for the menu using the style constant SWT.CASCADE. We attach a submenu to this menu title with setMenu(). This submenu is created directly under the shell, but with the style constant SWT.DROP_DOWN. Then we add the two menu items to the submenu as MenuItem instances.

The event processing for these MenuItem instances takes place in the method processMenuSelection().

```
/**
 * Method constructMenu.
 * Constructs the menu
 * @param shell - the parent shell
 */
private void constructMenu(Shell shell) {
  // We use this menu to create new playlists
  // and to open existing playlists
  Menu menuBar = new Menu(shell, SWT.BAR);
  shell.setMenuBar(menuBar);
  // Create File menu title
  MenuItem fileTitle = new MenuItem(menuBar, SWT.CASCADE);
  fileTitle.setText("File");
  // Create Submenu and attach it to the menu title
  Menu fileMenu = new Menu(shell, SWT.DROP_DOWN);
  fileTitle.setMenu(fileMenu);
  // Create menu items for the File menu title
  newPlaylistItem = createMenuItem(fileMenu, "New Playlist");
  openPlaylistItem = createMenuItem(fileMenu, "Playlist open");
}

/**
 * Method createMenuItem.
 * Creates a menu item
 * @param menu - The menu
 * @param text - Label for the menu item
 * @return MenuItem - the new MenuItem instance
 */
private MenuItem createMenuItem(Menu menu, String text) {
  MenuItem item = new MenuItem(menu, SWT.NULL);
  item.setText(text);
  // Add event processing
  item.addSelectionListener(new SelectionAdapter() {
    public void widgetSelected(SelectionEvent e) {
      processMenuSelection(e);
    }
  });
  return item;
}
```

Once again we use a FileDialog instance of type SWT.OPEN to open an existing playlist. The selected file name is then set as a new input source for the playlist model via the setInput() method. The viewer will notify the playlist model about this event via inputChanged(). This is possible because the playlist model implements the IContentProvider interface.

If we want to create a new playlist, we use a FileDialog of type SWT.SAVE. This dialog allows us to enter the file name explicitly. However, we must check for the existence of the specified file. If the file already exists, we use a MessageDialog to ask the end user whether the file should be overwritten. If the user answers positively, we first delete the existing file, then pass the file name to the viewer using `setInput()`. The playlist model then creates a new playlist file with the specified name automatically, and signals this via the `inputChanged()` method.

```
/*
 * Method processMenuSelection.
 * Process menu events
 * @param e – The event object
 */
private void processMenuSelection(SelectionEvent e) {
  // Retrieve MenuItem instance from event object
  Widget widget = e.widget;
  // Retrieve shell
  Shell shell = e.display.getShells()[0];
  if (widget == openPlaylistItem) {
    // Open playlist: Create and open file selection dialog
    FileDialog dialog = new FileDialog(shell, SWT.OPEN);
    dialog.setFilterExtensions(PLAYLISTEXTENSIONS);
    dialog.setText("Open Playlist ");
    String filename = dialog.open();
    // Set this file as new input for TableViewer
    if (filename != null) setInput(filename);
  } else if (widget == newPlaylistItem) {
    // New playlist: Create and open file selection dialog
    while (true) {
      FileDialog dialog = new FileDialog(shell, SWT.SAVE);
      dialog.setFilterExtensions(PLAYLISTEXTENSIONS);
      dialog.setText("Create new Playlist");
      String filename = dialog.open();
      if (filename == null)
        return;
      // Add file extension if necessary
      if (!filename.endsWith(PLS))
        filename += PLS;
      // Check if file already exists
      File file = new File(filename);
      if (!file.exists()) {
        // Set this file as new input for TableViewer
        setInput(filename);
        break;
      } else if (
        // File already exists.
        // Asks user if file is to be overwritten.
        MessageDialog.openQuestion(
          shell,
          "New Playlist",
          "File already exists.\nOverwrite?")) {
        file.delete();
        setInput(filename);
```

```
            break;
        }
      }
    }
  }
}
```

The PlaylistLabelProvider class

PlaylistLabelProvider is responsible for deriving the table cell contents from the playlist entries. It retrieves the corresponding feature value from a specified playlist entry and a specified column number by using the access methods of the playlist domain model.

In the case of sound and image files we check if these files exist. If not, we prefix the cell content with a warning icon via getColumnImage().

```java
package com.bdaum.jukebox;

import java.io.File;
import org.eclipse.jface.viewers.ILabelProviderListener;
import org.eclipse.jface.viewers.ITableLabelProvider;
import org.eclipse.swt.graphics.Image;
import org.eclipse.swt.widgets.Display;
import org.w3c.dom.Node;

/**
 * This class provides the table of the playlist viewer
 * with cell contents.
 */
public class PlaylistLabelProvider
  implements ITableLabelProvider {

  // Playlist domain model
  private IPlaylist playlistmodel;
  // Here we store the warning icon
  private Image alertImage;

  /**
   * Constructor for PlaylistLabelProvider.
   */
  public PlaylistLabelProvider(IPlaylist playlistmodel) {
    super();
    this.playlistmodel = playlistmodel;
  }
```

Returning a warning icon The method getColumnImage() is called by the Table instance when rows have to be redrawn. For the first and second column of our table we use the method getFile-Alert() to test whether the files specified in the table cells still exist. If not, we return the warning icon as an `Image` instance. The method caches this `Image` instance in the instance field `alertImage`, so we only have to load this image the first time it is used.

If the `PlayListLabelProvider` is no longer needed, we release the image by calling its `dispose()` method.

When loading the image from file, we need a `Display` instance to convert it into an `Image` instance. As this method does not have access to a widget from which we could obtain such a `Display` instance, we use a different approach. We fetch the `Display` instance from the current SWT thread via the static method `Display.getCurrent()`. This is possible because this method is executed within the SWT thread (otherwise we would obtain the value `null`).

```java
/**
 * @see org.eclipse.jface.viewers.ITableLabelProvider#
 * getColumnImage(java.lang.Object, int)
 */
public Image getColumnImage(Object element, int columnIndex) {
  Node nod = (Node) element;
  // For the features <soundfile> and <image> we test for
  // the existence of the specified files. If the file does not
  // exist we return a warning icon
  switch (columnIndex) {
  case 1 :
    return getFileAlert(playlistmodel.getFeature(nod,
      Player.SOUNDFILE));
  case 2 :
    return getFileAlert(playlistmodel.getFeature(nod,
      Player.IMAGEFILE));
  default :
    return null;
  }
}

/**
 * Method getFileAlert.
 * @param string – File name
 * @return Image – A warning icon if the specified does not exist
 * null otherwise.
 */
private Image getFileAlert(String name) {
  if (name == null || name.length() == 0) return null;
  // Test if file exists
  File file = new File(name);
  if (file.exists()) return null;
  // No, let's return the warning icon
  // If the icon is not yet loaded, we load it now.
  if (alertImage == null)
    alertImage = new Image(Display.getCurrent(),
```

```
        "icons/alert_obj.gif");
      return alertImage;
    }

    /**
     * @see org.eclipse.jface.viewers.IContentProvider#dispose()
     */
    public void dispose() {
      // Release the warning icon again
      if (alertImage != null) {
        alertImage.dispose();
        alertImage = null;
      }
    }
```

Cell text

The text content of the table cells is provided by the getColumnText() method. This is quite simple: the corresponding feature values are retrieved from the playlist model. In the case of file names we also apply a bit of formatting.

```
    /**
     * @see org.eclipse.jface.viewers.ITableLabelProvider#
     * getColumnText(java.lang.Object, int)
     */
    public String getColumnText(Object element, int columnIndex) {
      Node nod = (Node) element;
      // In case of file names we only return the short name
      switch (columnIndex) {
        case 0 :
          return playlistmodel.getFeature(nod, Player.TITLE);
        case 1 :
            return getShortName(playlistmodel.getFeature(nod,
              Player.SOUNDFILE));
        case 2 :
          return getShortName(playlistmodel.getFeature(nod,
            Player.IMAGEFILE));
        case 3 :
          return playlistmodel.getFeature(nod, Player.DESCRIPTION);
      }
      return null;
    }

    /**
     * Method getShortName.
     * Convert file path into short file name
     * @param filename — File path
     * @return String — Short file name
     */
    private String getShortName(String filename) {
      if (filename == null)
        return "";
      File file = new File(filename);
```

```
        return file.getName();
    }
```

The next two methods are required for implementing the interface IBaseLabelProvider. Here, we have the option of informing possible ILabelProviderListeners about changes in the state of the PlaylistLabelProvider. (This could require a refresh of the viewer table.) However, we don't need this functionality, and therefore leave these methods empty.

The method isLabelProperty() is used for optimization. Here we have the option to return the value false if the cell representation of a feature is independent of the value of the feature. We can thus avoid unnecessary updates of table elements. In our case, however, all cell representation depend on the corresponding feature values – therefore we always return the value true.

```
    /**
     * @see org.eclipse.jface.viewers.IBaseLabelProvider#
     * addListener(org.eclipse.jface.viewers.ILabelProviderListener)
     */
    public void addListener(ILabelProviderListener listener) {
    }

    /**
     * @see org.eclipse.jface.viewers.IBaseLabelProvider#
     * removeListener(org.eclipse.jface.viewers.ILabelProviderListener)
     */
    public void removeListener(ILabelProviderListener listener) {
    }

    /**
     * @see org.eclipse.jface.viewers.IBaseLabelProvider#
     * isLabelProperty(java.lang.Object, java.lang.String)
     */
    public boolean isLabelProperty(Object element, String property) {
      return true;
    }
}
```

The FileCellEditor class

Now we implement own cell editors for the table of the viewer (see Section 7.3.3). The class FileCellEditor is based on the JFace class DialogCellEditor. When such an editor is clicked twice (but *not* a double click), a small button appears on the right hand side of the cell. A further click on this button opens a dialog. In this case it is a file selection dialog.

As we want to use this class for two different features (sound files and image files), we allow this class to be configured via its constructor. The constructor accepts a parameter for the dialog's title line and a filter list for the file selection.

Then we override the method openDialog() of the parent class DialogCellEditor. From the table cell we fetch its contents (file name) via getValue() and pass it to the FileDialog instance. We therefore make sure that the file selection dialog is already positioned to the current file named in the table cell. We also set the specified title and the list of file extensions for the file selection filter. When the FileDialog is closed, we check if a file name has been returned. (null is returned if the dialog was canceled.) Using the method setValueValid() we set the state of the cell editor accordingly. Then we return the file name that we received from the FileDialog to the caller: the Dialog-CellEditor will replace the current cell contents with this value provided that it was marked as valid.

```
package com.bdaum.jukebox;

import org.eclipse.jface.viewers.DialogCellEditor;
import org.eclipse.swt.SWT;
import org.eclipse.swt.widgets.Composite;
import org.eclipse.swt.widgets.Control;
import org.eclipse.swt.widgets.FileDialog;

public class FileCellEditor extends DialogCellEditor {

  // Filter for the file selection
  private String[] extensions;
  // Title for pop-up dialog
  private String title;
  /**
   * Constructor for FileCellEditor.
   * @param parent – containing Composite
   * @param title – Title for pop-up dialog
   * @param extensions - Filter for file selection
   */
  public FileCellEditor(Composite parent, String title,
    String[] extensions) {
    super(parent);
    // Save parameters
    this.extensions = extensions;
    this.title = title;
  }
  /**
   * @see org.eclipse.jface.viewers.DialogCellEditor#
   * openDialogBox(org.eclipse.swt.widgets.Control)
   */
  protected Object openDialogBox(Control cellEditorWindow) {
```

Pop-up dialog

```
    // Create file selection dialog
    FileDialog dialog =
      new FileDialog(cellEditorWindow.getShell(), SWT.OPEN);
    // Position dialog to current file
    dialog.setFileName((String) getValue());
    // Set filter and title
    dialog.setFilterExtensions(extensions);
    dialog.setText(title);
    String filename = dialog.open();
    // Indicate if file name is valid
    setValueValid(filename != null);
    return filename;
  }
}
```

8.7   The description editor

The DescriptionCellEditor is also based on the class DialogCellEditor. In this case a click on the cell's edit button will bring up a pop-up dialog for convenient input of descriptive text. This dialog is implemented as a DescriptionEditorDialog instance, to which we pass the playlist model as a parameter. After we have constructed the dialog, we initialize it with the current cell contents. When the dialog is closed, we check whether it was closed with the *OK* button. If so, we fetch the modified text from the dialog and return it to the caller, after declaring it as valid.

The DescriptionCellEditor class

```
package com.bdaum.jukebox;

import org.eclipse.jface.dialogs.Dialog;
import org.eclipse.jface.viewers.DialogCellEditor;
import org.eclipse.swt.widgets.Composite;
import org.eclipse.swt.widgets.Control;

public class DescriptionCellEditor
  extends DialogCellEditor {

  // The playlist domain model
  IPlaylist playlistModel;

  /**
   * Constructor for DescriptionCellEditor.
   * @param parent - Containing Composite
   * @param playlistModel — The playlist domain model
   */
  public DescriptionCellEditor(Composite parent,
    IPlaylist playlistModel) {
```

```
                         super(parent);
                         // Save parameters
                         this.playlistModel = playlistModel;
                      }
```

Pop-up-dialog

```
                      /**
                       * @see org.eclipse.jface.viewers.DialogCellEditor#
                       * openDialogBox(org.eclipse.swt.widgets.Control)
                       */
                      protected Object openDialogBox(Control cellEditorWindow) {
                        // Create new DescriptionEditorDialog instance
                        DescriptionEditorDialog dialog = new DescriptionEditorDialog(
                          cellEditorWindow.getShell(), playlistModel);
                        // Create the dialogs GUI-elements
                        dialog.create();
                        // Initialize with current cell content
                        dialog.setText((String) getValue());
                        if (dialog.open() == Dialog.OK) {
                          // Indicate that value is valid
                          setValueValid(true);
                          // Return new text
                          return dialog.getText();
                        }
                        return null;
                      }
                    }
```

The DescriptionEditorDialog class

We go into the final round with the implementation of this class. However, it still offers us something to learn. It implements a pop-up dialog for entering descriptive text and is based on the JFace class `TitleAreaDialog` (see Section 7.2.1). A `SourceViewer` instance (see Section 7.4.2) is used as the editor for the descriptive text.

During this editing process we use syntax driven text coloring: keywords that begin with the '$' character are displayed in a different color. To support the input of such keywords, we offer a *Content Assistant* that can be invoked with *Ctrl-Spacebar*.

In addition, we configure an *Undo Manager* for the `SourceViewer`. This *Undo Manager* can be called via the keyboard shortcuts *Ctrl-Z* and *Ctrl-Y* for undo and redo. Copying, deleting, and pasting text via the keyboard shortcuts *Ctrl-C, Ctrl-X,* and *Ctrl-V* is already supported by the predefined `SourceViewer`.

```
        package com.bdaum.jukebox;

        import java.util.ArrayList;
        import java.util.Iterator;
        import java.util.List;
        import org.eclipse.jface.dialogs.TitleAreaDialog;
        import org.eclipse.jface.text.*;
```

```
import org.eclipse.jface.text.contentassist.*;
import org.eclipse.jface.text.presentation.IPresentationReconciler;
import org.eclipse.jface.text.presentation.PresentationReconciler;
import org.eclipse.jface.text.rules.*;
import org.eclipse.jface.text.source.ISourceViewer;
import org.eclipse.jface.text.source.SourceViewer;
import org.eclipse.jface.text.source.SourceViewerConfiguration;
import org.eclipse.swt.SWT;
import org.eclipse.swt.custom.VerifyKeyListener;
import org.eclipse.swt.events.KeyAdapter;
import org.eclipse.swt.events.KeyEvent;
import org.eclipse.swt.events.VerifyEvent;
import org.eclipse.swt.layout.GridData;
import org.eclipse.swt.widgets.Composite;
import org.eclipse.swt.widgets.Control;
import org.eclipse.swt.widgets.Display;
import org.eclipse.swt.widgets.Shell;
public class DescriptionEditorDialog extends TitleAreaDialog {
```

Code scanner   The inner class KeywordCodeScanner is responsible for the syntax highlighting of the
displayed text. The class is based on a RuleBasedScanner (see Section 7.4.2). In our
example we only need a single SingleLineRule to recognize the keywords. We specify
'$' as a start character and space as a end character. These keywords are then marked up
with the created Token instance. The last parameter specifies the escape character (in
this case '\'). The array with this single rule is then passed to the scanner via the
setRules() method.

```
public class KeywordCodeScanner extends RuleBasedScanner {

  public KeywordCodeScanner() {
    // We fetch the current Display instance
    // for later retrieval of system colors
    Display display = Display.getCurrent();
    // We create a token paint it green
    IToken tagToken =
      new Token(
      new TextAttribute(
      display.getSystemColor(SWT.COLOR_DARK_GREEN)));
    // We only need a single rule to recognize a keyword
    IRule[] rules = new IRule[1];
    // By using a SingleLineRule we make sure that
    // the keyword does not stetch across line breaks
    rules[0] = new SingleLineRule("$", " ", tagToken, '\\');
    // We set this rule for the scanner
    setRules(rules);
  }
}
```

Content assistant   The inner class KeywordContentAssistProcessor implements a *Content Assistant* (see
section Section 7.4.2) that makes proposals for keywords. This assistant is automatically

called when a '$' is entered. This is controlled via the getCompletionProposalAutoActivationCharacters() method.

All proposals are compiled in the method computeCompletionProposals(). In this method we first retrieve the current document from the viewer, check in the method getQualifier() to determine whether a part of the keyword has already been entered, and compute – based on input – the possible proposals. Finally we return all CompletionProposal instances as an array. Each of these instances contains the proposed character string, the position at which to insert it (the current cursor position minus the length of the keyword part already entered), the length of the text area that should be replaced by the proposal (the length of the keyword part already entered), and the new cursor position. In our case we always position the cursor behind the proposal.

In the method getQualifier() we read the document from the current position backwards, character by character, and store these characters into a StringBuffer. If we arrive at a space character or a line break, we return the empty string – obviously no keyword part was entered. If we arrive at a '$' character, we reverse the contents of the StringBuffer and return the reversed string as the result. This result is then used in the method computeProposals() to restrict the set of possible keywords to only the keywords that start with the string already entered.

The rest of this class contains standard implementations of the IContentAssistProcessor methods. We don't need the context related methods here – these only become important in the case of ambiguous proposals.

```java
// All keywords
private final static String[] TAGS =
  new String[] {
    "performers",
    "producer",
    "publisher",
    "pubDate",
    "title" };

public class KeywordContentAssistProcessor
  implements IContentAssistProcessor {
  /**
   * Method computeCompletionProposals.
   * Compiles an array of CompletionProposal instances.
   * @param viewer – The viewer, from which this method is called
   * @param documentOffset – The current position in the document
   */

  /**
   * We want automatic proposals after a $-character
   */
  public char[] getCompletionProposalAutoActivationCharacters() {
```

```
      // Make proposals automatically after the following characters
      return new char[] { '$' };
   }

   public ICompletionProposal[] computeCompletionProposals(
      ITextViewer viewer,
      int documentOffset) {
         IDocument doc = viewer.getDocument();
         String qualifier = getQualifier(doc, documentOffset);
         // Compile keyword list for proposals
         List propList = computeProposals(qualifier);
         // Create CompletionProposal array
         CompletionProposal[] proposals =
         new CompletionProposal[propList.size()];
         Iterator it = propList.iterator();
         int i = 0;
         while (it.hasNext()) {
            String proposal = (String) it.next();
            int cursor = proposal.length();
            // Create single proposal
            proposals[i++] =
               new CompletionProposal(
               proposal,
               documentOffset - qualifier.length(),
               qualifier.length(),
               cursor);
         }
         return proposals;
   }

   /**
    *
    * Method getQualifier.
    * @param viewer – The viewer under which we work
    * @param documentOffset – The current position in the document
    * @return String – Keyword part that already has been entered
    */
   private String getQualifier(IDocument doc, int documentOffset) {
      // We read the document backwards
      // until we encounter whitespace or a $-character
      StringBuffer buf = new StringBuffer();
      while (true) {
         try {
            // Get character in front of cursor
            char c = doc.getChar(--documentOffset);
            if (Character.isWhitespace(c)) {
               // Begin of line or begin of word -
               // no keyword was found.
               break;
            }
```

```
                        buf.append(c);
                        if (c == '$')
                          // Keyword was found.
                          // Revert the string and return it.
                          return buf.reverse().toString();
                    } catch (BadLocationException e) {
                      // Begin of document — no keyword found
                      break;
                    }
                  }
                  return "";
                }

                /**
                 *
                 * Method computeProposals.
                 * @param qualifier — Already entered keyword part
                 * to restrict proposals
                 * @return List — List of suggested keywords
                 */
                private List computeProposals(String qualifier) {
                  List propList = new ArrayList();
                  for (int i = 0; i < TAGS.length; i++) {
                    String insert = "$" + TAGS[i] + " ";
                    if (insert.startsWith(qualifier))
                    // We only allow those proposals that
                    // begin with the qualifier
                    propList.add(insert);
                  }
                  return propList;
                }

                /**
                 * Standard implementation for display of contexts
                 */
                public IContextInformation[] computeContextInformation(
                  ITextViewer viewer,
                  int documentOffset) {
                    return null;
                  }

                /**
                 * Standard implementation for activation of contexts
                 */
                public char[] getContextInformationAutoActivationCharacters() {
                  return null;
                }
```

```
/**
 * Standard implementation for validation of contexts
 */
public IContextInformationValidator
  getContextInformationValidator() {
    return null;
}

/**
 * Standard implementation for error messages
 */
public String getErrorMessage() {
    return null;
}
}
```

SourceViewer
configuration

Now, we must tell the SourceViewer about the syntax highlighting and the content assistant. This happens in the following code, where we create a new SourceViewer-Configuration (see Section 7.4.2) under the name KeywordViewerConfiguration. Using the KeywordCodeScanner declared above, we create a new DefaultDamagerRepairer that is responsible for the presentation of the text. This DefaultDamagerRepairer is then registered with a new PresentationReconciler instance as both a Damager and a Repairer. We do this for content category IDocument.DEFAULT_CONTENT_TYPE, which is the only content category we use.

A new ContentAssistant instance is created in method getContentAssistant(). For this instance we set the KeywordContentAssistProcessor declared above as the processor. We switch to automatic activation of the content assistant and specify 500 milliseconds as the delay.

Finally, we also add an *Undo Manager* to this configuration. We use the Eclipse standard implementation DefaultUndoManager here and allow nine undo steps.

```
// SourceViewer Configuration
class KeywordViewerConfiguration extends
  SourceViewerConfiguration {

  // Configure Presentation
  public IPresentationReconciler getPresentationReconciler(
    ISourceViewer sourceViewer) {
    // Create new PresentationReconciler instance
    PresentationReconciler reconciler =
      new PresentationReconciler();
    // We use a DefaultDamagerRepairer
    // as both Damager and Repairer
    DefaultDamagerRepairer dr =
      new DefaultDamagerRepairer(new KeywordCodeScanner());
    reconciler.setDamager(dr, IDocument.DEFAULT_CONTENT_TYPE);
    reconciler.setRepairer(dr, IDocument.DEFAULT_CONTENT_TYPE);
```

```
                return reconciler;
              }
              // Configure Content Assist
              public IContentAssistant getContentAssistant(
                ISourceViewer sourceViewer) {
                // Create new ContentAssistant instance
                ContentAssistant assistant = new ContentAssistant();
                // Set the ContentAssistProcessor for the
                // default content category
                assistant.setContentAssistProcessor(
                new KeywordContentAssistProcessor(),
                IDocument.DEFAULT_CONTENT_TYPE);
                // Allow automatic activation after 500 msec
                assistant.enableAutoActivation(true);
                assistant.setAutoActivationDelay(500);
                return assistant;
              }
```

UndoManager
```
              // We use the DefaultUndoManager as Undo Manager
              public IUndoManager getUndoManager(ISourceViewer
                sourceViewer) {
                // A maximum of 9 undo steps
                return new DefaultUndoManager(9);
              }
            }
```

SourceViewer

Now we can begin to implement the DescriptionEditorDialog. In the constructor we accept the parent shell and the playlist domain model.

We add the SourceViewer to the dialog in the method createDialogArea(). Before we do this, we add a title and a message text to the dialog.

The SourceViewer is then configured with the KeywordViewerConfiguration declared above. In addition, we equip the SourceViewer with a document instance. To make the SourceViewer fill the dialog area completely, we fetch the SourceViewer's StyledText widget and apply an appropriate GridData instance to it.

Then we look after the keyboard event. We add a VerifyKeyListener to the SourceViewer. With this listener we trap all key presses that are modified with the *Ctrl* key: we set the variable doit in the event object to false. The event is therefore vetoed and the key press is ignored.

In the KeyListener that we added to the SourceViwer's StyledText widget, however, all key presses modified with *Ctrl* get special treatment. Depending on the key combination pressed, an appropriate ITextOperationTarget operation is selected. Then we ask the SourceViewer, with the method canDoOperation(), if the operation can be performed: if yes, we execute it via the doOperation() method. This test with canDoOperation() is absolutely necessary!

```java
// Widgets
private SourceViewer sourceViewer;
// The SourceViewers Document instance
private Document doc = new Document();
// The playlist domain model
private IPlaylist playlistModel;

/**
 * Constructor DescriptionEditorDialog.
 * @param parentShell - Containing Shell
 * @param playlistModel - The playlist domain model
 */
public DescriptionEditorDialog(Shell parentShell,
  IPlaylist playlistModel) {
  // Save parameters
  super(parentShell);
  this.playlistModel = playlistModel;
}

/**
 * @see org.eclipse.jface.dialogs.Dialog#
 * createDialogArea(org.eclipse.swt.widgets.Composite)
 */
public Control createDialogArea(Composite parent) {
  // Set title
  setTitle("Description");
  // Set message
  setMessage("Enter description text.\n"+
    "Press Ctrl-Spacebar to invoke the Content Assistant.");
  // Create Composite
  Composite composite =
    (Composite) super.createDialogArea(parent);
  // Create SourceViewer
  sourceViewer = new SourceViewer(composite, null,
    SWT.MULTI | SWT.BORDER | SWT.WRAP
    | SWT.H_SCROLL | SWT.V_SCROLL);
  // Configure SourceViewer
  sourceViewer.configure(new KeywordViewerConfiguration());
  // Set Document instance
  sourceViewer.setDocument(doc);
  // Get StyledText widget
  Control styleTextWidget = sourceViewer.getControl();
  // Set the widget to maximum size
  styleTextWidget.setLayoutData(
  new GridData(
    GridData.GRAB_HORIZONTAL
      | GridData.GRAB_VERTICAL
      | GridData.HORIZONTAL_ALIGN_FILL
      | GridData.VERTICAL_ALIGN_FILL));
```

```
                        // Avoid hotkeys appearing in the text
                        sourceViewer.appendVerifyKeyListener(new VerifyKeyListener() {
                          public void verifyKey(VerifyEvent event) {
                            if ((event.stateMask & SWT.CTRL) != 0) {
                              // Veto, if CTRL was pressed
                              event.doit = false;
                            }
                          }
                        });
```

Key events and
operations
```
                        // Event processing for hotkeys
                        styleTextWidget.addKeyListener(new KeyAdapter() {
                          public void keyPressed(KeyEvent e) {
                            // Only if CTRL was pressed
                            if ((e.stateMask & SWT.CTRL) == 0)
                              return;
                            int operation = 0;
                            if (e.character == ' ') {
                              // Ctrl+Spacebar: Content Assist
                              operation = SourceViewer.CONTENTASSIST_PROPOSALS;
                            } else if ((e.character | '\u0040') == 'Z') {
                              // Ctrl +Z: Undo
                              operation = ITextOperationTarget.UNDO;
                            } else if ((e.character | '\u0040') == 'Y') {
                              // Ctrl +Y: Redo
                              operation = ITextOperationTarget.REDO;
                            }
                            // Check if operation is possible
                            if (operation != 0
                                && sourceViewer.canDoOperation(operation))
                              // Perform operation
                              sourceViewer.doOperation(operation);
                          }
                        });
                        return composite;
                      }

                      /**
                       * Method getText.
                       * Return the edited text.
                       * @return String — Edited text
                       */
                      public String getText() {
                        // Retrieve text from document and return it
                        return doc.get();
                      }
```

```
/**
 * Method setText.
 * Initialize document with text.
 * @param input. Default text for text field
 */
public void setText(String input) {
  doc.set((input == null) ? "" : input);
}
}
```

8.8   Deploying the Jukebox

It is not very difficult to deploy the jukebox as a stand-alone application. We only have to take care that all the required JAR files and the required native SWT libraries are included in the deployment.

First, we export the whole project into a directory of our choice as a JAR file. Please make sure you remove the checkmark from file jukebox.ini when selecting the files to be exported. This file is created automatically by the playlist model implementation when the application is executed for the first time.

When invoking the Jukebox, we must make sure, that all JAR files included in the *Java Build Path* are also included into the *Java Classpath*. In addition, it is necessary, to specify the native SWT library in the –D option of the java command.

8.9   Discussion

The player implemented on these pages is, of course, miles away from a really comfortable and powerful Jukebox. However, it can be used as a basis for extensions. My goal was to demonstrate core concepts of the SWT and the JFace libraries in the context of a non-trivial application.

As expected, this application looks like a native application of the host's operating system (here Windows 2000). The windows and dialogs behave like native window and dialogs – in fact, they *are* native windows and dialogs.

What is more difficult, as with a pure Java application, is deployment. Because the SWT archives and the native SWT library are platform specific, we need a different deployment package for each platform. Alternatively, we can pack all platform specific SWT archives and libraries into a single installation, but this then becomes large. What remains in our wish list is better deployment support by Eclipse, such as the possibility to automatically generate command files for running deployed application on the target platform.

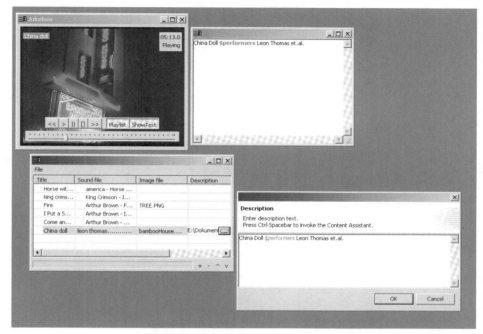

*Figure 8.4:   The various windows of the jukebox. At the top left we see the main
window with a background image, on the right is the window with the descriptive
text. At the bottom left is the playlist window, and to the right of this window is the
editor for the descriptive text.*

In fact the layout of our player can be improved quite considerably. The control
elements are currently somewhat minimalist. One idea would be to implement sliders
for volume and balance, and to allow for different operational modes (single pass, loop,
shuffle). For the background image, automatic scaling to the size of the canvas would
certainly be an improvement.

The management of the playlists could also be more comfortable. If the same song is
used in multiple playlists, the repeated entry of the song data becomes tiring. An option
would be to scan all existing playlists for a song when it is inserted into any playlist, and
to derive the features (title, background image, description) from existing entries. It
should also be possible to nest playlists. Another option would be to add other features
such as a transition time for cross-fading into the next song. This could be done by using
two *jlGui* engine instances.

However, all this must be left to the interested reader.

Another issue must be postponed to Eclipse 3.0. It would be nice to use HTML markup for the song descriptions. An HTML renderer, however, is currently not available under SWT/JFace. It is proposed for Eclipse 3.0 and will, hopefully, work better than the one implemented under Swing.[1]

1. After a first peek into Eclipse 3.0 M3, I'm sure it does. The new Browser widget wraps a native web browser such as Internet Explorer or Mozilla!

Part 3

Eclipse as an application platform

In the last two parts we developed applications that were deployed independently of Eclipse. In this part, in contrast, we discuss how we can use the Eclipse platform as a generic application framework. This option can shorten the development time for your own applications considerably, because you can reuse components of the Eclipse platform in your own Java applications. With Eclipse 2.1 this is, in particular, possible with IDE-like applications. Eclipse 3.0 will then enable Eclipse as a general application framework for client Java applications.

Our other topic in this part is the development of Eclipse plug-ins (which is, in fact, a prerequisite for application development with Eclipse). Plug-ins allow us to add extra functionality to the Eclipse platform or to a product developed on basis of the Eclipse platform. Finally, in Chapter 11 we show the implementation of a universal spell checking plug-in for Eclipse as an example.

9 Developing plug-ins for the Eclipse platform

Plug-in development sounds at first sight like a topic for Eclipse specialists. However, this quickly proves to be one of the main 'selling points' of the Eclipse platform. To understand this, we must briefly discuss the architecture of the Eclipse platform (see Section 9.1). Eclipse consists of a fairly small core application whose functionality is mainly restricted to the execution of plug-ins. In fact, every function the Eclipse workbench has to offer has been added to this core in the form of a plug-in.

To learn which plug-ins your current Eclipse SDK contains, just invoke the menu function *Help > About > Plug-in Details*. Another way to get an overview of the installed plug-ins is the *Plug-in Browser* that can be opened via *Window > Show View > Plug-ins*. Finally, the *Search* function supports the search for plug-ins, provided that it is used under the *Plug-in Development Perspective* (see Section 9.4.1).

This plug-in oriented architecture has two consequences:

- First, we can extend the Eclipse SDK almost indefinitely. Most of the third-party plug-ins currently offered for Eclipse deal with some aspect of application development. For example, there are plug-ins for modeling with UML or AOM, or plug-ins for special Java tools such as JavaCC (see Appendix A). Other plug-ins provide IDEs for programming languages such as C++ or AspectJ.

- Second, we can remove features from the Eclipse SDK. Theoretically, we can build on the 'naked' Eclipse core to construct applications that don't have very much to do with program development. In particular, this makes sense for applications that themselves require a certain degree of variability, so need to be implemented using a plug-in concept. We find such applications in areas like graphics and imaging applications, video editing, pre-press, content management, sound studios, and many others.

When developing such applications and plug-ins we can use the functionality of existing Eclipse plug-ins. In particular, we should mention the plug-ins for the Eclipse workspace resource management (projects, views, and files) and for the GUI components of the Eclipse workbench (editors, views, wizards, preferences, help system, and much more). Despite the steep learning curve of the Eclipse architecture, the time and effort saved by reusing these components by far outweighs the effort necessary to get acquainted with the architecture.

In this chapter we discuss the principles of the Eclipse plug-in architecture and introduce plug-in development. We refrain from presenting runnable example programs at this point, however, as the classes and interfaces discussed here only make sense within the context of a complete plug-in. Instead, we will implement a larger example plug-in in Chapter 11.

9.1   The architecture of the Eclipse platform

The only purpose of the tiny Eclipse core is to load and execute plug-ins. All the other functionality of the Eclipse platform is provided by plug-ins. In most cases – but not always – such a plug-in consists of a Java archive. In addition, it may contain other files such as images or help texts. An absolute requirement for each plug-in, however, is the plug-in manifest plugin.xml, which describes the configuration of the plug-in and its integration into the platform. We will discuss this manifest file in more detail in Section 9.4.

Extension points   *Extension Points* are a core concept of the plug-in architecture. Plug-ins may also define their own extension points to which other plug-ins may connect. In the manifest file plugin.xml each plug-in describes to which existing extension points it connects, and which new extension points it adds to the platform.

9.1.1   A minimal platform

The whole game begins with the platform core runtime org.eclipse.core.runtime. This is formally a plug-in, too, and consists of a Java library runtime.jar and a manifest file plugin.xml. This platform belongs – together with the plug-in org.eclipse.platform with the Java archive startup.jar and the plug-in org.eclipse.core.boot with the Java archive boot.jar – to the absolute minimum of plug-ins required for each Eclipse based application. boot.jar is – among other things – also responsible for completing the installation of a freshly installed Eclipse platform. The plug-in org.apache.xerces, with its *Xerces* Document Object Model (DOM) implementation, also belongs to the core software. A DOM is required to interpret the manifest files, as these files are stored in XML format.

In Section 9.2 we will discuss the platform core in more detail.

9.1.2   Resource management

Resources in Eclipse are projects, folders, and files of the Eclipse workspace. Since practically all Eclipse based applications rely in some form on such resources, the plug-in `org.eclipse.core.resources` also belongs to the core software of most Eclipse based applications. This plug-in provides the necessary functionality for accessing and managing resources independently of the host file system. In addition, it implements some services that are usually not provided by the host file system. Such services include a mechanism for managing resource annotations (*Marker*) and an event management for resource changes. In Section 9.4 we will discuss the resource management in more detail.

Ant

The resource management plug-in is based on a further plug-in: `org.eclipse.ant.core`. This plug-in organizes the support for the *Ant* tool. *Ant* (www.apache.com) is a Java based tool supporting the *Make* process (i.e. the assembly) of projects (see also Section 10.1). The reason why this tool is integrated into the resource management lies in Eclipse's support for the assembly process of projects at the resource level. The Ant functionality is therefore available virtually everywhere in the platform. The Eclipse plug-ins for resource management may be included in and deployed with our own applications. However, since some components (*Ant, Xerces*) are covered by the *Apache Software License 1.1*, products based on these plug-ins must refer explicitly to the Apache copyright and liability regulations.

9.1.3   User interface

Several plug-ins are available for the implementation of user interfaces. This includes SWT and JFace, which we already have discussed in Chapter 6 and Chapter 7, but also higher level components such as views and text editors. This functionality is divided into several plug-ins, such as:

```
org.eclipse.ui
org.eclipse.swt
org.eclipse.text
org.eclipse.jface
org.eclipse.jface.text
org.eclipse.ui.views
org.eclipse.ui.workbench
org.eclipse.ui.workbench.texteditor
org.eclipse.ui.editors
```

The Eclipse workbench is implemented with the help of these plug-ins. By using them in our own applications, we can achieve high quality and consistent user interfaces with relatively little effort. Also, there are no difficulties in terms of licenses – all the plug-ins in the Eclipse SDK are covered by the *Common Public License Version 1.0*. This licenses you to use these plug-ins in your own applications and to deploy them with your own applications. Section 9.5 introduces several components of these GUI plug-ins.

9.1.4   Help system

The plug-ins:

```
org.eclipse.help
org.eclipse.help.ui
org.eclipse.help.webapp
```

implement a complete system for end user help. The help functions of the Eclipse workbench are also based on these plug-ins. The complete help system is implemented as a Web server – the HTML help pages can be displayed with a standard Web browser such as *Internet Explorer* or *Mozilla*. Eclipse is able to use Web browsers found on the host system for this purpose. We will discuss the help system in more detail in Section 9.5.10.

9.1.5   Team support

Several plug-ins support the development of software artifacts in a team:

```
org.eclipse.team.core
org.eclipse.team.cvs.core
org.eclipse.team.cvs.ssh
org.eclipse.team.cvs.ui
```

The *Team Support* (see Section 5.1) of the Eclipse workbench is also implemented with these plug-ins. The support they provide is based on a client/server architecture with a central repository containing the team's artifacts, and on clients that implement the user interface. These plug-ins feature a relatively generic architecture. For example, it is possible to implement various user specific workflow strategies. Several repositories can co-exists in one application, and several clients are possible for a single repository. This allows for quite flexible workflow strategies.

9.1.6   Other plug-in groups

The plug-ins mentioned above are well suited for generic application development. Besides these plug-ins, the Eclipse SDK contains various other plug-in groups such as plug-ins for Java development, for debugging, and for plug-in development itself (the creation of the manifest and other configuration files). In this book we will not discuss the APIs of these plug-ins in detail, as they are only of interest for very specific application cases.

9.1.7   Summary

When we want to implement a new Eclipse based application, besides the core components we will usually use the plug-ins for resource management, the user interface, the help system, and perhaps the plug-ins for team support (Figure 9.1).

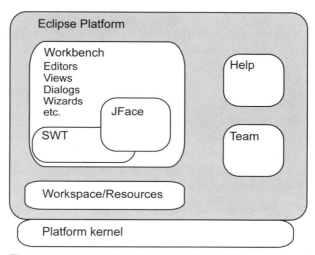

Figure 9.1:   The components of the Eclipse platform. We can use a rich arsenal of ready-made components, particularly when creating user interfaces.

The components contained in the Eclipse SDK cover most of the functions that are necessary for running the Eclipse platform and the Java IDE. If we implement an application from outside of this application spectrum, we may occasionally find that some required component is missing. For example, the Eclipse SDK contains neither a state-of-the-art graphics editor nor a spreadsheet component. Here we have to make use of third party plug-ins, which appear in ever increasing numbers on the market. Of course, we must check the individual license conditions of these plug-ins before we integrate them into our own applications. We list some of the most important third-party plug-ins for Eclipse based application development in Appendix A.

9.2   The core classes of the Eclipse platform

As we have already mentioned, the nucleus of the Eclipse platform is very small and contains only the functionality required to load and execute Eclipse plug-ins. In addition, it contains some interfaces and classes that are of general interest. All these interfaces and classes are contained in the package org.eclipse.core.runtime.

9.2.1   The Platform class

The Platform class is of general significance. It cannot be instantiated, and contains only static methods. It manages all the installed plug-ins, takes care of the access authorization to Eclipse workspace resources, and maintains the Eclipse protocol. In particular, we obtain the location of the workspace root directory via the method getLocation(). With the getCommandLineArgs() method we can get the command line options that were specified when the Eclipse platform was started. This allows us to control plug-ins by command line options. We can search a particular plug-in in the plug-in registry with getPlugin() by specifying its identification.

9.2.2   The Plugin class

The implementation of an Eclipse plug-in begins with a subclass of class Plugin. Here we implement the constructor of the new subclass. In the constructor we must create a single instance of this class (*singleton*), and store this instance into a static field. In addition, we implement the methods getInstance() and getDefault() respectively, from which we can later obtain the created instance.

In the constructor we will also initialize the plug-in preferences (see the next section) and any resource bundles that we may need (see Section 10.6). The API reference documentation provides a code example for such a Plugin subclass under *Help > Contents > Platform Plug-in Developer Guide > Reference > API Reference > Platform > Runtime > org.eclipse.core.runtime > Plugin*. This example program also shows how to use an INI file to save the state of a plug-in from one session to the next.

Most of the methods of the Plugin class deal with low-level resource management and the management of preferences. For example, the methods setPluginPreferences() and getPluginPreferences() store and retrieve the current preferences. With find() we can obtain the URL of a specified workspace resource, and with openStream() we can open an input stream on a specified workspace resource.

The method getDialogSettings() is equally important, with which we can retrieve the settings of all persistent dialogs of a plug-in (see also Section 7.2.3). Best practice is to create an individual section for each single dialog. Loading and saving of the settings is automatically performed by the plug-in.

9.2.3   The Preferences class

This class implements a persistent preference store. A single instance of this class contains all the preference of a given plug-in. Each single preference entry consists of a name/value pair. The name is a non-empty character string that is unique within the context of the plug-in. The value can be of type boolean, double, float, int, long, or

String. Using the methods getBoolean(), getDouble() and setValue(), we can retrieve the single preference values or set new preference values respectively. Changes in the preference store cause events of type Preferences.PropertyChangeEvent.

If a value was not previously set, querying that value returns the default value. For String type preferences this is normally the empty string; for all other preference types the default value is zero. It is possible to preset the default value of each preference entry via setDefault(). Note that these default values are not persistent and must be set when the plug-in is initialized.

Initializing preferences

To do this, we must override the method initializeDefaultPluginPreferences() in our Plugin subclass. All default preference values can be preset in this method. Examples are given in Section 11.4 and Section 11.9.1.

This initialization happens in several steps: the invocation of the method initializeDefaultPluginPreferences() is only the first step. In the second step, Eclipse evaluates the contents of the file preference.ini if such a file exists in the plug-in directory. The default values defined in this file will override the default values set in step one.

Here is an example of an entry in preferences.ini:

```
SPELL_THRESHOLD=99
```

Defining such a file allows us to modify the preference default values without re-compiling a plug-in. A typical use for this is debug switches for test output.

In the third step the plugin_customization.ini files defined in other Eclipse features are evaluated (see Section 10.4.1). The entries defined here will override the entries set in the first and second initialization steps.

9.2.4 Path specifications

The interface IPath and its standard implementation Path represent resource path specifications – for both workspace resources and resources outside the Eclipse workspace. The representation of these path is independent from the host system: The character '/' is always used as the separator between path steps. The specification of a device such as c: or server/disk1: is also possible. IPath and Path are equipped with a variety of methods that allow evaluation, synthesis, or modification of path specifications.

9.2.5 Monitoring long-running processes

The interface IProgressMonitor and the classes NullProgressMonitor, ProgressMonitorWrapper and SubProgressMonitor allow monitoring of long-running processes. During such a process we may display a progress bar and provide a button for aborting the process. Each IProgressMonitor object is informed about the start and the end of the process and about steps in between so that it can visualize the progress of the process accordingly.

The `NullProgressMonitor` does – guess what – nothing. We use it in those cases when we don't want to visualize the processes' progress. Should we actually want to show a progress bar, we can use two existing JFace classes:

```
org.eclipse.jface.dialogs.ProgressMonitorDialog
org.eclipse.jface.wizard.ProgressMonitorPart
```

While the latter implements a progress bar widget that can be embedded into other `Composites`, the first implements a complete dialog from which we can obtain an `IProgressMonitor` object via method `getProgressMonitor()`. We can initialize such an object via the method `beginTask()`. With the `worked()` method we can update the progress bar after each step. The end of the process is indicated via method `done()`. Using method `isCanceled()` we can check whether the process has been cancelled by the end user or by another program unit (via the method `cancel()`).

9.3 The Eclipse workspace

We introduced various resources of the Eclipse workspace in Section 2.2: projects, folders, and files. In this section we are going to discuss the resource management's API.

Unlike the Eclipse predecessor *Visual Age*, which stored resources in a central repository, Eclipse uses the file system of the host operating system directly. Project, folders, and files are mapped onto the corresponding items in the host's file system: projects and folders onto directories and files onto files. The advantage is that we may still access these resources when Eclipse is no longer installed or if it is not functional.

Eclipse does have an internal repository, of course. This sits in the workspace in subdirectory `.metadata` and stores all kind of metadata such as preferences for the various plug-ins, the configuration and the current state of the Eclipse platform, markers and annotations for problems, tasks, and breakpoints, the *Local History* of resources (see Section 1.10), specific *Resource Properties*, and much more. Programmers do not have direct access to this metadata.

9.3.1 Resources

Resources of the Eclipse workspace are described by the `IResource` interface. This interface, together with other interfaces and classes of the resource management, resides in the package `org.eclipse.core.resources`. The complete functionality of the resource management unit is deployed as a separate Eclipse plug-in.

The most common resources we know are projects, folders, and files. Projects may contain folders and files. Folders may contain sub-folders and files. Figure 9.2 shows the resource type hierarchy.

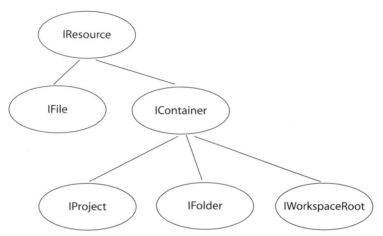

Figure 9.2:   The hierarchy of IResource interfaces.

As each resource in the workspace corresponds with a resource in the host file system, each resource has two addresses: the address within the workspace and the location in the host file system. (Consequently, there are two different ways to open files, depending on the location of the file: inside the workspace or outside the workspace.) We can retrieve the workspace address of a resource via its method getFullPath(), and the location within the host file system can be retrieved via getLocation(). Both of these addresses are represented as IPath instances (see Section 9.2.4).

Normally, the address obtained with getLocation() consists of the concatenation of Platform.getLocation() (see Section 9.2.1) and getFullPath() – but only normally. In the case in which we import a whole project into the workspace (via the menu function *Import > Existing Project into Workspace*) the imported files are *not* moved into the workspace directory. Instead, Eclipse creates only a mapping of workspace addresses to the imported project, so these files are not contained physically in the workspace folder. This is one of the reasons why we should never try to construct file system locations from workspace addresses manually, but always should use the IResource method getLocation().

IResource defines a rich arsenal of methods. In the following we list the major function groups:

- Methods for classical resource management such as `exists()`, `move()`, `copy()`, and `delete()`.

- Methods for the implementation of the *Visitor* design pattern [Gamma1995]. We can pass an `IResourceVisitor` instance to a resource with the `accept()` method. This resource then invokes the `visit()` method of the visitor instance. In the case of success, the `IResourceVisitor` instance is also passed to the child resources of the current resource via their respective `accept()` methods.

- Methods for managing *Markers*. Eclipse provides a concept for adding markers such as problems, tasks, or breakpoints to resources. The methods `createMarker()`, `findMarker()` and `findMarkers()`, `getMarker()`, and `deleteMarkers()` belong to this group. We will examine markers and the corresponding interface `IMarker` more closely in the next section.

- Methods for managing *Resource Properties*. This group allows the addition of an unlimited number of properties to each resource. The methods:

  ```
  setPersistentProperty()
  setSessionProperty()
  getPersistentProperty()
  getSessionProperty()
  ```

  respectively allow the setting and retrieval of single properties. The concept is quite similar to the WebDAV standard (www.webdav.org). Each property consists of a unique name and a string value. Usually, one would want to use an XML expression for the string value to allow for more complex structured values. What we write into such a property depends on the application. For example, we could remember the current state of a resource in such a property and could thus organize a workflow. Session properties are not persistent – they vanish when the session is closed. Persistent properties, in contrast, live across sessions because they are stored on disk (.metadata).

Containers

The interface `IContainer` is derived from `IResource`. Interfaces of resources that can contain other resources are based on this interface, such as `IProject`, `IWorkspaceRoot`, and `IFolder`. In addition to the `IResource` methods, the interface provides methods for localizing and retrieving child resources, such as `findMember()`, `getFile()`, `getFolder()`, and `members()`.

The workspace root

The interface `IWorkspaceRoot` represents the root directory of the Eclipse workspace. With `getProject()` and `getProjects()` we can obtain a specific project in the workspace and a list of all projects respectively. We can obtain the root directory from the current Plugin instance via getWorkspace().getRoot().

Projects and project natures

Projects are units that contain all the resources of a software product. Projects may contain other folders and files. The project acts as a root directory for these folders and files. In addition, a project may control how the final software product is assembled from its components. Projects may not contain other projects, although they can refer to other prerequisite projects. This information is stored in the project folder in a file named .project.

Projects can be equipped with one or several plug-in specific project natures. Each nature describes a specific behavioral aspect of a project. For example, a Java project has a Java nature. Natures can be defined and selected freely. However, it is also possible to restrict the selection of natures for a given project. We may even specify natures that rely on other natures as prerequisites. New natures can be implemented as subtypes of the interface IProjectNature. How project natures can be created and assigned to projects is described in detail under *Help > Contents > Platform Plug-in Developer Guide > Programmer's Guide > Resource and workspace API > Project natures.*

Build

In order to support all this additional functionality, the interface IProject offers – besides the methods inherited from IResource and IContainer – additional methods such as build() for the assembly of a software product, getReferencedProjects() and getReferencingProjects() for retrieving the dependencies between projects, and getNature(), hasNature() and isNatureEnabled() for the retrieval of project natures.

With create() we can create a new project. But to do so, we must first own an IProject instance. We can obtain such an instance from the IWorkspaceRoot instance with the help of getProject(). For example:

```
IWorkspace workspace = ResourcesPlugin.getWorkspace();
IWorkspaceRoot root = workspace.getRoot();
IProject project = root.getProject("newProject");
try {
  // progressMonitor=null
  project.create(null);
} catch (CoreException e) {
  e.printStackTrace();
}
```

In this example we first fetch an IWorkspace instance from the resources plug-in. From this instance we get the workspace root instance, and from there we can fetch an IProject instance with the specified name. Finally, we can create the project. For simplicity's sake we have specified the value null for the IProgressMonitor instance requested by the create() method.

Folders

The interface IFolder does not offer much more functionality than that inherited from interface IContainer. New folders are created via create() in the same way that projects are created. We can get an IFolder instance from an IWorkspaceRoot instance via getFolder().

Files

Files are described by the interface IFile. We can get an IFile instance from the workspace root via getFile(). New files are created with the IFile method create(). The IFile interface offers the following methods to manipulate the contents of a file: setContents() to overwrite the contents, appendContents() to append additional contents to a file, and getContents() to retrieve the complete contents of a file. In all these methods we can specify an IProgressMonitor instance as parameter to visualize the progress of the operation.

History

All these methods are history aware: When the contents of a file are changed or when a file is deleted, we can optionally keep a copy of the old file version in the *Local History* (see Section 1.10). getHistory() allows us to get a list of all previous versions of a file. This list is provided in the form of an IFileState array. From such an IFileState instance we get the previous contents of the file via getContents(), and we can get the time stamp of this version using getModificationTime(). Only file contents are subject to the *Local History*, not the file's properties (see Section 9.3.1).

In the following example we create a new file by concatenating two existing files. We also keep a copy of the intermediate versions in the *Local History*. We have set the parameter force to false because we don't want the file to be modified when the workspace entry (metadata) of the file does not match the file version in the host file system.

```
IFile file1 = project.getFile("hello.txt");
IFile file2 = project.getFile("world.txt");
if (file1.exists() && file2.exists()) {
  try {
    InputStream is1 = file1.getContents();
    InputStream is2 = file2.getContents();
    IFile file3 = project.getFile("helloWorld.txt");
    // force=false, no ProgressMonitor
    file3.create(is1, false, null);
    // force=false, keepHistory=true, no ProgressMonitor
    file3.appendContents(is2, false, true, null);
  } catch (CoreException e) {
    e.printStackTrace();
  }
}
```

9.3.2   Markers

As we have already demonstrated in Section 1.4, Eclipse offers the option of attaching annotations to resources. The interface `IMarker` describes a general interface for creating and managing such annotations. However, it is not expected that programmers implement this interface. Instead, `IMarker` instances are obtained via the `IResource` method `createMarker()`. This method accepts a string describing the marker type as a parameter. Eclipse already defines five standard marker types:

`org.eclipse.core.resources.marker`	Generic marker type
`org.eclipse.core.resources.taskmarker`	Markers for tasks
`org.eclipse.core.resources.problemmarker`	Markers for problems
`org.eclipse.core.resources.bookmark`	Markers for book marks
`org.eclipse.core.resources.textmarker`	Other text markers

Each `IMarker` instance has an identifier that identifies the marker within a resource uniquely. We can obtain this identification via `getID()`. In addition, we may equip any marker with an arbitrary number of attributes. Each attribute must be identified uniquely via a name and has a value of type `boolean`, `int`, `String`, or `Object`. With `setAttribute()` and `getAttribute()` we can set and retrieve such attributes individually. With `setAttributes()` and `getAttributes()` we can set and retrieve all attributes of a marker in one operation. Eclipse predefines the following standard attributes: `CHAR_START`, `CHAR_END`, `DONE`, `LINE_NUMBER`, `LOCATION`, `MESSAGE`, `PRIORITY`, `SEVERITY`. In the case of `SEVERITY`, we have the choice between the attribute values `SEVERITY_INFO`, `SEVERITY_WARNING`, and `SEVERITY_ERROR`.

In Section 9.4 we will discuss how plug-ins can be configured. During this configuration it is possible to declare our own marker types, and to construct marker hierarchies in which child marker types inherit attributes from ancestor marker types. For this reason the `IMarker` interface provides the method `isSubtypeOf()`. This method allows us to query the inheritance relationships between marker types.

We can declare individual marker types as *persistent* when declaring marker types in the plug-in configuration. Such markers 'live' across sessions. Normally we would use persistent markers to implement end user created task markers. Problem markers, in contrast, will usually be updated when a resource is opened. Nevertheless, it can make sense to make problem markers persistent, too. This allows the *Package Explorer* to decorate the corresponding resource with a problem indicator.

9.3.3   Reacting to resource changes

In some cases it may be necessary for an application to react to changes of workspace resources caused by other plug-ins. This is true in particular when the currently opened resources depend in some way on the modified resource, or when currently opened resources are reverted to a previous version by the end user via the *Replace...* function.

If we want to react to such changes, we must implement the interface IResourceChange-Listener and must register an instance of this interface with the workspace. First we need a workspace instance, which we get from the resources plug-in:

```
IWorkspace workspace = ResourcesPlugin.getWorkspace();
```

Then we can register an IResourceChangeListener with the IWorkspace instance:

```
IResourceChangeListener listener = new IResourceChangeListener() {
  public void resourceChanged(IResourceChangeEvent event) {
    System.out.println("A resource was changed!");
  }
};
workspace.addResourceChangeListener(listener);
```

Since changes to resources happen frequently, and consequently create some overhead, we should deregister the listener as soon as possible via the method removeResourceChangeListener(). ResourceChangeListener should work as effectively as possible to avoid performance problems.

The interface IResourceChangeListener features only the single method resourceChanged(), which accepts IResourceChangeEvent objects. Using the method getType() we can get information about the type of event. Normally, one would want to react to events of type POST_CHANGE. When registering an IResourceChangeListener, we can optionally specify an event mask, so that the listener method is only invoked for the selected event types.

IResourceChangeEvent objects do not necessarily represent a single resource change, but possibly a whole series of resource changes. All these changes are represented in form of an IResourceDelta instance, which forms the root node of an IResourceDelta tree. This tree mirrors the resource tree in the Eclipse workspace, but contains only the modified resources and their parent containers. All these resources are represented as IResourceDelta instances. To analyze all these changes we must therefore walk through the entire tree. For this purpose IResourceDelta offers the accept() method, to which we may pass an IResourceDeltaVisitor instance. The visit() method of this instance is then called for each node of the tree. (However, if we are only interested in a single resource, the method findMember() offers a quicker way to get there.)

Usually, we would first retrieve the kind of change (ADDED, REMOVED, CHANGED) for the specific resource delta in the visitor's accept() method. This can be done with the

IResourceDelta method getKind(). With getFlags() we obtain details, for example whether the contents or the type of the resource was changed, or if, in the case of REMOVED, the resource was deleted or moved to another location. In the latter case we obtain the new location via getMovedToPath(). We obtain the corresponding resource instance with getResource().

If we want to represent such resource changes in the user interface, we have to be cautious. The resourceChanged() method does not necessarily run in the SWT thread. The required changes in the GUI must therefore by wrapped into a suitable Display method such as asyncExec() or syncExec(). In the previous example application (see Section 8.3) we have already seen how this is done.

In addition, we should be aware of the fact that all resources are locked against modification while the resourceChanged() method is active, to avoid avalanches and loops. The event types PRE_AUTO_BUILD and POST_AUTO_BUILD are excluded from this rule, however.

We will leave our short overview about resource changes at this stage. Readers interested in details should refer to the excellent article about resource changes [Arthorne2002] in the *Eclipse Corner* (www.eclipse.org).

9.4   Configuring plug-ins

After a first look into the basics of the Eclipse resource management, we now turn our attention to plug-in creation. We will discover that some things here are quite different compared to the creation of independent Java applications. First, we must define how the plug-in is embedded into the Eclipse workbench. For example, we may need to add additional GUI elements as well as the menu and the toolbar of the workbench. The debugging phase of a plug-in is also different than that of a conventional application: to test a plug-in, a second plug-in must be started under which the test plug-in is executed. In the meantime, the first workbench controls the execution of the debug process.

9.4.1   The Plug-in Development Perspective

To support this development process, Eclipse provides a special perspective. Of course, it is possible to create plug-ins under the *Java Perspective* but the *Plug-in Development Perspective* makes life much easier (see Figure 9.3). In the same way as shown in Section 1.2, we can open the *Plug-in Development Perspective* with the *Open Perspective* symbol.

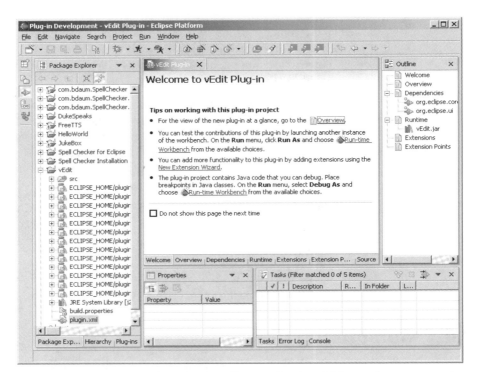

Figure 9.3: The Plug-in Development Perspective. In addition to the components familiar from the Java Perspective, this perspective features a browser for installed plug-ins, a window for showing the properties of selected items, and (under the Tasks window) windows for the error log file and the Java console. The last two windows are important for debugging: the error messages produced by the plug-in being tested are shown there.

A special function in the *Plug-in Development Perspective* is the wizard for the creation of new plug-in development projects. After a click on the *New* button, we select the category *Plug-in Development* and then *Plug-in Project* (instead of *Java*). On the following wizard pages we enter the project name and leave all other entries at their default value. Finally, we get to the selection of the plug-in template (Figure 9.4).

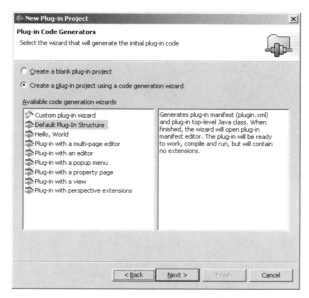

Figure 9.4: Several templates are available for the creation of a new plug-in. All these templates result in plug-ins that can be immediately executed and tested. Try some of these templates and look at the generated code to learn about the construction of the standard plug-in types!

Depending on our requirements, we select an appropriate template. For example, if our planned plug-in is based on a text editor, we select the template *Plug-in with an editor*. With the template *Default Plug-In Structure* we just obtain the minimum Plugin class and the manifest file plugin.xml, on which we can build later. After we press *Finish* the necessary folder structures and files of the new plug-in are created.

We can invoke this plug-in immediately via *Run > Run as... > Run-time Workbench*.

After a while a second workbench appears on the screen (Figure 9.5), equipped with the new plug-in to be tested. Of course, there is currently nothing to debug – we first have to add a few custom functions to the new plug-in. In the following sections we will call this workbench a *Test Platform*, and the workbench from which we started the new workbench, the *Development Platform*. Members of the OTI development team call these platforms 'Little Eclipse' and 'Big Eclipse'.

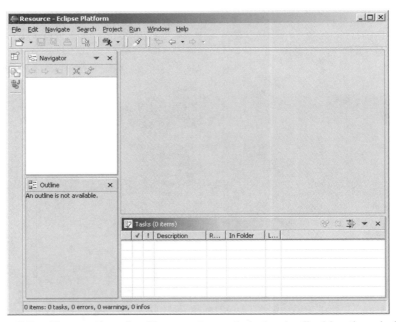

Figure 9.5:   The workbench with a newly created plug-in. Besides the windows that are usually present in the Resource Perspective (Navigator, Outline, Tasks) there is a large empty space that may be filled by the new plug-in.

One more word about the debug process. Since the invocation of a new workbench needs time, the debugging process can become a bit tiresome at times. Fortunately, however, Eclipse support*s hot swapping*: while the test platform is running, we can modify the plug-in code in the development platform and re-compile it using the *Save* function. These changes are carried through to the test platform. We can therefore avoid stopping and restarting the test platform in most cases. However, *hot swapping* only works in *Debug* mode, not in *Run* mode, and requires at least JRE 1.4.0.

9.4.2   The Plug-in Manifest

Now, let's close the test platform and return to the development platform. Here, we already see the welcome greeting (Figure 9.3) of the plug-in manifest `plugin.xml`. This file is the central instance for plug-in development. It controls how the plug-in is embedded into the workbench and controls the assembly of the plug-in from its components. The file extension `.xml` indicates that this file is stored in XML format. For our minimal plug-in the source of this file looks like this:

Source code

```xml
<?xml version="1.0" encoding="UTF-8"?>
<plugin
  id="vEdit"
  name="vEdit Plug-in"
  version="1.0.0"
  provider-name="Berthold Daum"
  class="vEdit.vEditPlugin">
  <runtime>
    <library name="vEdit.jar"/>
  </runtime>
  <requires>
    <import plugin="org.eclipse.core.resources"/>
    <import plugin="org.eclipse.ui"/>
  </requires>
</plugin>
```

However, only in rare cases do we need to edit the raw XML source code. It is much more comfortable to edit this file with the manifest editor. The various sections of the manifest file are distributed over several editor pages:

The Overview page

This page provides a summary of the most important properties of the plug-in (Figure 9.6).

The Dependencies page

This page lists all the plug-ins that are required for the successful execution of the current plug-in. For our minimal plug-in there are only two: the plug-in for resource management org.eclipse.core.resources, and the plug-in for the user interface, org.eclipse.ui. We can easily add other plug-ins to the list with the *Add* button. For example, if we want to provide end user help functions within our plug-in, we would add the plug-in org.eclipse.help. As soon as we save the manifest file (via *Ctrl-S*), the JAR files of these plug-ins appear in the *Package Browser*. The classes and interfaces contained in these JAR files can now be used by our own classes and interfaces.

On the right hand side of the *Dependencies* page we can make further specifications for a selected plug-in. For example, we can specify that the dependency from the selected plug-in also becomes visible for plug-ins using the current plug-in (*Reexport the dependency*). In addition, we can specify rules for selecting a specific version of the required plug-in. We can search for cyclic dependencies, and we can search for plug-ins that refer to our current plug-in.

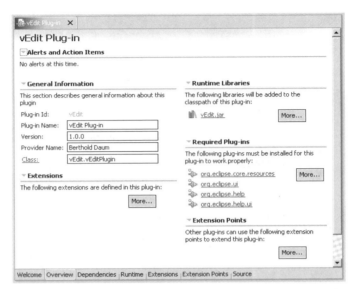

Figure 9.6:   The Overview page of the manifest editor. All the information from the other pages is repeated here in condensed form. A click on one of the 'More...' buttons leads to a more detailed view.

The Runtime page

All the JAR files that contain binaries of the current plug-in (.class files, .properties files, etc.) and that belong to the plug-in's *Classpath* are declared on this page. The first archive, named *projectname*.jar, is already pregenerated.

In the section below we can specify, for each selected archive, where the source files of that archive are located. When an archive is generated (see Section 10.3.2), the folders specified here are compiled and the resulting binaries are added to the corresponding archive.

At the right hand side at the top we can specify *Export* rules for each archive. The classes and interfaces of an exported archive are visible to foreign plug-ins; the other archive are private to the current plug-in.

Below this section we can specify the prefixes used by these packages. This specification is only needed to 'tune' an application – plug-ins with declared prefixes are loaded about 10 percent faster.

The Extensions page

This page provides an overview of the extension points used by the current plug-in. Since our minimal plug-in offers no functionality at all, this page is still empty. We can add new functionality such as editors, views, menu items or tool buttons to our plug-in with the *Add* button. When doing so, we have the choice between two wizard types:

- When selecting *Generic Wizards,* new extensions are created with the help of *Extension Point Schemas.* All plug-ins contained in the Eclipse SDK describe their extension points with the help of such schemas, and also third-party plug-ins usually do so. The classes created by this wizard must be completed by the programmer.

- When selecting *Extension Templates,* we have the choice of many standard extensions. After deciding on a specific template, we are prompted for various options. The wizard then generates the specified extensions completely, and we are able to execute the plug-in with the new extension immediately. Of course, depending on our requirements, we may need to modify the generated code.

We will discuss these extension points in more detail in Section 9.4.3.

The Extension Points page

On this page we can define which extension points the current plug-in provides for other plug-ins. By specifying such extension points we can prepare our plug-in for later extensions (even from third parties). A new extension point can be specified with the *Add* button.

We need to specify three values:

- *Extension Point ID.* Here we must specify an identification that is unique within the scope of the current plug-in. Other plug-ins may refer to the extension point by specifying its fully qualified extension point ID (i.e. the ID defined in the manifest prefixed with the plug-in ID). For example, if we specify the extension point vFilter within in plug-in vEdit, other plug-ins may refer to this extension point via the ID vEdit.vFilter.

  Since larger plug-ins may define hundreds or even thousands of extension points, we should avoid very long identification strings. Short identifications are processed faster and need less resources.

- *Extension Point Name.* The name of an extension point used for display purposes, such as Video Effect Filter.

- *Extension Point Schema.* Finally we provide a schema for each defined extension point. This schema will guide the user of the extension point and prompt for the required parameters when configuring a plug-in. Here, we may specify an existing schema or enter the name of a new schema. For the example above, Eclipse will suggest the schema `schema/vFilter.exsd`.

After specifying these three values the *Schema Editor* can be started automatically. In Section 9.4.4 we will discuss the *Schema Editor* in detail.

9.4.3   The most important SDK extension points

As we have already mentioned, all components of the Eclipse SDK are implemented as plug-ins. We can use this functionality in our own plug-in by using the extension points of the existing plug-ins, or we can add our own plug-in to an existing plug-in.

Schema based extension points

When using the wizard for schema-based extension points, we should make ourselves knowledgeable about the respective extension point. All extension points defined in the Eclipse SDK are documented in detail under *Help > Help Contents > Platform Developer Guide > Reference > Extensions Points Reference*. For third-party plug-ins, however, we need the corresponding documentation from the plug-in's manufacturer.

Let's select a schema based extension point such as `org.eclipse.ui.editors`. Optionally, we can define our own identification and a name for the selected extension point. After clicking the *Finish* button the new extension point appears in the list of extensions.

Schema controlled definition

So far only the schema is specified. This schema will guide us through the definition of the new extension. We select the extension `org.eclipse.ui.editors` and invoke the context function *New > editor*. In the *Properties* view we will now see all the parameters of the new editor. Identification and name are already predefined, as Figure 9.7 shows.

Now we only need to apply the right entries at the right places of the *Properties* table. Let's begin with the attribute `class`. Here we enter the name of the class that implements the new editor. This can be the name of an existing class. In most cases, however, we will enter the name of a not-yet-existent class. In this case, Eclipse generates a stub for the new class. In our case, this is a subclass of the abstract class `EditorPart`.

Most extension points have attributes that require the specification of Java classes. In our case there are three attributes: `class`, `contributorClass`, and `launcher`. The other parameters consist of Boolean values, character strings, or file paths. We can find a description of all these parameters in the help section *Platform Developer Guide > Reference > Extensions Points Reference > Workbench > org.eclipse.ui.editors*. In Section 9.5.3 we take a closer look at the editors of the Eclipse SDK.

Figure 9.7:   The schema for the extension point 'org.eclipse.ui.editors'.

GUI extension points   In the following table we have listed the most important extension points for creating user interfaces:

`~.ui.acceleratorSets`
`~.ui.acceleratorConfigurations`
`~.ui.acceleratorScopes`
	`acceleratorSets` defines groups of keyboard shortcuts. These groups can be assigned to `acceleratorConfigurations` (such as *Emacs* or *Standard*), which then can be activated by the end user. `acceleratorScopes` can restrict the scope of each group.
	
	Note that these extension points (which were introduced with Eclipse 2.0) and the extension point `actionDefinitions` (see below) are already deprecated in Eclipse 2.1, and were replaced by the extension point `commands` (see below). We document these extension points anyway, as first experiences with the new extension point `commands` indicate that it cannot be used in all scenarios.

`~.ui.actionSets`
`~.ui.actionDefinitions`
`~.ui.actionSetPartAssociations`
	`actionSets` define actions and action groups. An `action` in Eclipse is an abstract user action. This action can appear in various presentations such as menus, menu items, or tools buttons on a toolbar (see Section 9.5.5). Users may activate or deactivate individual action groups. Actions can be associated with keyboard shortcuts via the extension point `actionDefinitions`. `actionSetPartAssociations` can assign action groups to selected components of the workbench. If that component is no longer active, the corresponding actions vanish from the menu and the toolbar.

`~.ui.commands`	This extension point was introduced with Eclipse 2.1 and replaces the extension points `acceleratorSets`, `acceleratorConfigurations`, `acceleratorScopes`, and `actionDefinitions`. In Eclipse a *command* is an abstract user command without a defined semantic. To each command we can attach one or several keyboard shortcuts (`keyBinding`). Many of these keyboard shortcuts are already predefined in the manifest file `org.eclipse.ui_2.1.0/plugin.xml`. The correlation between command and actions (see above) happens via the ID of the command. This ID must be identical with the `definitionID` of the corresponding action. It is possible to restrict the scope of such a correlation. Besides predefined scopes (*global*, *text editor*, *Java editor*) it is also possible to define custom scopes.

	Keyboard shortcuts can be assigned for specific configurations. We can use one of the predefined configurations (*Standard, Emacs*) or provide our own `keyConfiguration`. Finally, we can assign the individual commands to existing or new categories to organize them into groups on the preferences page (*Window > Preferences > Workbench > Keys*).
`~.ui.dropActions`	`dropActions` define possible 'drag and drop' actions between the components of the workbench.
`~.ui.editors` `~.ui.editorActions`	The extension point `editors` adds new editors to the workbench. Here we can build on the standard text editor implementation contained in the Eclipse SDK. We can also use this extension point to invoke external editors. With `editorActions` we can equip existing editors with additional actions such as menu items or tool buttons (see Section 9.5.5).
`~.ui.exportWizards` `~.ui.importWizards`	These extension points allow us to add new choice points into the *Import* and *Export* wizards.
`~.ui.markerHelp` `~.ui.markerResolution`	`markerHelp` allows us to attach help texts to markers, such as problems or tasks. With the extension point `markerResolution` we can attach a `MarkerResolutionGenerator` to markers. These generators are used to generate correction suggestions (*QuickFix*).
`~.ui.newWizards`	This extension point allows us to add new choice points to the *New* wizard.

~.ui.perspectives ~.ui.perspectiveExtensions	The extension point perspectives is used to define new workbench perspectives. The class specified here defines the initial layout of the perspective. The extension point perspectiveExtensions allows us to add additional components to existing perspectives.
~.ui.popupMenus	This extension point allows us to add new menu items to existing context menus.
~.ui.preferencePages	This extension point allows us to add new pages to the workbench's *Preferences*.
~.ui.propertyPages	This extension point allows us to define new pages in the *Properties* dialog box. This is the dialog that appears when we invoke the context function *Properties* for a selected resource.
~.ui.resourceFilters	This extension point allows us to equip views displaying resources (such as the *Navigator* view) with additional file filters.
~.ui.startup	This extension point allows us to specify the plug-ins that should be started when the platform is started.
~.ui.views ~.ui.viewActions	The extension point views allows us to add new views to the workbench. The extension point viewActions enables new actions such as menu items and tool buttons, (see Section 9.5.5) to be added to existing views.
~.ui.workingSets	This extension point allows us to create new wizards for the definition of *Working Sets*. Working sets are used in various views such as the *Navigator* to restrict the displayed set of resources. Eclipse understands several working set types. For each type we can define our own wizard.

~.help.contexts ~.help.support ~.help.ui.browser	The extension point contexts allows us to define context sensitive help for the current plug-in. The extension point support specifies the class implementing the Help GUI. The extension point ui.browser can be used to specify a browser for displaying the HTML help texts.
Warning: The ui.browser extension point may change in future versions.	
~.help.toc ~.help.luceneAnalyzer	The extension point toc specifies a help text table of contents for the current plug-in. Eclipse uses Apache's *Lucene* engine for indexing help texts. With the extension point luceneAnalyzer we can equip *Lucene* with a custom program for text analysis.
~.search.searchPages ~.search.searchResultSorters	The extension point searchPages allows us to add additional pages to the search dialog in order to support specialized search operations. With the extension point searchResultSorters we can define specific sort strategies for the search results.

A documentation of all schema based extension points defined in the Eclipse SDK is found under *Help > Help Contents > Platform Plug-in Developers Guide > Reference > Extension Point Reference*.

Template based extension points

In contrast to schema based extension points, template based extension points support only a subset of the components contained in the Eclipse SDK. However, these extension points offer very extensive configuration possibilities, allowing us to save a lot of coding. As shown in Figure 9.8, the most popular workbench components are offered.

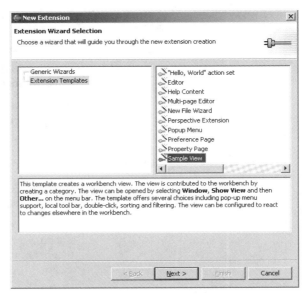

Figure 9.8: Template based extension points allow the selection of various predefined components. In particular, we find here various editors and views, a wizard for the creation of new files, pop-up menus, new perspectives, and preference pages.

First, we select a component template, for example the template *Sample View*. On the following wizard pages (see Figure 9.9 and Figure 9.10) we can configure this view according to our requirements.

After entering all the options and pressing the *Finish* button, the necessary classes and packages are generated, and the necessary entries are added to the manifest file plugin.xml. In our case, these are entries for the new category and the new view. After saving these files (*Ctrl-S*) we can execute the plug-in immediately by using *Run > Run as... > Run-time Workbench*.

First, the new view is invisible (we did not check the option *Add the view to the resource perspective*). With the function *Window > Show View > Other...* we can select the new view in category *Videoclips* and open it.

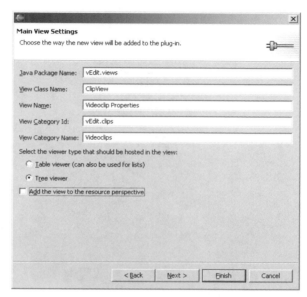

Figure 9.9:   Here we configure the component 'Sample View'. We specify a name for the package and the class of the view implementation. The specification of a View Category Id allows the combination of several views into groups when they are displayed under the function Window > Show View. Finally, we can determine the contents of a view – either a table or a tree – and whether we want to add the view to the Resource Perspective. We will discuss workbench views in more detail in Section 9.5.4.

We obtain a relatively well instrumented tree-based view, as shown in Figure 9.11. What remains is to equip this view with an application specific domain model.

Template-based extension points thus offer the possibility to produce pre-manufactured application components with just a few mouse clicks. Instead of having to hunt through dozens of APIs, we obtain well functioning code that we only have to modify according to our requirements.

Figure 9.10: On the third wizard page we can specify additional options for the new view. We discuss actions in Section 9.5.5, and the discussion of event processing follows in Section 9.5.2.

Figure 9.11: The new view contains a tree prototype, several example actions in the toolbar, a drop-down menu, and a context menu.

9.4.4   The Schema Editor

If we want to define our own extension points (see Section 9.4.2) it makes sense to define schemas with these extension points too. These schemas can guide programmers through the specification of extension point parameters, as we have already had seen in Section 9.4.3.

Eclipse uses a subset of the language XML Schema to define such schemas. In some respects, however, such as namespace usage or the spelling of some tags, the dialect used in Eclipse differs from the World Wide Web Consortium (W3C) defined standard [Daum2003]. For this reason, Eclipse schemas have the file extension .exsd instead of the usual extension .xsd.

Fortunately, Eclipse provides a *Schema Editor* with which we can create schemas without detailed knowledge of the schema language syntax. With the help of this schema editor we can easily create arbitrarily complex descriptions of extension points.

Schema elements A schema consists of one or several named *elements*. In addition, it is possible to decorate these elements with *attributes*. Elements are first defined independently of each other in the left hand part of the *Schema Editor*. Here we must specify the name of each element. We can also add icons to elements. Under *Label Attribute* we can specify which of the element's attributes specifies the display label of the element.

Attributes We have the choice between attribute types (*Kind*):

- An attribute of type *java* will later specify the path of a Java class.

- An attribute of type *resource* will later specify the path of a workspace resource.

- An attribute of type *string* will later contain a data value. The specification 'string' is a bit misleading at this point. In fact, this attribute type allows two different data types: Boolean attributes (*boolean*) can accept the values 'true' and 'false', and string attributes (*string*) accept any character string. It is possible to restrict the possible values by specifying an enumeration under *Restriction*.

Under the entry *Use* we can determine if the attribute must be specified (required) or if the attribute is optional. In addition, we can specify a default value in entry Value if we specified the value *default* under the entry *Use*.

Schema structure If we defined several elements, we must organize them into a tree structure. This is done in the right part of the *Schema Editor* (see Figure 9.12). Each schema must consist of a single root element – the first element in the element list in the left hand side window of the editor – to which the other elements are connected directly or indirectly.

Each element within this tree represents either a tree node with child elements or a leaf node. For each tree node with child elements we can specify a branching type by selecting from four *connectors*:

- *Sequence*. This connector organizes its child nodes into an ordered list. Schema instances must follow the sequence of child nodes in this node.

- *All*. This connector organizes the child nodes in an unordered list. Schema instances may use a different order of child nodes as specified for this node.

- *Choice*. This connector describes an alternative. In a concrete instance of the schema only one child node from the choice list must be specified.

- *Group*. This connector is not available in the W3C standard and seems to be quite superfluous. *Sequence*, *All*, and *Choice* are sufficient for the construction of schema trees.

All these connectors can be nested to an arbitrary depth. In addition, we may specify a repetition factor for each connector and each element. We can specify a lower bound (*minOccurs*) and an upper bound (*maxOccurs*) for repetitions. By specifying `minOccurs="0"` we can define optional tree nodes. If a node can be repeated without an upper bound, we specify `maxOccurs="unbounded"`.

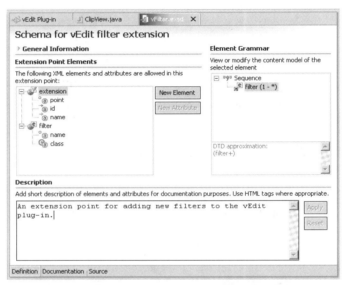

Figure 9.12: The schema editor with the opened schema file 'vFilter.exsd'. At the left we see a list of XML elements with their attributes. The window on the right shows the child elements for the element extension. The Description window at the bottom allows the specification of element specific and attribute specific documentation. More documentation can be entered on the Documentation page.

New schema file

When creating a new schema file (*File > New > Other > Plug-in Development > Extension Point Schema*), the wizard first prompts you for four values:

- The ID of the plug-in for which the schema file is created.

- The ID of the extension point relative to the plug-in.

- The name of the extension point for display purposes.

- The name of the new schema file.

The new schema file already contains the root element extension with the attributes point, id, and name. We will usually leave this element unmodified, since it only describes general properties of the extension point. Application specific elements are created by pressing *New Element* and then connecting the new element directly or indirectly to the root element.

Documentation   The *Schema Editor* is able to generate an HTML reference document from the defined schema. We can get a preview of this document with the context function *Preview Reference Document*.

9.5   Reusing existing workbench components

Applications that are implemented as Eclipse plug-ins and want to use the Eclipse user interface will reuse existing components of the Eclipse workbench in one way or another. The various workbench views belong to these components, as do the text based editors, as shown in Figure 9.13. Graphical editors such as diagram editors or bitmap editors are not available in the Eclipse SDK – if such components are required we can find appropriate third-party plug-ins (see Appendix A).

In particular, when using editors we would either use the class TextEditor or implement our own editor by extending one of the abstract or concrete editors from the editor hierarchy shown in Figure 9.14. For workbench views the situation is somewhat different. Several concrete view components such as TaskList, BookmarkNavigator, and ResourceNavigator are already active within the workbench. We can use these view instances from our own application – we gain access to these views by specifying the view identification to the workbench. If we want to implement our own view components, we can extend the existing abstract view classes such as ViewPart or PageBookView.

Adapters   All concrete workbench components implement the IAdaptable interface with the method getAdapter(). getAdapter() is a factory method: from a class specification (i.e. a Class instance) it can create an instance of that class.

This allows Eclipse to generate concrete instances from the class names specified in the manifest file plugin.xml (see Section 9.4.2). In addition, it becomes possible to save the current workbench state when the workbench is closed, and to open the workbench again with the same components active.

9.5.1   The architecture of the Eclipse workbench

The Eclipse workbench is represented by an IWorkbench instance. This is the root object for the whole Eclipse user interface. We obtain this instance by invoking the static method PlatformUI.getWorkbench().

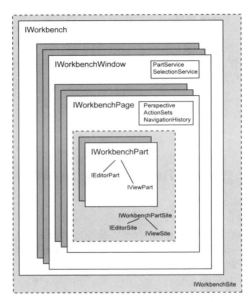

Figure 9.13: The Eclipse workbench has a clear hierarchical structure. At the top are the workbench instances, the lowest level is constituted from various workbench components (IWorkbenchPart) such as editors or views. 'I...Site' instances allow access to the manifest declarations and other information of the runtime environment.

Workbench window   The workbench may consist of one or several workbench windows (see Figure 9.13). By default, when Eclipse is started, the workbench is started with a single window. Optionally, it is possible to open each perspective in its own workbench window (*Window > Preferences > Workbench > Perspectives*). Consequently, the IWorkbench instance can own several workbench windows (IWorkbenchWindow) that we can retrieve via getWorkbenchWindows(). If the last workbench window is closed the workbench is also closed.

The workbench   Each workbench window can own one or several workbench pages (IWorkbenchPage).
page   These pages are used to display the various perspectives of a workbench window. Only one page per workbench window is active and visible to the end user at a time. We can retrieve the list of all pages by calling the IWorkbenchWindow method getPages(). We obtain the currently active page via getActivePage().

Workbench   Each workbench page is constituted from one or several workbench components
components   (IWorkbenchPart). These are either editors (see Section 9.5.3) or views (see Section 9.5.4). Workbench pages offer a series of methods for managing these editors and views. For example, we can obtain a list of references of all editors available in the current

workbench page with getEditorReferences(). With getActiveEditor() we get the currently active editor, with getDirtyEditors() we get all those editors where the content had been changed and must be saved when the workbench is closed. With open-Editor() we can open an editor, with closeEditor() or closeAllEditors() we can close editors.

Managing views is simpler: with getViewReferences() we obtain a list of references of all views available in the current workbench page. We can get a view instance with findView() by specifying its identification (as defined in the manifest file plugin.xml). We can make a view visible with showView(), while we can make it invisible with hideView().

Besides managing editors and views, workbench pages are also responsible for managing *Action Sets*. With showActionSet() and hideActionSet() we can make *Action Sets* visible or invisible respectively.

Since Eclipse 2.1 workbench pages are also able to manage the navigation history. We can retrieve INavigationHistory instances with getNavigationHistory().

Perspectives   It is the responsibility of the end user how the single components are placed onto a workbench page. However, an application may define the initial layout of a workbench page by specifying a perspective. The Eclipse platform provides some predefined perspectives, such as the *Resource Perspective* or the *Java Perspective*. Of course, applications are free to define their own perspectives.

We can get a reference (IPerspectiveDescriptor) to the currently active perspective of a workbench page using getPerspective(). With setPerspective() we can set a new active perspective for a workbench page, while resetPerspective() allows us to revert the layout changes made by the end user.

Manifest information   To the interfaces IWorkbench and IWorkbenchPart belong the corresponding interfaces IWorkbenchSite and IWorkbenchPartSite. With these interfaces we can get access to the runtime environment of the workbench and of each workbench component. The declarations made in the manifest file plugin.xml belong to this environment, as do registered context menus (see Section 9.5.5). We can gain access to instances of type IWorkbenchSite and IWorkbenchPartSite via the method getSite().

Two subtypes IEditorSite and IViewSite are available for the type IWorkbenchPart-Site. These types provide extended environment information for editors and views.

9.5.2   Event processing in the Eclipse workbench

Each application implemented on the basis of the Eclipse platform usually consists of several workbench components. An application may implement its own components, such as special editors or views, or it may use existing components such as a text editor, the *Navigator* view, or the *Tasks* view.

The coordination of these various components is organized via event processing, a common technique in object-oriented programming. Usually each component observes state changes in other components and reacts accordingly. To do so, the observing component registers with the observed component as a *listener*. It is then notified by the observed component when an event occurs via a call to a listener method. We have already demonstrated this kind of event processing in the example given in Chapter 8.

In an open architecture such as the Eclipse platform, however, this concept is not flexible enough. Since the platform can be extended at any time with new plug-ins, we cannot assume a fixed configuration: by using 'hard-wired' event processing between components we would prevent further extensions of a given configuration.

Central event management

For this reason, the Eclipse platform provides central event management. Components that create events register with the central event management as an event provider and inform the central management whenever events occur. All components that have registered with the central event management as listeners are then informed about the event accordingly. This strategy ensures that the platform remains extensible: new components must only register with the central event management as event providers or listeners.

Now let's have a look at the various event types.

Window events

IWorkbench events occur when a workbench window is opened (windowOpened()), activated (windowActivated()), deactivated (windowDeactivated()), or closed (windowClosed()).

Components that wish to receive these events must register with the IWorkbench instance as an IWindowListener via addWindowListener().

Component events

Component events, i.e. events that are caused by state changes of IWorkbenchPart instances, are obtained from the component service of the Eclipse platform. We obtain a respective IPartService instance from a IWorkbenchWindow instance via the method getPartService(). The concrete IPartService instance will usually be a workbench page, since IWorkbenchPage is a subtype of IPartService.

From this IPartService instance we can fetch the currently active component or a reference to the active component via the methods getActivePart() and getActivePartReference() respectively. In addition, we can register as an observer via addPartListener(). These observers are represented by two interfaces: IPartListener and IPartListener2. The latter interface is an extension of the first and reports about a few more event types.

partActivated()	Component was activated.
partBroughtToTop()	Component was brought to top.
partClosed()	Component was closed.
partDeactivated()	Component was deactivated.
partHidden()	Component was made invisible (IPartListener2).
partOpened()	Component was opened.
partVisible()	Component was made visible (IPartListener2).

Selection events

Selection events occur when a GUI element in the workbench is selected, for example when a resource is selected in the *Navigator*. We obtain selection events from the selection service (ISelectionService). ISelectionService instances can be obtained from an IWorkbenchWindow instance via getSelectionService(). Usually, this will be a workbench page, since IWorkbenchPage is a subtype ISelectionService.

We can retrieve the current selection from such an ISelectionService instance via the method getSelection(). With the help of the methods addSelectionListener() and addPostSelectionListener() we can register observers of type ISelectionListener. The difference between both methods is that the latter method supports only events from StructuredViewer instances (see Section 7.3.2), and that the event is fired after a short delay if it was caused by a keyboard event. ISelectionListener instances are notified about selection events via selectionChanged(). The event object contains information about the component that caused the event (IWorkbenchPart) and about the selection (ISelection). If we want to get access to the selection details, we must first typecast the generic ISelection object to a more concrete type such as IMarkSelection, IStructuredSelection, or ITextSelection.

Event notification   How can a component register with the selection service to notify it about selection events? To do this, the component only needs to implement the interface ISelection-Provider with the methods addSelectionListener(), removeSelectionListener(), getSelection(), and setSelection(). When a component is activated, the workbench always checks automatically if the component implements this interface. If this is the case, it registers the appropriate selection service with the activated component as an observer via `addSelectionListener()`. The central selection service is thus notified about selection events caused by this component when the component calls the method `selectionChanged()` as required. When the component is deactivated, the workbench automatically deregisters the selection service with the component.

Processing events correctly

It is normally not sufficient just to register with the selection service as a listener and wait for the event to arrive. For example, when a view is opened, it is not yet informed about the current selection state. Consequently it cannot display information relating to the selection. The view would be updated only when the end user changes the selection.

This problem also occurs when the workbench is started. The programmer has no influence over the order in which the components of a workbench page are initialized. For example, if we have a view that displays properties that depend on the selection state of an editor and the editor is initialized before the view is initialized, the view is not notified about the selection state of the editor. This is because it was not registered as a selection listener when the editor was started, and therefore not informed about the editor's selection state.

Initialization   When we initialize a component, we must therefore fetch the currently active component from the part service via `getActivePart()` and the current selection from the selection service via `getSelection()`. This is usually done at the end of the method `createPartControl()`, where the component is initialized.

When processing events, we cannot make assumptions about the sequence in which components are notified about these events. Components should therefore be implemented in such a way that they can act autonomously without relying on the state of other components. Their behavior should depend only on received events, and not make assumptions that other components already have processed such events.

Sequence   However, it can sometimes become necessary to do exactly that, for example to avoid costly recomputations for performance reasons. In such a case we can force a specific sequence in event processing by starting event processing after a short delay. This can be done via the method `Display.timerExec()`. With this trick, event processing is performed after all other components have processed an event – provided that these components don't use the same trick! We can then call methods from other components without running the risk of obtaining outdated information.

However, we must execute some caution when using the method `timerExec()`. The processing scheduled in this method can still be executed when the component that scheduled this task is already closed and its widgets are disposed. If we access widgets in such a delayed method, therefore, we must play it safe:

```
if (widget != null && !widget.isDisposed)
```

9.5.3 Editors

All workbench editors are based on the abstract class EditorPart. This class mainly implements the IEditorInput concept. The interface IEditorInput describes the data source of an editor in abstract form. This may be a file, but not necessarily so. The Eclipse platform understands two different concrete data sources: IFileEditorInput and IStorageEditorInput. While IFileEditorInput represents a file in a file system, IStorageEditorInput represents a general byte stream. The input source for an editor is set by the workbench via init() shortly after the EditorPart instance has been created. It can be retrieved with getEditorInput().

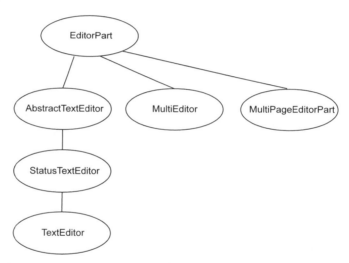

Figure 9.14: The hierarchy of text based editors. Other editor types such as graphical editors can be implemented on basis of EditorPart.

Editor classes that subclass EditorPart usually override the method createPartControl(). Within that method they create the concrete appearance of the editor by creating the necessary SWT widgets and JFace components.

Toolbars and menus We do not usually need to construct toolbars and menus manually, as Eclipse does this automatically by interpreting the definitions made in the manifest file plugin.xml (see Section 9.4.2). However, the option exists to create menus and toolbars manually. To do so, we first use the method getEditorSite() to fetch an IEditorSite instance. From this instance we can obtain an IEditorActionBarContributor instance with the help of getActionBarContributor(). This instance manages the menus, toolbars, and the status line. These tasks – managing menus, toolbars, and status line – cannot be left to the editor, because actions and menus would appear multiple times if several editors of the same type were opened in the same workbench page. The IEditorActionBarContributor, in contrast, can be shared between several editor instances. The standard implementation EditorActionBarContributor features the method getActionBars() with which we can fetch an IActionBars instance. From this instance we can obtain the menu manager (IMenuManager) via getMenuManager(), and the toolbar manager (IToolManager) via getToolManager(). If we want to construct a toolbar or a drop-down menu, we can just add actions (IAction instances) to these managers via their respective add() methods. Further details about menu managers are given in Section 9.5.5. In this section we also describe how to construct context menus for editors.

Keyboard shortcuts We also obtain access to the key binding service (IKeyBindingService) from the IEditorSite instance via getKeyBindingService(). Here we can restrict the scope for keyboard shortcuts to the current editor using setScopes(). This is necessary if we introduce a new editor type that uses key scopes that differ from the scopes defined for the standard editors (text editor). Such scopes can be declared in the extension point org.eclipse.ui.commands (see Section 9.4.3).

Status line The IActionBars instance also provides access to the workbench's StatusLineManager (see Section 7.5.2) via the method getStatusLineManager().

Saving files In addition, the EditorPart API contains a method group for saving the modified editor content:

```
doSave()
doSaveAs()
isDirty()
isSaveAsAllowed()
isSaveOnCloseNeeded()
```

Jump to marker Finally, there is the gotoMarker() method. By invoking this method and passing an IMarker instance as a parameter, we can select the marked area and position the cursor accordingly (see below).

All these methods can be overridden by EditorPart subclasses to implement the required functionality. The Eclipse SDK already contains three abstract subclasses of EditorPart: AbstractTextEditor, MultiEditor, and MultiPageEditorPart (see Figure 9.14).

The AbstractTextEditor class

The AbstractTextEditor class is the standard implementation of the interface ITextEditor, and represents the common basis for all text based editors in the Eclipse workbench. The standard text editor in Eclipse (the class TextEditor), among other, is a subclass of this class, as also are the various program editors. To implement concrete editors we will usually use the text processing classes defined in JFace, which we already have discussed in Section 7.4.

`AbstractTextEditor` implements some of the standard functions that are common to text based editors, such as:

- Standard functions for text processing, such as cut, copy, paste, find and replace.

- Visualization of annotations and markers.

- Update of markers when the text content is changed by the end user.

- Management of context menus.

- Reaction to resource changes in the workbench, for example, when a resource is refreshed, when projects are closed, or when a resource is deleted that is currently open in an editor.

A class that wants to extend `AbstractTextEditor` must first configure this editor. The Eclipse workbench must be notified about the extension points of the various context menus. This is done with the help of the methods `setEditorContextMenuId` and `setRulerContextMenuId`. The manifest file `plugin.xml` (see Section 9.4.3) can now refer to these identifications and link *Action Sets* to the editor's context menus.

Layout
We can change the appearance of the editor if desired. By default, the `AbstractTextEditor` consists of a `SourceViewer` and a vertical `Ruler` for markers at the left hand side of the `SourceViewer`. We can easily add further widgets by overriding or extending the method `createPartControl()`.

With the method `setStatusField()` we can determine a status field in which the status messages of the editor are shown. We can assign different status fields for different categories of status messages. The editor's status fields are displayed in the status line of the workbench when the editor becomes active. Status fields are described by the interface `IStatusField`. The default implementation of this interface is the class `StatusLineContributionItem`.

Document model
`ITextEditor` separates the document model from the user interface. The current document is given to the editor by a `IDocumentProvider` instance. This allows several editors to access the same document. `IDocumentProvider` manages documents of type `IDocument`, as discussed in Section 7.4.1. `IDocumentProviders` are responsible for saving and restoring the managed documents. The `AbstractTextEditor` uses the methods of the registered `IDocumentProvider` instance when performing editor operations such as `doSave()` or `doRevertToSaved()`.

These and other operations are usually invoked by user actions (menu function, click on tool button, context menu). How therefore does the communication between actions and editor function?

Actions
We can install an action (see Section 9.5.5) of type `IAction` with the editor using the method `setAction()`. When doing so, we assign an identification string to each `IAction`

instance. Using this string, we can query the editor for a specific action via getAc-tion(), we can assign keyboard shortcuts to actions via setActionActivationCode() and remove them again with removeActionActivationCode(). To implement a specific action, we would extend the standard implementation Action rather than implement the interface IAction. Its subclasses override the run() method to implement specific behavior. With the editor methods:

```
markAsContentDependentAction()
markAsPropertyDependentAction()
markAsSelectionDependentAction()
markAsStateDependentAction()
```

we can organize the various actions according to their behavior. This is important when actions must be updated after editor events.

Selection

The AbstractTextEditor also provides methods for setting and retrieving emphasized text ranges (setHighlightRange(), resetHighlightRange(), and getHighlight-Range()) and for retrieving the ISelectionProvider (getSelectionProvider()). This ISelectionProvider instance allows us to set and retrieve selections (ISelection) and to set and remove ISelectionChangedListeners.

Extending the AbstractTextEditor

Subclasses that extend the class AbstractTextEditor can override several method of this class to adapt their behavior as required. In particular, we may want to override the following methods:

createActions()	Creates the standard actions of the AbstractTextEditor: *Undo, Redo, Cut, Copy, Paste, Delete, DeleteLine, DeleteLineToBeginning, DeleteLineToEnd, SetMark, ClearMark, SwapMark, SelectAll, ShiftRight, ShiftLeft, Print, FindReplace, FindNext, FindPrevious, FindIncremental, AddBookmark, AddTask, Save, Revert, GotoLine.*
createPartControl()	Creates the vertical Ruler, at the left hand border of the editor area, and the SourceViewer.
dispose()	This class must be extended when the subclass needs to release resources (colors, fonts, printer, etc.) when the editor is disposed of.
doSave() doSaveAs() doRevertToSaved()	These methods save the current editor document and restore it to its last saved state respectively.

editorContextMenuAboutToShow()	This method is invoked before the editor's context menu is to be shown. The context menu must be constructed in this method.
init()	Initializes the editor with an IEditorSite instance and an IEditorInput instance.
isSaveAsAllowed()	The standard implementation always returns the value false for this method. Subclasses may override it as required.

The TextEditor class

The class TextEditor is the standard text editor of the Eclipse workbench and is based on the class AbstractTextEditor. In many cases we will prefer to extend this class instead of the AbstractTextEditor class. This editor has the identification org.eclipse.ui.DefaultTextEditor.

Example

An example for the extension of the class TextEditor is the ReadmeTool example program, which is found in the plug-in directory:

\eclipse\plugins\org.eclipse.ui.examples.readmetool_2.1.0

The class ReadmeEditor adds an *Outline* window to the text editor, i.e. a view in which a summary of the editor's contents is displayed. To implement this, the ReadmeEditor overrides the method getAdapter(). In the overridden getAdapter() it generates a suitable ReadmeContentOutlinePage from a received IFileEditorInput instance. It also overrides the method doSave() in order to update the content of the *Outline* page after saving the editor content; and it overrides the method editorContextMenuAbout-ToShow() to display an example context menu.

The MultiEditor class

A MultiEditor combines several editors to a single GUI component. To manage these editors (known as 'inner editors') the following methods are necessary:

createInnerPartControl()	This method creates the GUI of an inner editor.
getActiveEditor()	This method returns the currently active editor.
getInnerEditors()	This method returns all inner editors.

The MultiPageEditorPart class

The abstract class `MultiPageEditorPart` implements an editor with several pages. Each page can contain its own editor, consisting of arbitrary SWT control elements.

Subclasses that extend this class must override the following methods:

`createPages()`	This method creates all the editor pages. The method `addPage()` can also be used to do this.
`IEditorPart.doSave()` `IEditorPart.doSaveAs()`	These methods save the contents of the whole editor.
`IEditorPart.isSaveAsAllowed()`	This method return the value `true` if *Save As* is allowed.
`IEditorPart.gotoMarker()`	The editor window is brought to the marker position.

Working with markers

We have already discussed `IMarker` instances in Section 9.3.2 in connection with resources. Here we are going to discuss how we can declare our own marker types in the manifest file, and how markers can be used in the context of an editor.

Declaring markers   The declaration of a new marker type is achieved by specifying a new `extension` element at the extension point `org.eclipse.core.resources.markers`. The attribute `id` of this extension identifies the marker type, while the attribute `name` specifies a marker name for display purposes. The `extension` element can be equipped with several child elements:

- The element `attribute` declares a marker attribute. The attribute `name` specifies the name of that attribute.

- The element `persistent` declares whether the marker is persistent or not. The attribute `value` takes the values `true` for persistent markers and `false` for transient markers.

Inheritance   - The element super declares the parent marker type. In the `type` attribute we specify the identification of the parent marker type. The current marker inherits all attributes from the parent marker except the ones it overrides. It is possible to specify several super element (i.e. multiple inheritance). The persistency property is *not* inherited.

Example:

```
<extension id="diagramProblem"
  name="Diagram Problem"
  point="org.eclipse.core.resources.markers">
  <super type="org.eclipse.core.resources.problemmarker"/>
  <super type="com.bdaum.myApplication.diagramMarker"/>
  <persistent value="false"/>
  <attribute name="item"/>
  <attribute name="flags"/>
</extension>
```

Here we have defined a new marker type diagramProblem. This marker type inherits all attributes from the predefined marker type org.eclipse.core.resources.problem-marker and from the marker type diagramMarker, from which we assume that it has been declared previously. The new marker type is declared as transient and is equipped with the additional attributes item and flags.

In Section 9.3.2 we have already discussed how IMarker instances can be created, and how attributes are set and retrieved. These are just the methods we use when we want to implement the method gotoMarker() for a given editor.

GotoMarker

If a new marker is created, the *Tasks* view appears automatically on the screen, provided that the *Tasks* view filter does not inhibit this. If we double click an entry in the *Tasks* view, the resource to which the marker belongs is opened with its current default editor and the gotoMarker() method of this editor is invoked. What happens next depends on the editor type and the marker type. In the case of the text editor, the attribute IMarker.LINE_NUMBER or the attributes IMarker.CHAR_START and IMarker.CHAR_END are evaluated. The editor viewport is positioned to the corresponding text area and this text area is selected. For a diagram editor we would instead store the identification of a graphical element in an attribute item (as indicated above). A double click on the marker would lead to the selection of the element.

Marker lifecycle

When working with markers we should be aware that IMarker instances are not really 'first-class citizens', i.e. they don't contain the marker data. Instead, they only contain a handle to a data record that itself contains the marker attributes. It may therefore happen that the data record belonging to a given IMarker instance does not exist, for example if the resource to which the marker belongs has been deleted in the meantime. We should therefore safeguard all marker operations by first querying the marker's exists() method.

9.5.4   Views

Besides editors, views are the other basic ingredient of the Eclipse workbench. All views are based on the abstract class ViewPart. Unlike editors, views don't have their own input source. Instead, they show the state information of the active editor or of the workbench.

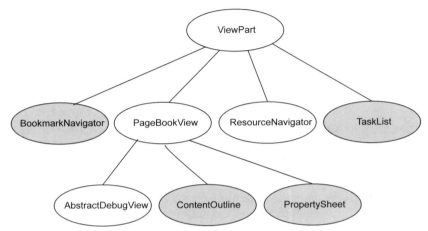

Figure 9.15: The hierarchy of view types. The grayed out components cannot be instantiated or subclassed.

The Eclipse SDK comes with a variety of predefined view types. Of course is it possible to implement our own view types as well, based on ViewPart or one of its subclasses. We give an example of such a custom view in Section 11.6. By overriding the ViewPart method init() we can implement a specific initialization for a custom view.

Persistency   This is necessary when we want to maintain the state of a view across sessions. We can archive the state by overriding the method saveState(). A parameter of type IMemento is passed to this method. In the next session the same IMemento instance is received by the init() method. Mementos are hierarchical structures – each memento can contain other mementos as child node – in which the state information of a view can be preserved. The Eclipse SDK provides a concrete implementation of the IMemento interface with the class XMLMemento. As its name indicates, this class stores the view's state information in the form of an XML file.

View toolbars   In contrast to editors, each view instance has its own toolbar, which can also be equipped with a view-specific drop-down menu. We can obtain this toolbar from the IViewSite instance via getActionBars(). (The IViewSite instance can be retrieved from the ViewPart via the method getViewSite().) The method getActionBars() delivers an IActionBars instance, from which we can obtain the menu manager (IMenuManager) via getMenuManager() and the toolbar manager (IToolManager) via getToolManager(). If we want to construct a toolbar or a drop-down menu, we just add IAction instances to these managers with the help of their respective add() methods.

Further information about menu managers can be found in Section 9.5.5. That section also describes how to construct context menus for views, just as it is done for editors.

The ResourceNavigator class

The `ResourceNavigator` class implements the navigator for Eclipse workspace resource (see Figure 9.16). Clients can configure the navigator via the `IResourceNavigator` interface.

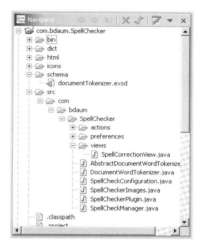

Figure 9.16: The standard appearance of a ResourceNavigator instance as we know it from day-to-day work with Eclipse.

The following methods can be used to configure the resource navigator:

`getFrameList()`	This method delivers a `FrameList` instance that contains the user's navigation history. For example, we can navigate to a previous resource view by calling the `back()` method of this instance (see also Section 2.2.4).
`getPatternFilter()`	This method delivers the active filter of the resource navigator. The class `ResourcePatternFilter` manages string arrays that contain the filter patterns. Each pattern specifies resources that are *not* to be shown in the navigator.

getSorter()	This method delivers the current ResourceSorter. ResourceSorter, which allows the displayed IResource instances to be sorted by name or type.
getViewer()	This method delivers the TreeViewer instance used by the ResourceNavigator to display the resources.
getWorkingSet()	This method delivers the currently active IWorkingSet instance, or null if no *Working Set* is currently active.
setFiltersPreference()	This method allows you to set new filter patterns. The end user can activate a filter pattern by selecting it from this list.
setSorter()	Using this method you can set a new ResourceSorter and thus modify the sort strategy.
setWorkingSet()	With this method you can set an IWorkingSet instance as a new active *Working Set*.

Various other navigators, such as the *Java Package Explorer*, are based on the ResourceNavigator and use the methods listed above to achieve their individual configurations.

The PageBookView class

The abstract class PageBookView serves as a basis for the implementation of the classes AbstractDebugView, ContentOutline, and PropertyView. The latter two classes are discussed in more detail below. We can also use the PageBookView as a basis for the implementation of custom views.

The class PageBookView supports views that display state information from particular workbench components (IWorkbenchPart) such as state information from the active editor. As the name indicates, a PageBookView instance can be equipped with several pages. The standard page usually shows state information from the currently active component. Additional pages may display state information from other workbench components.

Each subclass of PageBookView must implement the following methods:

createDefaultPage()	In the implementation of this method we must construct the default page. This page is always shown when no specific PageBookView page can be found for the currently active workbench component.
getBootstrapPart()	This method is used for determining the currently active workbench component. By overriding this method, clients can determine an active component that differs from the currently active component of the WorkbenchPage.
isImportant()	This method must return the value true if a PageBookView page is to be constructed for the received IWorkbenchPart component.
doCreatePage()	In the implementation of this method we construct the PageBookView pages for specific workbench components. The method is only invoked when the previously called method isImportant() returned the value true.
doDestroyPage()	In the implementation of this method we can dispose of PageBookView pages for specific workbench components.

Subclasses of PageBookView can override further methods, such as partActivated(), partBroughtToTop(), partClosed(), partDeactivated(), and partOpened(). By doing so, we can vary the page order – and, of course, the page contents – according to the state of the workbench page.

The outline view

The class ContentOutline implements a view that displays an outline for editor contents. The *Outline* view of the *Java Perspective* (see Section 2.5) is an example of such a view.

We cannot instantiate or subclass the ContentOutline class – its (only) instance is created and managed by the workbench when needed. This singleton can be displayed by calling the IWorkbenchPage method:

```
showView("org.eclipse.ui.views.ContentOutline");
```

Despite the fact that this class cannot be extended via subclasses, it supports the creation of outlines for all possible editor types. This works as follows: when the ContentOutline discovers that a component of type IEditorPart is activated, it asks that component if it can provide an *Outline* page. If the response is yes, the *Outline* page is included in the view. (Remember that ContentOutline is a subclass of PageBookView).

Editors that wish to contribute an *Outline* must provide a suitable adapter (see Section 9.5). The ContentOutline instance will fetch the *Outline* page with the following method call:

```
editor.getAdapter(IContentOutlinePage.class);
```

An example of this technique is found in the *Readme* editor contained in the Eclipse SDK as an example application.

The property view

Property views are used to display and edit specific properties of selected objects. An example is the property view of the manifest editor (see Section 9.4.2).

The PropertyView class works very similarly to the ContentOutline class. Property-View can also not be instantiated or subclassed – its (only) instance is created and managed by the workbench when needed. This instance can be displayed by calling the IWorkbenchPage method:

```
showView("org.eclipse.ui.views.PropertySheet");
```

When the PropertyView discovers that a component is activated, it asks that component if it can provide a PropertySheetPage instance. If the response is yes, the page is included into the view.

Components that wish to contribute a PropertySheetPage must provide a suitable adapter (seeSection 9.5). The PropertyView instance will fetch the PropertySheetPage instance with the following method call:

```
part.getAdapter(IPropertySheetPage.class);
```

The bookmark manager

The class BookmarkManager implements a view that displays bookmarks (see Section 1.4.3). If the end user double clicks a bookmark, the corresponding editor is opened and its viewport is positioned to the bookmark.

This class can also not be instantiated or subclassed – its (only) instance is created and managed by the workbench when needed. This instance can be displayed by calling the IWorkbenchPage method:

```
showView("org.eclipse.ui.views.BookmarkNavigator");
```

New bookmarks are not explicitly added to the bookmark manager, but are added as IMarker objects to the corresponding resource (see Section 9.3.2). They then appear automatically, depending on the filter settings in the bookmark manager.

The tasks list

Things are quite similar for the TaskList class, which displays the current problems and tasks (see Section 1.4.2). Again, this class cannot be instantiated or subclassed – its (only) instance is created and managed by the workbench when needed. This instance can be displayed by calling the IWorkbenchPage method:

```
showView("org.eclipse.ui.views.TaskList");
```

New tasks and problems are not explicitly added to TaskList, but are added as IMarker objects to the corresponding resource (see Section 9.3.2). They then appear automatically, depending on the filter settings in the *Tasks* view.

9.5.5   Actions

We have already mentioned the concept of *Actions* from time to time. In Eclipse this idea represents an abstract user action, such as writing to a file, searching for a string in text, or jumping to a marker. Actions are represented in Eclipse by the JFace interface IAction (see Section 7.5.1). This interface abstracts the action's semantics from the representation of the action in the workbench. When executing the action, it makes no difference whether the action was represented as a menu item, as a toolbar button, or as both.

Local and global actions

Eclipse offers two different action types: local actions and global actions. Global actions are useful if several editors have actions with the same name, such as *Undo*, *Save*, or *Find*. To avoid menus and toolbars becoming overcrowded with the individual actions from all active editors, it is possible to combine similarly named actions into global actions. The implementation of global actions is in fact quite different from local actions (see below). The Eclipse SDK already defines a set of constants in the interface org.eclipse.ui.IWorkbenchActionConstants that can be used as identifiers for global actions.

In particular, the following actions can be shared between different editors and views:

View			Editor	
File	**Edit**	**Navigate**	**File**	**Edit**
move *rename* *refresh* *properties*	*cut* *copy* *paste* *delete* *select all* *undo* *redo*	*go into* *back* *forward* *up* *next* *previous*	*revert* *print*	*find* *cut* *copy* *paste* *delete* *select all* *undo* *redo*

When implementing an action we have two main options:

- We can specify the action in an *Action Set* in the manifest file plugin.xml (see Section 9.4.3). In this case the IAction instances are instantiated by the workbench – the programmer does not need to implement IAction. However, in this case we must implement an action delegate (IActionDelegate). The manifest editor will generate an IActionDelegate stub for each new action.

- We can explicitly implement the IAction interface in our own application. In this case the application is also responsible for creating IAction instances. This is required for actions whose enabling does not depend on workbench selection, but rather on other criteria. It is also required for context menus that cannot yet be declared in the manifest.

Defining actions in the manifest

Let's deal with the first case first. Here we only need to describe the action sufficiently in the manifest (see Figure 9.17). This is usually the best practice because it allows easy extension of the plug-in's functionality later.

Actions can be defined in various extension points, such as org.eclipse.ui.action-Sets, org.eclipse.ui.editorActions, and org.eclipse.ui.viewActions (see Section 9.4.3).

Figure 9.17: The manifest attributes that we have defined for the action 'CheckSpelling' from Chapter 11.

For each action we can specify the following attributes:

id	A unique identifier of the action.
label	A display text for the action, to be shown, for example, in the menu item or the tool button. We can emphasize one letter of the text by prefixing it in the usual way with the character '&'. This letter will then act as a mnemonic code for the action. In addition, we may append a keyboard shortcut in form of a text string separated by the character '@'. Several key names can be concatenated with the help of the character '+' as in '@Ctrl+Shift+S'.
accelerator	The code for the keyboard shortcut as defined in the class SWT. If the shortcut consists of several keys, their code values are summed.
definitionId	The identification for an *action definition*. This is only needed when the key assignment is performed dynamically via the *Key Binding Service*. In this case the definitionId must match with the id used in the *action definition* and the id used for the action in the corresponding *Action Set*.

menubarPath	A path expression describing where the action should appear in the workbench menu. If this attribute is omitted, the action is not represented as a menu item.
	Each section in the path specification (except the last section) must specify the valid identifier of an existing menu item. The last section specifies either the name of a new group or an existing group to which the action is to be added.
	The necessary menu item identifiers are found in the interface `org.eclipse.ui.IWorkbenchActionConstants`.
toolbarPath	A path expression describing where the action should appear in the workbench toolbar. If this attribute is omitted, the action is not represented as a tool item.
	The first section of this path specification identifies the toolbar. (`Normal` stands for the default workbench toolbar.) The second section specifies either the name of a new group or an existing group to which the action is to be added.
icon	The path, relative to the location of `plugin.xml`, of an icon that represents the action in toolbars.
disabledIcon	Another icon that represents the action when it is disabled. If this icon is omitted, a gray version of the icon specified under the `icon` attribute is used.
hoverIcon	The icon that should appear when the mouse hovers over the enabled action. This icon is also used to represent enabled actions in menus. If this attribute is omitted, the icon specified under the `icon` attribute is used instead.
tooltip	A message that is displayed on the screen when the mouse hovers over the toolbar representation of the action.
helpContextId	A unique identifier of the action for context sensitive help. Please see Section 9.5.10 for details.
state	If this value is specified, the action can be toggled. The specified value (`true` or `false`) determines the initial state.

pulldown	An alternative to the state attribute, this attribute can specify that the action is equipped with a drop-down menu. In toolbars, a pull-down arrow appears at the right hand side of the action's representation.
class	The fully qualified name of a class implementing the interface org.eclipse.ui.IWorkbenchWindowActionDelegate (see below).
retarget	An alternative to the class attribute, we can specify the value true for this attribute if the action is a global action (see below).
allowLabelUpdates	This attribute is only used when true is specified for the attribute retarget. If the attribute allowLabelUpdates is set to true, clients may modify the display label and the tool tip of the global action.
enablesFor	This attribute specifies when the action is enabled: ! Nothing selected. ? Nothing or only a single element selected. + One or more elements selected. 2+ Two or more elements selected. n Exactly *n* elements selected. * Enabling is independent of selection. If the attribute is omitted, the action's enabling depends solely on program logic. In addition, actions can be enabled or disabled by the application.

In addition to the quite basic enablesFor attribute, we can make further specifications for enabling, disabling, and notification of actions. To do so, we select the action in the manifest editor and invoke the context function *New*. We then have the choice between selection and enablement.

Selection Under element selection we can specify the fully qualified name of a class or an interface (for example org.eclipse.core.resources.IResource) in the attribute class. By doing so, we enforce the selected objects to only be sent to the IActionDelegate when all selected elements are of the specified type. In all other cases the IActionDelegate method selectionChanged() will obtain the empty selection. Under the attribute name we can specify a filter pattern (such as '*.txt'). The names of all selected objects must match this pattern to enable the action.

Enabling and disabling actions

Further control about the enabling of actions is possible via the enablement element. Here we can declare the enabling of an action as a function of the type and current state of the selected object, and also of the state of the plug-in and the state of the whole system. These individual conditions can be combined with Boolean expressions. The various criteria and Boolean operators are declared as child elements of the enablement element (via context function *New*).

objectClass	Under the attribute name we can specify the fully qualified name of a class or an interface. If all selected objects belong to this type, the condition has the value true.
objectState	Under the attribute name we can specify the name of an object property, and under the attribute value the value of that property. If all selected objects have properties with such a value, the condition has the value true.
	To support the workbench in the evaluation of this condition, the selected objects must implement the interface IActionFilter, or must be able to provide an IActionFilter instance via getAdapter(). If this is not the case, the condition results in false. The workbench uses the testAttribute() method of the IActionFilter interface to test the state of an object.
	If we introduce new selectable objects into the workbench, we should always implement the IActionFilter interface. This allows for actions that are added later by plug-ins to react to state changes of selected objects.
	The Eclipse SDK already implements action filters for the object types IResource, IMarker, and IProject. Which properties may be queried for these object types is described in the interfaces IResourceActionFilter, IMarkerActionFilter, and IProjectActionFilter.

systemProperty	Under the attribute name we can specify the name of a system property. The workbench will use this name to query the corresponding system property via System.getProperty(), and will compare the result with the value specified under the attribute value. If equal, the condition returns true.
pluginState	Under the attribute id we can specify the identification of a plug-in. When we specify the value installed under the attribute value, the workbench will test whether the specified plug-in is installed. If the value activated was specified, the workbench will test whether the plug-in is active.

Delegates How do we connect an action with the application? This depends on whether the action is local or global. For local actions we specify a class of type org.eclipse.ui.IWork-benchWindowActionDelegate under the attribute class. Section 11.5 shows an example of such a delegate. The init() method here is invoked when the workbench is started. When the selection within the workbench changes, the method selectionChanged() is called. The method run() is invoked when the end user activates the action.

Global actions are defined by specifying the value true under the attribute retarget. In this case the class attribute is not specified. It is the application that is responsible for creating a concrete RetargetAction instance (or a LabelRetargetAction instance when allowLabelUpdates is set to true). Usually this is done in the createPartControl() method of the respective editor or view. The new action instance is then registered via:

```
getViewSite().getActionBars().setGlobalActionHandler(
    id, retargetAction);
```

In this code we first fetch a view's runtime environment via getViewSite(). From this view site we fetch the view's toolbar via getActionBars() (see Section 9.5.4). Then we register the action with the help of setGlobalActionHandler() by specifying the identification of the action (id) and the RetargetAction instance (retargetAction). The code for registering editor actions is similar. However, in this case an intermediate step via an IEditorActionBarContributor instance is required (see Section 9.5.3).

The example *Readme* editor contained in the Eclipse SDK demonstrates how to work with global actions quite explicitly.

Implementing actions manually

As an alternative to declaring actions in the manifest file plugin.xml we can, of course, implement actions the hard way in Java code. For global actions, we have already seen that the application is responsible for creating the respective IAction instances (such as RetargetAction or LabelRetargetAction instances).

We will usually not implement the IAction interface from scratch, but instead will extend one of the classes from the package org.eclipse.ui.actions. We can find a variety of actions for standard tasks in this package.

If we don't define an action within plugin.xml, we must ensure that the action appears in the respective toolbars and menus. This is, in particular, the case for context function actions, because context functions cannot be declared in plugin.xml.

In Section 11.6.1 we show how to hard-code actions for a view in an example plug-in. We first create the individual action instances, and then construct a toolbar, a drop-down menu, and a context menu with these actions. We create Separator instances, too, that act as anchor points, allowing other plug-ins to add actions to the so created menus.

We have already discussed how actions can be added to the toolbar of a view in Section 9.4. For context menus we must do a bit more work, making use of the respective JFace components, as discussed in Section 7.5.

9.5.6   Dialogs

We can find a set of ready-made Dialog classes that can be used within plug-ins in the package org.eclipse.ui.dialogs. Using these classes can save a lot of work and help to achieve a consistent 'look and feel' in an application.

Figure 9.18: The hierarchy of Dialog classes in the package 'org.eclipse.ui.dialog'.

SelectionDialog   All these dialog classes are based on the abstract class SelectionDialog, which is itself based on the JFace class (and therefore, too, on the JFace class Window), which has already been discussed in Section 7.2. Consequently this class is equipped with the methods inherited from Dialog, such as create(), open(), close(), etc. It implements additional methods, such as setInitialElementSelections() and setInitialSelections(), with which we can make an initial selection of dialog elements. The methods setTitle() and setMessage() allow setting a title and a longer text for the message area of the dialog. These methods must be used between the method calls create() and open().

We obtain the result of a dialog with the help of getResult(). If the dialog was not closed with the *OK* button, this method returns the value null.

We will now take a closer look at some of the concrete dialog classes of the package org.eclipse.ui.dialogs.

CheckedTreeSelectionDialog and ElementTreeSelectionDialog

These dialogs support the selection of elements from a tree. We can supply the viewer (see Section 7.3.2) of these dialogs with input data using the method setInput(), and we can determine which elements are initially expanded with setExpandedElements(). With addFilter() we can set a ViewerFilter instance. This instance determines which elements of the input data are shown in the tree. With setSorter() we can set a sorter for the tree elements. A validator can be specified with setValidator(). In the case of selection changes this validator checks whether all selected elements are valid and enables or disables the *OK* button accordingly. Finally, we can set the size of the tree area in characters via setSize().

ElementTreeSelectionDialog features, in addition, the methods setAllowMultiple() and setDoubleClickSelects() for allowing or disallowing multiple selection of tree elements, and determining the behavior in the case of double clicks. As both classes are derivatives of SelectionStatusDialog, they also have methods for managing the status line. Among these methods are the method setStatusLineAboveButtons() for determining the position of the status line, and the method updateStatus(), with which the status line can be updated. In addition, we may control the state of the *OK* button with method updateButtonsEnableState().

ElementListSelectionDialog

This dialog implements a simple list from which the end user can select elements. We can set the elements of this list via method setElements(). This dialog, too, is a derivative of SelectionStatusDialog, and thus inherits the above methods for status line management.

ListSelectionDialog

This dialog also implements a list from which elements can be selected by the end user. However, this dialog works with arbitrary domain models. The contents of the selection list is retrieved from an IContentProvider instance, and the representation is computed with the help of an ILabelProvider instance. We can pass the input object, an IStruc-

turedContentProvider instance, the ILabelProvider instance, and a message in the
ListSelectionDialog() constructor.

ContainerSelectionDialog

This dialog allows the end user to select a workspace container (project or folder). We
can specify the root directory of the selection tree in the constructor of this class. In
addition, we can specify whether new containers may be created.

ResourceListSelectionDialog

This dialog allows the end user to select workspace resources. We specify the root
directory of the selection tree in the constructor of this class, and we can specify an
initial selection with setInitialSelections().

SaveAsDialog

This dialog can be used to prompt the end user for the location and name for a file to be
stored. We can set a default selection with the method setOriginalFile(). This method
must be executed before create(). We obtain the specified file location as an IPath
object via getResult().

NewFolderDialog

We can prompt the end user for the name of a new directory with this dialog. The parent
container is specified in the constructor of this class. The dialog will immediately create
the new directory when the *OK* button is pressed.

ContainerGenerator

This class is not a dialog, but is nevertheless useful. It creates all missing resource
containers along a specified path. The path is specified in the constructor of the class.
We can then create all missing containers using generateContainer().

9.5.7   Workbench wizards

We have already discussed how wizards can be implemented with JFace classes in
Section 7.6. Here we discuss how the existing wizards of the Eclipse workbench can be
extended. In particular, this is required when an application needs to create new files or
new projects. In this case we should not create our own eccentric solution, but rather
should link into the *New* wizard of the Eclipse workbench.

The newWizard extension point

Integration into *New* wizard is quite easy to achieve: we simply define the extension in the manifest file plugin.xml. The extension point identification for the *New* wizard is org.eclipse.ui.newWizards. We can add three elements to this extension point:

- category. We can define a new category for the new wizard in this element. The attribute id identifies the category uniquely. Under the attribute name a display name for the new category is defined. We can define the identification of an existing category to which the new category is added as a child with the optional attribute parentCategory.

- wizard. This element is required to declare the new wizard. The attribute id identifies the wizard uniquely. A display name for the new wizard is defined under the attribute name. With the optional attribute category we can assign the new wizard to a category. If this attribute is not specified, the wizard is by default assigned to the category 'Others'. We can specify the relative path of an icon that represents the wizard in the selection list under icon. The implementation of the wizard is specified in attribute class. The class specified here must implement the interface INewWizard (see below).

  If the optional attribute project is set to true, the new wizard will not be used to create new files, but to create new projects – the wizard appears in the *New Project* dialog. In this case we can specify the attribute finalPerspective (see Section 9.5.9). This attribute specifies the identification of the perspective that should be opened when the new project is created.

  Finally, the child element description may be added to the wizard element. This element can contain a description text for the wizard.

- selection. Under the attribute class we can specify the fully qualified name of a class or interface (for example org.eclipse.core.resources.IResource). If all selected elements of the workbench belong to this type, the selection will be passed to the wizard when it is initialized. Otherwise it will obtain the empty selection. Under the attribute name we can specify a filter pattern (for example '*.txt') that must be satisfied by the names of all selected elements for the selection to be passed to the wizard.

Here is an example for a (fictitious) wizard for creating a new jukebox playlist (see Section 8.5). First we create a new category called Jukebox. In this category we create a new wizard called Playlist. When the wizard is activated, an instance of the class PlaylistCreationWizard is created and the run() method of this instance is invoked. Workbench selections are only passed to the wizard when all elements of the selection are workspace resources.

```
<extension
  point="org.eclipse.ui.newWizards">
  <category
    name="Jukebox"
    id="com.bdaum.jukebox.newWizard">
  </category>
  <wizard
    name="Playlist"
    icon="icons/basic/obj16/playlist.gif"
    category="com.bdaum.jukebox.newWizard"
    class="com.bdaum.jukebox.wizards.PlaylistCreationWizard"
    id="com.bdaum.jukebox.newPlaylistWizard">
    <description>
      Creates new Jukebox playlist file
    </description>
    <selection
      class="org.eclipse.core.resources.IResource">
    </selection>
  </wizard>
</extension>
```

The interface IWorkbenchWizard

Wizards that are created for the Eclipse workbench should implement the interface IWorkbenchWizard. The interface INewWizard is an extension of this interface. IWorkbenchWizard is based on the JFace interface IWizard, but specifies an additional method, init(). This is invoked when the wizard is started, and passes the Workbench instance and the current workbench selection to the wizard, provided that the selection satisfies the conditions specified in the selection element.

The class WizardNewFileCreationPage

When creating a *New File* wizard, we can save some work in many cases if we base the wizard's default page on the class WizardNewFileCreationPage. This class prompts the end user for the required input and creates the new file based on that input. We can use this class in its original form or can create our own subclasses. In particular, we may want to override or extend the methods getInitialContents(), getNewFileLabel(), and handleEvent(). The method getInitialContents() returns the initial contents of the new file in form of an InputStream – these contents will be written into the new file. The method getNewFileLabel() returns the display label for the input field of the file name. The method handleEvent() is called for any events caused by this wizard page. We can react adequately to user actions by extending this method.

For example, if we want to create a default page PlayListCreationWizardPage for our wizard PlaylistCreationWizard, it could look like this:

```
public class PlayListCreationWizardPage extends
  WizardNewFileCreationPage {
  private final static String XMLPROLOG =
    "<?xml version=\"1.0\" encoding=\"UTF-8\"?>";

  protected InputStream getInitialContents() {
    try {
      String input = XMLPROLOG + "<playlist></playlist>"
      return new ByteArrayInputStream(input.getBytes("UTF8"));
    } catch (UnsupportedEncodingException x) {
      return null;
    }
  }

  protected String getNewFileLabel() {
    return "Playlist name";
  }
}
```

The method getInitialContents() here creates an empty playlist in XML format.

9.5.8   Preferences

We discussed preference pages and preference trees in Section 7.7. We don't need to deal with the classes PreferenceNode, PreferenceManager, and PreferenceDialog in the context of the Eclipse workbench. The workbench already constructs a preference tree that can be opened by the end user via *Window > Preferences*. All we have to do is to add the preference pages provided by our plug-in to this tree.

Manifest   This is done by declaring an appropriate extension in the manifest file plugin.xml. The extension point in question is org.eclipse.ui.preferencePages. This extension point is quite simple and only consists of the single element page. We specify the identification of the new node in the preference tree under the attribute id. Under name we specify the display text for this node, and under attribute class we specify the fully qualified class name of the respective PreferencePage implementation. The workbench will later create an instance of this class when required. Finally, we can specify the path (see Section 7.7.4) for the identification of the parent node of the new node under category. If this attribute is not specified, the new node is appended directly to the root node of the preference tree.

We give some examples for the declaration of preference pages in plugin.xml in Section 11.3 and Section 11.11.2.

Initializing   As already mentioned in Section 7.7.1 and Section 9.2, it is necessary to initialize the PreferenceStore with default values when an application is started, because default values are not persistent. In the context of a plug-in, the best place for doing so is the Plugin class, or a special class that represents the preferences' domain model. Initializing the preference default values in the PreferencePage class is *not* recommended, as this would increase the start-up time of the Eclipse platform. In Section 11.4 and Section 11.9 we show how plug-in preferences can be initialized and modified.

9.5.9   Defining perspectives

Perspectives define the initial layout of a workbench page: they define where editors and views are placed and which *Action Sets* are visible.

Plug-ins may (but are not required to) add one or several perspectives to the workbench. This is recommended when the existing perspectives are not suitable for the tasks that are to be performed with the respective plug-in. Another thing to consider is that a plug-in may be installed in the minimal *Eclipse Runtime Environment*, and this environment only understands the *Resource Perspective*.

The definition of a new perspective begins, too, with an entry in the manifest file plugin.xml. The corresponding extension point is org.eclipse.ui.perspectives with the element perspective. This element may possess a child element description containing a description text for the perspective. The attribute id contains the identification of the perspective. The attribute name specifies the display text. The attribute icon refers to an icon that is displayed on the *Open Perspective* button of the perspective, on the left border of the workbench. Finally, the attribute class specifies the fully qualified name of a class that implements the interface IPerspectiveFactory. This class is responsible for the construction of the initial layout.

This is done in the only method of this interface, createInitialLayout(). This method accepts an instance of type IPageLayout as a parameter, representing the layout of a workbench page. In the API documentation of this interface we can also find an example of the implementation of the method createInitialLayout().

Perspective layout   Initially a perspective consists of a single area, occupied by the editor. We get the identification of this area from the IPageLayout object with the help of getEditorArea(). Starting from this area, we can now add additional *folder areas* of type IFolderLayout with the help of createFolder(). Such a folder area can contain one or several views, stacked on top of each other. The parameters needed for this method are the identification of the new area, the orientation (TOP, BOTTOM, LEFT, RIGHT), the size ratio to the reference area, and the identification of the reference area. The reference area can be the editor area or another previously created folder area. It is possible to construct deeply nested layouts.

We can now attach area an arbitrary number of views to each folder. This is done with `addView()`. This method accepts the identification of the respective view (as defined in `plugin.xml`) as a parameter. Alternatively, we can use the method `addPlaceholder()` to reserve space for a not-yet-visible view. When the end user opens this view at a later time with *Window > Show View*, the view will appear in the reserved area. We have the option of adding a view to the primary *Show View* list via `addShowViewShortcut()`. Without doing so, the view would only appear under *Window > Show View > Others*.

FastViews   As we saw in Section 2.7, we have the option of using views as *FastViews* instead of stacking them in a folder area. When defining a perspective, we may also initialize a view as *FastView*: the method `addFastView()` is used for this purpose.

Action sets   Finally, we have the option of activating *Action Sets* defined in the manifest file `plugin.xml` when initializing the perspective. This is done with `addActionSet()`.

We can place the *Open Perspective* button with the specified icon onto the left border of the workbench page with the method `addPerspectiveShortcut()`.

9.5.10   The Help system

We have mentioned the Eclipse help system in various sections of this book. While JFace still requires us to code help functions explicitly (for example by registering a help listener), things are quite different in the context of plug-in programming. Here, help pages are associated with GUI elements in the higher software layers.

There are two different ways to offer help. One way is to offer it via the help function of the Eclipse workbench (*Help > Help Contents*). Each plug-in can provide a help table of contents (*toc*) that can be embedded into the global table of contents. It may appear there as a separate chapter, or may be added further below in the tree of help pages.

The other way is to offer context sensitive help. When the user presses the *F1* key, the GUI element that has the focus determines the help page to be displayed. The central mechanism here is the *help identification*. It links the respective GUI element or the respective program function to one or several help pages.

Both the table of contents and the association of help pages with help identifications is encoded into separate XML files. The advantage is that the help system can be developed quite independent from the application. It is even possible to deploy the help system of a given plug-in as a separate plug-in.

Creating a Help table of contents

The *Table of Contents* of the help pages of a plug-in is defined in a file that is usually called `toc.xml` and stored in the project directory of the plug-in.

XML editor   As the file extension indicates, the table of contents is an XML file. No special editor for
                 this file type exists in the Eclipse SDK, but we can use the text editor. Another possi-
                 bility is to create a simple XML editor. This is done with just a few mouse clicks.

                 First, we create a new plug-in project (see Section 9.4). On the *Plug-in Code Generators*
                 page of the *New Project* wizard we select *Plug-in with an editor*. This will generate a
                 complete XML editor with syntax highlighting. We can install this editor by copying the
                 plug-in directory from the workspace directory into the directory plugins and then
                 restarting Eclipse.

                 If we want more features, there are some 'grown-up' XML editors available as third-
                 party plug-ins (see Appendix A).

                 The file toc.xml must contain a root element named toc. Usually, such a toc element
                 contains one or several topic elements that can be nested.

                 Here is the help table of contents from Section 11.10.1 as an example:

```
<?xml version="1.0" encoding="UTF-8"?>
<toc label="Spell Checker" topic="html/spelling.html">
  <topic label="Correction View" href=
    "html/SpellCheckerView.html"/>
  <topic label="Default Preferences"
    href="html/SpellCheckerPreferences.html">
    <anchor id="postPreferences"/>
  </topic>
  <topic label="Other Information">
  <topic label="Acknowledgements" href=
    "html/Acknowledgements.html"/>
      <topic label="Dictionaries" href="html/Dictionaries.html"/>
  </topic>
</toc>
```

                 The label attributes define the display text shown in the help page tree. A click on this
                 text will display the help page referenced by the attribute href. (If this attribute is not
                 defined, nothing will happen, of course.) If topic elements are nested, the inner
                 elements appear as a subsection of the other elements. It is possible to expand or
                 collapse the outer elements depending on the browser used and on the browser
                 preferences.

                 As we see in the code above, it is also possible to assign a help page to the toc element.
                 This is done in abbreviated form with the attribute topic.

                 The path expression in the href attributes and the topic attribute do not necessarily
                 need to remain within the boundaries of our own plug-in. However, the reference point
                 is always the own plug-in directory. By using appropriate path expressions, however, we
                 can also point to help pages in other plug-in directories. For example:

```
href="../org.eclipse.jdt.doc.user_2.1.0/tips/tips-1.html
```

A specialty is the anchor element shown in the example above. Such an element allows other plug-ins to link into this table of contents, or to organize a table of contents in form of several modules. We will show how this is done in Section 11.11.5.

Manifest   Of course it is still necessary to declare the help table of contents in the manifest file plugin.xml. This is done with the extension point org.eclipse.help.toc in the element toc. Here we specify under the attribute file the name of the XML file containing the table of contents (for example toc.xml). The attribute primary="true" identifies this table of contents as an autonomous table of contents. (primary="false" would indicate a table of contents that is to be embedded into another table of contents.) We can specify the relative path of a directory containing all help pages that cannot be reached via the table of contents (i.e. pages that can only be reached via context sensitive help or via the index) in the attribute extradir. When the help subsystem computes the help index, it will analyze all pages that are referenced in the table of contents and all pages contained in the directory referenced by extradir.

Section 11.3 and Section 11.11.2 show what such manifest declarations look like.

Creating help context associations

The association of help pages with help identifications for a plug-in is done in a file usually called contexts.xml. This file is stored in the project directory of the plug-in. The file must contain a root element named contexts. This element usually contains one or several context child elements. Each of these context elements corresponds to an *Infopop* (a little window that appears when the *F1* key is pressed). Section 11.10.2 shows an example of such a context association.

Each context has an attribute id, which declares the help identification with which the element is associated. In addition, a context element may contain a description child element and one or several topic child elements. Both of these have already been discussed.

Manifest   It is also necessary to declare the help–context association in the manifest file plugin.xml. This happens via the extension point org.eclipse.help.contexts with the element contexts. We specify the name of the context association file (for example contexts.xml) under the attribute file.

Section 11.3 and Section 11.11.2 show what such manifest declarations look like.

Setting context identifications

Help identifications can be assigned to individual GUI elements using the static method setHelp() of the class WorkbenchHelp. The respective GUI element and the help identification string are passed as parameters. The following GUI element types can be equipped with context sensitive help: Control, IAction, MenuItem, and Menu.

For example:

```
Button button = new Button(parent, SWT.PUSH);
WorkbenchHelp.setHelp(button,"example.plugin.button1_context");
```

We must specify the fully qualified context identification (including the plug-in identification) in this method.

Manifest   For some abstract constructs we have the option of declaring context identification in the manifest. In particular, this is possible for actions in *Action Sets*, by specifying the helpContextId attribute (see Section 9.5.5). An example is found in Section 11.3.

Also for markers of all kinds, we can declare help identification in the manifest file. This is done in the extension point org.eclipse.ui.markerHelp with the element markerHelp. Here we can define an association between marker type (specified in attribute markerType) and a help identification (specified in attribute helpContextId).

Instead of the attribute markerType, or in combination with this attribute, we can specify one or several attribute child elements. Each of these elements specifies a marker attribute name (name) and an attribute value (value). With this specification we can associate a help identification to markers that have at least one attribute that matches the specified attribute value. If several markerHelp declarations match a marker in such a case, the help identification of the markerHelp declaration with the most matching attributes is used, allowing the help information to depend on the content of the marker. For example, for a problem marker we could show a specific help text for each different problem type.

Packaging help for deployment

Help pages are implemented as HTML pages. They are located, together with the other resources (images, etc.), in a separate appropriately named folder (for example, html or doc). The href references in the topic elements in the table of contents and in the help-context association file refer to these files.

In the case of large help systems, however, this storage method wastes a lot of disk space. Help pages are usually quite small but allocate a full block (for example 64 Kbytes) on the disk. Eclipse therefore allows the packaging of all help resources into a Zip archive. This archive must have the name doc.zip. If the Eclipse help subsystem finds such an archive, it will search there first for requested help pages. Only if the page is not found is it searched for among the unpacked help pages.

Active help

Eclipse even allows workbench functions or plug-in functions to be offered in help pages. Instead of asking the user to perform a specific action, we can embed a hyperlink in the help page that performs the action for the user when clicked.

To offer this functionality, Eclipse uses the central JavaScript file `livehelp.js`. This must be declared in all help pages that wish to use this functionality. For example:

```
<script language=
  "JavaScript" src="../../org.eclipse.help/livehelp.js/>
```

We can then use this script in all HTML elements that accept scripts, for example in a hyperlink:

```
<a href='javascript:liveAction(
  "com.bdaum.SpellChecker",
  "com.bdaum.SpellChecker.actions.ActiveHelpAction",
  "start"
)'>Check Spelling</a>
```

The first parameter specifies the plug-in identification. The second parameter specifies the class that implements the action, and the third parameter is a string value that is transmitted to the action.

The class that represents the action must implement the interface `ILiveHelpAction`. Two methods must be implemented:

- The method `setInitializationString()` accepts the value of s third parameter in the JavaScript call. This allows this class to be used in different places with different parameter values and to react differently depending on those values.

- The method `run()` must perform the requested action.

An example of such a class and its invocation can be found in Section 11.10.3.

10 Developing your own Eclipse based products

From the implementation and testing of a plug-in to its deployment, we still have a few steps to cover. Fortunately, Eclipse offers support here too, but some steps may require manual intervention. The Eclipse functions offered in these areas are still subject to change, and the changes introduced in the final release version of Eclipse 2.1 were quite substantial.

When deploying a product, we should start with an idea of how to segment the product into modules. Eclipse offers three different constructs here: *features*, *plug-ins*, and *fragments*. Eclipse makes use of the Ant assembly tool for all these constructs when creating the deployment archives. The scripts used to control Ant are automatically created by Eclipse. However, manual modifications are possible.

We have several options for the installation format. For example, we can deliver a plug-in as a ZIP file. The user then simply unpacks the file into the directory `eclipse/plugins`. You may remember that the installation of the Eclipse SDK is quite similar. A further option is to use a commercial installation manager such as *InstallAnyWhere* or *InstallShield*. Finally, Eclipse offers its own elegant installation function, the *Eclipse Update Manager*. However, this function can only be used when deploying Eclipse add-ons, not for deploying stand-alone products.

For stand-alone products the question of customizing is important, too. For example, such a product should start with its own splash screen and not with the Eclipse splash screen. The configuration of the *About* pages and of the *Help* pages will also differ from the standard solution provided by the Eclipse SDK.

Finally, we will discuss the localization of an application. Eclipse offers several ways to adapt applications to different national or cultural contexts.

10.1 Embedded Ant

Ant is an *Apache* project (`ant.apache.org`). Ant offers similar functionality to make and other tools that assemble deployment archives from development artifacts. The big difference between Ant and make and other similar tools is that Ant does not use shell commands to perform tasks — all actions are performed with the help of Java classes. The Ant script is merely an XML file. The advantage is that Ant scripts are completely platform independent, as the Ant system itself.

Ant is already embedded into the Eclipse SDK. To run an Ant script, we just have to select the script file in the *Navigator* (the file must have the file extension `.xml`), then invoke the context function *Run ANT...* or the menu function *Run > External Tools > External Tools...*

Configuration   If no Ant configuration currently exists, we must first create a new configuration. This is done in a similar fashion to creating a *Run* configuration with the *Run...* function (see Section 5.2).

The configuration dialog (see Figure 10.1) offers various options spread over several pages:

- On the *Refresh* page of the configuration dialog we can determine the resources for which a *Refresh* function should be executed after an Ant run. The reason for this setting is that Ant is executed as an external tool. This means that it runs outside of the Eclipse workspace. By default the resource changes caused by Ant do not appear in the resource navigator of the Eclipse workbench. We therefore have to apply the context function *Refresh* to the project folder to synchronize the resources after running Ant.

- On the *Targets* page we can select individual Ant targets for execution.

- On the *Classpath* page we can modify the classpath under which Ant is running. Changes are only required if we have added our own Java classes to Ant.

- On the *Properties* page we can assign values to Ant variables. Alternatively, we may specify property files that contain name/value pairs for Ant variables.

If we want to modify Ant scripts we should, of course, learn the Ant script language. Detailed information about Ant can be found on the Apache Web site at `ant.apache.org`. Some comprehensive books about Ant are also available, such as [Hatcher2002] and [Tilly2002].

For typical Eclipse tasks such as the assembly of deployment archives for features, plug-ins, and fragments, Eclipse generates the required Ant scripts. The necessary script targets are stored in a file named `build.xml`. The generation of these scripts can be controlled via the file `build.properties` (see Section 10.3.2).

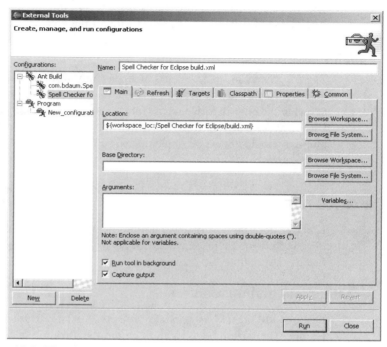

Figure 10.1: The dialog for the configuration of external tools. Depending on the tool – here we have selected Ant – we can create different configurations with different runtime parameters.

10.2 Plug-ins and fragments

In the minimal case a plug-in just consists of the manifest file plugin.xml. Normally, however, a plug-in contains additional binary Java files – in particular the class Plugin – as well as help pages, help table of contents, context associations, icons, schemas, and other resources.

In some cases it can make sense to subdivide a plug-in into several fragments. This allows the deployment of the core functionality of a plug-in as early as possible. Additional components such as national language support or support for other host operating systems can then be deployed separately later. Fragments make this possible.

Fragments are created in a similar way to plug-ins via the *New* wizard (see Section 9.4.1). However, instead of selecting *Plug-in Project* as project type, select *Fragment Project*. The wizard will then create a fragment.xml file instead of the file plugin.xml.

The fragment manifest file `fragment.xml` is quite similar to `plugin.xml`, but must specify the identification and the version of the corresponding plug-in. In addition, the wizard does not generate a `Plugin` class, as fragments are not allowed to have their own `Plugin` class.

The fragment can be developed independently from the rest of the plug-in and can be deployed separately. During the installation it is merged into the corresponding plug-in, allowing the plug-in to access the functionality of the fragment. The end user will not be able to distinguish between the fragment and the corresponding plug-in. Of course, plug-ins should always be implemented such that they can be executed without the additional fragments.

10.3 Features

Features describe one or several plug-ins that are deployed as a single functional unit. For example the Eclipse Java IDE is a single feature consisting of several plug-ins. The feature description also contains copyright information and license conditions.

10.3.1 Creating and editing features

Features are created as separate projects. Again, we use the *New* wizard to create a feature. The wizard leads us through the specification of the project name, the feature name, the feature identification, the version and the feature provider. Finally, we checkmark all plug-ins that belong to the feature. The wizard creates the manifest file `feature.xml` from these specifications, which is then opened in the *Feature Editor* (see Figure 10.2). Here, we can add additional specifications.

On the *Overview* page we can see all the specifications that we entered when we created the feature. We want to make sure that the identification of the feature matches the identification of the main plug-in. We can also specify two URLs: the *Discovery URL* can point to a Web page offering information about other products or technical support. The *Update URL* points to a Web address where the *Update Manager* (see Section 10.5) can find new versions of the feature.

The *Primary Feature* checkbox is marked if the current feature is not an add-on to already installed Eclipse platforms, but represents (together with the Eclipse platform itself) a stand-alone product. By marking the *Exclusive Install* checkbox, we can enforce the rule that no other features should be installed on the same platform. We can also specify a *Banner Image*, which appears when the plug-in is activated the very first time in a session.

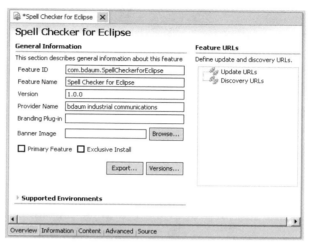

Figure 10.2: The Overview page of the Feature Editor.

In the *Supported Environments* section we can restrict the feature to certain host operating and windowing systems, to certain national language environments, and to certain processor architectures. If nothing is specified here, the feature can be installed anywhere.

The *Versions...* button offers several options for version numbering. We have the option of determining the version number of the feature from the plug-ins, or of forcing the version number of the feature into the plug-ins. To update the feature manifest it is important to press this button again after the version number of a plug-in has been changed! (The *Export...* button is discussed further below.)

The next page, *Information*, can contain auxiliary information such as a description text, a copyright notice, and license conditions. In addition to the explicitly defined text, we can also specify URLs that point to HTML pages containing the required information. However, the license conditions should always be given explicitly and as a URL. The explicit text is displayed during installation of the feature, whereas the URL target is displayed when the end user invokes the function *Help > About Eclipse Platform > Features > More...*

On the *Advanced* page we can add existing features and external archive files to the current feature. We also may specify custom *Install Handlers* (see Section 10.5).

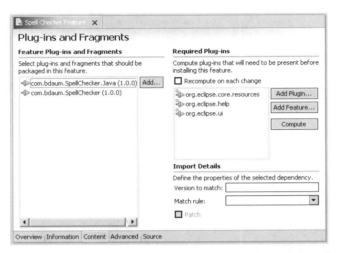

Figure 10.3: The Content page in the Feature Editor shows the plug-ins that belong to the feature on the left. The window on the right shows the plug-ins that are necessary for executing the feature. It is not necessary to create this list manually – a click on the 'Compute' button is sufficient.

10.3.2   Generating deployment scripts

The generation of Ant scripts is started by clicking on the *Export...* button in the *Overview* page of the *Feature Editor*. (The context function *Create Ant Build File* applied to *feature.xml* has the same effect.) A new Ant script file build.xml is generated for each plug-in belonging to the feature, and also for the feature project itself. If such a file already exists, it is overwritten. If we want to keep existing build.xml files, for example because we applied modifications manually, we must set the property custom=true in file build.properties.

The Ant scripts are executed automatically and the deployment archives are generated. We have the option of creating a single ZIP file (such a file is installed by simply unpacking it into the eclipse directory), or to create individual JAR files for an *Update Site* (see Section 10.4.2).

When generating deployment archives, the Ant scripts first generate JAR files that belong to the classpath of each plug-in. The names of the JAR files are specified on the *Runtime* page of the respective plug-in manifests plugin.xml (see Section 9.4.2).

Ant then generates the JAR files for the *Update Site*, one for each plug-in and one for the feature. Each of these files will contain the classpath JAR files and the manifest file `plugin.xml`. The feature JAR will, of course, contain no classpath JAR files, only the manifest file `feature.xml` plus auxiliary files.

Determining the archive content

At this point we should check the deployment archives for completeness, as we may have to remove some files that we don't want to deploy. To do this, we have two options:

- We can manipulate the Ant scripts `build.xml` directly. However, in this case we need some knowledge about Ant, as well as an understanding of the workings of the Eclipse Ant scripts. It will usually be sufficient to modify the Ant target `gather.bin.parts` to include new files and folders via the `includes` attribute or to exclude files or folders via the `excludes` attribute. We also have to include the property `custom=true` in the file `build.properties`, to prevent Eclipse from overwriting the modified script.

- We can modify the respective `build.properties` files. These files are created and maintained by the *Manifest Editor*, but can be modified manually. The variables defined in these files influence the creation of the Ant scripts. By modifying these variables we can thus control the *Export...* process for the deployment archives. I would recommend this option rather than the direct modification of the Ant scripts.

build.properties   In particular, the following variables are of interest:

`bin.includes`	We can add further resources to the deployment archive with this variable. For plug-ins this is, in particular, the manifest `plugin.xml`, all help files including `toc.xml` and `contexts.xml`, icons and images, schemas, and the documentation for extension points. Files and folders are specified using the Ant syntax (see below).
`bin.excludes`	We can exclude resources from the deployment archive with this variable. For example, if we had included the whole folder with help files and had used Microsoft FrontPage to create the help pages, we might want to exclude the auxiliary folders `_vti_cnf/` and `_vti_pvt/` created by FrontPage.

Warning: When using both variables simultaneously, always control the content of the generated deployment archives – sometimes the results can be surprising.

Eclipse provides a special editor for `build.properties` files that can be opened with a double click on the file. Note that such a file may be modified only if the corresponding manifest file `plugin.xml` (or `feature.xml`) is not open at the same time. The reason for this is that changes in the manifest file may lead to changes in the properties file.

In the *Properties Editor* we can select variables such as `bin.includes` or `bin.excludes` from a list on the left. At the right of the window we can specify a list of resources to be assigned to these variables. When specifying resources we can use Ant patterns:

?	Wild card representing an arbitrary character.
*	Wild card representing an arbitrary file name, directory name, or file extension. For example: `src/*.java`, `help/*.*`.
**	Represents all direct and indirect subdirectories. For example, the pattern `**/*.java` represents all Java source files within the project.
dir/	Represents the specified directory with all of its subdirectories. For example the pattern `icons/` represents the whole content of the `icon` directory.

We show the generation of deployment archives in the context of an example plug-in in Section 11.12.2.

10.3.3   The Welcome page

Each feature (see Section 10.3.1) can define a welcome page `welcome.xml` that introduces the end user to the feature. This page is not stored in the feature project, but in the project of the feature plug-in, i.e. the plug-in with the same identification as the feature. Welcome pages are active: they can offer functions that can be invoked by the end user via a click on a hyperlink.

There is no special editor for welcome pages: we can use the Eclipse text editor, or we can use an XML editor (see Section 9.5.10).

The root element of the welcome page has the name `welcomePage` and may be given an optional `title` attribute. The root element may contain an optional `intro` element and an unlimited number of `item` elements.

Both elements (`intro` and `item`) can contain text, and markup in this text is supported:

- `<b>`… `</b>` encloses bold text.

- `<action/>` elements specify possible user actions. We can specify the following attributes with such a tag:

  - `pluginId`. The identification of the plug-in that contains the action implementation.

- class. The fully qualified name of the class representing the action. The class must implement the JFace interface IAction and may be derived from the Action class. When the function is activated, the IAction method run() is invoked.

- <topic/> elements point to help pages. Here we can specify one of the following attributes:

  - id. Refers to a help table of contents. The reference consists of a plug-in identification followed by the name of the *toc* file (usually toc.xml), separated by a slash. For example: /com.bdaum.SpellChecker/toc.xml.

  - href. Refers directly to a help page. The reference consists of a plug-in identification followed by the relative path of the help page. For example: /com.bdaum.SpellChecker/html/Acknowledgements.html.

Here is a complete example of a welcome page:

```
<?xml version="1.0" encoding="UTF-8" ?>
<welcomePage title="Eclipse Multimedia Studio">

<intro>This page introduces you to the Eclipse Multimedia Studio.
Please read it thoroughly. You may also click on one of the hyperlinks
to start an action. </intro>

<item><b>Eclipse Multimedia Studio Perspective </b>
To unlock the whole power of the Multimedia Studio, please open the
Eclipse Multimedia Studio Perspective with
<action pluginId="com.bdaum.multimedia.studio"

class="com.bdaum.multimedia.studio.actions.OpenPerspectiveAction">Wind
ow > Open Perspective > Other… > Multimedia Studio</action>.</item>

<item><b>Install example files </b>
To populate the workspace with an example project and example files,
please click <action pluginId="com.bdaum.multimedia.studio"
class="com.bdaum.multimedia.studio.actions.InstallFirstProjectAction">
here</action>.</item>

<item><b>Starting with the tutorial </b>
To learn more about the studio, please open <topic href="/
com.bdaum.multimedia.studio/html/FirstSteps.htm">the tutorial</topic>.
The latest studio news is available under <topic id="http://
www.theStudio.org">http://www. theStudio.org</topic>.</item>
</welcomePage>
```

However, it is not sufficient to just define such a page: we must also refer to this page in the file about.ini (see Section 10.4.1).

10.4 Deployment

There are three main ways in which we can deploy our own products:

- As a complete product that includes the Eclipse runtime environment.
- As an extension to existing Eclipse platforms.
- As an SDK that includes the source code.

10.4.1 Deploying complete products

A product based on Eclipse needs, of course, the Eclipse runtime environment. It is not necessary to deploy the whole Eclipse SDK: it is sufficient to deploy the minimal Eclipse runtime environment, plus the plug-ins required by your own application. Minimal Eclipse runtime environments are available as separate downloads on the Eclipse Web site at `www.eclipse.org`.

Per ZIP

The *Dependencies* page of the manifest file `plugin.xml` provides a good overview about the plug-ins that must be deployed with any given plug-in. We therefore need the product's feature description, our own plug-ins, and the plug-ins required by our own plug-ins.

In the simplest case we can zip everything together and leave the installation to the user. The installation is just as simple as installing the Eclipse SDK. This works well as long as we provide a different deployment archive for each supported host platform.

Installation aids

In more complex cases – for example, if we want to combine files for different host operating systems or national languages into one deployment archive, or if we want to include a Java runtime environment – we should make use of an installation tool such as `InstallShield` or `InstallAnyWhere`. Such tools, of course, need scripts, and we have to create these scripts. Detailed instruction about this topic can be found in the Eclipse help system under *Platform Plug-in Developer Guide > Programmer's Guide > Packaging and delivering Eclipse based products > Product installation guidelines*.

Binary objects

In both cases we must determine what goes into the deployment archives. First, we need to create the classpath archives. The simplest method for creating these archives is by applying the context function *Run Ant...* to the `build.xml` files and the respective plug-in projects. If such a file does not yet exist, we can create it by applying the context function *Create Ant Build File* to the manifest file `plugin.xml`.

Other resources

We then export all our own plug-in projects, fragment projects, and feature projects to a deployment directory (*Export > File System*). The name of the directory must match the plug-in name. This means that fragment projects are exported to the deployment directory of the corresponding target plug-in. What we don't export are the source files (unless we explicitly want to include source files) and the binaries (these are already contained in the classpath archives). Meta files such as .project, .classpath, .template, build.xml, and build.properties are also not required. During installation, all the plug-in deployment directories are installed as subdirectories to the directory .../eclipse/plugins, and the feature deployment directory is installed as a subdirectory into the directory .../eclipse/features.

Example files

If we want to deploy example projects and files as well, we should refrain from populating the workspace directory during installation, because these projects and files would not normally appear in the Eclipse workspace: the necessary meta data is missing. In addition, the directory .metadata should *never* be included in a deployment: the files contained in this directory depend on configuration, platform, version, and session history.

A better way is to install all example files into the plug-in directory. But how do we get them into the workspace? One idea is make the Plugin class transfer these files to the Eclipse workspace during its very first activation. Unfortunately, however, this class is only activated when it is actually needed, as is the case when the first resource belonging to this plug-in is opened. It would not be very user friendly to show the example files in the *Navigator* at such a late stage.

Another possibility is to leave the initiative to the end user. On the welcome page (see Section 10.3.3) we can give the end user the option of whether to populate the workspace with example files. The following example shows how the implementation of a corresponding action might look:

```java
package com.bdaum.multimedia.studio.actions;

import java.io.FileInputStream;
import java.io.FileNotFoundException;
import java.io.IOException;
import java.net.URL;
import org.eclipse.core.resources.IFile;
import org.eclipse.core.resources.IProject;
import org.eclipse.core.resources.IWorkspace;
import org.eclipse.core.resources.IWorkspaceRoot;
import org.eclipse.core.resources.ResourcesPlugin;
import org.eclipse.core.runtime.CoreException;
import org.eclipse.core.runtime.IPath;
import org.eclipse.core.runtime.Path;
import org.eclipse.core.runtime.Platform;
import org.eclipse.jface.action.Action;
import com.bdaum.multimedia.studio.StudioPlugin;

public class InstallFirstProjectAction extends Action {

    private static String EXAMPLE_PROJECT = "firstStudio";
    private static String EXAMPLE_FILE = "HipHopStudio.mms";
```

```
// Constructor
public InstallFirstProjectAction() {
}

// Override run-Methode
public void run() {
  // Fetch workspace instance
  IWorkspace workspace = ResourcesPlugin.getWorkspace();
  // Get workspace root
  IWorkspaceRoot root = workspace.getRoot();
  // Create IProject instance with specified name
  IProject firstModel = root.getProject(EXAMPLE_PROJECT);
  if (!firstModel.exists()) {
    try {
      // Create project if it does not exist
      firstModel.create(null);
    } catch (CoreException e) {
      System.err.println(e);
    }
  }
  if (!firstModel.isOpen()) {
    try {
      // Open project if it is not open
      firstModel.open(null);
    } catch (CoreException e) {
      System.err.println(e);
    }
  }
  // Construct path of workspace file
  IPath path = new Path(EXAMPLE_PROJECT + "/" + EXAMPLE_FILE);
  // Create IFile instance with specified path
  IFile mFile = root.getFile(path);
  if (!mFile.exists()) {
    // If file does not yet exist, we fetch the URL
    // of the plug-in directory
    URL url =
    StudioPlugin.getDefault().getDescriptor().getInstallURL();
    try {
      // Resolve the Eclipse pseudo URL
      url = Platform.resolve(url);
      // Extract file path
      String urls = (url.getPath() + EXAMPLE_FILE);
      try {
        // Get file in plug-in directory
        java.io.File input = new java.io.File(urls);
        // Create new file in workspace and fill with content
        mFile.create(new FileInputStream(input), true, null);
      } catch (FileNotFoundException e) {
        System.err.println(e);
```

```
      } catch (CoreException e) {
        System.err.println(e);
      }
    } catch (IOException e) {
      System.err.println(e);
    }
  }
 }
}
```

Customizing   If we deliver our product in this form, however, it does not look like our own product, but like the Eclipse workbench with an installed plug-in. To really make it look like a product in its own right we must make a few more customizations. This can be done in a few extra files listed in the table below. All these files (except splash.bmp) are stored in the feature plug-in folder, i.e. the plug-in that has the same identification as the feature that constitutes the product.

about.ini	This file describes feature properties. The file format is the same as in a properties file (java.io.Properties). The following properties may be specified:
	• aboutText. The text to be shown in the *About* dialog.
	• windowImage. Refers to an icon of 16x16 pixels. The icon will appear at the top left corner of all windows. This specification is only necessary for primary features.
	• featureImage. Refers to an icon of 32x32 pixels. The icon will appear in the feature description section of the *About* dialog.
	• aboutImage. Refers to an image of 500x330 or 115x164 pixels. The image will appear in the product description section of the *About* dialog.
	• appName. Contains the application name. This specification is only necessary for primary features.

	• welcomePage. Refers to the feature's welcome page (see Section 10.3.3). This page is listed on the target platform under *Help > Welcome*. • welcomePerspective. Contains the identification of the perspective (see Section 9.5.9) under which the welcome page can be opened. • tipsAndTricksHref. Refers to a 'tips and tricks' HTML page. This page is listed on the target platform under *Help > Tips and Tricks*.
about.html	HTML page with additional text about the plug-in or about the feature. This page is displayed when the button *More Info* is pressed in the *About* dialog.
about.mappings	This page may contain parameter values that are inserted into the *About* texts. The file format is the same as in a Java properties file (java.io.Properties). For example, the property aboutText in file about.ini might contain the text 'This product has the registration number {0}'. about.mappings could then contain the text '0=2342-8A8S-234B', resulting in the final text 'This product has the registration number 2342-8A8S-234B'.
about.properties	Contains translations for about.ini. This is only necessary for multi-lingual deployment: see Section 10.6.

`plugin_customization.ini`	This file can contain default preferences for other plug-ins (see Section 9.2.3). The file format is the same as in a Java properties file (`java.io.Properties`). The condition is, of course, that the preference identifications of the target plug-ins are public. For example, we could start the Eclipse workbench under a different perspective:
	
	`org.eclipse.ui/defaultPerspectiveId=`
	`com.us.prod.ourPerspective`

`plugin_customization.properties`	Contains translations for `plugin_customization.ini`. This is only necessary for multi-lingual deployment: see Section 10.6.
`splash.bmp`	The splash screen is shown as long the platform is loaded. This image should be a 24-bit BMP file with a size of about 500x330 pixels. The file is used in the plug-ins `org.eclipse.platform` and `org.eclipse.core.boot`. A copy of this file is stored in the corresponding plug-in directories.
`welcome.xml`	The welcome page for the feature (see Section 10.3.3).

10.4.2 Deploying Eclipse extensions

Features whose purpose is to upgrade existing platforms in the field are best deployed in the format supported by the *Update Manager* (see Section 10.5). Don't be mislead by the name of this manager – you will be able to deploy even brand-new plug-ins and features. The term 'update' relates to the Eclipse platform being updated, not to the individual plug-ins and features.

You can of course also deploy a feature or plug-in in the form of a ZIP file, but using the Update Manager does have some advantages. During the installation, the Update Manager checks if all required plug-ins do exist, and if their versions are compatible. In addition, it can check if the host operating system, the windowing system, and the processor architecture match the installation requirements. Before the installation is performed the Update Manager can prompt the end user with the license conditions, and will only perform the installation when the end user accepts them. The Update Manager also supports installation over the Web via an installation URL, so that a separate download can be avoided.

Update site   To support installation via the Update Manager, we must create an *Update Site*. Such a site consists of two directories – the `features` directory and the `plugins` directory – and of a site manifest `site.xml`. An Update Site can contain several features that can be installed selectively.

Such a site can be created quickly with the help of the *New* wizard. For project type, we select *Plug-in Development > Update Site Project*. After entering the name of the site the manifest file `site.xml` is created and the *Site Editor* is opened (see Figure 10.4). We can now enter additional specifications using the pages of the Site Editor.

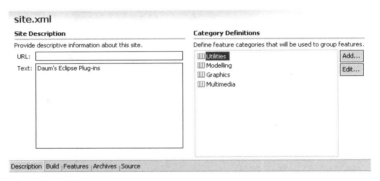

Figure 10.4: The Site Editor

- On the *Description* page we can enter some descriptive text, and optionally a URL pointing to a descriptive HTML page. In addition, we can define categories to which the features of the *Update Site* can be assigned.

- On the *Build* page we can specify the features that are to be included in the Update Site, and which of the features are to be offered to the end user for installation. (For complex features that consist of several sub-features we may not want to offer the sub-features separately for installation.) We can also specify the names of the feature directory and the plug-in directory (the default is `features` and `plugins`).

- On the *Features* page we can refine the specification of the features that are selectable for the user. In particular, we can checkmark to which categories a feature belongs.

Creating an update site

By pressing the *Build* button on the *Build* page of the Site Editor we can populate the Update Site with content. This process is controlled with Ant scripts whose definition is based on the specifications made previously in the *Feature Editor* (see Section 10.3.2).

10.4.3 Deploying source code

If we want to deploy the source code with a feature or plug-in, the best idea is to use the same format as in Eclipse. Eclipse packs all source files for a feature or a plug-in into a single ZIP file. The name of this ZIP file is constructed from the name of the feature or of the plug-in, followed by the string 'src'. If, for example, the classpath archive has the name SpellChecker.jar, the ZIP file containing the sources would have the name SpellCheckersrc.zip.

build.source

Such source code archives are not created manually, but by executing the target build.source in the Ant script build.xml. (If this script does not exist, we create it by applying the context function *Create Ant Build File* to the manifest file plugin.xml or feature.xml.) To execute this target, we select the script and invoke the context function *Run ANT*. In the following dialog we uncheck the default target on the *Targets* page and checkmark the target build.source (see Figure 10.5). Then we press the *Run* button.

Afterwards we invoke the *Refresh* context function on the project (alternatively, we could have set an appropriate *Refresh* area in the Ant configuration). The archive ….src.zip appears in the project folder. Now we only have to add this archive to the deployment archive, by setting the variable bin.includes in file build.properties accordingly. Afterwards, we rebuild the Update Site (see Section 10.4.2) to include the archive in the deployment.

10.5 The Update Manager

After creating the Update Site we can install the new feature immediately with the help of the Update Manager. To do so, we open the *Update Perspective* (by calling either *Window > Open Perspective > Install/Update* or *Help > Software Update > Update Manager*). In the *Feature Updates View* we now navigate to the Update Site. In the case of a local site we start with *My Computer*. In the case of a Web site we expand the item *Sites to Visit*. If the required site is not listed there, we can add it by calling the function *New > Site Bookmark...*

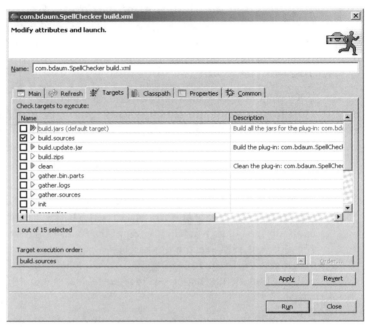

Figure 10.5: To create a source code archive, we modify the Ant configuration for 'build.xml'.

Installing features   After we have arrived at the Update Site we expand its tree node. Now the different categories of the site are displayed, and a further expansion lists the selectable features. If we now select one of those features, its details are shown in the *Preview* view. Now we proceed with the installation as suggested by the Update Manager. After the installation the workbench is restarted.

Deactivating features   If we want to deactivate a feature, or if we want to return to a previous platform configuration, we find the required function in the *Install Configuration* view. The details of the current configuration are listed there under *Eclipse Platform*. If we select one of the features listed there, the *Preview* view will offer the button *Disable Now*. After invoking this function, Eclipse is restarted. Note that the feature is only deactivated, not removed from the Eclipse directory.

If we want to return to a previous configuration, we expand the node *Configuration History*. There we can select one of the listed configurations, look at its details, and restore the selected configuration with a click on the *Restore* button. This function, too, requires a restart of the workbench.

Install handler   The Update Manager can be extended via so-called *install handlers*. These are Java classes that implement the interface IInstallHandler from package org.eclipse.update.core (usually they extend the standard implementation Base-InstallHandler). The methods of such a class are called at specific points of the installation or update process and can perform specific actions.

An install handler can be predefined as a global install handler. This is done in the manifest file plugin.xml of a suitable plug-in at the extension point org.eclipse.update.core.installHandlers. Alternatively, an install handler can be contained in the installation archive. However, in this case they can only be used within the current installation (a local install handler).

If we want to use an install handler during the installation of a feature, we must declare it on the *Advanced* page of the feature manifest feature.xml (see Section 10.3.1). There we specify, in the *Library* field, the name of the archive containing the install handler. In the *Handler* field we specify the name of the IInstallHandler class. If we use a global instead of a local install handler, the *Library* field remains empty and the *Handler field* specifies the identification under which the global install handler was installed.

A typical application of install handlers is the installation of resources outside of the Eclipse platform, for example if we want to deploy a specific Java Runtime Environment.

10.6 Internationalizing products

I am wary of writing anything about this topic, because there is an excellent article about internationalization by Dan Kehn, Scott Fairbrother, and Cam-Thu Le [Kehn2002] on www.eclipse.org. A short overview should therefore be sufficient.

Internationalization is often understood as merely translating texts presented to the end user into a national language. This is certainly an important aspect of internationalization, but not the only one. For example, the meaning of images may differ from culture to culture and should therefore be adapted to the target culture, too. We also all know the confusion that date formats (European vs. US) can cause. But the placement of GUI elements may also differ from culture to culture. Countries like the Arabic countries and Israel, for example, read from right to left, and many Asiatic countries read from top to bottom. A good example of how things can go wrong was an advertisement for a new detergent in Arabic countries. It read: 'Big effect in very little time' and displayed the dirty laundry on the left and the clean laundry on the right!

Similarly, people may have different expectations of where important form elements should be positioned. The different lengths of text constants in different languages may also influence the layout of screen masks.

Despite these layout problems, we will just concentrate here on text elements in different languages. Internationalizing other items such as images and icons, currency and date formats can often be mapped onto text strings (image name, format string).

10.6.1   Text constants in programs

The simplest case is the internationalization of text constants in programs. In the Java source editor, Eclipse offers excellent support for this with the context function *Source > Externalize Strings*. This wizard creates a list with all string constants used in a compilation unit. Afterwards, we may sort this string constants into three different categories:

- *Translate*. In this case the string constant is moved to a *Properties* file. In the source code, the string constant is replaced with a call to an access method. This method fetches the string constant at runtime from the *Properties* file with the help of a specified key. In addition, the source line is suffixed with a comment that looks like:

```
//$NON-NLS-1$
```

This comment indicates that the string constant (now the key) must not be analyzed when the function *Externalize Strings* is executed again. For example, the instruction

```
replaceAction.setText("Replace");
```

is translated into:

```
replaceAction.setText(
    Messages.getString("SpellCorrectionView.Replace_5")); //$NON-NLS-1$
```

- *Never Translate*. The string constant is equipped with a // $NON-NLS-...$ comment, so that it is not analyzed in future invocations of the function *Externalize Strings*. For example:

```
manager.add(new Separator("Additions"));
```

is translated into:

```
manager.add(new Separator("Additions")); //$NON-NLS-1$
```

- *Skip*. Nothing is changed. The string constant is offered for externalization in future invocations of the function *Externalize Strings*.

The wizard performs all the selected replacements in the source file. It also creates a properties file within the current package that contains the externalized string constants. It also creates a class Messages that organizes the access to the file via the getString() method.

All that remains to do is to translate the properties file into the target language. If we use the Java naming conventions basename_lang_region_variant.properties for the properties file, the Message class will automatically use the right properties file, depending on the national language of the target host platform. We can then add new languages in the form of new properties files without recompiling a single Java class.

In some cases it may be necessary to embed program generated values into the string constants. This can be done with the help of parameters. These are defined in the string literals in the properties file, in the following way:

```
Editor.save.SVG.error=Error saving SVG file {0} in folder {1}
```

If we use such parameters, it is a good idea to extend the `Messages` class with a parameterized variant of method `getString()`:

```
public static String getString(String key, Object[] params) {
  if (params == null)
    return getString(key);
  try {
    return java.text.MessageFormat.format(getString(key), params);
  } catch (Exception e) {
    return "!"+key+"!";
  }
}
```

10.6.2 Text constants in manifest files

To internationalize the various manifest files such as `plugin.xml`, `feature.xml`, `fragment.xml`, `site.xml`, `about.ini`, etc. requires a bit more work, as we have no tool support there.

Here, we create a corresponding properties file for each of these files: `plugin.properties`, `feature.properties`, `site.properties`, `about.properties`, etc. The exception is `fragment.xml`. Instead of `fragment.properties`, the file `plugin.properties` is used.

In the original file we replace the translatable string constants by key strings that are identified via a prefixed '%' character. In the corresponding properties file we give the key definition. We can translate these files into the target language afterwards, as discussed in the previous section.

Here is an example of the definition of an *Action Set* in the manifest file `plugin.xml`:

```
label="Check spelling"
```

We would change this into:

```
label="%checkSpelling"
```

and include in file `plugin.properties` the line:

```
checkSpelling=Check spelling
```

10.6.3   Help texts and welcome pages

In the case of help and welcome pages the above approach is not suitable. Instead, we need to translate the whole page. We create a separate folder for each language in which the translated pages are stored.

At runtime the right folder is selected by evaluating substitution variables. Eclipse understands four different substitution variables that can modify library paths:

os	This variable is substituted by a token representing the current operation system (linux, macosx, qnx, solaris, win32).
ws	This variable is substituted by a token representing the current windowing system (carbon, gtk, motif, photon, win32).
nl	This variable is substituted by the current Java *locale*.
arch	This variable is substituted by a token representing the current processor architecture (PA_RISC, ppc, sparc, x86).

When we want to test a plug-in that uses these variables, we can set the variables under *Window > Preference > Plug-in Development > Target Environment*.

For example, if we specify a welcome page (see Section 10.4.1) in about.ini, we can use a substitution variable for the folder name:

```
welcomePage=$nl/welcome.xml
```

During execution the variable $nl is replaced by the current *locale*, for example by DE_de. The welcome page is then fetched from DE_de/welcome.xml.

This works quite similarly for help pages, too (see Section 9.5.10). Here we would not only translate the HTML pages, but also the table of contents toc.xml and the context associations contexts.xml, since these files not only contain references but also display texts. References to toc.xml and contexts.xml (for example from plugin.xml) would then be prefixed with a $nl/. This is normally not required for the references specified in toc.xml and contexts.xml, since these references are usually specified relative to the current location.

Unfortunately, this approach has a severe disadvantage: if a specific language package is not available, Eclipse will simply show nothing instead of the English standard version. Fortunately there is an alternative, which works without substitution variables. This alternative approach relies solely on naming conventions. If we want, for example, to create help and welcome pages in German, we would store them under directory nl/de (for all German language areas) and nl/de/DE (for Germany only) respectively. At runtime Eclipse evaluates the Locale information of the JVM and tries to find an appropriate folder under the nl/ directory. If such a folder is not found, the standard help and welcome pages (usually in English) are used. These pages are not stored under the nl/ directory.

10.6.4   Deploying national language resource bundles

The best idea is to deploy language bundles as separate fragments (see Section 10.2). To do so, we create a package structure within the new fragment that mirrors the package structure of the corresponding plug-in. However, the fragment packages contain only the properties files that have been translated into the target language. The translated nl/ folders are also imported into the fragment. We must declare these folders in the bin.includes variable in file build.properties (see Section 10.3.2). An exception from the rule are the plugin_*locale*.xml files, which must be stored in the src/ directory instead of the project folder.

Example   For deploying a German language bundle for the plug-in com.bdaum.SpellChecker we create an extra fragment com.bdaum.SpellCheckerDE. The fragment has the same package structure as the plug-in, but each package contains only a translation of the respective Messages.properties file, which we rename following the Java naming conventions as Messages_de_DE.properties. These files will later be included automatically in the classpath JAR file SpellCheckerDE.jar.

In the folder nl/de we store the translated welcome page, the translated help table of contents, the translated context associations, and the folder html, which contains all the translated HTML pages. We add this folder, nl/de, to the variable bin.includes in the file build.properties.

We can now apply the context function *Create ANT Build File* to the file fragment.xml to create the necessary Ant script build.xml. We execute this Ant with the context function *Run Ant...* In the following configuration dialog we checkmark the targets build.jars and build.update.jar and press the *Run* button. We thus get both the classpath archive SpellCheckerDE.jar and the deployment archive com.bdaum.SpellCheckerDE_1.0.0.jar (which also contains the classpath archive).

11 Project 3 – A spell checker as an Eclipse plug-in

Our third example application is a fully functional spell checker for the Eclipse SDK. It enables the end user to check text based resources for spelling errors and to correct these errors. The plug-in developed here will be able to apply spell checking to any editor in the Eclipse platform that implements the interface ITextEditor, and also to any Text and StyledText widget that currently has the focus.

During the implementation of this spell checker we demonstrate the following plug-in development techniques:

- Definition of a plug-in manifest.

- Integration of third-party JARs into our own plug-ins.

- Use of the API for the ITextEditor interface and the MultiEditor class.

- Addition of menu items to the menu structure of the Eclipse workbench.

- Addition of tool buttons to the toolbar of the Eclipse workbench.

- Association of actions with keyboard shortcuts.

- Implementation of a workbench view (for correction proposals).

- Creation of a view toolbar and a view menu.

- Location and opening of view instances.

- Creation of new preference pages.

- Creation of a help system, including table of contents, context sensitive help (*InfoPops*), and active help.

We also show how to write a plug-in that can be extended by others. We don't implement the spell checking functionality in the form of a single plug-in, but as a group of cooperating plug-ins. This allows us to implement different spell checking strategies for different document types and to install these strategies separately when required. We therefore implement the spell checker as a base plug-in that defines its own extension points. These points allow the addition of file type specific plug-ins. As an example we implement an extension plug-in for spell checking in Java source files. This gives the end user the optional ability to perform spell check in Javadoc comments, non-Javadoc comments, and in string literals. When implementing this plug-in, we demonstrate the following techniques:

- Definition of an extension point, including a schema.

- Definition of dependencies between plug-ins.

- Integration of help systems from several plug-ins.

11.1 The Spell Checker core classes

11.1.1 The Engine

We don't implement the core spell checking classes ourselves, but instead use the engine of the *jazzy* spell checker. This engine is completely implemented in Java and is available as an Open Source project at sourceforge.net/projects/jazzy. The algorithms used in this engine belong to the most effective current spell checking algorithms. What is amusing about this spell checking engine is that the comments in the source code are full of spelling errors! Our plug-in for Java source code spell checking should indeed offer some help here.

We use version 0.4 of *jazzy* here. The archive jazzy-0.4-bin.zip also contains the source code. In addition, we need the dictionary english.0.zip, which is available on the SourceForge web site.

The *jazzy* archive also contains the JAR file jazzy-core.jar. This is the archive that we need for our project. It contains the packages com.swabunga.spell.engine and com.swabunga.spell.event.

11.1.2 Overview

Figure 11.1 shows the most important classes in our spell checker and how they interact. In addition, we have the Plugin class, the classes for managing the preferences, and the configuration of the spell checking engine. The process of spell checking is initiated by the CheckSpellingActionDelegate class. The SpellCheckManager class acts as a central controller. The SpellCheckCorrectionView class displays spelling errors and interacts with the end user. The DocumentWordTokenizer class is used by the jazzy engine to tokenize a document into single words.

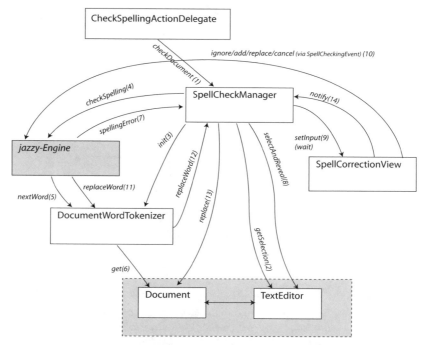

Figure 11.1: A simplified overview of the interaction between the spell checker classes. The numbers in parenthesis indicate the sequence of method calls. The Document and TextEditor classes don't belong to our spell checker, but serve as spell checking targets.

11.2 Setting up the project

First we must set up the target platform. Testing and debugging a plug-in does not happen in the development platform, but in a separate Eclipse session. The configuration of this platform can differ considerably from the configuration of the development platform. For example, we may want to run the new plug-in in the minimal Eclipse runtime environment, i.e. in a platform that does not have a Java IDE or a PDE. So we must first determine with which plug-ins our target platform is equipped. This can be done using the function *Window > Preferences > Plug-in Development > Target Platform* (see Figure 11.2).

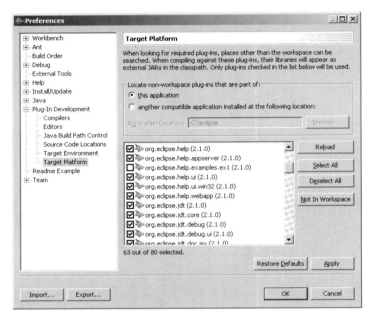

Figure 11.2: We can exclude certain plug-ins during the configuration of the target platform, and we can include other plug-in that are not in the Eclipse workspace using the 'Not In Workspace' button.

However, we want to test our spell checker plug-in in an environment that is equipped with a Java IDE and a PDE, as we want to use spell checking in the editors of those features. We therefore checkmark all plug-ins of the target platform with the exception of the example plug-ins and the source code plug-ins.

Plug-in project   Now we can create our project. In contrast to the first two example applications, we don't create a Java project for this example. Instead, we select *File > New > Project... > Plug-in Development > Plug-in Project*. This wizard leads us step by step through the creation of a plug-in project:

- On the next wizard page we enter the project's name. This will also be the name of the plug-in. We should therefore choose a name that is not chosen by manufacturers of other plug-ins. Common practice is to prefix the plug-in with the identification of the authoring organization. I have named the plug-in `"com.bdaum.SpellChecker"` in this case.

- On the next page we select *Java Project* and leave all other controls at their default values.

- On the next page we select the *Custom plug-in wizard* from the list of available wizards. This wizard will generate substantial parts of the new plug-in for us.

- On the next page we enter a provider name. We remove the checkmarks from the items *Add support for resource bundles* and *Add access to the workspace*. In this example we do not use resource bundles and we do not need direct access to workspace resources.

- On the next page we can now select which components should be pre-generated by Eclipse. We checkmark the following components and uncheck all other components respectively: *Sample Action Set, Sample Help Table of Contents, Preference Page,* and *Sample View*.

Now we need to configure the generators for these components. On the following pages we enter the details:

- On the *Sample Action Set* page we change *Action Class Name* to Check-SpellingActionDelegate.

- On the *Sample Help Table of Contents* page we change *Label of table of contents* to Spell Checker. We remove the checkmarks from all options.

- On the *Sample Preference Page* page we change *Page Class Name* to SpellChecker-PreferencePage. Under *Page Name* we enter Spell Checker.

- On the *Main View Settings* page we change *View Class Name* to SpellCorrection-View. Under *View Name* we enter Spell Correction View. Under *View Category Id* we enter com.bdaum.SpellChecker.views, and under *View Category Name* we enter Spell checker. (The view category identifies the group under which the new view appears when the function *Window > Show View* is invoked.) We select *Table viewer* as the viewer type (this table will later contain the correction proposals). In addition, we uncheck the option *Add the view to the resource perspective*. The view therefore remains invisible initially – we will only show it when the spell checker is in action.

- On the *View Features* page we uncheck the options *View should react to selections in the workbench* and *Add support for sorting*.

Now we are done and can generate the plug-in with a click on the *Finish* button. Then, Eclipse opens the new plug-in manifest plugin.xml in the PDE editor. Eclipse has also generated the packages com.bdaum.SpellChecker, com.bdaum.SpellChecker.actions, com.bdaum.SpellChecker.preferences, and com.bdaum.SpellChecker.views with the classes SpellCheckerPlugin, CheckSpellingActionDelegate, SpellCheckerPreferencePage, and SpellCorrectionView. We are now in possession of the base classes for the new plug-in, and only need to modify and complete these classes.

We must now make the spell checker engine `jazzy-core.jar` available to our project. This time we don't add the JAR as an external JAR to the project, but import the complete JAR to the project (*Import from File System*). Then we add this JAR to the *Java Build Path* with the button *Add Jars...*. This approach makes it easier for us to integrate this JAR file into the deployment archive later.

In addition we need a dictionary. Directly under our project we create a new folder called `dict`. We unpack the file `english.0.zip` that we downloaded from the Source-Forge site and import the file `english.0` into the new folder. This can be done with a drag-and-drop mouse action.

11.3 The plug-in configuration

We are now going to describe the features of our new plug-in in the manifest file `plugin.xml`. If this file is not yet open, we can open it with a double click (Figure 11.3). Since we are going to define our own extension point for this plug-in, we also will need to define a schema (see Section 11.3.2).

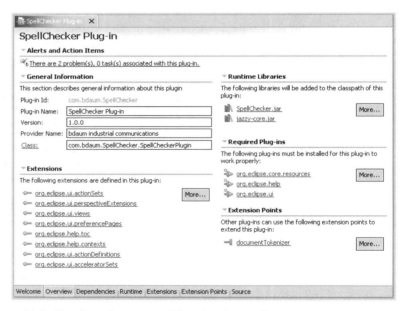

Figure 11.3: The Overview page of the plug-in manifest.

11.3.1 The manifest plugin.xml

The following source code shows the manifest in its final state. All changes and additions applied by us are printed in bold. Now, what do we change?

- On the *Runtime* page of the PDE editor we change the suggested archive name to SpellChecker.jar. We also add the imported JAR file jazzy-core.jar to the list of required libraries. On the right hand side of this page we checkmark the option *Export the whole library* for both libraries. This allows later extensions to use the classes defined in these libraries.

- We add the Eclipse help plug-in as a required plug-in.

- We define a new extension point documentTokenizer. This extension point will allow us to add extensions for specific file types later, such as the plug-in for Java source code spell checking. The name of this extension point was chosen on the grounds that later extensions more or less consist of specific tokenizers that break the text into single words following file type specific rules.

- We make the generated example action more concrete. Our spell checking plug-in contains only a single action 'Check spelling'.

  – In particular, we set a display text (*label*), an explanation text (*tooltip*) and an *icon* for this action.

  – With helpContextId we define the anchor point for context sensitive help (*Infopop*). We define a new toolbar com.bdaum.SpellChecker.spell_checker, so the action will appear in a separate group in the workbenches toolbar.

  – For the menu path menubarPath we specify edit/spelling. Consequently, the action will appear under the *Edit* menu title.

  – By specifying enablesFor="*" we ensure that the action's enabling does not depend on the number of selected resources.

  – With definitionId we refer to the following action definition.

- The definition of actions for our plug-in is done in the section *Spell Checker Actions*. Here we declare the identification that we already have used in definitionId for our sole action (see above). This definition serves as a link to the declarations for keyboard shortcuts. In addition, we define a description. This is not required, but it saves Eclipse from running into a null pointer problem when invoking the function *Window > Preferences > Workbench > Keys*!

- These keyboard shortcuts are defined in the section *Spell Checker Accelerators*. We use here the (outdated) extension points actionDefinition and acceleratorSet. (The new extension point commands that was introduced with Eclipse 2.1 did not work properly in this example.) Since we want to use the spell checking function independently of editors and views, we specify the global scope for keyboard short-cuts. For the configuration we use the standard configuration, and assign the function key *F9* to the action that we declared above. Readers that are familiar with Emacs keyboard shortcuts may wish to add an extra section for the Emacs configuration (org.eclipse.ui.emacsAcceleratorConfiguration).

- We add an icon to the *Spell Correction View*.

- Finally, we refer in the extension point org.eclipse.help.contexts to the file con-texts.xml describing the association of context identifications with help pages. We will discuss this later in more detail.

```
<plugin
  id="com.bdaum.SpellChecker"
  name="SpellChecker Plug-in"
  version="1.0.0"
  provider-name="bdaum industrial communications"
  class="com.bdaum.SpellChecker.SpellCheckerPlugin">

  <runtime>
    <library name="SpellChecker.jar">
    <export name="*"/>
    </library>
    <library name="jazzy-core.jar">
    <export name="*"/>
    </library>
  </runtime>
  <requires>
    <import plugin="org.eclipse.core.resources"/>
    <import plugin="org.eclipse.help"/>
    <import plugin="org.eclipse.ui"/>
  </requires>

  <extension-point id="documentTokenizer"
    name="Document Tokenizer"
    schema="schema/documentTokenizer.exsd"/>
  <extension point="org.eclipse.ui.actionSets">
  <actionSet label="Spell Checker"
    visible="true"
    id="com.bdaum.SpellChecker.actionSet">
    <action
      toolbarPath="com.bdaum.SpellChecker.spell_checker"
      id="com.bdaum.SpellChecker.action1"
      class=
        "com.bdaum.SpellChecker.actions.CheckSpellingActionDelegate"
      icon="icons/basic/correction_view.gif"
      helpContextId="com.bdaum.SpellChecker.action_context"
      label="Check spelling"
      menubarPath="edit/spelling"
```

```
              definitionId="com.bdaum.SpellChecker.check_spelling"
              tooltip="Checks the spelling of any text"/>
        </actionSet>
    </extension>
    <extension name="Spell Checker Actions"
        point="org.eclipse.ui.actionDefinitions">
        <actionDefinition
          name="Check Spelling"
          description="Starts Spell Checking"
        id="com.bdaum.SpellChecker.check_spelling"/>
    </extension>
    <extension name="Spell Checker Accelerators"
        point="org.eclipse.ui.acceleratorSets">
        <acceleratorSet
          scopeId="org.eclipse.ui.globalScope"
          configurationId=
            "org.eclipse.ui.defaultAcceleratorConfiguration">
          <accelerator key="F9"
            id="com.bdaum.SpellChecker.check_spelling"/>
        </acceleratorSet>
    </extension>
    <extension point="org.eclipse.ui.perspectiveExtensions">
        <perspectiveExtension
          targetID="org.eclipse.ui.resourcePerspective">
          <actionSet id="com.bdaum.SpellChecker.actionSet"/>
        </perspectiveExtension>
        <perspectiveExtension
          targetID="org.eclipse.ui.resourcePerspective">
        <view ratio="0.5"
          relative="org.eclipse.ui.views.TaskList"
          relationship="right"
          id="com.bdaum.SpellChecker.views.SpellCorrectionView"/>
        </perspectiveExtension>
    </extension>
    <extension point="org.eclipse.ui.views">
        <category name="Spell checker"
          id="com.bdaum.SpellChecker.views"/>
        <view name="Spell Correction View"
        icon="icons/basic/correction_view.gif"
        category="com.bdaum.SpellChecker.views"
        class="com.bdaum.SpellChecker.views.SpellCorrectionView"
        id="com.bdaum.SpellChecker.views.SpellCorrectionView"/>
    </extension>
    <extension point="org.eclipse.ui.preferencePages">
        <page name="Spell Checker"
        class=
          "com.bdaum.SpellChecker.preferences.SpellCheckerPreferencePage"
        id="com.bdaum.SpellChecker.preferences.defaultPreferences"/>
    </extension>
    <extension point="org.eclipse.help.toc">
```

```
        <toc file="toc.xml" primary="true"/>
    </extension>
    <extension point="org.eclipse.help.contexts">
        <contexts file="contexts.xml"/>
    </extension>
</plugin>
```

11.3.2   The schema documentTokenizer.exsd

The schema documentTokenizer is already generated by the manifest editor – we only
have to complete it. The completed schema is listed below (we have shortened it a bit by
removing the documentation parts).

First, the schema consists of the usual extension root element. Besides the attributes
point, id, and name, such an extension may – in our case – contain an unlimited
number of tokenizer elements.

These tokenizer elements are equipped with the following attributes:

name	Name of the tokenizer.
id	Identification of the tokenizer.
class	A class that must extend the class AbstractDocumentWordTokenizer.
preferences	The class implementing the tokenizers preferences. This class must extend the class SpellCheckerPreferences. If this attribute is omitted, the default spell checking preferences will be used for this tokenizer.
extensions	A list of file extensions for which this tokenizer should be activated.

```
    <?xml version='1.0' encoding='UTF-8'?>
    <!-- Schema file written by PDE -->
    <schema targetNamespace="SpellChecker">
        <element name="extension">
            <complexType>
                <sequence>
                <element ref=
                    "tokenizer" minOccurs="1" maxOccurs="unbounded"/>
                </sequence>
                <attribute name="point" type="string" use="required"/>
                <attribute name="id" type="string"/>
                <attribute name="name" type="string"/>
            </complexType>
        </element>
```

```
    <element name="tokenizer">
      <complexType>
        <attribute name="name" type="string" use="required"/>
        <attribute name="id" type="string" use="required"/>
        <attribute name="class" type="string" use="required"/>
        <attribute name="preferences" type="string"/>
        <attribute name="extensions" type="string" use="required"/>
      </complexType>
    </element>
</schema>
```

11.4 The Plugin class

For the generated class SpellCheckerPlugin we have to make some application specific modifications.

In the constructor of this class, SpellCheckerPlugin, we set the system property jazzy.config to the value 'com.bdaum.SpellChecker.SpellCheckConfiguration'. This tells the configuration model of the *jazzy* engine to fetch the configuration data not from the *jazzy* .properties files but instead from the class SpellCheckConfiguration, which we will implement later.

The pre-generated method getDefault() returns the single instance (*Singleton*) of class SpellCheckerPlugin.

Finally, we implement the utility method getId(). This method fetches the plug-in identification string from the plug-in descriptor as it was defined in plugin.xml.

```
package com.bdaum.SpellChecker;

import java.io.IOException;
import java.net.URL;

import org.eclipse.core.runtime.IPluginDescriptor;
import org.eclipse.core.runtime.IStatus;
import org.eclipse.core.runtime.Platform;
import org.eclipse.core.runtime.Status;
import org.eclipse.jface.preference.IPreferenceStore;
import org.eclipse.ui.IWorkbenchWindowActionDelegate;
import org.eclipse.ui.plugin.AbstractUIPlugin;

import com.bdaum.SpellChecker.preferences.SpellCheckerPreferences;


public class SpellCheckerPlugin extends AbstractUIPlugin {

    // Default dictionary
    public static final String DEFAULTDICT = "dict/english.0";
```

```
// The singleton
private static SpellCheckerPlugin plugin;

// Active SpellCheckManager
private SpellCheckManager manager;
// Active ActionDelegate
private IWorkbenchWindowActionDelegate spellCheckingActionDelegate;
// Default preferences
private SpellCheckerPreferences preferences;

/**
 * The Constructor.
 */
public SpellCheckerPlugin(IPluginDescriptor descriptor) {
  super(descriptor);
  plugin = this;
  // Set configuation for jazzy engine. We make jazzy fetch
  // the configuration from our own configuration implementation.
  System.setProperty(
    "jazzy.config",
    "com.bdaum.SpellChecker.SpellCheckConfiguration");
}

/**
 * Returns the plug-in singleton
 */
public static SpellCheckerPlugin getDefault() {
  return plugin;
}

/**
 * Method getId.
 * Fetches the plug-in identification.
 * @return String – the identification.
 */
public static String getId() {
  return getDefault().getDescriptor().getUniqueIdentifier();
}
```

Dictionary URL We have defined the location of the default dictionary as a string constant relative to the installation directory of the plug-in. This constant is resolved into an absolute path in the getDefaultDictionaryFileName() method. Please note that the dictionary is not in the Eclipse workspace, but belongs to the installation files located in the plug-in directory.

To retrieve the location of these files, we first must fetch the plug-in descriptor (IPluginDescriptor). Such a descriptor contains general information about the plug-in, among other information, and also the URL of its installation location. However, this URL is given in a format that only Eclipse can interpret correctly: it starts with the protocol specification 'platform:'. To resolve this URL into a conventional file URL (i.e. a URL beginning with 'file:') we must first apply the resolve() method. Afterwards we can remove the protocol's specification 'file:' and append the relative path specification for the dictionary.

```
/**
 * Method getDefaultDictionaryFileName.
 * Returns the absolute path of the default dictionary file.
 * @return String - Default dictionary file path
 */
public static String getDefaultDictionaryFileName() {
  // First, we getch the URL of the plug-in.
  URL pluginURL = getDefault().getDescriptor().getInstallURL();
  // This URL starts with the pseudo protocol "plugin:"
  // We therefore resolve this URL into a real URL
  try {
    URL resolvedURL = Platform.resolve(pluginURL);
    // Now we have a URL that starts with "file:".
    // We extract the path information and append the
    // relative path of the dictionary.
    return resolvedURL.getPath() + DEFAULTDICT;
  } catch (IOException e) {
    SpellCheckerPlugin.logError(4,
      "Error resolving dictionary URL", e);
  }
  return null;
}
```

Initializing preferences

Now we must initialize the default values of the preferences. Remember that when the Eclipse platform is started, only the manifest files of the various plug-ins are interpreted, but no plug-in specific code is executed. The PreferenceStore is therefore not initialized at that time.

However, the Plugin class invokes the initializeDefaultPluginPreferences() during the very first call of the getPluginPreferences() method. We can override this method to apply the necessary initializations. To perform these, we create a new instance of the class SpellCheckerPreferences and delegate the details of initialization to this instance. We cache this new instance in field preferences. This allows us later to access the preferences quickly via method getPreferences().

```
/**
 * Initialization of the PreferenceStore
 */
protected void initializeDefaultPluginPreferences() {
  if (preferences != null) {
    IPreferenceStore store = getPreferenceStore();
    preferences.initializeDefaults(store);
  }
}
```

```
/**
 * Returns the preferences of this plug-in
 */
public static SpellCheckerPreferences getPreferences() {
  if (plugin.preferences == null)
    plugin.preferences = new SpellCheckerPreferences();
  return plugin.preferences;
}
```

Central controller　Further, we implement the method getManager(). The manager mediates the communication between the user interface and the spell checking core classes. To be able to access this manager from all classes, we store an instance of the manager here in the class SpellCheckerPlugin. During its very first call getManager() creates an instance of the class SpellCheckManager. This lazy creation ensures that this component is only created when it is actually needed.

The spellCheckingActionDelegate field with its get...() and set...() access methods acts as a registry for the ActionDelegate instance created by the workbench. We will need this field in the context of active help (see Section 11.10.3).

Finally, we implement the utility method logError(). This method passes internal errors to the Eclipse log file – a much better way than reporting errors on System.err. We obtain the log file instance from the plug-in singleton via the getLog() method.

```
/**
 * Method getManager.
 * Returns the manager.
 * @return SpellCheckManager
 */
public static SpellCheckManager getManager() {
  // Create SpellCheckManager instance if necessary
  if (plugin.manager == null)
    plugin.manager = new SpellCheckManager();
  return plugin.manager;
}

/**
 * Method setSpellCheckingActionDelegate.
 * Registers the active SpellCheckingActionDelegate.
 * @param delegate - active SpellCheckingActionDelegate
 */
public static void setSpellCheckingActionDelegate(
  IWorkbenchWindowActionDelegate delegate) {
  plugin.spellCheckingActionDelegate = delegate;
}

/**
 * Method getSpellCheckingActionDelegate.
```

```
 * Returns currently active SpellCheckingActionDelegate.
 * @return IWorkbenchWindowActionDelegate - active action delegate
 */
public static IWorkbenchWindowActionDelegate
  getSpellCheckingActionDelegate() {
  return plugin.spellCheckingActionDelegate;
}

/**
 * Method logError.
 * Writes internal errors to log file.
 * @param code – Plug-in specific error code
 * @param message – message text
 * @param ex - Throwable that caused the error or null.
 */
public static void logError(int code,
  String message, Throwable ex) {
  getDefault().getLog().log(
    new Status(IStatus.ERROR, getId(), code, message, ex));
}
}
```

11.5 The action 'Check Spelling'

The CheckSpellingActionDelegate class is also generated already. In the init()
method the workbench window that was passed via a parameter is stored in an instance
variable so that it can be used in other method calls. In this method, we also start a
tracking mechanism that always informs us which SWT Control element currently has
the focus.

Furthermore, we register this CheckSpellingActionDelegate instance with the Spell-
CheckerPlugin instance.

```
package com.bdaum.SpellChecker.actions;

import org.eclipse.jface.action.IAction;
import org.eclipse.jface.viewers.ISelection;
import org.eclipse.swt.custom.StyledText;
import org.eclipse.swt.events.FocusEvent;
import org.eclipse.swt.events.FocusListener;
import org.eclipse.swt.widgets.Control;
import org.eclipse.swt.widgets.Display;
import org.eclipse.swt.widgets.Text;
import org.eclipse.ui.*;
import org.eclipse.ui.part.MultiEditor;
import org.eclipse.ui.texteditor.ITextEditor;
import com.bdaum.SpellChecker.SpellCheckManager;
import com.bdaum.SpellChecker.SpellCheckerPlugin;
```

```
import com.bdaum.SpellChecker.views.SpellCorrectionView;
/**
 * This class implements the action "Check Spelling"
 * @see IWorkbenchWindowActionDelegate
 */
public class CheckSpellingActionDelegate
  implements IWorkbenchWindowActionDelegate, FocusListener {

  private IWorkbenchWindow window;
  /** The spell checking thread **/
  private Thread spThread;
  /** The current IAction instance **/
  private IAction action;
  /** The current focus control element **/
  private Control currentFocusControl;

  /**
   * @see IWorkbenchWindowActionDelegate#init
   */
  public void init(IWorkbenchWindow window) {
    this.window = window;
    // Register with the PartService as a listener
    setCurrentFocusControl();
    // Register with the Plugin class.
    SpellCheckerPlugin.setSpellCheckingActionDelegate(this);
  }
```

Tracking the focus Focus tracking is done in setCurrentFocusControl(). This method first asks the current Display instance which control currently has the focus. We register a FocusListener with this focus owner that tells us when the owner loses the focus. In such a case we retrieve the next focus owner. If this is not possible, we just retry it 100 milliseconds later. In particular, this can happen during the first call of this method from init(). At this time a focus may not yet be assigned to a Control element.

```
    // Tracking the focus

    private void setCurrentFocusControl() {
      Display display = window.getShell().getDisplay();
      if (currentFocusControl != null)
        currentFocusControl.removeFocusListener(this);
      currentFocusControl =
        display.getFocusControl();
      if (currentFocusControl != null)
        currentFocusControl.addFocusListener(this);
      else {
        // We lost track
        // Retry later
        display.timerExec(100,new Runnable() {
          public void run() {
            setCurrentFocusControl();
```

```
        }
      });
    }
  }

  /* FocusListener methods */
  public void focusGained(FocusEvent e) {
    updateActionEnablement(action);
  }

  public void focusLost(FocusEvent e) {
    setCurrentFocusControl();
  }
```

During each focus change we also re-evaluate the action's enabled status. If no document was found that can be spell checked, the action is disabled.

```
  // Enable or disable action
  private void updateActionEnablement(IAction action) {
    // The action is only enabled if we have a spell check target
    if (action != null)
      action.setEnabled(getSpellCheckingTarget() != null);
  }
```

The getDisplay() method was written to support active help. Active help actions require a Display instance and also need to know if they can be executed or not.

```
  // Return a Display instance if action is enabled
  public Display getDisplay() {
    if (window == null || action == null || !action.isEnabled())
      return null;
    return window.getShell().getDisplay();
  }
```

Workbench events   All IActionDelegates react to workbench events: the method selectionChanged() is invoked when another item is selected in the workbench. The method receives the IAction instance (the CheckSpellingActionDelegate class is only a delegate of that action) and, of course, the selection, as parameters.

In selectionChanged() we just remember the IAction instance in an instance field so that we can refer to it later. Also, we take the opportunity – now that we know the IAction instance – to register the action with the KeyBindingService via the setActionDefinitionId() method.

```
  /**
   * The current workbench selection has changed.
   * @see IWorkbenchWindowActionDelegate#selectionChanged
   */
  public void selectionChanged(IAction action,
    ISelection selection) {
    // Remember action
```

```
      this.action = action;
      // Set definition ID for key binding service
      action.setActionDefinitionId(
        "com.bdaum.SpellChecker.check_spelling");
  }
```

Run action   When the action is activated by the user the run() method is invoked. Here we start the
spell checking task. First we fetch the currently active editor or the Text of StyledText
element that currently has the focus, via the getSpellCheckingTarget() method. If
such an editor or text control is present we open the SpellCorrectionView. To do so, we
first fetch the currently active page of the workbench window. Then we open the view
via the showView() method by passing the view identification defined in the manifest
file plugin.xml. Then we start the spell checking process via the SpellCheckManager in
a new thread.

Why a new thread? The spell checking process may generate a whole series of spelling
error events. These events must be processed by SpellCorrectionView event by event.
In our implementation we organize this in such a way that the spell checking process
waits until an event is processed by the SpellCorrectionView, when the next event can
be fired. If we were to do this (waiting) in the SWT thread, the whole user interface
would lock up.

Before we start a new thread, we first cancel existing spell checking threads via the
SpellCheckManager method abortSpellChecking(). Otherwise an unlimited number of
pending threads would come into existence if the spell checking action is executed
repeatedly without completing the previous spell checking processes.

```
    /**
     * @see IWorkbenchWindowActionDelegate#run
     */
    public void run(IAction action) {
      // Get spell checking target
      final Object target = getSpellCheckingTarget();
      if (target != null) {
        // Fetch current workbench page
        IWorkbenchPage activePage = window.getActivePage();
        if (activePage == null) return;
        // Get current Display instance
        final Display display = getDisplay();
        if (display == null) return;
        try {
          // Now find the SpellCorrectionView and open it
          final SpellCorrectionView view =
            (SpellCorrectionView) activePage.showView(
            "com.bdaum.SpellChecker.views.SpellCorrectionView");
          // Getch the SpellCheckManager
          final SpellCheckManager manager =
            SpellCheckerPlugin.getManager();
```

```
                      // The spell checking process must be executed
                      // in a new thread.
                      // First cancel any pending spell checking processes.
                      if (spThread != null && spThread.isAlive())
                      manager.abortSpellChecking();
                      spThread = new Thread("SpellCheckThread") {
                        public void run() {
                          if (target instanceof ITextEditor)
                            manager.checkDocument((ITextEditor) target,
                            display, view);
                          else
                            manager.checkDocument((Control) target,
                              display, view);
                        }
                      };
                      // Start thread
                      spThread.start();
                  } catch (PartInitException e) {
                      SpellCheckerPlugin.logError(6,
                      "Cannot initialize SpellCorrectionView",e);
                  }
                }
              }
```

Spell checking target

The spell checking process can, of course, only be executed if we have a valid spell checking target. We try to get such a target via getSpellCheckingTarget(). First, we fetch the currently active workbench component from the workbench's PartService. If this is a MultiEditor, we fetch its currently active inner editor. If we don't find a suitable text editor, we return the Control instance that currently holds the focus, but only if this is a Text or StyledText instance, otherwise we return null. In this case we cannot perform spell checking.

```
              /**
               * Method getSpellCheckingTarget.
               * Returns active ITextEditor instance or a Text or
               * StyledText instance that has the focus
               * @return ITextEditor, Text, StyledText or null.
               */
              private Object getSpellCheckingTarget() {
                // Get workbench component
                IWorkbenchPart activePart =
                  window.getPartService().getActivePart();
                // Is it a MultiEditor?
                // If yes, get the active inner editor.
                while (activePart instanceof MultiEditor)
                  activePart = ((MultiEditor) activePart).getActiveEditor();
                // (Unfortunately, we cannot look into MultiPageEditorPart
                // editor. The method getActiveEditor() of this class
                // is not public.)
                // Is it a text editor?
```

```
        if (activePart instanceof ITextEditor)
          return activePart;
        // No text editor found, let's try it with a text field.
        if (currentFocusControl instanceof Text
          && (( Text) currentFocusControl).getEditable())
          return currentFocusControl;
        if (currentFocusControl instanceof StyledText
          && (( StyledText) currentFocusControl).getEditable())
          return currentFocusControl;
        return null;
      }
```

Disposal　　　　When the IActionDelegate is disposed, we must deregister it as a FocusListener. We also deregister it with the Plugin instance.

```
      /**
       * Dispose action
       */
      public void dispose() {
        // Remove from listener list to allow this object
        // to be recycled by the Java garbage collection.
        if (currentFocusControl != null
          && !currentFocusControl.isDisposed())
          currentFocusControl.removeFocusListener(this);
        currentFocusControl = null;
        // also deregister from the Plugin class
        SpellCheckerPlugin.setSpellCheckingActionDelegate(null);
      }
    }
```

11.6　The correction window

In this section we discuss the implementation of the *Spell Checker View*, and in this context also the management of image files (for the toolbar buttons).

11.6.1　The SpellCorrectionView class

The SpellCorrectionView class is quite large. In addition to the pre-generated table, we have to create a text field above the table. This field will contain the erroneous word or a replacement for the word.

Then we need to implement a toolbar, a drop-down menu, and a context menu (all with six actions), and a special action for handling double clicks. We decide to hard code these actions, instead of defining them in the plug-in manifest. The reason is that the enabling of these actions does not depend on workbench selections, but from other criteria that are difficult to specify via the manifest.

We first create a few fields for the actions of the view:

```
package com.bdaum.SpellChecker.views;

import java.util.List;

import org.eclipse.jface.action.*;
import org.eclipse.jface.viewers.*;
import org.eclipse.swt.SWT;
import org.eclipse.swt.events.KeyAdapter;
import org.eclipse.swt.events.KeyEvent;
import org.eclipse.swt.graphics.Image;
import org.eclipse.swt.layout.GridData;
import org.eclipse.swt.layout.GridLayout;
import org.eclipse.swt.widgets.Composite;
import org.eclipse.swt.widgets.Display;
import org.eclipse.swt.widgets.Menu;
import org.eclipse.swt.widgets.Text;
import org.eclipse.ui.IActionBars;
import org.eclipse.ui.help.WorkbenchHelp;
import org.eclipse.ui.part.ViewPart;
import com.bdaum.SpellChecker.SpellCheckManager;
import com.bdaum.SpellChecker.SpellCheckerImages;
import com.bdaum.SpellChecker.actions.CorrectionViewAction;
import com.swabunga.spell.engine.Word;
import com.swabunga.spell.event.SpellCheckEvent;

public class SpellCorrectionView extends ViewPart {

  /* Text constant for cases where we have
   * no correction proposals */
  private static final String[] NOPROPOSALS =
    new String[] { "(No suggestions)" };

  /* Widgets */
  // The current Display instance
  private Display display;
  // The Text widget for displaying the bad word
  private Text badWord;
  // The TableViewer of this view
  private TableViewer viewer;

  /* View actions */
  // Toolbar and menu actions
  private IAction ignoreAction;
  private IAction ignoreAllAction;
  private IAction cancelAction;
  private IAction replaceAction;
  private IAction replaceAllAction;
  private IAction addToDictionaryAction;
```

```
// The double click action
private Action doubleClickAction;

/* The manager */
private SpellCheckManager spellCheckManager;
/* The current spelling error event */
private SpellCheckEvent currentEvent;
/* Indicator if replacements are allowed */
private boolean documentIsEditable;
```

ContentProvider   These definitions are followed by the definitions of two inner classes: ViewContentProvider and ViewLabelProvider. These classes support the display of the table. The class
ViewContentProvider supplies the table with table entries. This is done in the getEle-
ments() method. In our case these entries are correction proposals. A list of such
correction proposals – wrapped into a SpellCheckEvent object – is passed to the view
via setInput(). This event is then signaled from the table to the ViewContentProvider
by calling the method inputChanged(). We transform this list into a suitable format
using getElements(). If the list of correction proposals is empty, we just return the
default message defined above as the sole table element.

```
/**
 * The ViewContentProvider creates the table content from the
 * spelling error event.
 */
class ViewContentProvider implements IStructuredContentProvider {

  // current spelling error event
  private Object spEvent;

  /**
   * This method is called by the TableViewer after setInput()
   * was called.
   */
  public void inputChanged(
    Viewer v, Object oldInput, Object newInput) {
    spEvent = newInput;
  }

  /**
   * This method is called when the table is refreshed
   */
  public Object[] getElements(Object parent) {
    // Fetch correction proposals from the spelling error event
      if (spEvent instanceof SpellCheckEvent) {
      List suggestions =
        ((SpellCheckEvent) spEvent).getSuggestions();
      int s = suggestions.size();
      // Check if we have proposals
      if (s > 0) {
```

```
                              // Return correction proposals as an array
                              // to the TableViewer
                              Word[] sugArray = new Word[s];
                              suggestions.toArray(sugArray);
                              return sugArray;
                          }
                      }
                      return NOPROPOSALS;
                  }

                  public void dispose() {
                  }
              }

              /**
               * The ViewLabelProvider creates the individual table entries
               */
              class ViewLabelProvider extends LabelProvider
                  implements ITableLabelProvider {

                  /*
                   * Process text for table entry
                   */
                  public String getColumnText(Object obj, int index) {
                      return getText(obj);
                  }
                  public Image getColumnImage(Object obj, int index) {
                      return null;
                  }
                  public Image getImage(Object obj) {
                      return null;
                  }
              }
```

Construct view contents

For the spell correction view Eclipse has already pre-generated the method `createPart-Control()`. We extend this method by adding the `Text` widget `badWord` above the table. This text field will be used to display the erroneous word. To combine the text field with the table, we use `Composite` a `GridLayout` for the parent.

In addition, we implement the event handling for the table viewer. If a proposal is selected from the table, we want to copy it to the text field `badWord`. The exception is the string `NOPROPOSALS`, which we don't want to copy into the text field. This string is not a `Word` instance, so we use its type as a knock-out criterion.

The `KeyListener` allows the invocation of some of the menu and toolbar actions via keyboard shortcuts.

The following pre-generated calls create the actions and construct the menus and the toolbar. We have completed this code with method calls for updating the actions and for registering the view with the help system.

The implementation of the method setFocus() is a requirement from the parent class ViewPart. Here, we set the focus to the table.

```java
public void createPartControl(Composite parent) {
  // Fetch Display instance for later usage
  display = parent.getDisplay();
  // Set GridLayout
  parent.setLayout(new GridLayout());
  // Create Text widget for display of bad word
  badWord = new Text(parent, SWT.BORDER);
  badWord.setLayoutData(new GridData(GridData.FILL_HORIZONTAL));
  // Create table viewer
  viewer =
    new TableViewer(parent,
      SWT.H_SCROLL | SWT.V_SCROLL | SWT.BORDER);
  viewer.getControl().setLayoutData(
    new GridData(GridData.FILL_BOTH));
  // Set ContentProvider and LabelProvider
  viewer.setContentProvider(new ViewContentProvider());
  viewer.setLabelProvider(new ViewLabelProvider());
  // Listener for selection of table elements
  // Selected elements are copied to text field badWord gebracht.
  viewer.addSelectionChangedListener(
    new ISelectionChangedListener() {
    public void selectionChanged(SelectionChangedEvent event) {
      ISelection sel = event.getSelection();
      if (sel instanceof IStructuredSelection) {
        Object obj =
          ((IStructuredSelection) sel).getFirstElement();
      // Check for Word type to exclude NOPROPOSALS
      // from selection
      if (obj instanceof Word)
        badWord.setText(obj.toString());
    }
  }
});
  // Add KeyListener to support keyboard shortcuts
  viewer.getControl().addKeyListener(new KeyAdapter() {
    public void keyPressed(KeyEvent e) {
      if (e.character == '+')
        addToDictionaryAction.run();
      else
        switch (e.keyCode) {
          case 13 :
            if ((e.stateMask & SWT.CTRL) != 0)
            replaceAction.run();
```

```
                    else
                      ignoreAction.run();
                      break;
                    case SWT.ESC :
                      cancelAction.run();
                      break;
                }
              }
            });
            // Create actions
            makeActions();
            // Add the context menu
            hookContextMenu();
            // Add the double click action
            hookDoubleClickAction();
            // Create the toolbar
            contributeToActionBars();
            // Initialize the actions
            updateActionEnablement();
            // Create help context
            WorkbenchHelp.setHelp(
              parent,
              "com.bdaum.SpellChecker.correctionView_context");
          }

          /**
           * Set focus to TableViewe
           */
          public void setFocus() {
            viewer.getControl().setFocus();
          }
```

Create actions   The construction of the menus, the toolbar, and the double click action are nearly completely pre-generated. For the double click action an anonymous DoubleClickListener is registered. This listener invokes the action's run() method in the case of an event. The menu manager is equipped with a MenuListener. Every time the menu is to be displayed this listener constructs a new menu in the fillContribution() method.

To construct the toolbar, the method contributeToActionBars() fetches the managers for the drop-down menu and for the toolbar from the ViewSite. Then the method fill-Contribution() is invoked to add the required actions to these managers. Eclipse had originally generated separate methods for menus and toolbars, but here we have combined both methods into a single method fillContribution().

```
          // Add double click action
          private void hookDoubleClickAction() {
            viewer.addDoubleClickListener(new IDoubleClickListener() {
              public void doubleClick(DoubleClickEvent event) {
                doubleClickAction.run();
```

```
        }
      });
    }

    // Add context menu
    private void hookContextMenu() {
      // Create new menu manager
      MenuManager menuMgr = new MenuManager("#PopupMenu");
      // Remove all menu items before building the menu
      menuMgr.setRemoveAllWhenShown(true);
      // Event processing for context menu
      menuMgr.addMenuListener(new IMenuListener() {
        public void menuAboutToShow(IMenuManager manager) {
          SpellCorrectionView.this.fillContribution(manager);
        }
      });
      // Create menu
      Menu menu = menuMgr.createContextMenu(viewer.getControl());
      viewer.getControl().setMenu(menu);
      // Register context menu with workbench site
      getSite().registerContextMenu(menuMgr, viewer);
    }

    private void contributeToActionBars() {
      // Fetch action bar from workbench site
      IActionBars bars = getViewSite().getActionBars();
      // Create the drop-down menu
      fillContribution(bars.getMenuManager());
      // Create the toolbar
      fillContribution(bars.getToolBarManager());
    }

    // Fill menus or toolbar with actions
    private void fillContribution(IContributionManager manager) {
      manager.add(replaceAction);
      manager.add(replaceAllAction);
      manager.add(new Separator());
      manager.add(addToDictionaryAction);
      manager.add(new Separator());
      manager.add(ignoreAction);
      manager.add(ignoreAllAction);
      manager.add(cancelAction);
      // Other plug-ins can insert new actions here
      manager.add(new Separator("Additions"));
    }
```

We create all actions in the makeActions() method. We fetch the icons from the Spell-
CheckerImages class, which is listed in Section 11.6.3. We use the convenience method
createAction() to create an action. This method creates instances of type Correction-
ViewAction, which are quite simple (see below). The run() method of these actions just

calls the view's performOperation() method. There we perform – depending on the operation code – the main processing. Finally, we call the method signalEventProcessed() to indicate to the SpellCheckManager that the processing of the current event has finished and that a new event may be sent.

```
// Create actions
private void makeActions() {
  replaceAction = createAction(CorrectionViewAction.REPLACE,
    "Replace", "Replace occurrence",
    SpellCheckerImages.IMG_REPLACE);
  replaceAllAction = createAction(
    CorrectionViewAction.REPLACEALL,
    "Replace all", "Replace all occurrences",
    SpellCheckerImages.IMG_REPLACEALL);
  addToDictionaryAction = createAction(CorrectionViewAction.ADD,
    "Add to dictionary", "Add word to dictionary",
    SpellCheckerImages.IMG_ADDTODICTIONARY);
  ignoreAction = createAction(CorrectionViewAction.IGNORE,
    "Ignore", "Ignore spelling problem",
    SpellCheckerImages.IMG_IGNORE);
  ignoreAllAction = createAction(CorrectionViewAction.IGNOREALL,
    "Ignore all", "Ignore for all occurrences",
    SpellCheckerImages.IMG_IGNOREALL);
  cancelAction = createAction(CorrectionViewAction.CANCEL,
    "Cancel", "Cancel spell checking",
    SpellCheckerImages.IMG_CANCEL);
  doubleClickAction =
    new CorrectionViewAction(this,
    CorrectionViewAction.DOUBLECLICK);
}

// Create a single action
private IAction createAction(int operation, String label,
  String toolTip, String imageID) {
  IAction action = new CorrectionViewAction(this, operation);
  action.setText(label);
  action.setToolTipText(toolTip);
  SpellCheckerImages.setImageDescriptors(action,
    "lcl16", imageID);
  return action;
}

/**
 * Method performOperation.
 * Perform operation for an action
 * @param operation - der Operationscode
 */
public void performOperation(int operation) {
  if (currentEvent == null)
    return;
```

```
switch (operation) {
  case CorrectionViewAction.DOUBLECLICK :
    if (!documentIsEditable)
      return;
    ISelection selection = viewer.getSelection();
    Object obj =
      ((IStructuredSelection) selection).getFirstElement();
    if (!(obj instanceof Word))
      return;
    currentEvent.replaceWord(obj.toString(), false);
    break;
  case CorrectionViewAction.REPLACE :
    currentEvent.replaceWord(badWord.getText(), false);
    break;
  case CorrectionViewAction.REPLACEALL :
    if (!documentIsEditable)
      return;
    currentEvent.replaceWord(badWord.getText(), true);
    break;
  case CorrectionViewAction.ADD :
    if (!documentIsEditable)
      return;
    currentEvent.addToDictionary(badWord.getText());
    break;
  case CorrectionViewAction.IGNORE :
    currentEvent.ignoreWord(false);
    break;
  case CorrectionViewAction.IGNOREALL :
    currentEvent.ignoreWord(true);
    break;
  case CorrectionViewAction.CANCEL :
    currentEvent.cancel();
    break;
}
signalEventProcessed();
}

// Signal end of event processing
private void signalEventProcessed() {
  // Release waiting manager
  spellCheckManager.continueSpellChecking();
  // Reset current event
  currentEvent = null;
  // Update viewer
  updateView();
}
```

Updating the user interface

We enable or disable actions in the updateActionEnablement() method. If no more events are waiting, we disable all actions. If at least one event is waiting, the actions are enabled. However, the actions replaceAction and replaceActionAll are only enabled when the current document is editable.

```
// Disable or enable actions
private void updateActionEnablement() {
  boolean pendingEvent = (currentEvent != null);
  replaceAction.setEnabled(pendingEvent & documentIsEditable);
  replaceAllAction.setEnabled(
    pendingEvent & documentIsEditable);
  ignoreAction.setEnabled(pendingEvent);
  ignoreAllAction.setEnabled(pendingEvent);
  addToDictionaryAction.setEnabled(pendingEvent);
  cancelAction.setEnabled(pendingEvent);
}
```

These operations and other modifications to the user interface are invoked via the updateView() method. Here all of these updates are executed in the familiar way within a syncExec() method (see Section 6.5.3). This is necessary because some of these changes come from a different thread – the spell checking thread. In particular, we update the TableViewer via its setInput() method here, which event in turn is signaled to the ContentProvider of the TableViewer via the inputChanged() method. In addition, we update the text field and the view title.

```
// Update view
private void updateView() {
  // Execute via syncExec method as we are called
  // from other thread
  display.syncExec(new Runnable() {
    public void run() {
      // Update TableViewer
      viewer.setInput(currentEvent);
      // Update Text field and title
      if (currentEvent == null) {
        badWord.setText("");
        setTitle("Spell Check (done)");
      } else {
        badWord.setText(currentEvent.getInvalidWord());
        setTitle("Spell Check (in progress)");
      }
      // Update actions
      updateActionEnablement();
    }
  });
}
```

The `setInput()` method supplies the whole view with input data. In our case, this is a `SpellCheckEvent` containing the correction proposals from the *jazzy* engine. We accept this data and update the view.

```
/**
 * Method setInput.
 * Supplies the Spell Correction View with a
 * new spelling error event
 * @param event — the spelling error event
 * @param manager — the manager to be notified when finished
 * @param documentIsEditable - true, if document may be modified
 */
public void setInput(SpellCheckEvent event,
    SpellCheckManager manager, boolean documentIsEditable) {
    // Accept event, manager, and flag
    this.currentEvent = event;
    this.spellCheckManager = manager;
    this.documentIsEditable = documentIsEditable;
    // Update the view
    updateView();
}
}
```

11.6.2 View actions

The `CorrectionViewAction` class implements all of the `SpellCorrectionView` actions and is almost trivial. In its constructor we accept the view and the operation code of the concrete action. This data is then used in the `run()` method to invoke the view's `performOperation()` with the respective operation code.

```
package com.bdaum.SpellChecker.actions;

import org.eclipse.jface.action.Action;
import com.bdaum.SpellChecker.views.SpellCorrectionView;

public class CorrectionViewAction extends Action {

    public static final int DOUBLECLICK = 0;
    public static final int REPLACE = 1;
    public static final int REPLACEALL = 2;
    public static final int IGNORE = 3;
    public static final int IGNOREALL = 4;
    public static final int ADD = 5;
    public static final int CANCEL = 6;

    private SpellCorrectionView view;
    private int operation;
```

```
public CorrectionViewAction(SpellCorrectionView view,
    int operation) {
    this.view = view;
    this.operation = operation;
}

/*
 * Perform action
 */
public void run() {
    view.performOperation(operation);
}
}
```

11.6.3 Managing images

We fetch the icons for all actions of the SpellCorrectionView from the SpellChecker-Images class. This technique has the advantage that we keep an overview of the images used, because they are managed by a central instance. We could also easily extend this class into a central image repository for storing images for reuse. However, this is not necessary in our case, as all icons are only used once when the actions are created via makeActions(). Caching of images to reduce repeated image loading is therefore not required.

For the various images we use the following organizing principles:

Organizing images All images are stored in subfolders of the folder icons. Each action can accept three states: *disabled*, *enabled*, and *hot* (when the mouse hovers over the icon). We therefore need three different icons for each action:

- We set colored icons for hot actions with the method setHoverImageDescriptor(). These icons are stored in the icons/full/clcl16 folder.

- We set black and white icons for enabled actions with the method setImageDescriptor().These icons are stored in the icons/full/elcl16 folder.

- We set gray icons for disabled actions with the method setDisabledImageDescriptor().These icons are stored in the icons/full/dlcl16 folder.

The number '16' refers to the size of the icons: they are all 16x16 pixels in size.

The icon correction_view.gif is a special case. It is only used in the manifest file plugin.xml – a specification in the SpellCheckerImages class is therefore not necessary. This icon is also independent of state changes, so we only need a single version. Such icons are stored in the basic folder rather than the full folder.

In principle this is possible for all icons. If we don't want to create three different icons for each action, it is sufficient to create a single colored icon and to specify it in the setImageDescriptor() method. Eclipse then automatically computes the black and white and gray variants. We will usually arrive at graphically more satisfying solutions by creating each of the three state icons manually, however.

```java
package com.bdaum.SpellChecker;

import java.net.MalformedURLException;
import java.net.URL;

import org.eclipse.jface.action.IAction;
import org.eclipse.jface.resource.ImageDescriptor;

/**
 * Compilation of the images used in com.bdaum.SpellChecker plug-in.
 */
public class SpellCheckerImages {

  // Get URL for icon folder
  private static URL fgIconBaseURL = null;

  static {
    try {
      fgIconBaseURL = new URL(SpellCheckerPlugin.getDefault()
        .getDescriptor().getInstallURL(),
        "icons/");
    } catch (MalformedURLException e) {
      SpellCheckerPlugin.logError(
        7, "Bad URL when loading image", e);
    }
  }

  /**
   * Filenames for the images in this registry
   */

  public static final String IMG_IGNORE = "ignore.gif";
  public static final String IMG_IGNOREALL = "ignoreAll.gif";
  public static final String IMG_CANCEL = "cancel.gif";
  public static final String IMG_REPLACE = "replace.gif";
  public static final String IMG_REPLACEALL = "replaceAll.gif";
  public static final String IMG_ADDTODICTIONARY =
    "addToDictionary.gif";
```

```
/**
 * Method setImageDescriptors.
 * @param action - Action for which the icon shall be set
 * @param type - icon type
 * @param relPath - relative path of icon
 */
public static void setImageDescriptors(
  IAction action, String type, String relPath) {
    int c = 0;
    try {
      ImageDescriptor id =
        ImageDescriptor.createFromURL(
          makeIconFileURL("full/d" + type, relPath));
      if (id != null) {
        c++;
        action.setDisabledImageDescriptor(id);
      }
    } catch (MalformedURLException e) {
      SpellCheckerPlugin.logError(
        8, "Bad URL when loading disabled image", e);
    }
    try {
      ImageDescriptor id =
        ImageDescriptor.createFromURL(
          makeIconFileURL("full/c" + type, relPath));
      if (id != null) {
        c++;
        action.setHoverImageDescriptor(id);
      }
    } catch (MalformedURLException e) {
      SpellCheckerPlugin.logError(
        9, "Bad URL when loading hover image", e);
    }
    try {
      action.setImageDescriptor(
        ImageDescriptor.createFromURL(
          makeIconFileURL("full/e" + type, relPath)));
    } catch (MalformedURLException e) {
      SpellCheckerPlugin.logError(
        9, "Bad URL when loading enabled image", e);
      action.setImageDescriptor(
      ImageDescriptor.getMissingImageDescriptor());
    }
    if (c == 1)
      SpellCheckerPlugin.logError(10,
        "Supply either the default icon only, or all three icons",
        null);
  }

  // Construct URL for icon file
```

```
private static URL makeIconFileURL(String prefix, String name)
throws MalformedURLException {
  if (fgIconBaseURL == null)
    throw new MalformedURLException();
  return new URL(fgIconBaseURL, prefix + "/" + name);
}
}
```

As you have probably already found out, we don't work here directly with Image instances, but with ImageDescriptor instances. These image descriptors work as proxies for images and don't allocate resources in the host operating system. The workbench evaluates these descriptors and loads the images only when needed. As the workbench also takes care of for the required disposal of these Image instances, we don't have to.

11.7 Coordinating core classes with GUI classes

Now it is time to take care of the interaction between the spell checking engine and the user interface (actions and views). This interaction is organized by the SpellCheckManager class. When this class is initialized, the manager creates a new configuration instance (SpellCheckConfiguration). This instance is responsible for managing the preferences from the various PreferencePages and for passing these preferences to the spell checking engine. (Remember that we may have to deal with several plug-ins implementing different spell checking strategies, and each may have its own preference page.)

```
package com.bdaum.SpellChecker;

import java.io.File;
import java.io.FileNotFoundException;
import java.io.IOException;
import java.util.HashMap;
import java.util.Map;
import java.util.StringTokenizer;

import org.eclipse.core.runtime.*;
import org.eclipse.jface.text.BadLocationException;
import org.eclipse.jface.text.Document;
import org.eclipse.jface.text.IDocument;
import org.eclipse.jface.text.ITextSelection;
import org.eclipse.jface.viewers.ISelectionProvider;
import org.eclipse.swt.custom.StyledText;
import org.eclipse.swt.graphics.Point;
import org.eclipse.swt.widgets.Control;
import org.eclipse.swt.widgets.Display;
import org.eclipse.swt.widgets.Text;
```

```
import org.eclipse.ui.IEditorInput;
import org.eclipse.ui.IFileEditorInput;
import org.eclipse.ui.texteditor.IDocumentProvider;
import org.eclipse.ui.texteditor.ITextEditor;

import com.bdaum.SpellChecker.preferences.SpellCheckerPreferences;
import com.bdaum.SpellChecker.views.SpellCorrectionView;
import com.swabunga.spell.engine.SpellDictionary;
import com.swabunga.spell.event.SpellCheckEvent;
import com.swabunga.spell.event.SpellCheckListener;
import com.swabunga.spell.event.SpellChecker;

/**
 * This class organizes the interaction between the SpellChecker,
 * the user interface, and the spell checker configuration.
 */
public class SpellCheckManager implements SpellCheckListener {

  /* The engines for the spell checker */
  private Map engineMap = new HashMap(10);
  private SpellChecker currentEngine;

  /* The spell checking view */
  private SpellCorrectionView correctionViewer;

  /* Currently active preferences */
  private SpellCheckerPreferences currentPreferences;

  /* The configuration */
  private SpellCheckConfiguration config =
    new SpellCheckConfiguration();

  /* The current document */
  private IDocument document;

  /* The current selection */
  private int currentOffset;
  private int currentLen;

  /* The editor who owns the current document */
  private ITextEditor editor;

  /* The Text or StyledText element who owns the current document */
  private Control text;

  /* SelectionProvider des Editors */
  private ISelectionProvider selectionProvider;

  /* current Display */
  private Display display;
```

```
/* Indicator for aborting the current spell checking process */
private boolean abort = false;
```

Selecting the plug-in

In both methods called checkDocument() we prepare the spell checking process. If we have an active ITextEditor instance, we fetch the file extension from the IEditorInput and search for a suitable plug-in. To do so, we fetch the extension point documentTokenizer from the plug-in registry and search through the tree structure of this extension point. We then compare the file extensions that are defined in the extensions to this extension point, and compare it with the file extension of the IEditorInput object (are you still with me?).

If a matching plug-in is found, we first try to create a plug-in specific Preferences instance, which gives us access to the plug-in specific preference settings. If such a Preferences class is not defined in the plug-in manifest, we use the default preferences instead. We can then retrieve the preferences instance that was determined in that way using getPreferences().

Similarly, we create a specific tokenizer as defined in the respective plug-in. It is the tokenizer's responsibility to break a document into words. Consequently it has a big influence on the spell checking function.

```
/**
 * Method checkDocument.
 * Checks the document content
 * @param editor – the current text editor
 * @param display – the current Display instance
 * @param correctionViewer – the spell checking view
 */
public void checkDocument(ITextEditor editor, Display display,
  SpellCorrectionView correctionViewer) {
  this.display = display;
  this.editor = editor;
  // First reset the current preferences to the
  // default preferences
  currentPreferences = SpellCheckerPlugin.getPreferences();
  // Get file extension form editor input
  IEditorInput input = editor.getEditorInput();
  String doctype =
    (input instanceof IFileEditorInput)
    ? ((IFileEditorInput) input)
    .getFile()
    .getFullPath()
    .getFileExtension()
    : "*";
  // The spell checking view
  this.correctionViewer = correctionViewer;
  // We search for extensions to extension point
  // "documentTokenizer"
```

```java
// First get the plug-in registry
IPluginRegistry reg = Platform.getPluginRegistry();
// Now get the extension point
IExtensionPoint exPoint = reg.getExtensionPoint(
  SpellCheckerPlugin.getId(), "documentTokenizer");
// Fetch all installed extensions for this extension point.
// This can be more than one if several plug-ins
// were installed.
IExtension[] tokenizers = exPoint.getExtensions();
for (int i = 0; i < tokenizers.length; i++) {
  IExtension extension = tokenizers[i];
  // Now fetch all tokenizer specifications
  // Each extension can define several of these specifications
  IConfigurationElement[] configurations =
    extension.getConfigurationElements();
  for (int j = 0; j < configurations.length; j++) {
    IConfigurationElement element = configurations[j];
    // For each tokenizer we step through the list
    // of declared file extensions
    StringTokenizer st =
      new StringTokenizer(
        element.getAttribute("extensions"));
    while (st.hasMoreElements()) {
      String ext = st.nextToken();
      if (ext.equalsIgnoreCase(doctype)) {
        // Positive
        try {
          // We now fetch the plug-in specific preferences
          currentPreferences =
            (SpellCheckerPreferences) element
              .createExecutableExtension("preferences");
        } catch (CoreException e) {
          // no luck, we use the default preferences
        }
        try {
          // We try to create a tokenizer instance
          AbstractDocumentWordTokenizer documentTokenizer =
            (AbstractDocumentWordTokenizer) element
              .createExecutableExtension("class");
          // Now, having determined the configuration
          // we can start spell checking.
          doCheck(editor, documentTokenizer);
        } catch (CoreException e) {
          SpellCheckerPlugin.logError(1,
            "Could not create tokenizer",e);
        }
        return;
      }
    }
  }
}
```

```
      }
      // No matching extension found. We use the default tokenizer.
      doCheck(editor, new DocumentWordTokenizer());
    }

    /**
     * Method getPreferences.
     * @return SpellCheckerPreferences
     */
    public SpellCheckerPreferences getPreferences() {
      return currentPreferences;
    }
```

Performing spell checking

The actual spell checking process is prepared in the doCheck() method. There we first fetch the document to be checked from the text editor and the SelectionProvider with the current selection. We then initialize the tokenizer with the document and the current selection in performCheck() and call the *jazzy* engine.

```
        // Initialize tokenizer and perform spell check
        private void doCheck(
          ITextEditor editor,
          AbstractDocumentWordTokenizer documentTokenizer) {
            // Fetch document
            IDocumentProvider documentProvider =
              editor.getDocumentProvider();
            document =
              documentProvider.getDocument(editor.getEditorInput());
            // Evaluate current selection – this must be
            // done in the SWT thread
            selectionProvider = editor.getSelectionProvider();
            display.syncExec(new Runnable() {
              public void run() {
                ITextSelection sel =
                  (ITextSelection) selectionProvider.getSelection();
                currentOffset = sel.getOffset();
                currentLen = sel.getLength();
              }
            });
            // Invoke engine
            performCheck(documentTokenizer, editor.isEditable());
        }
```

When we don't have an active ITextEditor instance, we use the Text or StyledText instance that was passed to method checkDocument(), instead. We extract the text from these Controls and create a new Document instance with it. Then the spell check is applied on this document via performCheck(). In this case the default tokenizer and the default preferences are used.

```
/**
 * Method checkDocument.
 * Checks the content of a Control
 * @param control - Text or StyledText widget
 * @param correctionViewer — The correction window
 */
public void checkDocument(Control control, Display display,
  SpellCorrectionView correctionViewer) {
  this.display = display;
  this.text = control;
  this.correctionViewer = correctionViewer;
  // We use the default preferences
  currentPreferences = SpellCheckerPlugin.getPreferences();
  // We create a Document instance containing the contents of
  // the Control, so we can perform the spell check on
  // a Document instance. We also fetch the text selection
  display.syncExec(new Runnable() {
    public void run() {
      Point sel;
      if (text instanceof Text) {
        document = new Document(((Text) text).getText());
        sel = ((Text) text).getSelection();
      } else {
        document = new Document(((StyledText) text).getText());
        sel = ((StyledText) text).getSelection();
      }
      currentOffset = sel.x;
      currentLen = sel.y - sel.x;
    }
  });
  // Invoke engine (always use default tokenizer)
  performCheck(new DocumentWordTokenizer(), true);
}
```

Running the engine   We first initialize the tokenizer thus determined in performCheck() by passing the document, the beginning and the length of the selection. (A length of zero indicates that the whole document is to be checked.)

We then fetch a suitable engine via getEngine(), then execute the spell check via checkSpelling(). The engine will then use the tokenizer to analyze the document and fire a series of SpellCheckEvents if spelling errors are found. Because we had registered the manager with the engine as a SpellCheckListener when we created the engine, the events now arrive in the spellingError() method (see below).

When the spell checking process has ended, we dispose of the tokenizer, reset the SpellCorrectionView, and restore the original selection in the document, because this selection may have been destroyed before by highlighting a bad word.

```
/**
 *
 * Method performCheck.
 * Runs the jazzy engine
 * @param documentTokenizer - current tokenizer
 * @param isEditable — true, if the document can be modified.
 */
private void performCheck(
  AbstractDocumentWordTokenizer documentTokenizer,
  boolean isEditable) {
    // Initialize the tokenizer
    documentTokenizer.init(document, currentOffset, currentLen);
    // Reset the abort flag
    abort = false;
    // Fetch the engine
    SpellChecker engine = getEngine();
    if (engine == null)
      return;
    // Run the engine
    engine.checkSpelling(documentTokenizer);
    // Done — dispose the tokenizer
    documentTokenizer.dispose();
    // Reset the spell checking view
    correctionViewer.setInput(null, this, isEditable);
    // Restore original selection
    setSelection(currentOffset, currentLen);
}
```

In getEngine() we manage several engines. If we use more than one dictionary (plug-ins may define their own dictionaries), we require a different engine for each dictionary.

```
// determine suitable engine
private SpellChecker getEngine() {
  // Get dictionary file name
  String dict =
    config.getString(SpellCheckerPreferences.SPELL_DICTIONARY);
  // Try to get engine for this dictionary from map
  SpellChecker newEngine = (SpellChecker) engineMap.get(dict);
  if (newEngine == null) {
    // Not yet created
    // Create a new engine
    newEngine = createNewEngine(dict);
    if (newEngine == null)
      return currentEngine;
    // Store the engine in the map for next time
    engineMap.put(dict, newEngine);
  }
  if (newEngine != currentEngine) {
    // If the engine has changed we must modify the
    // listener registration
    if (currentEngine != null)
```

```
                              // Deregister with the previous engine
                              currentEngine.removeSpellCheckListener(this);
                              // and register with the new engine
                              newEngine.addSpellCheckListener(this);
                              currentEngine = newEngine;
                          }
                          return currentEngine;
                      }
```

The method createEngine() is a factory method for creating engine instances. Here we load the dictionary and then create a new engine for this dictionary.

```
                      /**
                       *
                       * Method createNewEngine.
                       * Create a new jazzy engine
                       * @param dict - dictionary file name
                       * @return SpellChecker
                       */
                      private SpellChecker createNewEngine(String dict) {
                          try {
                              if (dict != null) {
                                  // Load dictionary file
                                  SpellDictionary dictionary =
                                      new SpellDictionary(new File(dict));
                                  // Create engine with this dictionary
                                  return new SpellChecker(dictionary);
                              } else
                                  SpellCheckerPlugin.logError(
                                      5, "No dictionary file declared", null);
                          } catch (FileNotFoundException e) {
                              SpellCheckerPlugin.logError(
                                  2, "Dictionary file not found", e);
                          } catch (IOException e) {
                              SpellCheckerPlugin.logError(
                                  3, "Error reading dictionary file", e);
                          }
                          return null;
                      }
```

Select bad word The spelling error events fired by the engine arrive in spellingError(). First we retrieve the position and the length of the bad word from the SpellCheckEvent object. With these values we set a new text selection in setSelection() to highlight the bad word. We either set this selection in the text editor, or in the Text or StyledText widget, depending which of these acts as the spell checking target.

Then we pass the event object as input to the SpellCorrectionView, which then constructs a table with correction proposals, and go into the waiting state. We leave this state again upon notification from the SpellCorrectionView. Because of this we must execute the method spellingError() as a synchronized method.

The SpellCorrectionView performs this notification by invoking the continueSpell-Checking() method. There the waiting thread is released again via notifyAll() – we can now continue spell checking and possibly fire another event. If no more events are present, the spell checking view is reset, the original selection is restored, and the method performCheck() returns.

```
/**
 * Event processing for the jazzy engine
 * @see com.swabunga.spell.event.SpellCheckListener
 * #spellingError(com.swabunga.spell.event.SpellCheckEvent)
 */
public synchronized void spellingError(SpellCheckEvent event) {
  // Select bad word
  setSelection(
    event.getWordContextPosition(),
    event.getInvalidWord().length());
  // Inform the spell checking view about the event
  boolean isEditable =
    (editor != null) ? editor.isEditable() : true;
    correctionViewer.setInput(event, this, isEditable);
  try {
    // Here, we must wait until the event was
    // processed by the view.
    wait();
  } catch (InterruptedException e) {
  }
  // If view asks to abort, tell jazzy (via the event object)
  if (abort)
    event.cancel();
}

// Set selection in editor – must happen in SWT thread
private void setSelection(final int offset, final int len) {
  display.syncExec(new Runnable() {
    public void run() {
      if (editor != null)
        editor.selectAndReveal(offset, len);
      else if (text instanceof Text)
        ((Text) text).setSelection(offset, offset + len);
      else
        ((StyledText) text).setSelection(offset, offset + len);
    }
  });
}
```

```
/**
 * Method continueSpellChecking.
 * Notification that event processing was finished.
 */
public synchronized void continueSpellChecking() {
  // Release waiting thread
  notifyAll();
}
```

Operations We can cancel the current spell checking process with abortSpellChecking(). To do so, we just set a flag. Then the spellingError() method is awakened once again and just terminates itself after terminating the spell checking process by calling the event object's cancel() method.

```
/**
 * Method abortSpellChecking.
 * Cancels the current spell checking process.
 */
public void abortSpellChecking() {
  abort = true;
  continueSpellChecking();
}
```

The replaceWord() method is used to apply the end user's corrections to the current document. This is again done via a syncExec() method, because modifications in the document may cause changes in its user interface representation – and these changes must be run in the SWT thread (see Section 6.5.3). As the change request originates in the spell checking thread, this construction is necessary to avoid thread errors.

```
/**
 * Method replaceWord.
 * Replace word in the current document
 * @param pos - absolute position im document
 * @param count – Number of characters to be replaced
 * @param newWord – The replacement string
 */
public void replaceWord(
  final int pos,
  final int count,
  final String newWord) {
    // We must execute this via syncExec,
    // since it originates from the spell checking thread.
    display.syncExec(new Runnable() {
      public void run() {
        try {
          String oldWord = document.get(pos, count);
          if (!oldWord.equals(newWord)) {
            // True change – replace word in document
            document.replace(pos, count, newWord);
            currentLen += newWord.length() - count;
```

```
                        // In case of auxiliary document apply change to
                        // Text or StyleText widget, too.
                        if (text instanceof Text)
                          ((Text) text).insert(newWord);
                        else if (text instanceof StyledText)
                          ((StyledText) text).insert(newWord);
                      }
                  } catch (BadLocationException ex) {
                }
              }
            });
          }
        }
```

11.8 Analyzing documents

The tokenizer is implemented by two classes:

- The class AbstractDocumentWordTokenizer serves as a base class for all tokenizer implementations within the spell checker.

- The default tokenizer DocumentWordTokenizer is based on this class.

Later, in a further plug-in, we will find another tokenizer class based on Abstract-DocumentWordTokenizer.

As these classes are fairly irrelevant in the context of Eclipse plug-in implementation, we refrain from discussing them here. Interested readers find their source code on the book's Web site at www.bdaum.de.

11.9 Configuring the Spell Checker

In this section we discuss how preference pages are implemented, and how we evaluate the settings in these preference pages. The SpellCheckPreferencePage class has already been generated by Eclipse during project set-up. Of course, we have to apply a few changes to represent the spell checking options as Eclipse preferences.

In addition, we split the preference domain model into the separate class SpellChecker-Preferences. This has the advantage that we don't need to load the relatively large GUI class SpellCheckPreferencePage when the preferences are initialized.

11.9.1 Preferences

First we must find out which options need to be implemented. All the options of the *jazzy* engine are listed in file configuration.properties. There are two option groups:

the options with the prefix EDIT_ are used for fine tuning the spell checking algorithm, while the options with the prefix SPELL_ represent user options. To achieve consistent management for these configuration parameters, we adopt both groups into the PreferenceStore (and initialize their default values), but only provide field editors for the values starting with prefix SPELL_.

We also add one more option: the dictionary path. The corresponding key for the PreferenceStore is named SPELL_DICTIONARY. The default value for this key is set to the path of the default dictionary as defined in class SpellCheckerPlugin.

We use the method getPluginPreferences() to load the whole set of plug-in specific preferences, as each plug-in has its own set of preferences. This allows us to configure the spell checker individually for each file type. For example, Java source files may have a different spell checking configuration than plain text files.

```java
package com.bdaum.SpellChecker.preferences;

import org.eclipse.core.runtime.Preferences;
import org.eclipse.jface.preference.IPreferenceStore;

import com.bdaum.SpellChecker.SpellCheckerPlugin;
import com.swabunga.spell.engine.Configuration;

public class SpellCheckerPreferences {

  /* Key for dictionary path */
  public static final String SPELL_DICTIONARY = "SPELL_DICTIONARY";

  /**
   * Method initializeDefaults.
   * Sets the defaults for all preferences
   * @param store - the PreferenceStore instance
   */
  public void initializeDefaults(IPreferenceStore store) {
    // Only initialize if not already initialized
    // Otherwise preference.ini and plugin_customization.ini
    // would not work.
    if (store.getDefaultString(SPELL_DICTIONARY).length() == 0) {
      initializePublicPreferences(store);
      initializeHiddenPreferences(store);
    }
  }

  /**
   * Method initializePublicPreferences.
   * @param store - the PreferenceStore instance
   */
  protected void initializePublicPreferences(
    IPreferenceStore store) {
```

```
    store.setDefault(SPELL_DICTIONARY,
      SpellCheckerPlugin.getDefaultDictionaryFileName());
    store.setDefault(Configuration.SPELL_THRESHOLD, 140);
    store.setDefault(Configuration.SPELL_IGNOREDIGITWORDS, true);
    store.setDefault(
      Configuration.SPELL_IGNOREINTERNETADDRESSES, false);
    store.setDefault(Configuration.SPELL_IGNOREMIXEDCASE, false);
    store.setDefault(
      Configuration.SPELL_IGNOREMULTIPLEWORDS, false);
    store.setDefault(
      Configuration.SPELL_IGNORESENTANCECAPITALIZATION,false);
    store.setDefault(Configuration.SPELL_IGNOREUPPERCASE, false);
  }

  /**
   * Method initializeHiddenPreferences.
   * non-public configuration data for spell check algorithm
   * @param store - the PreferenceStore instance
   */
  protected void initializeHiddenPreferences(
    IPreferenceStore store) {
    store.setDefault(Configuration.EDIT_DEL1, 95);
    store.setDefault(Configuration.EDIT_DEL2, 95);
    store.setDefault(Configuration.EDIT_SWAP, 90);
    store.setDefault(Configuration.EDIT_SUB, 100);
    store.setDefault(Configuration.EDIT_SIMILAR, 10);
    store.setDefault(Configuration.EDIT_MIN, 90);
    store.setDefault(Configuration.EDIT_MAX, 100);
  }

  /**
   * Method getPluginPreferences.
   * @return Preferences
   */
  public Preferences getPluginPreferences() {
    return SpellCheckerPlugin.getDefault().getPluginPreferences();
  }
}
```

11.9.2   The GUI

The implementation of the SpellCheckerPreferencePage class closely follows the pre-generated pattern. In the constructor we decide on a grid layout. In the init() method we just add a descriptive text for the preference page. We have also extended the method createControl() to set help identification for context sensitive help (*Infopops*) (see Section 11.10).

We construct a field editor for each (public) spell checking option in create-FieldEditors().

```
package com.bdaum.SpellChecker.preferences;

import org.eclipse.jface.preference.*;
import org.eclipse.swt.widgets.Composite;
import org.eclipse.ui.IWorkbench;
import org.eclipse.ui.IWorkbenchPreferencePage;
import org.eclipse.ui.help.WorkbenchHelp;

import com.bdaum.SpellChecker.SpellCheckerPlugin;
import com.swabunga.spell.engine.Configuration;

/**
 * This class implements a preference page for the
 * the basic options of the spell checker.
 * It can be subclassed if required.
 */

public class SpellCheckerPreferencePage
  extends FieldEditorPreferencePage
  implements IWorkbenchPreferencePage {

    /* Constructor */
    public SpellCheckerPreferencePage() {
      super(GRID);
    }

    /**
     * Initialization
     */
    public void init(IWorkbench workbench) {
      setDescription("All changes will take effect for the next "
      + "spell checking pass.\n\n");
    }

    /*
     * Get Plug-in specific PreferenceStore instance
     */
    public IPreferenceStore doGetPreferenceStore() {
      return SpellCheckerPlugin.getDefault().getPreferenceStore();
    }

    /**
     * Construct page content
     */
    public void createControl(Composite parent) {
      super.createControl(parent);
      WorkbenchHelp.setHelp(parent.getParent(),
        getPreferenceHelpContextID());
    }
```

```
/**
 * Method getPreferenceHelpContextID.
 * @return String - the ID for context sensitive help.
 */
protected String getPreferenceHelpContextID() {
  return "com.bdaum.SpellChecker.preferences_context";
}

/**
 * Create field editors
 */

public void createFieldEditors() {
  Composite composite = getFieldEditorParent();
  addField(new FileFieldEditor(
    SpellCheckerPreferences.SPELL_DICTIONARY,
    "Spell &Dictionary File", composite));
  addField(new IntegerFieldEditor(Configuration.SPELL_THRESHOLD,
    "Spell &Threshold", composite ));
  addField( new BooleanFieldEditor(
    Configuration.SPELL_IGNOREDIGITWORDS,
    "Ignore &Numbers", composite ));
  addField(new BooleanFieldEditor(
    Configuration.SPELL_IGNOREMIXEDCASE,
    "Ignore &Mixed Case", composite ));
  addField(new BooleanFieldEditor(
    Configuration.SPELL_IGNORESENTANCECAPITALIZATION,
    "Ignore Sentence &Capitalization",
    getFieldEditorParent()));
  addField(new BooleanFieldEditor(
    Configuration.SPELL_IGNOREUPPERCASE,
    "Ignore &Upper Case", composite ));
}
}
```

11.9.3   Reading from the PreferenceStore

Now we only need a method to pass the options set in the preferences pages to the spell checking engine. We have already told the *jazzy* engine to fetch its configuration parameters from class SpellCheckConfiguration in the SpellCheckerPlugin class by setting the system property jazzy.

This is quite simple. The SpellCheckConfiguration class extends the *jazzy* class Configuration and overrides the methods getBoolean(), setBoolean(), getInteger(), and setInteger(). In addition we have added the method getString() to be able to fetch the dictionary path. When a get...() method is invoked, the value belonging to the specified key is fetched from the respective Preferences class. Which plug-in the Preferences class belongs to is determined by the SpellCheckManager, which has selected the plug-in and created the respective Preferences instance depending on the type of the file to be checked.

The set…() methods do nothing, as all preferences are modified via the Preference-Pages and not via the Configuration class.

```
package com.bdaum.SpellChecker;

import org.eclipse.core.runtime.Preferences;
import com.bdaum.SpellChecker.preferences.SpellCheckerPreferences;
import com.swabunga.spell.engine.Configuration;


public class SpellCheckConfiguration extends Configuration {

  // Fetch preferences

  private Preferences getPreferences() {
    SpellCheckerPreferences preferences =
      SpellCheckerPlugin.getManager().getPreferences();
    return preferences.getPluginPreferences();
  }

  /**
   * Fetch integer value from Preferences.
   * @param key - identification of value
   * @return - value belonging to the key
   */
  public int getInteger(String key) {
    return getPreferences().getInt(key);
  }

  /**
   * Fetch Boolean value from Preferences.
   * @param key - identification of value
   * @return - value belonging to the key
   */
  public boolean getBoolean(String key) {
    return getPreferences().getBoolean(key);
  }

  /**
   * Fetch string value from Preferences.
   * @param key - identification of value
   * @return - value belonging to the key
   */
  public String getString(String key) {
    return getPreferences().getString(key);
  }
```

```
/**
 * All preferences are set via the PreferencePages.
 * Therefore, the setXXX() implementation do nothing here.
 */
public void setInteger(String key, int value) {
}

public void setBoolean(String key, boolean value) {
}
}
```

11.10 The help system

The Eclipse help system is designed in a way that allows the implementation of help pages independently from the application, using a standard HTML editor. The association of the individual help pages to help topics (or in a context sensitive way to GUI components) is defined via XML files.

For space reasons we don't show the HTML pages here.

11.10.1 The help table of contents

The path of the help table of contents has already been declared in the manifest file plugin.xml (see Section 11.3).

The file toc.xml looks like this:

```xml
<?xml version="1.0" encoding="UTF-8"?>
<toc label="Spell Checker" topic="html/spelling.html">
  <topic label="Correction View" href="html/SpellCheckerView.html"/>
  <topic label="Preferences"
  <topic label="Default Preferences"
    href="html/SpellCheckerPreferences.html"/>
  <anchor id="postPreferences"/>
  </topic>
  <topic label="Other Information">
    <topic label=
      "Acknowledgements" href="html/Acknowledgements.html"/>
    <topic label="Dictionaries" href="html/Dictionaries.html"/>
  </topic>
</toc>
```

An HTML page is assigned to each topic element and also to the root element of the table of contents (toc). Topics may branch into subtopics, i.e. topics may be nested. We can define a display text for each topic with the attribute label. In the help browser the topics are displayed as a tree structure on the left hand side. We can open the associated HTML page with a click on a topic.

Anchor points   The definition of the anchor element under the topic Default Preferences is a special case. Here we create an extension point to which the help systems of other plug-ins can refer. Thus the help systems of several plug-ins can merge.

11.10.2 Context sensitive help

The path of the file containing the associations of help pages with GUI elements has also already been declared in manifest file plugin.xml (see Section 11.3).

The file contexts.xml looks like this:

```
<?xml version="1.0" encoding="UTF-8"?>
<contexts>
  <context id="action_context">
    <description>Help for Spell Checker Action Set</description>
    <topic href="html/spelling.html" label="Spell Checker"/>
  </context>
  <context id="preferences_context">
    <description>Help for Spell Checker Preferences</description>
    <topic href="html/SpellCheckerPreferences.html"
      label="Spell Checker Preferences"/>
  </context>
  <context id="correctionView_context">
    <description>Help for Spell Checker Correction View</description>
    <topic href="html/SpellCheckerView.html"
      label="Spell Checker Correction View"/>
  </context>
</contexts>
```

All the individual context associations are listed in the element contexts. Each context definition refers to a context ID that identifies the corresponding GUI element. This ID is always specified here relatively to the plug-in. Each context definition contains a description element, which later appears in the *Infopop*, and a topic element that refers to the associated HTML page.

Where do the context IDs come from? This is not really handled consistently in Eclipse, and we may see changes in future versions. In some cases, context IDs are defined in the manifest for plugin.xml (for example for actions), while in other cases the context IDs must be set in the Java code. We have already seen this in the classes SpellCheckPreferencePage Section 11.9.1) and SpellCorrectionView (Section 11.6.1). In these cases, the context IDs are set in the Eclipse help system with the help of the static Workbench-Help method setHelp().

11.10.3 Active help

At the end of this section on help we want to demonstrate how active help works. On the main help page `spelling.html` we have attached a hyperlink. By activating this hyperlink, the end user can start spell checking.

Here is an HTML fragment of this page. The link to the script `livehelp.js` and the invocation of the script in the hyperlink are printed in bold type:

```
<head>
  <script language="JavaScript"
    src="../../org.eclipse.help/livehelp.js"></script>
</head>
<h1>Spell Checker Help</h1>
<hr color="#66FFFF">
<p>The spell checker is started by placing the cursor inside a text or
editor area, then invoking the function
<i><b><a href='javascript:liveAction("com.bdaum.SpellChecker",
"com.bdaum.SpellChecker.actions.ActiveHelpAction",
"start")'>Edit&gt;Check
Spelling</a></b></i> or by pressing the spell checker tool button.</p>
<p>Incorrect words are shown in the <i><b>Spell Correction View</b></
i>. You may replace such words, ignore them, or add them to the
dictionary.</p>
```

We have specified the class `ActiveHelpAction` as the second parameter of the script invocation. We must still implement this class.

The ActiveHelpAction class

In this class we first implement the method `setInitializationString()`. Here we accept the third parameter of the JavaScript invocation (in this case the value 'start'). This parameter allows us to implement different actions depending on the parameter value.

```
package com.bdaum.SpellChecker.actions;

import org.eclipse.help.ILiveHelpAction;
import org.eclipse.swt.widgets.Display;
import org.eclipse.swt.widgets.Shell;
import org.eclipse.ui.IWorkbenchWindow;
import org.eclipse.ui.IWorkbenchWindowActionDelegate;
import org.eclipse.ui.PlatformUI;

import com.bdaum.SpellChecker.SpellCheckerPlugin;
```

```
/**
 * Invoking spell checking via active help
 */
public class ActiveHelpAction implements ILiveHelpAction {
  // Third parameter from JavaScript invocation
  String data;

  public void setInitializationString(String data) {
    // Remember the parameter
    this.data = data;
  }
```

Running the help action

In the run() method we first fetch the SpellCheckingActionDelegate instance from the class SpellCheckerPlugin. Remember that this instance has registered itself with the class SpellCheckerPlugin. We fetch the current Display instance from the Spell-CheckingActionDelegate instance. The method getDisplay() returns the value null if the action cannot be executed.

The rest of the action is performed in the SWT thread. Here we first fetch the current workbench window from the platform. We get its Shell instance, bring this shell into the foreground, and start the spell checking action by calling the run() method of the SpellCheckingActionDelegate instance.

```
public void run() {
  final IWorkbenchWindowActionDelegate delegate =
    SpellCheckerPlugin.getSpellCheckingActionDelegate();
  if (delegate == null)
    return;
  // We must fetch a Display instance from the
  // CheckSpellingActionDelegate since we have no access to a
  // widget that could provide us with such an instance.
  Display display =
    ((CheckSpellingActionDelegate) delegate).getDisplay();
  if (display == null)
    return;
  // Active help does not run in the SWT thread.
  // Therefore we must encapsulate all GUI accesses into
  // a syncExec() method.
  display.syncExec(new Runnable() {
    public void run() {
      // Get active workbench window
      IWorkbenchWindow window =
        PlatformUI.getWorkbench().getActiveWorkbenchWindow();
      // If none is active get just a workbench window
      if (window == null)
        window =
          PlatformUI.getWorkbench().getWorkbenchWindows()[0];
      // We bring the workbench into the desktop foreground
      Shell shell = window.getShell();
      shell.setMinimized(false);
```

```
                  shell.forceActive();
                  // Then we execute the spell checking action
                  if (data.equals("start"))
                    delegate.run(null);
              }
          });
      }
  }
```

11.11 A plug-in for Java

After we have finished the implementation of the main spell checker plug-in, we are going to implement a specialized spell checker plug-in for Java source files in this section. This plug-in connects to the previous plug-in via the extension point document-Tokenizer. We don't plan to check Java code for spelling errors, of course. But Java source files contain sections where spell checking can be useful, such as comments and string literals (see Figure 11.4).

To implement such a specialized spell checker on the basis of the previous plug-in, besides the manifest file plugin.xml we only need four Java classes: a small Plugin class, a tokenizer specialized for Java source code, a class for the specialized Preferences, and the corresponding PreferencePage. We will also add further pages to the help system.

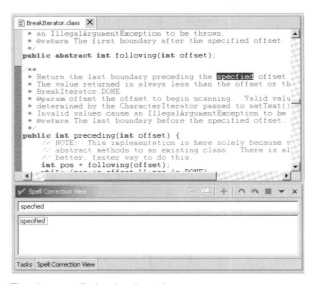

Figure 11.4: The Java spell checker in action.

11.11.1 Setting up the project

We implement the Java spell checker as a separate project. Again, we invoke the *New* wizard with the function *File > New > Project... > Plug-in Development > Plug-in Project*. On the following wizard page we enter the name of the project: 'com.bdaum.SpellChecker.Java'.

On the next wizard page we select *Java Project* and leave all other settings at their default values. On the following page we switch to *Create a blank plug-in project* and press the *Finish* button. The wizard now generates only the manifest file plugin.xml in the new project.

11.11.2 The manifest

In this blank plug-in we have to create most of the manifest file ourselves:

- On the *Overview* page of the PDE editor we enter the name of the plug-in, the provider name, and the name of the plug-in class (JavaSpellCheckerPlugin).

- On the *Dependencies* page it is sufficient to mark the plug-in com.bdaum.Spell-Checker that we created in the previous sections as a prerequisite. This allows us to use the classes of this plug-in during the implementation of the new plug-in. All other dependencies are automatically computed from this plug-in and are added to the list.

- On the *Runtime* page we change the name of the JAR file into JavaTokenizer.jar.

- On the *Extensions* page we add extensions to the extension points com.bdaum.SpellChecker.documentTokenizer, org.eclipse.ui.PreferencePages, org.eclipse.help.toc, and org.eclipse.help.contexts. For all these points we use schema based extensions. The corresponding schemas, among which is the previously created schema documentTokenizer.exsd for the extension point com.bdaum.SpellChecker.documentTokenizer, help us in completing the extension point specification. See the listing below for details.

Tokenizer extension Let's step, for example, through the specification of the extension point com.bdaum.SpellChecker.documentTokenizer. The ID for this extension point is 'com.bdaum.SpellChecker.Java' and its name is 'Java Spell Checker'. We now click on this extension point with the right mouse button and select the menu item *New > tokenizer*. A new element com.bdaum.SpellChecker.JavaTokenizer1 is now created as a child element of com.bdaum.SpellChecker.documentTokenizer. When we select this element, we see the individual attributes of this element in the *Properties* view as they where defined in schema documentTokenizer.exsd.

In the *class* entry we click on the small button at the right hand side of the entry and select *Create a new Java class*. In the following dialog we enter 'com.bdaum.SpellChecker.Java' under *Package Name* and 'JavaWordTokenizer' under *Class Name*. This will automatically generate a stub for the new class.

Under the entry *extensions* we enter the file extension 'java', and under the entry *id* 'com.bdaum.SpellChecker.Java.JavaWordTokenizer'. Under *name* we enter 'Java Spell Checker'. Also, under *preferences* we press the little button at the right hand side and create a new Java class JavaSpellCheckerPreferences in the package com.bdaum.SpellChecker.Java. In this case, too, a stub is generated immediately.

Manifest

```xml
<?xml version="1.0" encoding="UTF-8"?>
<plugin
  id="com.bdaum.SpellChecker.Java"
  name="SpellChecker for Java"
  version="1.0.0"
  provider-name="bdaum industrial communications"
  class="com.bdaum.SpellChecker.Java.JavaSpellCheckerPlugin">

  <runtime>
    <library name="JavaTokenizer.jar"/>
  </runtime>
  <requires>
    <import plugin="org.eclipse.ui"/>
    <import plugin="org.eclipse.core.resources"/>
    <import plugin="org.eclipse.help"/>
    <import plugin="com.bdaum.SpellChecker"/>
  </requires>

  <extension point="org.eclipse.ui.preferencePages">
    <page name="Java"
      category=
        "com.bdaum.SpellChecker.preferences.defaultPreferences"
      class=
        "com.bdaum.SpellChecker.Java.JavaSpellCheckerPreferencePage"
      id="com.bdaum.SpellChecker.Java.preferencePage"/>
  </extension>
  <extension point="org.eclipse.help.toc">
    <toc file="toc.xml"/>
  </extension>
  <extension point="org.eclipse.help.contexts">
    <contexts file="contexts.xml"/>
  </extension>
  <extension id="com.bdaum.SpellChecker.Java"
    name="Java Spell Checker"
    point="com.bdaum.SpellChecker.documentTokenizer">
    <tokenizer preferences=
      "com.bdaum.SpellChecker.Java.JavaSpellCheckerPreferences"
      name="Java Spell Checker"
```

```
            extensions="java"
            class="com.bdaum.SpellChecker.Java.JavaWordTokenizer"
            id="com.bdaum.SpellChecker.Java.JavaWordTokenizer"/>
        </extension>

    </plugin>
```

11.11.3 The Plugin class

The class `JavaSpellCheckerPlugin` is minimal. The only extension is the initialization of the preferences. However, we delegate the initialization details to the `JavaSpellCheckerPreferences` class (see the next section).

```
package com.bdaum.SpellChecker.Java;

import org.eclipse.core.runtime.IPluginDescriptor;
import org.eclipse.jface.preference.IPreferenceStore;
import org.eclipse.ui.plugin.AbstractUIPlugin;

import com.bdaum.SpellChecker.preferences.SpellCheckerPreferences;


public class JavaSpellCheckerPlugin extends AbstractUIPlugin {

  // The plug-in singleton.
  private static JavaSpellCheckerPlugin plugin;

  /**
   * The Constructor
   */
  public JavaSpellCheckerPlugin(IPluginDescriptor descriptor) {
    super(descriptor);
    plugin = this;
  }

  /**
   * Returns the shared instance.
   */
  public static JavaSpellCheckerPlugin getDefault() {
    return plugin;
  }

  /**
   * Initialize PreferenceStore
   */
  protected void initializeDefaultPluginPreferences() {
    IPreferenceStore store = getPreferenceStore();
    SpellCheckerPreferences preferences =
      new JavaSpellCheckerPreferences();
    preferences.initializeDefaults(store);
```

```
      }
   }
```

11.11.4 The preferences

In the case of the preferences we build on top of the preferences of the previous plug-in. We inherit all the preferences from SpellCheckerPreferences but use a plug-in specific PreferenceStore. The preferences for Java files and text files can therefore be identically named but may have different values. We have also added some Java specific options, and use different default settings for the inherited options, therefore overriding the method initializePublicPreferences().

```java
package com.bdaum.SpellChecker.Java;

import org.eclipse.core.runtime.Preferences;
import org.eclipse.jface.preference.IPreferenceStore;

import com.bdaum.SpellChecker.SpellCheckerPlugin;
import com.bdaum.SpellChecker.preferences.SpellCheckerPreferences;
import com.swabunga.spell.engine.Configuration;


public class JavaSpellCheckerPreferences
   extends SpellCheckerPreferences {

   public static final String CHECKJAVADOC = "checkJavadoc";
   public static final String CHECKCOMMENTS = "checkComments";
   public static final String CHECKSTRINGLITERALS = "stringLiterals";
   public static final String IGNORECOMPOUNDS = "ignoreCompounds";

   /**
    * Method initializePublicPreferences.
    * Java specific default values for public options.
    * @param store - the PreferenceStore instance
    */
   protected void initializePublicPreferences(IPreferenceStore store) {
      store.setDefault(SPELL_DICTIONARY,
        SpellCheckerPlugin.getDefaultDictionaryFileName());
      store.setDefault(Configuration.SPELL_THRESHOLD, 140);
      store.setDefault(Configuration.SPELL_IGNOREDIGITWORDS, true);
      store.setDefault(
        Configuration.SPELL_IGNOREINTERNETADDRESSES, true);
      store.setDefault(Configuration.SPELL_IGNOREMIXEDCASE, true);
      store.setDefault(Configuration.SPELL_IGNOREMULTIPLEWORDS, false);
      store.setDefault(
        Configuration.SPELL_IGNORESENTANCECAPITALIZATION, false);
      store.setDefault(Configuration.SPELL_IGNOREUPPERCASE, true);
      store.setDefault(IGNORECOMPOUNDS, true);
      store.setDefault(CHECKJAVADOC, true);
```

```
      store.setDefault(CHECKCOMMENTS, true);
      store.setDefault(CHECKSTRINGLITERALS, true);
    }

    /**
     * Method getPluginPreferences.
     * @return Preferences
     */
    public Preferences getPluginPreferences() {
      return
        JavaSpellCheckerPlugin.getDefault().getPluginPreferences();
    }
  }
```

11.11.5 The preference page

The JavaSpellCheckerPreferencePage class is similar to the default preference page, so we have defined it as a subclass of SpellCheckerPreferencePage. In addition, we have implemented the GUI for the Java specific options. We use a different context ID for the help pages than the default preference page, of course. We retrieve a PreferenceStore instance from the current plug-in with the doGetPreferenceStore() method and thus guarantee that we work with our own set of preference values.

```
package com.bdaum.SpellChecker.Java;

import org.eclipse.jface.preference.BooleanFieldEditor;
import org.eclipse.jface.preference.IPreferenceStore;
import org.eclipse.swt.widgets.Composite;

import com.bdaum.SpellChecker.preferences.SpellCheckerPreferencePage;

/**
 * This class implements a PreferencePage for Java spell checking
 */
public class JavaSpellCheckerPreferencePage
  extends SpellCheckerPreferencePage {

  /**
   * @see org.eclipse.jface.preference.
   * PreferencePage#doGetPreferenceStore()
   */
  public IPreferenceStore doGetPreferenceStore() {
    return JavaSpellCheckerPlugin.getDefault().getPreferenceStore();
  }

  /**
   * @see com.bdaum.SpellChecker.preferences.
   * SpellCheckerPreferencePage#getPreferenceHelpContextID()
   */
```

```
protected String getPreferenceHelpContextID() {
  return "com.bdaum.SpellChecker.Java.java_preferences_context";
}

/**
 * Add Java specific options to the field editors.
 * @see org.eclipse.jface.preference.FieldEditorPreferencePage
 * #createFieldEditors()
 */
public void createFieldEditors() {
  // Initialize the default values
  super.createFieldEditors();
  Composite composite = getFieldEditorParent();
  addField(new BooleanFieldEditor(
    JavaSpellCheckerPreferences.IGNORECOMPOUNDS,
    "Ignore &Compounds (Words containing '.' or ':')", composite));
  addField(new BooleanFieldEditor(
    JavaSpellCheckerPreferences.CHECKJAVADOC,
    "Check &JavaDocs", composite));
  addField(new BooleanFieldEditor(
    JavaSpellCheckerPreferences.CHECKCOMMENTS,
    "Check &other Comments", composite));
  addField(new BooleanFieldEditor(
    JavaSpellCheckerPreferences.CHECKSTRINGLITERALS,
    "Check String &Literals", composite));
}
}
```

11.11.6 The Java tokenizer

The Java tokenizer is also implemented as a subclass of `AbstractDocumentWordTokenizer`. This class mainly consists of a small parser that scans the Java source code and identifies Javadoc comments, non-Javadoc comments, string literals, and program code. Depending on the preferences – which are fetched from the `SpellCheckConfiguration` class – the respective text section is admitted to the spell checking process or not.

Since this tokenizer does not contain Eclipse specific code, we don't list it here. Interested readers find the complete code at www.bdaum.de.

11.11.7 The help system

For this plug-in we also define the files `toc.xml` and `contexts.xml`, together with the corresponding HTML pages.

Reference to anchor point Here is the code for `toc.xml`. Please note the attribute `link_to` in the `toc` element. This attribute creates a link to the anchor point defined in Section 11.10.1.

```
<?xml version="1.0" encoding="UTF-8"?>
<toc link_to="../com.bdaum.SpellChecker/toc.xml#postPreferences"
  label="Java Spell Checker">
  <topic label="Java Preferences" href="html/JavaPreferences.html"/>
</toc>
```

The file `contexts.xml` defines only a single new context (for the Java preference page):

```
<?xml version="1.0" encoding="UTF-8"?>
<contexts>
  <context id="java_preferences_context">
    <description>Help for Spell Checker Java Preferences</description>
    <topic href="html/JavaPreferences.html"
      label="Spell Checker Java Preferences"/>
  </context>
</contexts>
```

11.12 Deploying the Spell Checker

11.12.1 Reducing start-up time

We will finally do some fine tuning to both the manifest files `plugin.xml`. In the manifest editor we open the *Runtime* page, select the JAR file, expand the section *Package Prefixes*, press the *Add* button, and select the respective package prefixes from the list.

In the case of the `com.bdaum.SpellChecker` plug-in, we add the prefix `com.bdaum` for the archive `SpellChecker.jar` and the prefix `com.swabunga.spell` for the archive `jazzy-core.jar`.

The corresponding section in `plugin.xml` looks then like this:

```
<library name="SpellChecker.jar">
  <export name="*"/>
  <packages prefixes="com.bdaum"/>
</library>
<library name="jazzy-core.jar">
  <export name="*"/>
  <packages prefixes="com.swabunga.spell"/>
</library>
```

In the case of the plug-in `com.bdaum.SpellChecker.Java`, we select the prefix `com.bdaum.SpellChecker` for the archive `JavaTokenizer.jar`. The corresponding section `plugin.xml` looks then like this:

```
<runtime>
  <library name="JavaTokenizer.jar">
    <packages prefixes="com.bdaum.SpellChecker"/>
  </library>
</runtime>
```

With these simple modifications we can reduce the loading time for plug-ins by 10 percent because these prefixes serve as a hint for Eclipse where to search plug-in binaries.

11.12.2 Defining the Spell Checker feature

We want to deploy the spell checker as an installable feature for the Eclipse platform. This feature should contain the default spell checker plug-in plus the spell checker plug-in for Java source files.

Feature project   To do so, we create a new, feature project. We invoke the function *File > New > Project* and select *Plug-in Development* and *Feature Project*. Under *Project Name* we enter a suitable name such as 'Spell Checker for Eclipse'. On the next wizard page we replace the proposed *Feature Id* with 'com.bdaum.SpellChecker'. This feature identification matches the identification of our spell checker plug-in. The *Feature Provider* should also be completed, for example 'bdaum'.

On the next page we can determine which plug-ins should be added to the feature. We checkmark both the plug-ins com.bdaum.SpellChecker and com.bdaum.Spell-Checker.Java. After pressing the *Finish* button, the *Feature Editor is* opened. The information on the *Overview* page is already complete. The field *Primary Feature* is not marked – this is only required for stand-alone products. In terms of Eclipse, however, our spell checker is not a stand-alone product, but an add-on to the Eclipse platform. For this reason we also refrain from implementing product related files such as welcome.xml or about.ini.

On the *Information* page we can complete the sections *Feature Description*, *Copyright Notice*, and *License Agreement* directly using text, or we may refer to a relevant document via a URL. For example, we may create an HTML file license.html describing the license conditions in this feature project. In the section *License Agreement* we then specify the value license.html in the field *Optional URL*. However, it is sensible to specify important license conditions as text, too, because the end user is only prompted with this text information during the installation of the feature.

On the *Content* page we just press the *Compute* button. This will determine all the plug-ins that are required on the target platform for running the feature successfully.

Feature manifest   This completes the definition of the feature manifest. Here is the code of the file feature.xml:

```
<?xml version="1.0" encoding="UTF-8"?>
<feature
  id="com.bdaum.SpellChecker"
  label="Spell Checker for Eclipse"
  version="1.0.0"
```

```
    provider-name="bdaum industrial communications">

    <description>
    This feature provides a general purpose spell checker for Eclipse.
    In addition a special purpose spell checker for Java source
    files is provided.
    </description>

    <copyright>
      (c) 2003 Berthold Daum
    </copyright>

    <license url="license.html">
    License
    This Plug-in is provided to you under the terms and conditions
    of the Common Public License Version 1.0. A copy of the CPL is
    available at http://www.eclipse.org/legal/cpl-v10.html.
    Third Party Content
    The Content includes items that have been sourced from third
    parties as follows:
    Jazzy 0.4
    Jazzy is licensed under the LGPL.
    </license>

    <requires>
      <import plugin="org.eclipse.core.resources"/>
      <import plugin="org.eclipse.help"/>
      <import plugin="org.eclipse.ui"/>
    </requires>

    <plugin
      id="com.bdaum.SpellChecker"
      download-size="0"
      install-size="0"
      version="1.0.0"/>

    <plugin
      id="com.bdaum.SpellChecker.Java"
      download-size="0"
      install-size="0"
      version="1.0.0"/>

  </feature>
```

Configuring Ant scripts

We now can start to prepare the feature for deployment (see Section 10.3.2). To do so, we modify the build.properties files in the respective projects.

build.properties

We open the *Properties Editor* (Figure 11.5) with a double click on this file. When doing so, we want to make sure that the corresponding manifest file plugin.xml is not open at the same time – in this case `build.properties` would be locked against modifications.

For both plug-in projects we specify:

```
bin.excludes = src/,bin/,temp.folder/,*.classpath,*.project,\
    build.properties,build.xml
```

With this definition all the files and folders of the respective project except the specified files and folders will be included into the deployment archive.

For the feature project we specify instead:

```
bin.includes = feature.xml,license.html
```

Here only the specified files will be included in the deployment archive.

We also want to make sure that `custom=true` is *not* specified, otherwise the above specifications would have no effect on the generation of the Ant script.

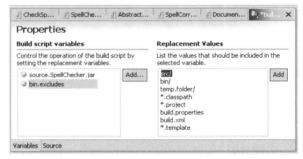

Figure 11.5: The Properties Editor. In the left window we have added the variable 'bin.excludes'. In the right window we have listed all the folders and files that we want to exclude from the deployment archive.

11.12.3 Defining the update site

We can now offer our feature on an *Update Site*. To create such a site, Eclipse provides a simple wizard that generates the *Update Site* in a format understood by the Eclipse *Update Manager*. We invoke the function *File > New > Project > Plug-in Development > Update Site Project*. On the next wizard page we enter as a name 'Spell Checker Installation' and press the *Finish* button. The wizard now creates the file `site.xml` and opens it in the PDE editor.

In this editor we enter a short description of the site on the *Description* page. On the *Build* page we press the *Add* button and select the feature `com.bdaum.SpellCheckerFea-`

ture. This feature then appears on the *Build* page. However, we must still checkmark it to offer it to the end user during the installation process.

This is the code for the manifest file `site.xml`:

Site manifest

```
<?xml version="1.0" encoding="UTF-8"?>
<site>
  <description>
  This site contains the installation files for the Eclipse Spell
Checker.
  </description>
  <feature url="features/com.bdaum.SpellChecker_1.0.0.jar"
    id="com.bdaum.SpellCheckerforEclipse" version="1.0.0"/>
</site>
```

Generating a site
By pressing the *Build* button we start the generation of the *Update Site*. During this process two new folders, `plugins` and `features`, are created. These folders contain the installation archives that are created with the `build.xml` Ant scripts that we configured in Section 11.12.2.

11.12.4 Installation

Now we can invoke the *Update Manager* via the function *Help > Software Updates > Update Manager*. In the section *Installing New Features* we click on the hyperlink *Feature Updates*. In the *Feature Update* view that now opens we navigate from *My Computer* to the element …/`eclipse/workspace/Spell Check Installation/Other/ Spell Check Feature 1.0.0`. When we select this element the *Update Manager* displays information about this feature on the right hand side. We can now start the installation. After accepting the license conditions, the installation is executed. Afterwards, Eclipse must be restarted.

After Eclipse has restarted we cannot see any trace of the spell checker. First, we must activate the spell checker's *Action Set*. To do so, we invoke the function *Window > Customize Perspective > Other* and check the field *Spell Checker*. If everything works correctly we should now see the spell checker icon in the toolbar. We can now start spell checking!

11.13 Experiences

In this chapter we have implemented a fully working spell checker that integrates into the Eclipse workbench. What experiences – negative and positive – did we have with Eclipse during the development of this tool?

If there is anything to criticize, it would only be minor issues. What I do not like is the inconsistent treatment of help context IDs, or the fact that we were not able to access the inner editors of the `MultiPageEditorPart` class.

Very positive experiences include the extremely short time needed to implement this feature. From the first idea, though discovering, downloading, and exploring the *jazzy* package, to running a first working prototype did not take me more than one working day. The fine tuning of this plug-in was done when I wrote this chapter. (Which *did* take more than one working day!) The option to pre-generate plug-in parts was very useful. This not only saves a lot of typing, but, even more important, it saves a lot of exploring and browsing the documentation, and a lot of trying and testing until the first plug-in is executable. Using this function, I could start with a plug-in template that could be executed right 'out of the box', and could add the spell checking functionality bit by bit, following the XP motto '*Code a little, test a little*'.

One piece of advice: when designing Eclipse based applications, you should adopt the Eclipse 'style'. This is particularly true when designing user interfaces. Here you should accept what Eclipse has to offer and design your applications accordingly, instead of insisting stubbornly on your own conceptions!

A Useful plug-ins for Eclipse

Many useful plug-ins have been created for Eclipse, and many of them are freely available on the Web. Here we list some of these plug-ins. We refrain from presenting plug-ins that are only in the planning stage, or are at a pre-alpha stage. It may be worth visiting the Web sites listed from time to time to look out for new developments.

Good starting points for searching plug-ins are, of course, the official Eclipse Web site at www.eclipse.org and SourceForge at sourceforge.net. In addition, there are some Web sites dedicated to Eclipse plug-ins, such as eclipse-plugins.2y.net and www.eclipse-workbench.com.

Name	Description	Home page
Databases		
Attrezzo per Xindice	A graphical user interface for the Xindice XML database. Free.	`attrezzo.sourceforge.net`
easysql	SQL editor and executor. Free.	`sourceforge.net/ projects/easysql`
JFaceDbc	A JDBC client. Free.	`sourceforge.net/ projects/jfacedbc`
Graphics		
Batik and SVG Support	Supports the display of SVG drawings on an SWT canvas. Free.	`www.holongate.org`
GEF	*Graphical Editor Framework*. A framework for implementing diagram editors. Free.	`www.eclipse.org/gef`
Java Advanced Imaging	JAI as an Eclipse plug-in. Free.	`www.holongate.org`
Java2D for SWT	Java2D integration into SWT (see Section 6.7.5). Free.	`www.holongate.org`
SWT Flash	A Flash player for Eclipse. Free.	`www.docuverse.com/ eclipse/swtflash.jsp`
GUI design		
JellySWT	An XML-based script language for SWT-based user interfaces. Free.	`jakarta.apache.org/ commons/sandbox/ jelly/jellyswt.html`
Luxor-SWT	An adaptation of the Mozilla XUL script language for the definition of SWT-based user interfaces. Free.	`luxor-xul.sourceforge.net`

Name	Description	Home page
V4ALL Visual Designer for Eclipse	A visual GUI designer for SWT and SWING. Free edition for non-commercial use.	`www.assisiplugins.com`
W4Eclipse	Visual Web-GUI designer for the SWT, manufactured by INNOOPRACT (`www.innoopract.de`). Commercial product, but free for the first 5000 objects.	`w4toolkit.com`
SWT-Designer	Visual GUI designer for SWT and JFace. Commercial product, but free community version.	`www.swt-designer.com`
Modeling		
EMF	Eclipse Modeling Framework.	`www.eclipse.org/emf`
KLEEN	A design tool for Asset Oriented Modeling (AOM). Free.	`www.aoModeling.org`
MagicDraw	A UML design tool. Commercial product.	`www.magicdraw.com`
Omondo	A UML design tool. Integrates with the Eclipse Java IDE. Free for non-commercial use.	`www.eclipseuml.com`
Rational ClearCase	A UML based CASE tool. Commercial product.	`www.rational.com`
Slime UML	A UML design tool. Commercial product.	`www.mvmsoft.de/ content/plugins/ slime/slime.htm`
Together WebSphere Studio Edition	A UML based CASE tool. Commercial product.	`www.togethersoft.com`

Name	Description	Home page
Software management		
VSS Plugin	Plug-in supporting the use of Microsoft Visual SourceSafe as a team repository. Free.	`sourceforge.net/ projects/vssplugin/`
Eclipse-ccase	Plug-in for using Rational ClearCase as a team repository. Free.	`sourceforge.net/ projects/eclipse- ccase/`
Programming languages and compiler-compiler		
AspectJ	AspectJ IDE. AspectJ is an aspect-oriented programming language based on Java. Free.	`sourceforge.net/ projects/ajc-for- eclipse`
CDT	C/C++ IDE. For C and C++ development (currently only under Linux). Free.	`www.eclipse.org/cdt`
Improve C#-Plugin	C# editor and builder. Free.	`www.improve- technologies.com/ alpha/esharp`
xored WebStudio	PHP IDE. Free.	`www.xored.com`
JavaCC	A popular compiler-compiler implemented as an Eclipse plug-in. Free.	`sourceforge.net/ projects/eclipse- javacc`
ANTLR	A powerful compiler-compiler implements as an Eclipse plug-in. Free.	`sourceforge.net/ projects/antlreclipse`
XML		
X-Men	An XML editor for Eclipse. Supports XML Schema and DTDs. Offers source view, table view. Good navigation via outline view. Free.	`sourceforge.net/ projects/xmen`

Name	Description	Home page
JXML	A complete XML editor for Eclipse. Editing happens in a separate SWING window. Free.	`sourceforge.net/ projects/jxmleditor`
XML Buddy	An XML editor with content assist, outline, DTD generator, and much more. Free.	`www.xmlbuddy.com`
Web projects		
Sysdeo Eclipse Tomcat Launcher	Starting, stopping, and configuring Tomcat from within the Eclipse workbench. Supports comfortable debugging of JSP and servlet-based projects. Free.	`www.sysdeo.com/ eclipse/ tomcatPlugin.html`
Systinet WASP Server for Java	Creates WebServices from Java classes. Supports the execution and debugging of WebServices from within Eclipse. Free for end users.	`www.systinet.com`
MyEclipse	Various tools for J2EE development, in particular a JSP editor and debugger. MyEclipse is the product of a joint venture between Genuitec (`www.genuitec.com`) and the Saxonian start-up BebboSoft (www.bebbosoft.de). Commercial license.	`www.myeclipse.org`

Name	Description	Home page
Embedded systems		
TimeStorm 2.0	Cross-Platform IDE for embedded-Linux target platforms. Commercial product.	`www.timesys.com`
and of course …		
SpellChecker for Eclipse	The spell checker developed in this book, and enhanced versions. Free.	`www.bdaum.de/eclipse`

B Migrating projects to a new Eclipse version

The migration of a project to a new version of the Eclipse platform is a special situation.

Projects

The best way is to install a new Eclipse version into a different directory and then to import the projects and your own or third-party plug-ins into this new version.

When doing so, you have the following options:

- 'Import' the complete workspace into the new version. Here you only need to modify the command line parameter -data accordingly when invoking Eclipse. For example:

  ```
  eclipse.exe -data C:\eclipseSDK2.0.2\eclipse\workspace
  ```

  Here the existing workspace remains at its old location and becomes the workspace of the new Eclipse platform.

- Import single projects from the old workspace with the help of the *Import* function. To do so, select the *Import* category *Existing Project into Workspace*. Here too the physical location of the imported project is not changed – the project remains in the old workspace directory!

In both cases it may be necessary to adapt the *Java Build Path* of the imported projects. In particular, if JAR files of the Eclipse distribution were specified as external JARs, you must make some adjustments:

- If the JAR file was specified relative to the environment variable ECLIPSE_HOME, this variable now points to the storage location of the new Eclipse version. However, the JAR files in the new Eclipse version usually have different version numbers, so you will have dangling references.

- If the JAR file was specified via an absolute path expression, this path expression is still pointing to the JAR file in the old Eclipse version. If you want to update this to the new version, you must modify the respective path expression.

In both cases, first remove the existing references to external JARs, then add them again with the function *Add external JARs*.

In the case of plug-in projects, however, an update is more easily achieved by applying the context function *Update Classpath...*

Plug-ins

If your project is a plug-in project the migration is somewhat simpler, provided that the project is already in an installable state. In this case, first install the plug-in on the old platform (including the source files). By doing this you ensure that the plug-in resources appear in the directory's `plugins` and `features` respectively.

Now you can migrate the plug-in to the new platform with the help of the *Import > External Plug-ins and Features* function. On the second wizard page, select all plug-ins required by the imported plug-in from the list. Based on this selection, the *Java Build Path* is adapted automatically. The workspace of the new platform now contains the complete development project for the imported plug-in.

C Important downloads

This appendix lists the addresses for all the third-party software used in the context of this book.

Project 1

FreeTTS (Version 1.1.1) can be found at sourceforge.net/projects/freetts. Make sure to use version 1.1.1, the API was changed in later versions!

Project 2

The source files for playing sound files (*jlGui 2.1.1*) can be found at www.javazoom.net/jlgui/sources.html.

Project 3

The spell checker engine (Version 0.4) can be found at sourceforge.net/projects/jazzy. Make sure to use version 0.4, the API was changed in later versions!

Book Web site

All the required resources are replicated on a special Web site dedicated to this book. This Web site is located at www.bdaum.de/eclipse.

There you can find the source code for the three projects, plus a ready-made spell checker plug-in.

Bibliography

[Arthorne2002]   John Arthorne, *How You've Changed! Responding to resource changes in the Eclipse workspace*, Eclipse Corner Article, www.eclipse.org, 2002.

[Daum2003]   Berthold Daum, *Modeling Business Objects with XML Schema*, Morgan Kaufman Publishing, 2003.

[Fogel2003]   Karl Fogel, Bar Moshe, *Open Source Projects with CVS*, Paraglyph Publishing, 2003.

[Fowler1999]   Martin Fowler, Kent Beck, John Brant, William Opdyke, Don Roberts, *Refactoring: Improving the Design of Existing Code*, Addison-Wesley, 1999.

[Gamma1995]   Erich Gamma, Richard Helm, Ralph Johnson, John Vlissides, *Design Patterns*, Addison-Wesley, 1995.

[Hatcher2002]   Erik Hatcher, Steve Loughran, *Java Development with Ant*, Manning Publications Company, 2002.

[Hightower2001]   Richard Hightower, Nicholas Lesiecki, *Java Tools for Extreme Programming: Mastering Open Source Tools Including Ant, JUnit, and Cactus*, John Wiley & Sons, 2001.

[Kehn2002]   Dan Kehn, Scott Fairbrother and Cam-Thu Le, *How to Internationalize your Eclipse Plug-In*, 2002.

[MacLeod2002]   Carolyn MacLeod and Shantha Ramachandran, *Understanding Layouts in SWT*, Eclipse Corner Article, www.eclipse.org, 2002.

[Moody2001]   *SWT Color Model, Eclipse Corner* article, James Moody & Carolyn MacLeod, www.eclipse.org, 2001.

[Robinson2000]   Matthew Robinson and Pavel Vorobiev, *Swing*, Manning Publications, 2000.

[Tilly2002]   Jesse Tilly, Eric M. Burke, *Ant: The Definitive Guide*, O'Reilly & Associates, 2002.

[Vesperman2003]   Jennifer Vesperman, *Essential CVS*, O'Reilly & Associates, 2003.

Index